CW00386338

Is Shakespeare Any Good?

1

Also available:

The Novel Now: Contemporary British Fiction
Richard Bradford

A Future for Criticism
Catherine Belsey

30 Great Myths About Shakespeare
Laurie Maguire and Emma Emith

30 Great Myths About the Romantics
Duncan Wu

Is Shakespeare Any Good?

*And Other Questions on How to
Evaluate Literature*

Richard Bradford

WILEY Blackwell

This edition first published 2015
© 2015 John Wiley & Sons, Ltd

Registered Office
John Wiley & Sons, Ltd, The Atrium, Southern Gate, Chichester, West Sussex, PO19 8SQ, UK

Editorial Offices
350 Main Street, Malden, MA 02148-5020, USA
9600 Garsington Road, Oxford, OX4 2DQ, UK
The Atrium, Southern Gate, Chichester, West Sussex, PO19 8SQ, UK

For details of our global editorial offices, for customer services, and for information about
how to apply for permission to reuse the copyright material in this book please see our website
at www.wiley.com/wiley-blackwell.

The right of Richard Bradford to be identified as the author of this work has been asserted in
accordance with the UK Copyright, Designs and Patents Act 1988.

All rights reserved. No part of this publication may be reproduced, stored in a retrieval system,
or transmitted, in any form or by any means, electronic, mechanical, photocopying, recording or
otherwise, except as permitted by the UK Copyright, Designs and Patents Act 1988, without the
prior permission of the publisher.

Wiley also publishes its books in a variety of electronic formats. Some content that appears in
print may not be available in electronic books.

Designations used by companies to distinguish their products are often claimed as trademarks.
All brand names and product names used in this book are trade names, service marks,
trademarks or registered trademarks of their respective owners. The publisher is not associated
with any product or vendor mentioned in this book.

Limit of Liability/Disclaimer of Warranty: While the publisher and author have used their best
efforts in preparing this book, they make no representations or warranties with respect to the
accuracy or completeness of the contents of this book and specifically disclaim any implied
warranties of merchantability or fitness for a particular purpose. It is sold on the understanding
that the publisher is not engaged in rendering professional services and neither the publisher nor
the author shall be liable for damages arising herefrom. If professional advice or other expert
assistance is required, the services of a competent professional should be sought.

Library of Congress Cataloging-in-Publication Data

Bradford, Richard, 1957–
    Is Shakespeare any good? : and other questions on how to evaluate literature / Richard Bradford.
       pages   cm
    Includes bibliographical references and index.
    ISBN 978-1-118-22001-6 (cloth)) – ISBN 978-1-118-21997-3 (paper)
1. Canon (Literature)   2. Literature–Philosophy.   I. Title.
    PN81.B64 2015
    809–dc23

                                        2014050196

A catalogue record for this book is available from the British Library.

Cover image: William Shakespeare, English poet and playwright. Engraving from The Leisure
Hour Magazine April 1864. © shutterstock/Stocksnapper
Decorative collage – bright vertical background © shutterstock/ Lukiyanova Natalia / frenta

Set in 10.5/13pt Minion by SPi Global, Pondicherry, India
Printed and bound in Malaysia by Vivar Printing Sdn Bhd

1   2015

For Ames

Contents

Acknowledgments

As usual, Dr Amy Burns has played a vital part in the preparation of this book, and my position as Visiting Professor at the University of Avignon, where literary aesthetics is a key aspect of research, has proved a stimulus for several of the chapters. Thanks in particular are due to Professor Madelena Gonzalez. The University of Ulster has provided an excellent environment for my research. A brief passage in Chapter 7 first appeared in *Crime Fiction: A Very Short Introduction* (Oxford University Press, 2015) and sections of Chapters 5 and 6 first appeared in *Poetry: The Ultimate Guide* (Palgrave-Macmillan, 2010).

Introduction

I gave some thought to including in the title of this book, or perhaps the subtitle, some reference to "literary aesthetics." It was a brief and untroubling thought. Literary aesthetics, the artistic qualities and value of literature if you will, is a long-serving concept – as old as Plato, Aristotle, and Longinus – which has been so savagely dismembered and battered both by literary critics and philosophers as to defy even the most liberal, capacious attempt at a definition.

Longinus, for example, was responsible for the concept of the sublime. He argued that sublimity is a supplement to the persuasive power of rhetoric, something that transports the reader's emotions to a state of exaltation. Burke and Kant had doubts about the value of this linguistic drug; Pater and Wilde worshipped it irrationally; Adorno and Lyotard ridiculed it as proof of the limitations of bourgeois thinking. Had these been simply differences of opinion then the matter might in itself be interesting, but when we read these thinkers we encounter not so much disagreement as a lack of consensus on what they are discussing. No one seems clear on what the sublime actually involves, and even if some thread of continuity can be traced back to Longinus's original thesis a question remains. Did he argue that the sublime was a defining characteristic of literature? If so what is literature supposed to do for us? Make us feel better?

Is Shakespeare Any Good?: And Other Questions on How to Evaluate Literature,
First Edition. Richard Bradford.
© 2015 John Wiley & Sons, Ltd. Published 2015 by John Wiley & Sons, Ltd.

For those who did debate the function and purpose of literature, their exchanges resemble a conversation between figures speaking in different languages, each with only a slight knowledge of what the others are saying.

Plato treated poets as superfluous to the proper functions of the state. Shaftesbury and Hobbes, in the eighteenth century, saw them as shifty chroniclers of the harmony, or otherwise, of the society they represented and wrote about. Friedrich Schiller, conversely, regarded the instability of literary works as part of a dialogue between art and the undercurrents that society tried to disguise; in this he anticipated such Marxist critics as Lukács and Jameson.

My point is that whenever you start to follow a trail that will, you hope, lead toward a conclusive principle of literary aesthetics, all you will encounter are byways, unanswered and seemingly unanswerable questions about what literature is and what it does. I will not ignore completely the subdiscipline of literary aesthetics; contemporary practitioners will feature prominently in the concluding chapter. But I will not allow its digressive self-absorption to divert us from the question at hand: how we distinguish between good and bad literature.

If the most frequently cited contributors to the subdiscipline of literary aesthetics have anything in common it is a collective reluctance to say anything specific about literature. Instead, poems, plays, and novels become an adjunct to their pursuit of other agendas, usually far more elemental and philosophically profound. Matthew Arnold, Samuel Taylor Coleridge, and Friedrich Nietzsche appear to disagree on virtually all elements of literature and art, but look closer at their writings and a common feature emerges. They are not really interested in literature per se at all. Coleridge uses it as a model for his faintly bizarre ideas regarding perception; Arnold sees it as a substitute for the decline in Christian belief; Nietzsche treats it as symptomatic of what Arnold fears that nineteenth century society is about to become: a delusional preoccupation with high emotion as a substitute for thinking. We read them and find ourselves clutching at unfulfilled promises, begging them to address basic questions, such as: "What is literature?" and "Why are some writers superior to others?" – questions they studiously avoid.

All of this was a horrible forecast for the present state of things. The chapter on "Literature" in *The Routledge Companion to Aesthetics* begins by instructing us that literature cannot be defined, either in terms of its intrinsic formal properties or as a cultural and social institution. The author, Peter Lamarque, is a professional philosopher but his sentiments are routinely echoed in all branches of academic literary studies. The standard formula is to inform, or remind, the reader that in years gone by the boundary between literary and nonliterary texts was often unrecognizable; that the King James Bible was admired for its "literary" qualities, that more recently Bertrand Russell and Winston Churchill received the Nobel Prize for Literature without having composed a novel or poem between them. After that, in case you are not yet convinced, you are shown that the supposedly defining elements of verse and fiction all feature in television advertisements, newspapers, and road signs.

I will tackle these contentious issues in more detail but I must first reflect on their ludicrous nature. A professional philosopher or academic critic might feel it appropriate to ask if the King James Bible is intrinsically different from the first generation of novels produced a century later by Defoe and others, but are sane, intelligent individuals troubled by such questions when they browse through the opening pages of a novel in a bookshop or even on Amazon? Let me ask you: do you have to remind yourself that a volume by Jamie Oliver is not, in truth, a work of fiction or a selection of his verse? The hypothesis is too absurd to merit a response. We know the difference between literary and nonliterary works much as we know the difference between a refrigerator and a motor car: our ability to make this distinction involves a facility generally referred to as common sense.

To summarize: Academia has decided that literature cannot be defined and has also therefore absolved itself from addressing the question of literary quality. If we don't know what it is we can't evaluate it, can't compare this novel or that poem with another in terms of its stylistic execution and general significance.

The situation is preposterous in that we have a canon of authors, and books, which is the mainstay of literary studies at every point from GCSE through A levels to degree courses. But since we can't come to any conclusion on what literature is, nor can we justify our elevation of a particular group of writers to the status of greatness.

Evaluation – that is, deciding on whether we enjoy, admire, and respect one author above another – is the elephant in the sitting room of the literary establishment. Every day – if we read literary works – we make decisions on whether we enjoy or admire authors, and so do reviewers in newspapers. But in doing so we refer to no abstract model for literary merit – even as something we might wish to disagree with – because schools and universities do not enable us to comment on issues such as quality.

It is the principal purpose of this book to build bridges between instinctive judgments and reasoned assessment. I will not attempt to impose upon readers a standard formula for the rating literary tests – in the end personal preference has to play an important part in this – but what I will do is to enable readers to articulate and formulate arguments.

I offer readers case studies on key aspects of literature and evaluation. Each is proactively controversial and although I shall attempt to maintain a degree of evenhandedness I will be merciless in exposing the conspiracies and inherent contradictions that inform the world of writing, publishing, selling, and discussing books. In Chapter 6 I provide readers with an evaluative forum, a means of articulating their opinions on literature; they are offered a platform from which they can confidently take on professional critics and the academic establishment.

I should add that my opinions on literature, as expressed in this book, are to an extent an extension of my temperamental characteristics. But no one is impartial. I shall in the book do two things. I will be honest and provocatively nonconformist; I will challenge shibboleths and make readers reconsider what they have taken for granted. I will also shift the focus to what in cold analytical terms literary evaluation actually involves.

1

A Brief Essay on Taste

This essay might seem not only brief but somewhat random, yet there is method in it. I have chosen points in the history of literature when authors have, for whatever motive, gone against the general expectations of what literature is supposed to be and do. Literary history is punctuated mainly by revolutions; some gradual, even benign, others sudden and momentous. Since the sixteenth century, thanks to the printing press, there has been a recorded dialogue between literature and criticism and from this we can discern trends in the way that the literary establishment, ostensibly acting on behalf of the reader, has responded to these changes. Prior to the middle of the twentieth century a general rule was maintained. When writers did something different, most notably when they tinkered with or transgressed established conventions, they were largely treated as sub-standard or as a capricious oddity. That a considerable number of these authors are now regarded as the greats of our literary heritage raises the question of why and how their reputations were transformed. There is no simple answer to this but by the end of this chapter we will, I hope, be better equipped to address it. The related question of why this game of transgression, adverse response, and acceptance is no longer played is equally complex and one that will be properly considered in the next chapter, but I will, to an extent, spoil the surprise: after modernism literary history came to a close.

Is Shakespeare Any Good?: And Other Questions on How to Evaluate Literature,
First Edition. Richard Bradford.
© 2015 John Wiley & Sons, Ltd. Published 2015 by John Wiley & Sons, Ltd.

Let us begin with a hypothesis. Each of us has our private opinions on the most celebrated writers of the so-called "canon," opinions usually formed when we were obliged to first read them at school. It is possible that not all of us particularly enjoy or even respect the work of some of these giants, but in what circumstances would we feel it appropriate to voice such misgivings, let alone write them down or put them into print? It is probable that we would reserve our views for those closest to us, or at least to companions who we trust as similarly disposed, and even then usually in informal circumstances, perhaps when drink has been taken. In short, what we feel does not necessarily correspond with what we feel able to say.

I'll now shift from the hypothetical to the specific. Do you enjoy and respect the poetry of T.S. Eliot? He is held by many to be if not the most important then one of the three or four most significant poets writing in English in the twentieth century. His work is enshrined in anthologies of English verse and his status as a figure who *must* be studied in order for us to understand and appreciate modern poetry is unassailable. So, whatever your genuine response to the question the answer that you will record officially is most likely to be "yes." With this in mind consider the following reviews of Eliot's first significant collection of poems, *Prufrock and Other Observations*, which included the poem "The Love Song of J. Alfred Prufrock" regarded by many as prefiguring *The Waste Land*.

> Mr Eliot is one of those clever young men who find it amusing to pull the leg of a sober reviewer. We can imagine him saying to his friends: "See me have a lark out of the old fogies who don't know a poem from a pea-shooter. I'll just put down the first thing that comes into my head, and call it 'The Love Song of J. Alfred Prufrock.' Of course it will be idiotic; but the fogies are sure to praise it, because when they don't understand a thing and yet cannot hold their tongues they find safety in praise." … We do not wish to appear patronising, but we are certain that Mr Eliot could do finer work on traditional lines. With him it seems to be a case of missing the effect by too much cleverness. All beauty has in it an element of strangeness, but here the strangeness overbalances the beauty. (From an anonymous review, *Literary World*, 5 July 1917)

> Among other reminiscences which pass through the rhapsodist's mind and which he thinks the public should know about, are "dust in crevices, smells of chestnuts in the street, and female smells in shuttered rooms, and cigarettes in corridors, and cocktail smells in bars."

> The fact that these thing occurred to the mind of Mr Eliot is surely of the very smallest importance to anyone one – even to himself. They certainly have

no relation to "poetry," and we only give an example because some of the pieces, he states, have appeared in a periodical which claims that word as its title. (From an anonymous review, *TLS*, 21 June 1917)

Certainly much of what he writes is unrecognisable as poetry at present … and it is only fair to say that he does not call these pieces poems. He calls them "observations" and the description seems exact [because] we do not pretend to follow the drift of "The Love Song of J. Alfred Prufrock" (From an anonymous review, *New Statesman*, 18 August 1917)

Swift, brilliant images break into the field of vision, scatter like rockets, and leave a trail of flying fire behind. But the general impression is momentary; there are moods and emotions, but no steady current of ideas behind them. (Arthur Waugh, *Quarterly Review*, October 1916, reviewing *The New Poetry*, a collection which contained "The Love Song of J. Alfred Prufrock")

I should point out that these four members of the literary establishment – sophisticated, well-read, open-minded individuals – were not in the minority. They represented what was a general consensus on Eliot's verse, ranging from indulgent puzzlement to downright contempt.

Eliot was at the vanguard of literary modernism, a phenomenon too complex and varied to summarize easily, except to say that all of its advocates wished to unshackle themselves from the established traditions of writing, circa 1900. It is evident from the critics quoted above that Eliot's debut collection departed from convention in two notable ways. It seemed to the *TLS* and *New Statesman* reviewers not to qualify as "poetry" at all, and from this we should assume that they refer to the extravagant and seemingly incoherent use of metaphor and to Eliot's somewhat irregular meter. For Arthur Waugh, the meaning of the verse, such as it is, appears "momentary" and transient: there are effects, but no "current of ideas." A persistent objection among these and other critics against early modernism was to what appeared to be the cultivation of striking and unusual impressions which defied understanding.

These critics might have been somewhat reactionary by temperament – those who praised Eliot were generally allied to the new aesthetic of modernism – but they were not stupid. They spoke as they found, and they found themselves unable to make sense of Eliot's verse. It does not seem to me entirely implausible to imagine that some individuals a century later – that is, now – might experience a similar sense of being dumbfounded by it, aware that something is being brought about by the unrelenting clash of disparate images, but unable, perhaps unwilling, to venture an opinion on what exactly this is.

'Prufrock' opens:

> Let us go then, you and I,
> When the evening is spread out against the sky
> Like a patient etherised upon a table;
> Let us go, through certain half-deserted streets,
> The muttering retreats
> Of restless nights in one-night cheap hotels
> And sawdust restaurants with oyster-shells:
> Streets that follow like a tedious argument
> Of insidious intent
> To lead you to an overwhelming question …
> Oh, do not ask, "What is it?"
> Let us go and make our visit.

We never find out any more about "you" referred to in this passage. He, or she, might be a figure who the speaker knows intimately, or casually, but is reluctant to describe in further detail; they might be a figment of the speaker's imagination, or they might even be us, the reader, invited to join the speaker on his peculiar journey. This passage is merely a taster for even more baffling and apparently unanswerable questions raised as the speaker continues with his account. We are never clear if the "journey" is a jumbled version of events that might actually have occurred, a glimpse into a gallery of recollected memories from various conflicting experiences, or a piece-meal sample of the latter combined with images that are pure fantasy and unrelated to the lived existence of the speaker – if indeed we can treat this disembodied chain of images as enabling us to conceive of the speaker as a composite human being.

Let us be clear that, in making these observations, I am not simply indulging or attempting to explain the misconceptions of Eliot's hostile critics. Quite the contrary; I am demonstrating that their points were valid. What is clear, however, is that what was said then would not be countenanced now. If you were a professional critic and literary journalist commissioned to write a piece on the centenary of the publication of Eliot's collection and your principal point was that the collection was an intriguing curiosity but essentially incoherent and incomprehensible your article would be treated either as a parody of its century-old precursors or a symptom of your having taken leave of your senses. If, as a sixth former or undergraduate, you were to venture a similar opinion in an examination or essay your honesty would probably earn you a fail.

Within a decade of the publication of "Prufrock" the consensus had shifted and the majority of commentators were beginning to praise Eliot as one of the most original and brilliant poets of the era. Eliot's *The Waste Land* appeared in 1922, in what would turn out to be modernism's annus mirabilis, which also saw the publications of James Joyce's *Ulysses*, D.H. Lawrence's *Aaron's Rod*, W.B. Yeats's *Later Poems,* and Virginia Woolf's *Jacob's Room*. Eliot's poem is now recognized as probably his finest piece of writing and more significantly as a work that exemplified a turning point in the history of literature; in short, a masterpiece. The early reviews were still mixed but the begrudgers and doubters were now matched in numbers by those who felt it their duty to explain to the reading public why exactly this was a work of genius. Conrad Aiken, for example: "'The Waste Land' is unquestioningly important, unquestionably brilliant." He goes on to substantiate his claim.

> If we leave aside for the moment all other considerations, and read the poem solely with the intention of understanding, with the aid of the notes, the symbolism, of making out what it is that is symbolized, and how these symbolized feelings are brought into relation with each other and with the other matters in the poem; I think we must, with reservations, and with no invidiousness, conclude that the poem is not, in any formal sense, coherent. We cannot feel that all the symbolisms belong quite inevitably where they have been put; that there is anything more than a rudimentary progress from one theme to another; nor that the relation between the more symbolic parts and the less is always as definite as it should be. (*New Republic,* 7 February 1923)

Aiken seems here to be transfixed by the very same features that in the view of his predecessors rendered "Prufrock" unsatisfactory as verse, and it should be pointed out that in *The Waste Land* the confusing pattern of allusions to other cultural reference points of the earlier verse become all the more dense and frequent, and the avoidance of continuity more emphatic. Aiken, when referring specifically to the anti-Eliot critics, makes it clear that what they objected to should be treated as a key element of the poem's excellence.

> We reach thus the conclusion that the poem succeeds – as it brilliantly does – by virtue of its incoherence, not of its plan; by virtue of its ambiguities, not of its explanations. Its incoherence is a virtue because its "donnée" is incoher-ence. Its rich, vivid, crowded use of implication is a virtue, as implication is

always a virtue; – it shimmers, it suggests, it gives the desired implication beautifully – conveys by means of a picture–symbol or action–symbol a feeling – we do not require to be told that he had in mind a passage in the Encyclopedia, or the color of his nursery wall; the information is disquieting, has a sour air of pedantry. We "accept" the poem as we would accept a powerful, melancholy tone-poem. We do not want to be told what occurs; nor is it more than mildly amusing to know what passages are, in the Straussian manner, echoes or parodies. We cannot believe that every syllable has an algebraic inevitability, nor would we wish it so. We could dispense with the French, Italian, Latin and Hindu phrases – they are irritating. But when our reservations have all been made, we accept "The Waste Land" as one of the most moving and original poems of our time. It captures us.

Let us be clear on this. Aiken does not berate Eliot's enemies because of their interpretive blindness, their failure to recognize the innovative aspect of his verse discovered by him. He makes it clear that he sees exactly the same essential characteristics as they do, except that in his opinion they are what make this poetry an achievement of such immense importance, and not, as they judged it, a passing curiosity. To return to my previous analogy, he comes across as a benign, indulgent tutor to a group of first-years who have been brave enough to confess that it sounds like gibberish. Yes, he condescendingly agrees; it does. And with my help it will be your gateway to a new conception of art and thinking.

Within a few weeks of Aiken's article Harold Monro published in *Chapbook* (no 34, February 1923) what he called "An Imaginary Conversation with T.S. Eliot," to which Eliot's contributions are brief and gnomic. The seemingly flippant tone of the piece encapsulates a serious point, already broached by Aiken: specifically, there is a communications breakdown between Eliot – or more accurately his verse – and much of the literary establishment. Monro states, somewhat archly,

I know it was not written for me. You never thought of me as among your potential appreciative audience. You thought of nobody, and you were true to yourself. Yet, in a sense, you did think of me. You wanted to irritate me, because I belong to the beastly age in which you are doomed to live. But, in another sense, your poem seems calculated more to annoy Mr Gosse, or Mr Squire, than me. I imagine them exclaiming: "The fellow *can* write; but he *won't*." That would be because just when you seem to be amusing yourself by composing what they might call *poetry*, at that moment you generally break off with a sneer. And, of course, they can't realise that your faults are as virtuous as their virtues are wicked, not that your style is, as it were, a mirror that distorts the perfections they admire, which are in truth only imitations of perfections. Your truest passages seem to them like imitations of imperfections.

He goes on to explain why those who doubt its qualities are unable, despite themselves, to appreciate Eliot's endeavor.

Most poems of any significance leave one definite impression on the mind. This poem makes a variety of impressions, many of them so contradictory that a large majority of minds will never be able to reconcile them, or conceive of it as an entity. Those minds will go beyond wondering why it so often breaks itself up so violently, changes its tone and apparently its subject.

The charge so frequently laid against Eliot – that he deliberately abjures coherence and continuity, and for apparently arbitrary reasons refuses to enable the reader to make sense of his poetry – is here treated as his formative stylistic signature, something which, when struggled against, is unappreciated and misinterpreted. Monro expands on this.

Most poets write of *dreaming*, and use the expression that they *dream* in its conventional rhetorical sense, but this poem actually is a dream presented without any poetic boast, bluff, or padding. (Monro, *Chapbook*)

Monro's point is that in traditional verse dreaming, and by implication all other sub-rational activities, is translated into the ordered linguistic discourse of the waking or conscious world. This, he contends, is a falsification of a unique experience. Eliot attempts, via his disorderly pattern of private and cultural allusions, to replicate these sensations.

Monro's and indeed Aiken's case is reasonably convincing: Eliot, they argue, demonstrates that poetry is capable of achieving far more with language, and indeed creating an experience for the reader, than had previously been thought possible. In going beyond precedent he creates a double bind for those who have invested their aesthetic expectations in what is known and established. The latter recognize that his medium is "poetic," in a very flexible sense of the term, yet feel confused and aggrieved by his refusal to conform to the given regulations on what poems must be and do.

Knowing what we do of Eliot's elevation to a status of unassailable greatness we might feel it proper to treat the work of Monro, Aiken, and others as early instances of the replacement of hidebound prejudice with insight and discovery. But a question is begged by the revelations, if such they are, that his verse transformed our expectations of the breadth and capabilities of poetry. One might ask: are originality and innovation worthy undertakings in their own right? Monro, to an extent, anticipates such queries and offers a justification for Eliot's departure from conformity.

> This poem is at the same time a representation, a criticism, and the disgusted outcry of a heart turned cynical. It is calm, fierce, and horrible: the poetry of despair itself become desperate. Those poor little people who string their disjointed ejaculation into prosaic semblances of verse – they pale as one reads "The Waste Land." They have no relation to it: yet, through it, we realise what they were trying, but have failed, to represent. Our epoch sprawls, a desert, between an unrealised past and an unimaginable future. "The Waste Land" is one metaphor with a multiplicity of interpretations.

Monro's doleful yet unspecific references to the plight of "our epoch", and to "an unimaginable future" would have registered vividly for his readers. A war which seemed for many to have undermined the claims of Europe to civilization had ended barely 4 years earlier. The allegedly dehumanizing consequences of modern technology – including everything from the wireless to the motor car – were, some argued, encroaching more and more upon the capacity of human beings to determine their own destiny. Indeed, all of these are now part of the standard explanation for why modernism – in literature and elsewhere – came about; its motivation was its radical purchase upon a world in a state of torment and dissolution.

The case would seem to be closed. Eliot's detractors are consigned to the history of interpretation and aesthetics, stubborn footnotes to its rightful progress. This, at any rate, would be the verdict of the vast majority of literary writers and commentators after the 1920s and 1930s, followed closely by their academic counterparts. But without necessarily allying ourselves with the critics who doubted the value and significance of Eliot's work, we should I think revisit this period of debate and transformation because there are questions raised by it that remain unanswered.

To reiterate: Monro's conclusion was that Eliot was not involved in the arbitrary or self-interested pursuit of innovation but rather that his implicit pretext both justified and illuminated his experiments. He was marshalling the so far unexplored potential of literary art as a means of reflecting unvoiced states of mind. There is an issue that underpins this that has been ignored completely by subsequent literary historians and critics. Monro takes it for granted – and assumes that all others will too – that it is the given function of literature to work as some form of index to shifts and variations in the real world, and his assumption opens doors upon a vast range of correlate problems. Even if we accept that literature can do, or at least achieve with a degree of special discernment, what is beyond the standard registers of contemporary debate – journalism, political writing, and so on – does this not relegate it to an activity whose primary function is polemicism or dogmatism? Literary art is generally treated – both by its champions and enemies – as a form of writing defined by its lack of accountability to fact and actuality. Even the so-called realist novel carries its own implied set of inverted commas: it might seem a little more realistic than its less trustworthy counterparts but it is still by its nature pure fiction. If we accept Monro's case – and he is certainly not alone in advocating it – and concede that literature should, even to a partial extent, commit itself to the process of excavating and illuminating aspects of lived experience that might otherwise remain undisclosed, or at least left to experience rather than captured in language, then we must also concede that one of the principal criteria for evaluating a literary work – judging its qualities and assessing it in relation to other works – must be grounded in its perceived success in this twin role of disclosure and representation. Paradoxically, then, modernism is by its nature superior to realism because it is more realistic.

This cascade of questions and attendant dilemmas is, I accept, too taxing for anything close to a straightforward resolution, at least at this point. I present it to you because it encapsulates the nature and purpose of the whole of this book. It is too easy to treat the conflict between Eliot's supporters and detractors as a battle won by the former and part of the undisputed chronicle of literary history.

Consider again the pretext of Monro's case. He contends that in order for literature to properly engage with change in society it must radicalize itself, as most modernist works did. The implications of the model are disturbing, given that it consigns virtually every type of writing that preceded Eliot – generally classified as traditional writing – as by its nature incapable of dealing with the raw material of present day (circa 1920s) existence. Even if we grant that the argument is only in part tenable then it still had far-reaching consequences. Modernism did not extinguish traditional writing and nor did it overturn the latter's ascendency as the preferred option for the ordinary reader. Therefore, in agreeing with Monro we are effectively prejudging conventional writing as second rate. Can we really accept that realist novels and conventional poems are inherently unsuitable as a means of addressing the complexities and turmoils of society, particularly society in a state of flux – given that most historians would contend that society is continually in a state of flux? This returns us once more to an overarching question already raised: why should we judge the value and quality of literature according to how effectively, or otherwise, it tackles contemporary life? The poems of John Donne are acclaimed as brilliant examples of the short lyric but do they tell us any more about early seventeenth century England than we might learn from historical records? And if not, are they any the worse, as literature, for that?

Let us now consider another giant of modernism whose transformative effect on the history of the novel was, arguably, equal to that of Eliot with poetry: James Joyce. Joyce's *A Portrait of the Artist as a Young Man* (1916) begs comparison with Eliot's "Prufrock" in that both were their respective author's initial assaults upon the bastions of tradition in their chosen genre. *A Portrait* is unconventionally lacking in the solid narrative storyline of the nineteenth century novel but the most radical feature of the novel involves the relationship between the main character, Stephen Dedalus, and the third person narrator. Stephen does not tell his own story but the narrator sympathetically adjusts the style of the novel to suit his mood. Indeed, as Stephen becomes more preoccupied with his ambitions as an "artist" the style becomes correspondingly more intensive and mature. Joyce, however, was treated far more sympathetically by reviewers than Eliot.

> When one recognizes genius in a book one can perhaps best leave criticism alone … There are many pages, and not a few whole scenes, in Mr. Joyce's book which are undoubtedly the work of a man of genius, nevertheless, it leaves us combative. The reader – who is as much ignored, and as contemptuously, as it is possible for him to be in a printed work – revolts and asserts himself from time to time, and refuses to sit down passively under the writer's scorn. Once criticism is let loose, it finds range enough and many marks to hit.
>
> Not for its apparent formlessness should the book be condemned. A subtle sense of art has worked amidst the chaos, making this hither-and-thither record of a young mind and soul … a complete and ordered portrait.
>
> ("A.M." of the *Manchester Guardian*, 2 March 1917)

"A.M." is impressed by Joyce's experiment with narrative but unsettled by the consequences.

> Not all the scenes are touched by genius. Some read like disagreeable phonographic records of the stupid conversations of ill-born and ill-bred youths,

composed of futile obscenities, aimless outrages against reasonable decencies – not immoral, but non-moral in a bad-mannered fashion. Perhaps Mr. Joyce wants to show what may be, and often is, the ugly background of fairer things which consent astonishingly to grow in a sordid neighbourhood.

On the one hand "A.M." accepts enthusiastically that Joyce's technique causes us to reconsider our standard notions of what fictional representations involve, yet he/she is slightly appalled by what this uncovering of inner thoughts – variously random, obscure, vulgar, base, and so on – actually comprises. "A.M." certainly does not dispute that what Joyce shows us is a truthful portrait of what happens beneath the façade of manners and courtesy – he/she concurs that all humans are equal in this respect – but he/she is distressed by the fact that the disclosures have been made public and, even worse, that literature has been employed to do so.

Francis Hackett, writing in *The New Republic* (3 March 1917) can claim to be the most insightful of the early commentators. He describes astutely the symbiotic relationship between Stephen's mental landscape and the sympathetically shifting temper of the narrator, a considerable achievement on his part given that nothing quite like this had been attempted in the English novel.

> What gives its intensity to the portrait is the art Mr. Joyce has mastered of communicating the incidents of Stephen's career through the emotions they excited in him. We do not perceive Stephen's father and mother by description. We get them by the ebb and flood of Stephen's feelings, and while there are many passages of singularly life-like conversation – such, for example, as the wrangle about Parnell that ruined the Christmas dinner or the stale banter that enunciated the father's return to Cork – the viridity is in Stephen's soul.

Hackett next confronts the dilemma that caused for "A.M." feelings of admiration and revulsion.

> A novel in which a sensitive, critical young man is completely expressed as he is can scarcely be expected to be pleasant. *A Portrait of the Artist as a Young Man* is *not entirely pleasant*. But it has such beauty, such love of beauty, such intensity of feeling, such pathos, such candor, it goes beyond anything in English that reveals the inevitable malaise of serious youth.

The two critics deal differently with the same contentious issue, and Hackett mounts a defense of Joyce almost exactly the same as Monro's of

Eliot. Both treat transgressions of the accepted purpose of literature as tokens of its ability to transform otherwise stilted, inhibited perceptions of a turbulent moment in history. And once more two interconnected questions are raised: why is literature uniquely equipped to perform such tasks and does its role, as such, compromise its status as art and cause it instead to become primarily an index for our conceptions of who we are and what we experience? While the latter is a commendable achievement it challenges the enduring sense of literature as art-in-language, absolved of obligations to reason and fidelity. Does this matter? It does, because it causes further confusion for the long debated issue of what is, and what is not, good literature. Consider for a moment the criteria that underpin Hackett's championing of Joyce. He, Hackett, is walking a very fine line between a celebration of high quality writing (and in this respect he does not make it clear why Joyce's method is more intellectually challenging, even enjoyable, than the methods of the previous century) and an exemption of writing from aesthetic judgments; these, he argues, are less important than its relevance, its ability to record a sense of social discord and malaise.

I give greater attention to this issue in the next chapter, but now I shall turn back the clock to a point more than a century before the birth of modernism when the trajectory of literary writing faced another moment of disjunction, Romanticism.

The *Lyrical Ballads, With a Few Other Poems* (a collection of poems by William Wordsworth and Samuel Taylor Coleridge, first published in 1798) is taken by most to be the inaugurating moment of Romantic verse, and it embodies the perversities and unresolved paradoxes that inform all aspects of the movement. In the second edition, published in 1800, Wordsworth, in the newly added Preface, proclaims that his intention is to make available in poetry "the real language of men," to catch the unmediated "spontaneous overflow or powerful feeling." He is, however, somewhat guarded and obtuse on how exactly he intends to realize these objectives. The vast majority of the poems in the collection concern the lives and experiences of the uncultured denizens of the rural landscape of eighteenth century England. The best known and most widely discussed are "The Idiot Boy," "Simon Lee," and "The Mad Mother." Wordsworth presented these figures as possessed of an intrinsic wisdom uncomplicated and undiminished by the intellectual constraints of the educated city dweller, and the poems that caused the most controversy among early reviewers of the collection were those that centered upon characters who were neither quaint nor particularly heroic and who presented the reader with few opportunities to reflect upon their dire state as being the cause of some tangible form of social injustice or symbolic of an ungenerous branch of fate. They simply existed, and Southey (1798), in a much-cited review, sums up the puzzling unprecedented character of this exercise. "The Idiot Boy," he claimed, "resembles a Flemish picture in the worthlessness of its design and the excellence of its execution." "Worthlessness" should not be mistaken as evidence of Southey's complete disapproval; he meant that the poem lacks any sense of allegory or pregnant meaning, that it is simply a naturalistic portrait of fact without comment. Similarly, Dr Burney in *The Monthly Review* (1799) compared the rural ballads with "pictures," "as dark as those of Rembrandt." The principal subjects of these poems, Johnny in "The Idiot Boy," Martha Ray in "The Thorn," the unnamed Mad Mother, or the eponymous Simon Lee, are never the commanding presences of their pieces. Sometimes their speech is reported but the story is always told by someone else, never quite the same person but serving a similar purpose in Wordsworth's sociocultural confidence trick. His speakers are intermediaries between his own condition of high cultural erudition, a state he regrets but from which he knows he can never detach himself, and a region unpolluted by art and philosophy where tactile experience and emotion enjoy unostentatious purity. Wordsworth conducted an exercise in cultural ventriloquism. He went down-market in an attempt to invest ordinary, manifestly ill-educated presences with transcendental significance. "The Thorn" begins:

> There is a thorn; it looks so old,
> In truth you'd find it hard to say,
> How could it ever have been young,
> It looks so old and grey.
> Not higher than a two-years' child,
> It stands erect this aged thorn;
> No leaves it has, no thorny points;
> It is a mass of knotted joints,
> A wretched thing forlorn.
> It stands erect, and like a stone
> With lichens it is overgrown.

> Like rock or stone, it is o'ergrown
> With lichens to the very top,
> And hung with heavy tufts of moss
> A melancholy crop:

> Up from the earth these mosses creep,
> And this poor thorn they clasp it round
> So close, you'd say they were bent
> With plain and manifest intent,
> To drag it to the ground;
> And all had joined in one endeavour
> To bury this poor thorn for ever.

The critical reception of *Lyrical Ballads* was largely unsympathetic and in his piece in the *Critical Review* (1798) Southey indicated the nature of the disdainful consensus, commenting on "The Thorn":

> The advertisement says that it is not told in the person of the author but in that of some loquacious narrator. The author should have recollected that he who personates tiresome loquacity becomes tiresome himself.

Southey's point is that the speaker is, if not entirely unsuitable for serious poetry, then at least capable of trying the patience of the cultivated reader. Southey again:

> The "experiment", we think, has failed, not because the language of conversation is little adapted to "the purposes of poetic pleasure", but because it has been tried *upon uninteresting subjects...* every piece discovers genius.

Wordsworth and Coleridge faced a problem: if, as they stated, their objective was to capture a mood, a state of mind, that transcended high culture they must either reinvent themselves as peasants – and that, as *Lyrical Ballads* proved, was both inauthentic and preposterous – or they must be honest about their own status as educated erudite writers and do something radical with conventional verse. The rustic pieces of *Lyrical Ballads* are stories, of a sort, but they propose no straightforward philosophic or moral truisms. On the one hand Wordsworth and Coleridge did not want to turn their countryfolk into weird, plain-speaking replicas of Kant or Hume but at the same time nor did they wish them to relinquish their quiet, instinctive wisdom. Southey was right; the "experiment" with rustic odes was a failure. Wordsworth and Coleridge were awed by ordinary uneducated people but they knew nothing about them and subjected them to a patronizing brand of intellectual anthropomorphism, imparting to them a kind of rough sagacity that was part of their own intellectual fantasy. After the volume was published the experiment died and the rustic ballads endure only within the educational establishment. Any elementary degree course on English will involve hapless students in an encounter with them. What will be lacking, however, is the opportunity to assess these pieces as literary artworks and, potentially, reach the conclusion that Wordsworth and Coleridge (mainly the former, who was primarily responsible for the rustic project) produced poor quality poetic hybrids. True, they are *interesting* as testaments to how innovation can go wrong but they are not in their own right of much value. So why have they survived in the canon, preserved like their fellow artefacts from the capricious questionings of the ordinary reader? They might not have worked as attempts to buy access to a nirvana of primitivism but they can be regarded as precursors to an upmarket brand of self-absorption – made up both of narrative poems and odes – which displays a similar reluctance either to complete their tales or to allow us to unravel their themes and enigmas. Wordsworth's "Ode: Intimations of Immortality," Coleridge's "The Rime of the Ancient Mariner" and "Christabel," Keats's "The Eve of St. Agnes" all seem to promise some kind of conclusion to their story or clarification of what they really mean, and all fail to deliver.

John Hazlitt on Coleridge's "Christabel" and "Kubla Khan," now regarded as quintessential classics of Romanticism, typifies contemporary responses.

> The fault of Mr. Coleridge is, that he comes to no conclusion. He is a man of that universality of genius, that his mind hangs suspended between poetry and prose, truth and falsehood, and an infinity of other things, and from an excess of capacity, he does little or nothing. Here are two unfinished poems, and a fragment.
>
> In parts of "Christabel" there is a great deal of beauty, both of thought, imagery, and versification; but the effect of the general story is dim, obscure, and visionary. It is more like a dream than a reality. The mind, in reading it, is spell-bound. The sorceress seems to act without power – Christabel to yield without resistance. The faculties are thrown into a state of metaphysical suspense and theoretical imbecility

Josiah Conder is similarly confounded:

> The conclusion of the second part of "Christabel", about "the little limber elf," is to us absolutely incomprehensible. "Kubla Khan", we think, only shews that Mr Coleridge can write better *nonsense* verses than any man in England. It is not a poem, but a musical composition.

> A damsel with a dulcimer
> In a vision once I saw:
> It was an Abyssinian maid,
> And on her dulcimer she play'd,
> Singing of Mount Abora.

We could repeat these lines to ourselves not the less often for not knowing the meaning of them…

In the mean time, we cannot conceal that the effect of the present publication upon readers in general, will be that of disappointment. It may be compared to a mutilated statue, the beauty of which can only be appreciated by those who have knowledge or imagination sufficient to complete the idea of the whole composition. The reader is obliged to guess at the half-developed meaning of the mysterious incidents, and is at last, at the end of the second canto, left in the dark, in the most abrupt and unceremonious manner imaginable. (*Eclectic Review*, June 1816)

The anonymous reviewer in the *Anti-Jacobin* is probably the most impatient and bad-tempered. On "Christabel":

Had we not known Mr Coleridge to be a man of genius and of talents, we should really, from the present production, have been tempted to pronounce him wholly destitute of both. In truth, a more senseless, absurd, and stupid, composition, has scarcely, of late years, issued from the press.

William Roberts fumes as vehemently as his fellow sceptics and his comments on Coleridge and Romanticism in general are fascinating.

The epidemic among modern poets is the disease of affectation, which is for ever carrying them into quaint, absurd, and outrageous extremes. *One* is determined to say nothing in a natural way, *another* is for saying every thing with infantile simplicity, while a *third* is persuaded that there is but one language for the drawing room, the Royal Exchange, the talk of the table, and the temple of the Muses. One consequence of this fatal propensity to affectation among out poets is a terrible sameness or mannerism in each of those who have been encouraged to write much; and the worst of it is that each of these luminaries, while he moves in his own orbit in perpetual parallelism with himself, has a crowd of little moons attending him, that multiply the malignant influence, and propagate the deceptious glare. But the most insufferable of all the different forms which modern affectation is composition has assumed is the cant and gibberish of the German school which has filled all the provinces, as well of imagination as of science, with profound nonsense, unintelligible refinement, metaphysical morals and mental distortion ...

We shall hail the day, as a day of happy auspices for the moral muse, when our present fanatic race of poets shall have exhausted all their "monstrous shapes and sorceries", and the abused understandings of our countrymen shall break these unhappy spells, forsake the society of demons, and be divorced from deformity. (*British Review,* viii, August 1816)

The parallels between Roberts's summation of where Romanticism is at fault and many of the early responses to modernism, poetry and fiction, are extraordinary. Irrespective of how we feel about Roberts's refusal to indulge this new phenomenon his argument, technically, is sound enough. Throughout the closing decades of the seventeenth century and the entirety of the eighteenth prevailing opinion was that poetry should equal the essay or the pamphlet in its claim upon coherence and transparency; the most celebrated verse of this period served as a lens to clarify complexities of thought and impression. As Roberts and his contemporaries note, Romanticism caused the pendulum to swing as far as possible in the opposite direction. Romantic poems, allegedly, had become vehicles for making the already unfathomable even more so, an arena for self-indulgence that alienates the ordinary reader. These very same charges were laid against T.S. Eliot. What, we might be forgiven for asking, had happened during the intervening century? Did the conservatives and doubters of the early twentieth century not realize that all of this had happened before? Not quite. What actually occurred was a process that can best be described as the domestication of revolt. By the mid–late nineteenth century the radicalism of the Romantics had been refined into an inconclusive thoughtfulness, encompassing such fundamentals as disillusionment, loss, often despair but in a manner that allowed for contemplation rather than confusion.

John Keats was a member of the second generation of Romantic poets and the reception of his work reflects the gradual sense among the literary establishment of a willingness to enquire, even celebrate, rather than condemn. Some reviewers treated him as depressing continuation of a trend begun by Wordsworth and Coleridge.

For ourselves, we think that Mr Keats is very faulty. He is often laboriously obscure; and he sometimes indulges is such strange intricacies of thought, and peculiarities of expression, that we find considerable difficulty in discovering his meaning. Most unluckily for him, he is a disciple in a school in which these peculiarities are virtues: but the praises of this small *coterie* will hardly compensate for the disapprobation of the rest of the literary world. (Unsigned piece in *The Monthly Review*, July, 1820)

A few months earlier the *London Magazine's* correspondent proposed that the faults were not with Keats, but with the incapacity of readers to adjust their ingrained expectations of what poetry should be and do.

Endymion is totally unlike all these, and all other poems. As we said before, it is not a *poem* at all. It is an ecstatic dream of poetry – a flush – a fever – a burning light – an involuntary out-pouring of the spirit of poetry – that will not be controuled. Its movements are the starts and boundings of the young horse before it has felt the bitt …

Almost entirely unknown as this poem is to general readers, it will perhaps be better to reserve what we have further to say of its characteristics, till we have given some specimens of it. We should premise this, however, by saying, that our examples will probably exhibit almost as many faults as beauties. But the reader will have anticipated this from the nature of the opinion we have already given – at least if we have succeeded in expressing what we intended to express. In fact, there is scarcely a passage of any length in the whole work, which does not exhibit the most flaring faults – faults that in many instances amount almost to the ludicrous. (*London Magazine*, ii, April 1820)

Romanticism had not changed and it had certainly not, through Keats, been purged of its radicalism, but, urges the reviewer, if we soften our inflexible notions of literary expectation, allow that something previously unknown might exceed what the known could achieve, then we might discover in these new works something more exalting, and challenging, than had been thought possible. Again we encounter a replica of what would occur with modernism, 100 years later: a new way of seeing would cause the cautious reader to cross the boundary between a region of doubt and perplexity to one of enlightenment.

I have compared these two periods to emphasize how the process of acceptance, the absorption of the unprecedented into common practice, tends to be a generic feature of response to radicalism: shock and rejection are followed by thoughtful consolidation. And I have done so to raise some questions. What changes? Do the critics, and as a consequence readers, become less intolerant and able to discover qualities previously overlooked or are such "responses" actually symptomatic of an addiction to change for its own sake, something that automatically overturns rational evaluation? Third, and most significantly, we must consider the unclear relationship between what the establishment, at a given time, considers acceptable as literature and the ability of a particular writer as a literary craftsman. Few if any of the critics who display hostility to the works of Eliot, Joyce, Wordsworth, Coleridge, and Keats would condemn them as incompetent writers. Rather, to offer an analogy, they are seen as talented sportsmen of some promise who have decided, without consulting the governing body, to alter the rules of the game. These initial transgressions are eventually adapted to a new set of conventions, but how do these modifications, these changes to what is and it not acceptable, affect the more fundamental question of the difference between good and bad writing? There are no easy answers to any of these questions but to better address them it is useful to consider the fact that not all changes in the critical consensus have been brought about by precipitate responses to innovative writing. In one notable instance the literary establishment took it upon itself to look backwards and re-evaluate work produced more than a century earlier.

The poets who are thought to have best embodied the spirit of English Renaissance literature are those of the so-called Metaphysical School. They thrived in the early seventeenth century and their most celebrated representatives, notably John Donne, George Herbert, Henry Vaughan, Robert Herrick, Richard Crashaw, Thomas Traherne, and Andrew Marvell, now occupy an esteemed place in the canon of nondramatic poetry, their elevated status unquestioned by literary cognoscenti and their work granted confirmation of classic status by the reading lists of university courses. Like many others we have already considered they are effectively immune from critical disfavor. Consider then the following opinion on them expressed by another writer, and critic, to whom we are expected to accord largely unquestioning respect, Samuel Johnson:

> But wit, abstracted from its effects upon the hearer, may be more rigorously and philosophically considered as a kind of *discordia concors*; a combination of dissimilar images, or discovery of occult resemblances in things apparently unlike. Of wit, thus defined, they have more than enough. *The most heterogeneous ideas are yoked by violence together* [emphasis added], nature and art are ransacked for illustrations, comparisons, and allusions; their learning instructs, and their subtlety surprises; but the reader commonly thinks his improvement dearly bought, and, though he sometimes admires, is seldom pleased. (Johnson, 1779–1781, p. 218)

Johnson objects to, as he sees it, the overadventurous and irresponsible use of figurative language (or "wit" as he puts it). In this respect, he was speaking on behalf of the general consensus of eighteenth century ideas regarding poetry. His principal point is that the Metaphysicals deliberately used language to undermine orderly perceptions of reality. By the phrase "heterogeneous ideas are yoked by violence together" he meant that ideas, concepts, and images that had no natural or logical relation to each other were caused to seem as though they did; the innately paradoxical was made to seem self-evidently logical and plausible. In his "Second Anniversary," Donne tells of how

> Her pure and innocent blood
> Spoke in her cheeks, and so distinctly wrought
> That one might almost say, her body thought.

Typically, he engages with that perennial debating point of philosophers and theologians, the relationship between the corporal and the spiritual, and, although one might take issue with Johnson's use of the term "violence," there is without doubt a hypnotizing "yoking together" of "heterogeneous ideas." Johnson and his contemporaries were aware that figurative language was a collateral feature of all poetic writing but in their view it should be used with discrimination and as a means of clarifying or buttressing a point of logical disputation. Donne, however, performs the verbal equivalent of illusionism, causing her cheeks to speak and her body to think. T.S. Eliot stated:

> It is the difference between the intellectual poet and reflective poet. Tennyson and Browning are poets, and they think, but they do not feel their thought as immediately as the odour of a rose. A thought to Donne was an experience; it modified his sensibility. *When a poet's mind is perfectly equipped for its work, it is constantly amalgamating disparate experience* [emphasis added]; the ordinary man's experience is chaotic, irregular, and fragmentary. The latter falls in love, or reads Spinoza, and these two experiences have nothing to do with each other, or with the noise of the typewriter or the smell of cooking; in the mind of the poet these experiences are always forming new wholes.
>
> (Eliot, 1921, p. 2024)

Eliot agrees almost exactly with Johnson on the nature of Metaphysical technique: "A thought to Donne was an experience." But Eliot regards the ability to undermine the logical and empirical specifications of reality as the essential calling of the poet: to use poetic language to oblige us to re-examine our rational processes of thinking and our perceptions of actuality. For Johnson, the eighteenth century rationalist, the distinction between, say, bodily sensations and the workings of the intellect should be maintained as much in poetry as in a philosophical essay. For Eliot, the modernist, it is the duty of the poet to challenge, even undermine, such orthodox classifications: "in the mind of the poet these experiences are always forming new wholes." While these two critics differ with regard to the value of Metaphysical writing, they agree precisely on its character and effect.

Once more we encounter a discord between an estimation of a writer's ability and the way they have chosen to execute it. Johnson and his peers rarely doubted the capacities of Donne, Herbert, and others as poetic writers but they treated them largely as wasted geniuses.

Johnson's premise is as follows: "If the father of criticism [Aristotle] has rightly denominated poetry ... *an imitative art*, these writers will without great wrong lose their right to the name of poets, for they cannot be said to have imitated anything: they neither copied nature nor life, neither painted the forms of matter nor represented the operations of the intellect." Whether or not Aristotle's verdict on the purpose of poetry should be treated as decisive can be left until Chapter 8. What is important here is to note that Johnson never regards the Metaphysical poets as sub-standard writers but his estimation of their work is effectively pre-decided. Before he reads a poem, by the Metaphysicals or anyone else, Johnson has made up his mind about what criteria it should meet and if it fails to do so, even if the poet displays an abundance of creative talent, it is automatically downgraded aesthetically.

To a certain degree all of us, from critics to general readers, are guided in our estimation of a work by ingrained expectations, even prejudices. Very often these vary according to temperament and disposition, but in the case of Johnson and his contemporaries their ideas on what did or did not qualify as good literature were formed according to a commonly accepted critical consensus. Something similar to this notion of the literary establishment bound together in a fabric of received wisdom obtains in most periods, but with fluctuating allowances for indulgence and conjecture. The eighteenth century was probably the most resolute and inflexible in the history of English, for several reasons. Given that the vast majority of commentators dated the provenance of English literature to the sixteenth century, it was barely then two centuries old. It came into the world accompanied by classical antecedents on what literature should be and do but it had no indigenous rules of its own. This in itself caused a sense of collective insecurity among the new cultural establishment, a preoccupation with designing a new set of conventions that matched classicism in terms of rigor and comfortable predictability. This first generation of critics and rule-makers was greatly influenced also by the political mood of the period. The eighteenth century began within living memory of the Civil War and its equally turbulent aftermath and there was a general determination to establish a sense of coherence and order within society, a model based upon an ideal of classical civilization.

The Royal Society was founded after the Cromwellian Protectorate during the first months of the Restoration and in the succeeding decades established itself as a kind of barometric guide to developments in the key areas of thinking and writing. Its best-known and most widely quoted statement of purpose occurs in Thomas Sprat's "The History of the Royal Society (and for "history" we might read "manifesto"):

> The resolution of the Royal Society has been … to reject all amplifications, digressions, and swellings of style; to return back to the primitive purity and shortness, when men deliver'd so many *things* almost in an equal number of *words*. They have extracted from all their members a close, naked, natural way of speaking, positive expressions, clear senses, a native easiness, bringing all things near the Mathematical plainness as they can, and preferring the language of Artizans, Countryman, and Merchants, before that of Wits or Scholars.
>
> (Sprat, 1667 (1908), pp. 117–118)

Sprat detects a danger in "amplifications digressions and swellings" of expression – which is virtually a definition of poetry – mannerisms that might as much mislead as entertain; he prefers the "Mathematical plainness" of the language of those who work for the good of the country. Before apportioning to Sprat an intolerance of literature per se we should note that John Dryden restates his proposition in his 1677 manifesto on the proper use of poetry: "the definition of wit … is only this: that it is the propriety of thoughts and words; or, in other terms, thoughts and words elegantly adapted to the subject." The parallels between both commendations of clarity, order, and coherence in writing and Johnson's attack on the Metaphysicals, a century later, are self-evident.

Though frequently praised during the eighteenth century even Shakespeare did not escape censure. In fact, the majority of those who enthused about him did so in response to the quality of contemporary performances. As literary works in their own right his plays were treated with widespread circumspection, which sometimes bordered on condemnation. George Colman in his *Critical Reflections on the Old English Dramatic Writers* (1761) claims that the popularity of Shakespeare has been sustained by his appeal to our baser appetites for verbal gymnastics and thrilling stories, which cause us to overlook his failings as a serious writer.

> The conduct of these Extravagant Stories is frequently uncouth, and infinitely offensive to that Dramatick correctness prescribed by late Critics and practised (as they pretend) by the French Writers.

Colman's principal objection to Shakespeare is that he is overambitious to the point of hyperbole, that he attempts to force the universality of experience into dramas which become overloaded with incongruities.

> What patient Spectators are we of the Inconsistencies that confessedly prevail in our darling Shakespeare! What critical Catcall ever proclaimed the indecency of introducing the Stocks in the Tragedy of *Lear*? How quietly do we see Gloster take his imaginary Leap from Dover Cliff! Or to give a stronger instance of Patience, with what a Philosophical Calmness do the audience doze over the tedious and uninteresting Love-Scenes, with which the bungling hand of Tate has coarsely pieced and patched that rich Work of Shakespeare! – To instance further from Shakespeare himself, the Grave-diggers in *Hamlet* (not to mention Polonius) are not only endured but applauded; the very Nurse in *Romeo and Juliet* is allowed to be Nature; the Transactions of a whole History are, without offence, begun and completed in less than three hours; and we are agreeably wafted by the *Chorus*, or oftener without so much ceremony, from one end of the world to another.

Colman is pursuing an argument similar to Johnson's on the Metaphysicals: the lens of literary representation has become too distorting and refractory. In her *Shakespeare Illustrated: or The Novels and Histories on which the Plays of Shakespeare are Founded* (1753–4), Charlotte Lennox seems ostensibly set upon a scholarly account of the sources of Shakespeare's works, in history and literature, but it soon becomes apparent that she is as much concerned with the extent to which his drama defies credulity and causes individual characters to speak and behave in ways that defy logic and the basic rules of consistency. On *Measure for Measure*:

> As the Character of the Duke is absurd and ridiculous, that of *Angelo* is inconsistent to the last Degree. His Baseness to *Mariana*, his wicked Attempts on the Chastity of *Isabella*, his villainous Breach of Promise and Cruelty to *Claudio* prove him to be a very bad Man, long practised in Wickedness; yet when he finds himself struck with the Beauty of *Isabella* he starts at the Temptation, reasons on his Frailty, asks Assistance from Heaven to overcome it, resolves against it, and seems carried away by the Violence of his Passion to commit what his better Judgement abhors.
>
> Are these the Manners of a sanctified Hypocrite, such as *Angelo* is represented to be? Are they not rather those of a good man overcome by a powerful Temptation? That *Angelo* was not a good Man appears by his base Treatment of *Mariana*; for certainly nothing can be viler than to break his Contract with a Woman of Merit because she had accidently become poor and, to excuse his own Conduct, load the unfortunate Innocent with base Aspersions and add Infamy to her other Miseries. Yet this is the Man who, when attacked by a Temptation, kneels, prays, expostulates with himself, and while he scarce yields in Thought to do wrong his Mind feels all the Remorse which attends actual Guilt.

Her analysis of the characters, their apparent motivations, and their relationship with each other is not inaccurate, but she raises, without explicitly addressing, a question. Is she basing her criteria for good literature upon what might be expected of a nonliterary work, such as a historical account of an actual event, in which truth, plausibility, and in the end authenticity overrule inventive license? We might treat her comments indulgently, as a curiosity, and we would do so on the assumption that we have progressed to a more sophisticated conception of what is and is not allowable in literature. We might, but what if we were then asked to chart the progress of evaluation and name the points at which the moments of enlightenment occurred? In short, does historical progress always confer improvement upon habits of interpretation?

One of the most celebrated dramatists, poets, and commentators of the century was Oliver Goldsmith. He does not offer as detailed a reading as Colman or Lennox but his unsympathetic judgment is based on similar premises.

> We seem to be pretty much in the situation of travellers at a Scotch inn: vile entertainment is served up, complained of and sent down; up comes worse, and that also is changed; and every change makes our wretched cheer more unsavoury. What must be done? Only sit down contented, cry up all that comes before us, and admire even the absurdities of Shakespeare.

Let the reader suspend his censure; I admire the beauties of this great father of our stage as much as they deserve but could wish, for the honour of our country, and for his honour too, that many of his scenes were forgotten. A man blind of one eye should always be painted in profile. Let the spectator who assists at any of these new revived pieces only ask himself whether he would approve such a performance if written by a modern poet; if he would not, then his applause proceeds merely from the sound of a name and an empty veneration of antiquity. In fact, the revival of those pieces of forced humour, far-fetch'd conceit, and unnatural hyperbole which have been ascribed to Shakespeare, is rather gibbeting than raising a statue to his memory; it is rather a trick of the actor, who thinks it safest acting in exaggerated characters, and who by out-stepping nature chuses to exhibit the ridiculous outré of an harlequin under the sanction of this venerable name. ("Of the Stage" from *An Enquiry into the Present State of Polite Learning in Europe,* 1759)

In Goldsmith's view, Shakespeare's work is an example of low culture which appeals to those who prefer "forced humour, far-fetched conceit and unnatural hyperbole" over the more prudent and discriminating qualities of great literature. He asks if we "would approve such a performance if written by a modern poet," implying that public taste has improved considerably since Shakespeare and his contemporaries introduced audiences to modern drama. To respond, as many of us would, that public appreciation of Shakespeare's greatness has improved since the mid-eighteenth century brings us to a dilemma. In our move to our present state of intellectual and cultural maturity have we actually gone backwards, to a point before Goldsmith when Shakespeare was uninhibited by such expectations as a resemblance between the play and the world? Goldsmith again:

What strange vamp'd comedies, farcical tragedies, or what shall I call them, speaking pantomimes, have we not of late see. No matter what the play may be it is the actor who draws an audience. He throws life into all; all are in spirits and merry, in at one door and out at another; the spectator, in a fool's paradise, knows not what all this means till the last act concludes in matrimony. The piece pleases our critics, because it talks of old English, and it pleases the galleries, because it has fun. True taste, or even common sense, are out of the question.

The most detailed and withering attack on Shakespeare comes from Henry Home, Lord Kames, a figure little known today but whose work matches modern criticism in its attention to detail. In his voluminous *Elements of Criticism* (1762) Kames picks relentlessly through passages of Shakespeare's drama in a manner that prefigures twentieth century New Criticism and on the basis of his findings draws conclusions on the Bard's value as a poet and playwright. Typically, on what he treats as the overambitious use of figurative devices:

> It is remarkable that this low species of wit has among all nations been a favourite entertainment in a certain stage of their progress toward refinement of taste and manners, and has gradually gone into disrepute. As soon as a language is formed into a system and the meaning of words is ascertained with tolerably accuracy, opportunity is afforded for expressions that, by the double meaning of some words, give a familiar thought the appearance of being new; and the penetration of the reader or hearer is gratified in detecting the true sense disguised under the double meaning. That this sort of wit was in England deemed a reputable amusement during the reigns of Elizabeth and James I is vouched by the works of Shakespeare, and even by the writings of grave divines. But it cannot have any long endurance: for as language ripens and the meaning of words is more and more ascertained words held to be synonymous diminish daily, and when those that remain have been more than once employ'd the pleasure vanisheth with the novelty.

This is based on the same evaluative pretext as Johnson's dismissal of the verse of the Metaphysicals and it should be made clear that those who begrudged Shakespeare a claim to true literary quality were in the majority throughout the eighteenth century. Anyone who would express such opinions today would at best be indulged as an eccentric, a figure who could be tolerated because their views are self-evidently preposterous. When did the consensus alter? The Romantics found in Shakespeare crucial parallels with their own creative manifestoes. What the eighteenth century critics treated as a careless abundance of invention and stylistic experiment, the Romantics seized upon as a triumph of the unfettered imagination over stifling conventions, literary and philosophical. Shelley went so far as to proclaim that Shakespeare had attained a God-like quality which rendered him immune from any sort of criticism, even that which praised him ("On the Knocking at the Gate in Macbeth," 1823). Since then a degree of sanity has intervened, but something of what George Bernard Shaw called the "bardolatry" of the Romantics endures. Contra Shelley, we now allow ourselves to criticize him but there are implicit boundaries that no communicator will dare cross.

We return to Shakespeare in Chapter 3 and close this one with a consideration of how the novel was dealt with during the eighteenth century, the period of its birth in England.

Tobias Smollett's *Humphrey Clinker* (1771) was published more than 50 years after the book that is generally agreed to have launched the genre, Defoe's *Robinson Crusoe* (1719), but it is evident from responses to it that there was still no clear agreement on what novels were.

The anonymous reviewer in *The Critical Review* is impressed by the letters between Mr Brimble and Mr Melford:

> Upon their expedition to North Britain, contain so many interesting observations, that they must not only gratify every reader of curiosity, but also tend to correct many wrong notions concerning that part of the Island. We would willingly give an account of many of the particulars related of Edinburgh and its inhabitants, but as our readers are probably less acquainted with the manners of the people farther North, we shall extract the representation which is given of the economy in the house of a Highland gentleman.
> (*The Critical Review, XXXII*, 1771, pp. 81–88)

Reviewers often praise novelists for the attention they give to detail and setting as a means of lending more credibility to the story and its characters, but the *Critical Review* correspondent is preoccupied exclusively with Smollett's reliability as a source of information on lesser known parts of England and Scotland.

> We find, from another passage in the work, that Lough Lomond, from whence the river Leven issues, is a body of pure highland water, unfathomably deep in many places, six or seven miles broad, and four and twenty miles in length. This contains above twenty green islands, covered with wood; some of them cultivated for corn, and many of them stocked with red deer.

This might, to us, come across as a somewhat bizarre way of assessing the qualities of a novel. The modern equivalent would be a review of Tom Wolfe's *The Bonfire of the Vanities* that is made up entirely of comments on how well the author informs those unacquainted with life in New York of the luxurious interiors of Broadway apartments, ongoing trends in furniture and décor, types of shoes favored by well-appointed stockbrokers, and the inhospitable standards of public transport, particularly the Subway, compared with chauffeured private limousines. This reviewer's seemingly obsessive focus on fact was not uncommon during the eighteenth century and towards the end of the piece we come upon an inadvertent explanation for it.

> Instead of visionary scenes and persons, the usual subjects of Romance, we are frequently presented with many uncommon anecdotes, and curious expressions of real life, described in such a manner as to afford a pleasure even superior to what arises from the portraits of fancy. We are every where entertained with the narration or description of something interesting and extraordinary, calculated at once to amuse the imagination, and release the understanding from prejudice.

Some in the 1770s still referred to fiction as "Romance," though "the novel" had by then overtaken this term in common usage. During the early decades of the century it was the custom to conflate the new brand of prose storytelling with the romance epics of the medieval period and the Renaissance. Most of these were in verse rather than prose but they at least offered later, often confused, commentators with some kind of precedent for the novel. This reviewer notes that Smollett dispenses with "visionary scenes and persons, the usual subjects of Romance," by which he means that Romance – and Spenser's *The Faerie Queene* falls into this category – was licensed to experiment with the boundaries between reality and the fantastic. The reviewer, albeit somewhat belatedly compared with most of his peers, is accepting that what we now understand to be classic realism – that is, the world we live in recorded convincingly in prose – was now the modus operandi of the new genre. However, having apparently recognized this he is perplexed by what exactly realism is supposed to do, and compensates by treating the novel as if it belonged in the same genre as Defoe's *A Tour of Britain*; that is, as documentary travel writing.

The review encapsulates a problem that faced critics, and readers, throughout the eighteenth century. As we have seen with Romanticism and modernism, writing that transgressed against convention could be celebrated or condemned for doing so, but what if there was no obvious precedent for a work or works to be compared with? Often we find in published responses to novels and in private correspondence expressions of enjoyment, appreciation, and quite often disgust, but in each instance the remarks will be cautiously offered, sometimes accompanied by a sense of guilt, even anger. People were clearly deeply affected by the experience of reading this new kind of literature – it would have been the equivalent of showing a film to an audience that had never before encountered cinema – but they were often unsettled by having to deal with emotive reactions for which there were no filtering systems. No one was quite sure what the novel was and as a consequence the mechanisms that routinely enabled them to measure or rationalize their feelings about literature or any other form of art became inadequate.

Daniel Defoe is credited with laying the foundations for the English novel with his best known works, notably *Robinson Crusoe* (1719), *Colonel Jack* (1722), and *Moll Flanders* (1722). Newspapers were in their infancy during this period but one will search in vain through them for contemporary coverage of his fiction. It was not that his work failed to attract public attention – quite the opposite, all his fiction was immensely popular – simply that reviewers did not know how to deal with a genre with no obvious literary parentage.

When retrospective accounts of his work began to appear in the 1770s and 1780s commentators remained uncertain of how to treat it:

> *Robinson Crusoe* must be allowed by the most rigid moralist, to be one of those novels, which one may read, not only with pleasure, but also with profit. It breathes throughout a spirit of piety and benevolence: it sets in a very striking light … the importance of the mechanick arts, which they, who do not know what it is to be without them, are apt to undervalue: it fixes in the mind a lively idea of the horrors of solitude, and, consequently, of the sweets of social life, and of the blessings we derive from conversation, and mutual aid: and it shows, how, by labouring with one's own hands, one may secure independence, and open for oneself many sources of health and amusement.
>
> (James Beattie, *Dissertations Moral and Critical,* 1783)

Ethics and morality are still regarded by some as significant elements of literature, but the number of such advocates is dwindling: 50 years ago the court case unbanning Lawrence's *Lady Chatterley's Lover* effectively demolished the idea that art should encourage good behavior. Beattie, professor of moral philosophy at the University of Edinburgh and highly respected critic, is obviously dumbfounded by what he elsewhere terms the "new romance." Unlike poetry and drama the novel lacked anything resembling an abstract formal structure. Stories seemed to meander from one point to another without any obvious evidence of planning, rather like life as we know it. Indeed, the controversy that first surrounded *Robinson Crusoe* – that Defoe had plagiarized Alexander Selkirk's autobiographical account of his actual experience as a castaway – was fuelled in part by the confusion provoked by Defoe's insistence that he had invented Crusoe and his narrative.

Such things were unknown and unclassifiable so he must either be lying or copying someone else's version of the truth. Beattie, following a line taken by many of his peers who faced the same dilemma, elects to treat the novel as something close to a modern parable. He was no doubt aware that some people derived excitement and often prurient pleasure in witnessing the successes and woes of fictional characters but this would hardly qualify fiction as literary art. Hugh Blair agrees that *Robinson Crusoe* is morally edifying, yet his praise carries a hint of caution, causing him to warn the reader against becoming too easily beguiled by the story while forgetting its instructive purpose.

> While it is carried on with that appearance of truth and simplicity, which takes a strong hold of the imagination of all Readers, it suggests, at the same time, very useful instruction; by showing how much the native powers of man may be exerted for surmounting the difficulties of any external situation.
> (*Lectures on Rhetoric and Belles Lettres*, 1783)

Critics were less sympathetic when Defoe offered his characters more license in terms of conscience, behavior, and lack of repentance. In his *Life* (1785) of the novelist, George Chalmers comments that in *Moll Flanders* "Defoe was aware, that in relating a vicious life, it was necessary to make the best use of a bad story; and he artfully endeavours, that the reader shall be more pleased with the moral than the fable … with the end of the writer than the adventures of the person." By this he means that despite her record of crime and licentiousness Moll is lightly punished, escaping the gallows, and settles with her husband into a life of quiet contrition. In short, he gives nominal attention to the "moral" while allowing the reader, like Moll, to enjoy her risqué "fable." Chalmers is seemingly bemused by Defoe's *Life of Roxana*.

> Scenes of crimes can scarcely be represented in such a manner, says Defoe, but some make a criminal use of them; but when vice is painted in its low-prized colours, it is not to make people love what from the frightfulness of the figures they ought necessarily to hate. Yet, I am not convinced, that the world has been made much wiser, or better, by the perusal of these lives: they may have diverted the lower orders, but I doubt if they have much improved them; if however they have not made them better, they have not left them worse. But they do not exhibit many scenes which are welcome to cultivated minds.

He finds it difficult to decide, from one sentence to the next, if he is dealing with a book illustrating the true nature of "vice" – and by implication

arousing repugnance for those of "cultivated minds" – or if these "scenes …
painted in … low prized colours" are dangerous literary entertainments
prized by "the lower orders."

Confusion reigns in commentaries by Blair, Chalmers, and others because
the novel, barely six decades old, had announced its presence without
disclosing its purpose. Chalmers, in his prefatory remarks, classifies these
novels as "fictitious biography" which, he declares, "may be more instructive
than a real life." Absurd as it might seem to us, critics and readers in the eighteenth century suffered persistently from interpretive double-vision, unsure
of where to draw the line between treating the inhabitants of novels as candid
representations of fellow human beings or as pure inventions. As a
consequence estimations of the aesthetic and formal qualities of a work
became entangled with, sometimes subsumed by, the kind of valuations that
enable us to assess incidents and individuals who are part of our world. Such
difficulties did not arise with poetry because the formal mechanisms of the
genre – meter, rhyme, figurative usage, and so on – were recognizable to all
literate persons and enabled them to distinguish between verse and every
other form of language. Crucially, this benchmark further allowed for a
consensus on what could be done in poetry. Ordinary language – from
conversation through pamphleteering to the philosophical essay – was
expected to be truthful and coherent while verse was a combination of
invention and gratuitous effect. A reliable definition of what was and what
was not poetry was also the foundation for evaluation. Imagine hearing a
piano played very badly, or someone singing to themselves in a manner that
is toe-curlingly dreadful. Even if we cannot name the concerto or the song
we can sense that something is wrong. But if we have no knowledge whatsoever of musical notation how do we describe the nature of the performer's
problem? This was the dilemma faced by eighteenth century commentators
on the novel. They read novels, were affected by them in different ways, but
the genre – unlike poetry – lacked a reliable definition and terminology for
describing how they worked and what they did.

The figure who caused the most controversy, and confusion, was Henry
Fielding. *Tom Jones* prompted a long letter from "Aretine", in effect an article
addressed directly to Fielding (*Old England*, 27 May 1749). From the first
part one imagines Aretine coming close to bursting a blood vessel as he
attempts to channel his poorly suppressed rage into coherent sentences.
One might indeed judge him faintly deranged, at least before detecting the
method beneath his obsessive preoccupation with minutiae and authenticity. For example, he spends a considerable amount of time on Fielding's

placing of the Allworthy's Gothic Seat "on the *South-East* Side of a Hill, sheltered from the *North-East* by a Grove of Oaks; and from a Lake at the foot of a Hill, issued a River that for several Miles *was seen* to meander thro' Meadows and Woods, 'till it emptied itself itself into *the Sea.*'" He accuses Fielding of a gross misrepresentation of the true topography of "the Counties of *Devon* and *Dorset*" and explains in tortuous detail how it is impossible to "reconcile this Description with Probability." One might of course attempt to steady the fuming Aretine by pointing out that Mr Allworthy and his entire estate do not exist but this would merely point up the difference between the way novels were perceived then and now, and would not necessarily reinforce the superiority of our point of view.

Aretine's case is more subtle than it first seems. His complaint against Fielding's reconfiguring of the known landscape of south-west England is a preamble to the second part of his letter where he details a comparable mismatch between the behavior of figures in the novel, and their implications for morality and social integrity, and the world beyond the covers of the book. He does not claim simply that Fielding is irresponsibly licensing bad behavior – that is, degrading principle in the same way that he modified Devon and Dorset – rather that to have so many people act in such a determinedly improper manner in an evolved, largely Christian society (a "History of Bastardism, Fornication and Adultery" as he puts it) defies credibility. It is, I think, too easy to dismiss Aretine as a delusional idealist. Many during the eighteenth century perceived the world as a formulated model. They did not blind themselves to human tendencies that failed to conform to it but they treated these as aberrations rather than, as we might, permutations on a limitless diversity of motives, acts, and consequences. In Aretine's opinion the abundance of corruption and depravity in the novel was a wilful misrepresentation of the achievements of civilized society. It was, in short, unrealistic.

Am I overindulging Aretine? A little perhaps, but we might pause before regarding ourselves as his enlightened betters. Consider Will Self's *Cock and Bull* (1992), a work consisting of two novellas. In the first, Carol, an otherwise submissive wife, grows a penis and rapes her husband, Dan. In the second, John Bull, a quintessentially male rugby player, acquires a vagina at the back of his knee and is seduced by his (male) doctor by whom he – or to be more anatomically specific, his leg – becomes pregnant. Despite the fact that what happens to these individuals seems unimaginably grotesque, they are characters portrayed as normal and believable to the point of cliché. There are enormous differences between *Tom Jones* and

Cock and Bull. Principally, even if we accept that the behavioral extremism of the former is, at least in Aretine's view, improbable, Self confounds accepted biological fact. But there are parallels too. Both demonstrate that fiction is, by its nature, the most realistic form of literary representation while at the same time that which is most capable of unsettling our notion of reality.

Samuel Johnson did his best to draw up regulations that might steady these conflicting properties. Fielding is not mentioned by name but it was evident to all who read the following that Johnson was dealing with the controversies caused by his novels.

> Many Writers for the sake of following Nature, so mingle good and bad Qualities in their principal Personages, that they are both equally conspicuous; and as we accompany them through their Adventures with Delight, and are led by Degrees to interest ourselves in their Favour, we lose the Abhorrence of their Faults, because they do not hinder our Pleasure, or perhaps, regard them with some Kindness for being united with so much Merit. (*The Rambler*, No 4, 31 March 1750)

This ability to shift the focus between good and bad qualities is a back-handed compliment to Fielding's achievement in *Tom Jones*, but Johnson tempers praise with censure. He concedes that characters such as Jones can partly conceal their flaws by their mercurial presence, causing the reader to involuntarily suspend the caution that governs their relationships with real people. Johnson treats fiction, and Fielding's use of it in particular, as subversive. In his view its capacity to create a version of the world we live in enables us to sidestep the responsibility that the latter entails.

> There have been Men indeed splendidly wicked, whose Endowments throw a Brightness on their Crimes, and whom scarce any Villainy made perfectly detestable, because they never could be wholly divested of their Excellencies; but such have been in all Ages the great Corrupters of the World, and their Resemblance ought no more to be preserved, than the Art of murdering without Pain.

Johnson goes so far as to imply that such novels have the power to override the reader's distinction between the real and the invented, particularly those which "confound the Colours of Right and Wrong, and instead of helping to settle their Boundaries, mix them with so much Art, that no common Mind is able to disunite them."

Even by our postmodern standards, this is a quite extraordinary claim: fiction, he contends, alters our preconceived opinions and discernments. It is likely that Johnson based his observation on his experience of talking to readers because if the private correspondence of the era is anything to go by the novel did indeed "confound the Colours of Right and Wrong" and blur their "Boundaries."

It is still common, at least in informal conversation, to refer to characters from a novel in familiar terms, as if our acquaintance with them via the book is the equivalent of having met them. But in most instances we are aware that this is a capricious indulgence. The private correspondence of eighteenth century novel readers discloses that for them invented figures commanded a more enduring, almost metaphysical presence.

> As to Tom Jones, I am fatigued with the name, having lately fallen into the company of several young ladies, who had each a Tom Jones in some part of the world, for so they call their favourites; (and ladies, you know, are for ever talking of their favourites). Last post I received a letter from a lady, who laments the loss of her Tom Jones; and from another, who was happy in the company of her Tom Jones. In like manner, the gentlemen and ladies (who had their Tom Jones's and their Sophias), a friend of mine told me he must shew me his Sophia, the sweetest creature in the world, and immediately produced a Dutch mastiff puppy. (Lady Dorothy Bradshaigh to Samuel Richardson, November 1749)

There is certainly a degree of self-caricature in this image of a platoon of Tom Joneses seemingly escaped from the novel but at the same Lady Bradshaigh hints that Fielding (whom Richardson detested) has hit upon a so-far untouched seam of credibility, verging on illusionism. Lady Henrietta Luxborough thinks Fielding

> Produces personages but too like those one meets with in the world; and even among those people to whom he gives good characters, he shews them as in a concave glass, which discovers blemishes that would not have appeared to the common eye, and may make every modest reader fear to look in such a glass, as some do who have been beauties, and would choose to fancy them- selves so still. The Beauty herself might shun it equally; for that sort of glass would not flatter, and defects would appear, as there is no perfection in us mortals. – If Mr Fielding and Mr Hogarth could abate the vanity of the world by shewing its faults so plainly, they would do more than the greatest divines have yet been capable of: But human nature will still be the same, and would,

I am afraid, furnish them, if they lived till the world ended, with such imperfect objects to represent. (Lady Henrietta Luxborough to William Shenstone, 23 March 1749)

Lady Luxborough seems both disturbed by the novel's power to draw one into a world remarkably similar to the one she inhabits, and enchanted by the experience. She indicates that fiction enables the literary writer, for the first time, to disarm the reader of their protective self-delusions on who they are or what their society is like. She celebrates that which horrified Chalmers and which Johnson censured. A vivid demonstration of her point comes in an exchange of letters between Catherine Talbot and Elizabeth Carter:

> The more I read Tom Jones, the more I detest him, and admire Clarissa Harlowe – yet there are in it things that must touch and please every good heart, and probe to the quick many a bad one, and humour that it is impossible not to laugh at. (Catherine Talbot to Elizabeth Carter, 22 May 1749)

Johnson's mixed boundaries are clearly evident here, and there is something almost confessional in Talbot's manner, as though she feels at once enchanted and uneasy about finding in a novel something she might be wary of admitting to in the world. Her friend replies, not perhaps to put her at her ease but at least to explain how Fielding has held both of them in a trance.

> I am sorry to find you so outrageous about poor Tom Jones; he is no doubt an imperfect, but not a detestable character, with all that honesty, goodnature, and generosity of temper. Though nobody can admire Clarissa more than I do, yet with all our partiality, I am afraid, it must be confessed, that Fielding's book in the most natural representation of what passes in the world, and of the bizarreries which arise from the mixture of good and bad, which makes up the composition of most folks. Richardson has no doubt a very good hand at painting excellence, but there is a strange awkwardness and extravagance in his vicious characters. (Elizabeth Carter to Catherine Talbot, 20 June 1749)

Richardson, she finds, is in fear of causing readers to see in disagreeable characters aspects of themselves, or worse be attracted to them. Fiction was proving itself capable of achieving something that until then was thought to define literature by its absence from it. Literature, primarily poetry, was expected to set itself at a distance both from ordinary language and from the world in which ordinary language was predominant. The novel, in the hands of Fielding and the like, encroached upon it.

Sterne's *Tristram Shandy* is today routinely cited as an act of prescient genius, being the forerunner of works by James Joyce, Virginia Woolf, Milan Kundera, Carlos Fuentes, and Salman Rushdie, to name but a few. It is celebrated as modernism two centuries before its time, which would cause one to expect contemporary reviewers to respond with varying degrees of utter astonishment. It divided opinion, certainly, but no more so than Fielding's more controversial pieces of a decade earlier. Owen Ruffhead complains mainly of boredom:

> But your Indiscretion, good Mr Tristram, is not all we complain of in the volumes now before us. We must tax you with what you will dread above the most terrible of all imputations – nothing less than DULLNESS. Yes, indeed, Mr Tristram, you are dull, *very dull*. Your jaded Fancy seems to have been exhausted by two pigmy octavos, which scarce contained the substance of a twelve-penny pamphlet; and we now find nothing new to entertain us.
>
> (*Monthly Review*, XXXIV, February 1761)

The anonymous reviewer of the *Critical Review*, on the other hand, is amused:

> The reader will not expect that we should pretend to give a detail of a work, which seems to have been written without any plan or any other design than that of shewing the author's wit, humour, and learning, in an unconnected effusion of sentiments and remarks, thrown out indiscriminately as they rose in his imagination. Nevertheless, incoherent and digressive as it is, the book certainly abounds with pertinent observations of life and characters, humourous incidents, poignant ridicule, and marks of taste and erudition. We will venture also to say, that the characters of the father and uncle are interesting and well sustained, and that corporal Trim is an amiable picture of low life.
>
> (*The Critical Review*, xi, April 1761)

If the plotless, digressive, sometimes fathomlessly introspective nature of this book is indeed the forerunner of experiments by Joyce and others why is it then that reviewers of the latter gasped in incomprehension and often condemned modernism as shameful disfigurement of the true principles of writing while Sterne's contemporaries felt that he was a little eccentric but not greatly unusual? The critics of the 1760s, unlike their successors in the early twentieth century, had no clear notion of what fiction was and what it was supposed to do. As each year went by another author would place a question mark against what their immediate predecessors had contributed to this continually evolving mass of precedent.

A consensus on these matters would not be arrived upon until the early nineteenth century, when for roughly the following hundred years the prevailing convention was that while the techniques evolved in the eighteenth century – generally "realist" in nature – should be perfected, the novelist must also practice a degree of self-censorship. Our baser and certainly our more disturbing instincts and motives should be reconditioned to suit the conventions of Victorian society regarding what could be said about the human condition, despite what was known. A similar regime of filtering obtained for representations of what actually went on in the streets, living rooms, servants' quarters, and of course the bedrooms of the nation. Realism endured not because, as in the eighteenth century, it enabled us via the novel to look again at ourselves but because it licensed a collective delusion.

As I made clear at the beginning, this account would not be comprehensive. It has, however, been my intention to show how we react to changes in literary protocol.

The most obvious conclusion one might draw from the critics and commentators covered is that evaluation is essentially a capricious and unreliable activity. But look closer and some common factors begin to emerge. The generally hostile reception that greeted the more unconventional Romantic and modernist writers evolved into accommodation and appreciation. These writers were deprecated, sometimes feared, because they transgressed the commonly agreed rules on what literature was expected to be and do. Within decades, however, the rules would be rewritten and this raises a point that I fully address in the following chapter: was this alteration of what was and what was not acceptable a recognition of something that genuinely expanded the boundaries of literary art or was it a totemic glorification of experiment for its own sake? More significantly, did the acceptance of what was first seen as discomfiting relate in any way to an improvement for the reader in what we might call, for want of a better word, their enjoyment of the novel, the play, or the poem? Pleasure is something that most of us, if we are honest, associate with our attraction to literature. In basic terms, if a book is the opposite of pleasurable we will probably not finish it and will in all likelihood guard ourselves against a future encounter with anything similar to it. Publishers, agents, booksellers, and publicity specialists base their jobs on this simple maxim but when we come to the more abstruse environment of literary criticism and analysis the notion of "pleasure" is not only less easy to grasp, it is something that is rarely spoken of. Few, if pressed, would deny its existence but its exact nature is treated like a shameful instinct.

It is clear enough that those who disagreed vehemently on virtually all other aspects of early modernism had one thing in common. They thought that the new writers had shifted literature away from the mass market by making it more difficult to comprehend. True, its advocates regarded this as to the benefit of all concerned, even those who would find it difficult to cope with the challenge; it would stir intellectual challenge and improvement. Such elevated engagements would certainly be different from the satisfactions enjoyed by fans of Dickens– basically, the fascination of melodrama and a good story – but it might, just, be classified as a form of pleasure. But let us drop the façade. The enjoyment offered by the verse of Eliot is completely different from that gained from readings of the verse of, say, his near contemporary, Edward Thomas. Equally, the Romantics – despite their ludicrous claims to being attuned to elementary human experience – shifted poetry to a state of introverted self-consciousness that would prevail for a further century until the modernists decided to turn a middle-class ritual into something even more elitist. Perhaps they, the Romantics, did achieve something; some people obtain a form of pleasure from being part of an intellectual cadre, particularly if it involves the opportunity for spiritual enlightenment as promised by the Romantics and their successors. To complicate matters, how do we deal with Johnson and his near contemporaries? They seemed to harbor an almost puritanical fear of poetry and drama, Shakespeare in particular, which tempted the reader into the fantastic possibilities of language. Wild metaphor and the transformation of human limitations through the excesses of language (Shakespeare again) seemed for the critics of the eighteenth century almost bestial, something that catered to the demands of the dangerous populace. It was, they came close to admitting, a form of rough pleasure. Similarly, the arrival of the novel stirred in commentators all manner of confusions and fears regarding the nature of how readers would respond to this new phenomenon. At the heart of the debate was the question of whether the reader thought they were witnessing a fictional version of their world, a replica of it, or some weird amalgam of the two. Throughout, there was a conflict between the attraction of suspending disbelief and an anxiety regarding the results, in particular the temptation to forget the moral obligations of life beyond the book.

It would be wrong to draw easy conclusions from all of this but at the same time one cannot help noticing that there is often a causal relationship between those moments when literary writers attempted to shrug off the ongoing conventions of their genre and the appeal of the new types of writing to what we have come to refer to as the general reader: in short, the intellectual establishment made room for the avant garde while the ordinary consumer tended to avoid it.

The novel is a most challenging phenomenon in that before the end of the eighteenth century there was no genuine consensus on what it was and what it might do: change is difficult to conceive of when we are not certain of what is being altered. Nonetheless, the European novel evolved into the prevailing though by no means unswerving ritual of classic realism in the nineteenth century, a monolith challenged by the reflective self-examinations of modernism. Here we come upon a point that propels us into the next chapter. Certainly, we treat the likes of Joyce and Woolf as classics but who "reads" them in the sense that their mannerisms have become a routine feature of what we expect of in fiction? Alternately, are they secretly classified as artefacts, treated as a dead language? This question is singularly pertinent to fiction but it raises another which forces us to address the progress of literature itself. Is experiment something we can perennially treat as the attainment of aesthetic potential? Or will it at some point draw literary history to close and cause us to think again about the benefits of innovation? With these questions in mind we should now turn our attention to modernism.

2

The Dreadful Legacy of Modernism

The title of this chapter offers a clear enough indication of its content and viewpoint. To imagine that we might rid ourselves of the legacies of modernism is preposterous but we should, I contend, accept that their effects upon literature and culture in general have been malign.

Clearly, the novelists and poets who contributed to the birth of modernism shared the vision of a new form of representation and communication. It would generally inherit the family name of literature but it would also make a complete break with the past. The question of why these individuals strove towards a similar objective is usually answered thus: The developed world changed so radically at the close of the nineteenth and beginning of the twentieth century that established artistic conventions could no longer deal with the new reality. The nature and extent of this change is difficult to quantify but some obvious examples come to mind: the mass traumatizing effects of World War I; the rise of socialism, communism, and anarchism; new and previously unimaginable forms of energy and transport; electronic communication; the encroachment of science and humanist–nihilist thinking upon traditional ideas, particularly religious faith.

This cause-and-effect explanation for the arrival of modernism is the one that will be found – with various embellishments and adjustments – in

Is Shakespeare Any Good?: And Other Questions on How to Evaluate Literature,
First Edition. Richard Bradford.
© 2015 John Wiley & Sons, Ltd. Published 2015 by John Wiley & Sons, Ltd.

virtually all studies of the phenomenon. It is sound enough, in that no other obvious motive is evident, but because of this it enables us to ignore its inadequacies. It takes for granted the assumption that what the modernists did with their turbulent world was appropriate and fitting. A simple question. Within a decade of 1922 – the annus mirabilis of High Modernism – Western Europe and America were struck by events just as traumatizing as any listed above: the Great Depression. Why is it that the best known, widely celebrated novel of these years epitomizes the methods of classic realism? John Steinbeck in *The Grapes of Wrath* (1939) chose to represent the lives and experiences of ordinary, desperate Americans in a manner that his immediate predecessors had abandoned as irrelevant to the new cultural and social ethos. Would a novel that replicated the technique of Woolf and Joyce tell us more than Steinbeck about the horrible effects of the Depression? That is, of course, a matter for speculation, but when forming an opinion it should be borne in mind that *Ulysses* is determinedly "about" nothing at all, except the different ways in which a day in the life of an ordinary Dubliner can be represented. Perhaps a similar telescoping of perspectives would reveal new levels of distress and perplexity in the habits and mind-set of Tom Joad? Perhaps.

Treating modernism as something that arose out of and addressed a complex historical crisis sidelines important questions about its true nature and significance.

In 1992 John Carey produced *The Intellectuals and the Masses: Pride and Prejudice among the Literary Intelligentsia 1880–1939*. Modernism's heyday occurred roughly at the middle of this period and Carey's venom is directed against a number of its leading players although he also takes aim at individuals who are unflinching traditionalists, notably Gissing and Wells. His point is that "modern" literary culture licensed an outbreak of elitism in which the "Masses" were routinely perceived as repulsive, irredeemably ignorant, and worthless. It is an excellent book though it should be remarked that Carey draws most of the evidence for his case from the *ex cathedra* nonliterary writings of these figures. There is, I would contend, something intrinsic to modernism as an aesthetic movement, and latent in many of its works, which indicates a collective sense of superiority, a desire to alienate the common reader from access to an exclusive field of appreciation. One might, of course, contend that serious literature has always entailed an elevated sphere of activity, bringing with it an expectation of intellectual investment on the reader's part. With modernism, however, something more occurred. If it were simply the case that these works presented far more complex aesthetic, even existential, questions to the reader than had previously been raised – and this, briefly summarized, is the position maintained by its supporters (that is, virtually everyone) in academia and the cultural hierarchy – then, yes, one must concede that modernism overall is a force for the good. One might even adopt the, in my view patronizing, position that in posing a greater challenge for the ordinary reader who wishes to improve their standing as a connoisseur of the arts it has provided an inadvertent public service. This is the opinion now countenanced by the cultural establishment and I dispute it. Modernism did not merely insult the ordinary reader by making itself more difficult to read than traditional literature. Rather it turned intellectual elitism into a cult, with a number of disagreeable consequences. It created a legacy of ideas about literature that are dangerous, in part because they carry the inflexible support of the intelligentsia, and are therefore immune from dissent, and also because they sanction forms of writing of quite dreadful quality which are, for the same reason, protected from criticism.

Ulysses, now regarded as by most respectable literary commentators as the most important novel of the twentieth century, was greeted by the mainstream press, and those popular papers that bothered to mention it, with almost widespread derision: of the latter, "Aramis" of *The Sporting Times* is typical.

> As readers of the *Pink 'Un* know, I have dealt appreciatively with many unconventional books in these pages; but I have no stomach for *Ulysses*, and do not care to expose my editor to the imminent risk of appearance in court for countenancing the unprintable. James Joyce is a writer of talent, but in *Ulysses* he has ruled out all the elementary decencies of life and dwells appreciatively on things that sniggering louts of schoolboys guffaw about. In addition to this stupid glorification of mere filth, the book suffers from being written in the manner of a demented George Meredith. There are whole chapters of it without any punctuation or other guide to what the writer is really getting at. Two thirds of it is incoherent, and the passages that are plainly written are devoid of wit, displaying only a coarse salacity intended for humour. (*The Sporting Times*, 1 April 1922)

The unsigned reviewer of *The Evening News* seems in a state of dumfounded incomprehension, in that he/she is unwilling, or unable, to say much about the content of the book, electing instead for fact-based observations.

> Copies have just arrived in London from Paris of the new book *Ulysses* ...
> The volume is to be had by those who take the trouble to seek it out for about
> £3.10s ... The book itself in its blue cover looks at first glance like nothing so
> much as a telephone directory. It contains 739 pages ... Mr Joyce was born in
> 1992 in Dublin; he lived in Zurich, Trieste and Rome; and has now settled
> with his family in Paris ... *Ulysses* is published by an American woman, Miss
> Sylvia Beach, whose shop "Shakespeare and Co," in the Rue de L'Odéon is a
> great resort of the younger literary folk.

Having apparently exhausted their treasury of bland detail, the reviewer
draws breath and tries to say something about what can be found between
the covers.

> Mr Joyce is as cruel and unflinching in respect to poor humanity as Zola. His
> style is in the new fashionable kinematic vein, very jerky and elliptical ... It
> seems a pity that Mr Joyce ... restricts the appeal of his work by so many
> Zolaesque expressions, which are, to say the least, disfiguring. (*The Evening
> News*, 8 April 1922)

The preposterous comparison with Zola, arch realist of the nineteenth
century French novel, was, one must assume, a clutch at straws, evidenced
by the reviewer's apparent inability to put into words what Joyce actually
does, aside from the enigmatic reference to his "jerky," "elliptical," "kinematic"
manner.

C.C. Martindale, a Jesuit writing for the *Dublin Review*, set aside his
sense of being led "down to a level where seething instinct is not yet illuminated by intellect" and tried to find an aesthetic pretext for Joyce's
endeavor, which in his view is a literary version of the formlessness of
futurist painting where "not only in the picture there was no 'whole' but you
were quite unable to surmise a future Whole, and so you felt as mad as the
picture looked."

> Well, Mr Joyce gets as far down as he can to this level of animality which
> exists, of course, as an ultimate in every man, and then, consciously and by
> art, tries to reproduce it. And this requires the most strong mental effort. For
> he has to *hold together* what yet must somehow *remain* incoherent; never to
> forget that the conscious memory has never been in possession of; to put into
> the impressions of the evening all that the morning held but was never known
> to hold, and to put it there, not in the shape in which morning offered it, but
> in the shape into which noon and all the hours between have distorted it.

> Thus the author, by a visible violent effort of memory and intelligence, had to show us what essentially was never consciously known, still less remembered. Hence an angry sense of contradiction in the reader. Mr Joyce is trying to think *as if* he were insane. (*The Dublin Review*, clxxi, 1922)

Martindale refers to the lengthy passages of the novel where Joyce abandons coherence, as buttressed by grammar and syntax, and opts instead for a form of writing never previously attempted. The reviewer, albeit grudgingly, concedes that this is an unprecedented, daring experiment, an attempt to render as art that which is otherwise unrecorded – thoughts that precede speech, impressions, and sensations that are, in their prelinguistic state, fragmented and disorderly. Yet, contends Martindale, there is a "contradiction" in this: how can he put into language what by its nature exists only beyond language?

Sisley Huddleston discovers in the novel the same effect described by Martindale but comes to different conclusions.

> As for the matter, I think I can best convey some idea of *Ulysses* by reminding the reader how odd is the association of ideas when one allows all kinds of what are called thoughts, but which have nothing to do with thinking, to pass in higgledy-piggledy procession through one's mind – one's subconscious mind, I suppose it is called in present-day jargon. Psycho-analysis is, I believe, very strong about this … Now the purpose of Mr. Joyce is, of course, much larger than to jot down all the incongruous notions that rattle around the arena of the cranium; but described narrowly, that is what he does. Has anybody done it before? I do not know, but I am certain that no one ever did it at such length and with such thoroughness. It is obvious that if one tries to put down everything in the life of a man, a single day in that life will fill many volumes. The external events are really of little importance except as forming a starting-point for reflection. Mr. Joyce's style is such that it is sometimes difficult to distinguish between what is taking place externally and what is taking place internally. The internal action is put on the same plane as the external action. Mr. Joyce indicates both with infinite humour and with extraordinary precision. One feels that these things are essentially, ineluctably, true. These are exact notations of trivial but tremendous motions, and these are truly the inconsequential but significant things that one says to oneself. There is Mr. Bloom at the funeral wondering how he can discreetly shift the tablet of soap which he has purchased and put in his tail pocket. As he passes the gasworks in the mourning carriage he wonders whether it's true that to live near a gasworks prevents whooping-cough. (*The Observer*, 5 March 1922)

Huddleston too recognizes that something unprecedented has occurred but rather than dismissing it as a "contradiction" celebrates Joyce's technique as a moment of illumination, a bridging of the gap between "the higgledy-piggledy procession [of thoughts] through one's mind" and the external world of rational orderly existence. It goes without saying that the post-1922 consensus of opinion on *Ulysses* favors Huddleston's reading. The latter goes on to acknowledge that in parts, particularly the "*monologue intéreur*" of Molly Bloom, "Blasphemy and beauty, poetry and piggishness, jostle each other" but rather than condemn this, as most early critics did, he celebrates it as a new aesthetic of truthtelling, something that had previously been the victim of self-denial on the part of the writer: "Is that not high art?" Since Huddleston appears to be one of the few reviewers to have set aside, while acknowledging, the initial feelings of unease, distaste, or confusion that accompany a first encounter with the book should we not simply acknowledge his judgment as extraordinarily prescient and perceptive and leave it at that? He knew that a book such as this would have to await a measured verdict on its importance, or otherwise, and that within a few years the overall response to his daring suggestion might be a resounding "no." He was wise to be cautious because other reviewers – some pro, some anti – supplemented the question of whether the book opened doors on new notions of perception and representation with another: what sort of person would want to read it? Holbrook Jackson in *To-Day* (June 1922) runs through the standard retinue of shock-and-awe comments on "the arrangement of the book" which is, apparently, "a chaos." "All the conventions of organised prose which have grown with our race ... which have been reverently handed on by the masters ... have been cast aside as so much dross." Holbrook generally allows fascination and a grudging sense of approval to sideline his intimations of dismay. Like Huddleston he admits to being in the presence of something pioneering, possibly groundbreaking. But: "Mr Joyce evidently believes in making it difficult for his readers but perhaps he wants to scare them away ... It seems gratuitous to put unnecessary difficulties in the way of a proper understanding of his message, story or record." Without referring to any specific manifesto for correct fiction writing – because none existed, beyond the examples set by the largely realist authors of the previous century and a half – Jackson implies that the generally accepted task of the novelist was to enable the reader to easily suspend disbelief, to find in the novel a near replica of the world they lived in.

> The result is that the reader is continually losing his way and having to retrace his steps. *Ulysses* is like a country without roads. But it is a novel, and if it will not amuse the idle novel reader, or even attract the lewd by its unsavoury franknesses, it must claim the attention of those who look upon fiction as something more than confectionery. With all its faults, it is the biggest event in the history of the English novel since *Jude*.

Jackson, like Huddleston, tempers enthusiasm with caution. *Ulysses* is, he admits, difficult to navigate but he also suggests that a refusal to take up the challenge is the response of the "idle reader," the sort of person who is content with fiction as "confectionery" by which he means easy entertainment. In the *Dublin Review* (September 1922) Shane Leslie, writing as "Domini Canis" also finds that it is a novel deliberately designed to frustrate and even alienate the "general reader," but while Holbrook treats this as a worthy raising of the intellectual bar Leslie perceives the general reader as the conscience of the literary world, its electorate. In this respect Joyce has, he avers, merely fed "the curiosity of the *literati* and *dilletanti*." For everyone else *Ulysses* is "so much rotten caviar." Leslie, while largely agreeing with Jackson on what the book does, treats it as an exercise in elitism. "Nothing could be more ridiculous than the youthful dilettantes in Paris or London who profess knowledge and understanding of a work which is often mercifully obscure."

It is not entirely uncommon to find two critics who, after reading the same book, reach entirely different conclusions as to its qualities or otherwise, but this tends to be a reflection of their inherent tastes and predispositions. With Holbrook and Leslie the difference arises from something more complex. They diverge completely on what fiction is supposed to do and what purpose it is supposed to serve for the reader. Leslie claims to speak on behalf of the "general reader" who we must assume he perceives as a stable anchor for literary taste, while Jackson regards this same individual, the consumer who sustains the solvency of publishing houses and their authors, as the purblind victim of "cosmetic" populism. Who was correct? Subsequent history would favor Holbrook given that few, if any, in the literary establishment or academia of the present day would dare to side with Leslie. But shift the perspective slightly and consider who is responsible for the elevation of *Ulysses* to a seemingly unassailable level of greatness. One must assume, by a process of deduction, that its status was conferred by those at the upper echelons of the literary and cultural world, especially during the period after the

1930s when universities became far more significant as mediators of opinion on modern writing and not, as previously, encampments for the scholarly pursuit of classical learning. If it were not for the growth of a pro-modernist consensus among what Leslie refers to as the literati *Ulysses* would very likely have become something of an aesthetic curiosity, a work that caused a controversy for a while but did not otherwise disturb the progress of the nineteenth century realist form then in the hands of respected and popular writers such as Arnold Bennett and a little later George Orwell. There are very few among that class which Leslie calls the "general reader" who would over the past 90 years have voluntarily read let alone purchased the volume: for those who did it was most often an involuntary encounter brought about by the massive post-war expansion of higher education and the fervent, unquestioning support for innovation and experiment by those who taught in the new universities. There is evidence, then, that Leslie's charge of elitism was prescient, that the reputation of Joyce and his alleged masterpiece has been sustained despite the tastes and opinions of the so-called general reader.

Popularity is not, of course, a guarantee of quality, but consider a variation on Leslie's charge of elitism. There are, at present, a considerable number of novelists whose sales outsoar by far even the best known proponents of the so-called literary novel. Jeffrey Archer is an obvious case as is Stephen King and J.K. Rowling. Of late – that is, 2013 in particular – a previously unknown presence, E.L. James, has sold over 100 million copies of a series of sado-erotic novels that seem to appear on a monthly basis, a phenomenon that began with *Fifty Shades of Grey*. I have, so far, attempted to be evenhanded regarding differences of opinion on the qualities of literary works but in these instances generosity can be dispensed with. Perhaps with the exception of Rowling and King who are reasonably accomplished within their somewhat limited genres these novels are atrocious rubbish. This is, I accept, a rash unfounded judgment and I shall look more closely at how to justify such evaluations in Chapter 7. For the time being I stand by my assessment. The fact that they are far more popular than anything produced or celebrated by members of the literati proves that a reliance upon audience numbers as an index for taste is a dangerous strategy. But should we treat the people who buy and presumably enjoy this dross as the modern equivalent of Leslie's general reader? Given the changes that have taken place in the publishing industry since the 1920s the answer to that is "no." In actuality there are spectrums of attraction and indifference that allow individual readers to transcend attempts to classify them as belonging to a particular group. It is quite plausible that a reasonably well-educated reader – perhaps with a university degree in the humanities, or perhaps not – will purchase and read books on the basis of past experience of what satisfies their particular melange of pleasure, satisfaction, and appreciation. Somewhere in this mixture will be found a glimmer of what in higher learning is termed aesthetic discernment, but for the time being let us make a clear discrimination between two levels of preference that are rarely if ever entertained by a single reader, and which are more accurate than, say, Leslie's division of the "literati" from the "general reader" as an index to taste.

Some readers, I would contend, read novels primarily because they expect to find therein a version of the world they know and inhabit. Inevitably, this will be distorted to suit the conventions of storytelling in prose. We will get to know characters not by meeting them but through the skills a novelist brings to bear upon the building of an individual, mainly by the use of dialogue and an accumulation of descriptive registers, from what they look like and how they behave to their private thoughts. More importantly these personnel will be involved in a story, one which holds our attention because if the novelist is any good we are as interested in the participants as we are in real people and as a consequence we will want to know what happens next. This is the formula upon which virtually all so-called realist novels are based. Joyce and a number of other modernist fiction writers founded their endeavors upon the pretext that the realist method was both limited and delusional, that it created, via the novel, the impression that reality is orderly and subject to rational modes of interpretation by those who inhabit it. In short, realist fiction is not "realist" at all; its claim to be mimetic is a pretence. The alternative, tested in *A Portrait of the Artist as a Young Man* and more daringly explored in *Ulysses*, involved making language recreate the true nature of the human condition, made up, randomly, of insignificant recollections, unconnected observations on matters both mundane and fundamental, and unspecified allusions, while abandoning the framework of individual motivation and interpersonal drama.

Even those who condemned Joyce as immoral or self-indulgent conceded that he had attempted something quite remarkable and his supporters and begrudgers were also in agreement on another point: that *Ulysses* was at once unprecedented and unrepeatable. Huddleston, one of his most enthusiastic early champions, typifies this sentiment: "the book is a staggering first which, once attempted and more than half achieved, may never be attempted again – the way of a cosmic atom under heaven during a day and a night." The rationale for this opinion is provided at length by that stalwart of the realist technique that Joyce was attempting to unseat from its predominant position, Arnold Bennett, who reviewed *Ulysses* in *Outlook* (29 April 1922). Bennett, to his credit, begins in a self-parodic manner, affecting a mood of bafflement at the storm of praise that followed all of Joyce's publications in France, particularly the essay by Valery Larbaud in *La Nouvelle Revue Française* which declared *Ulysses* a masterpiece beyond compare. He is playing the part of a dyspeptic member of the old guard rendered uncomprehending by his usurpers. But gradually a far more commanding presence takes over and the review mutates into one of the most thought-provoking early responses.

> Of course the author is trying to reproduce the thoughts of the personage, and his verbal method can be justified – does indeed richly justify itself here and there in the story. But upon the whole, though the reproduction is successful, the things reproduced appear too often to be trivial and perfectly futile in the narrative. I would not accuse him of what is absurdly called "photographic realism". But I would say that much of the book is more like an official shorthand writer's "note" than a novel. In some of his moods the author is resolved at any price not to select, not to make even the shortest leap from one point of interest to another. He has taken oath with himself to put it all down and be hanged for it … He would probably defend himself and find disciples to defend him. But unless the experience of creative artists since the recorded beginning of art is quite worthless, James Joyce is quite wrong headed. Anyhow, with his wilfulness, he has made novel reading into a fair imitation of penal servitude … The author seems to have no geographical sense, little sense of environment, no sense of the general kindness of human nature, and not much poetical sense. Worse than all, he has positively no sense of perspective. But my criticism of the artist in him goes deeper. His vision of the world and its inhabitants is mean, hostile, and uncharitable.

Bennett's point is that there is a symbiotic relationship between what the reader expects of a novel and what the novelist delivers, that the taste for realism that had prevailed so far was not an unambitious refusal to move beyond the routine and familiar, but rather the consequence of two centuries of gradual metamorphosis, in which novelists continually re-examined the relationship between this relatively untested brand of writing and its audience. Bennett's stance involves more than a reactionary intolerance of innovation. He charges Joyce with a failure in his duty to the reader. "*Ulysses* would have been a better book and a much better appreciated book if the author had extended to his public the common courtesies of literature." By this he does not mean that literature should for the reader be a passive, unchallenging experience. Rather that the features of fiction that Joyce dispenses with – such as a "sense of environment," "a sense of perspective," the "poetical sense" of prose which causes us to adjust our expectations – are what enable fiction to engage the reader in its unique game of hide and seek, with a narrative as addictive yet as unpredictable as life itself and characters who are sufficiently life-like to be able to dissemble but also, often surprisingly, to disclose "the general kindness of human nature." Bennett might appear to oversentimentalize the duties of the writer when he accuses Joyce of presenting "the world and its inhabitants" as "mean, hostile, and uncharitable." He was not so naïve as to perceive humanity as exempt from these features or to advocate that literature should pretend that we are. What he found unpalatable about *Ulysses* was its employment of a radical technique to leave the reader with no option but to comprehend only the "mean, hostile, and uncharitable" dimensions of existence.

The reservations and objections of Bennett, Leslie, and many others have been swept aside by the overwhelming force of the literary and academic zeitgeist but it is, I think, unfair to ignore the principle that underpins Bennett's article. Which is this: even if a work of literature is a magnificent example of innovation should we question its inherent quality if it also in some way limits the reader to the role of alienated spectator rather than participant? Most would now contend that the latter was one of modern-ism's great accomplishments and that the failure of many early readers to appreciate this was the result of stubborn intolerance on their part rather than some defect in the work. In short, the more enlightened among us learned to experience that to which their predecessors had blinded them-selves. I would disagree. This is the conventional opinion on what occurred but it enables its advocates to sweep under the carpet fundamental ques-tions raised by the doubters.

The charges against modernism in its early years and at its zenith were that it was gratuitously difficult and elitist, and among its defenders was Mark Van Doren, an academic, who offered solace to readers "who find themselves a bit bewildered among modern poets." He concedes that "Poetry which is both new and good is also difficult to read. In a sense all good poetry is difficult to read, but we are not aware of the fact when we are considering the classics [by which he means the exalted authors in English as well as their "Classical" forebears], which centuries of human experience have taught us how to read" (Van Doren 1930, p. 10) There are a number of glaring inconsistencies in this statement which all subsequent commentators have for some reason overlooked. Van Doren takes for granted that literary quality – "good poetry" – must necessarily involve difficulty, but does not bother to justify this sweeping generalization. Further, nor does he explain what he means by "difficult." For example, the Imagists – one of whose founders was Ezra Pound – were committed to making poetry far less complex than ever before; their objective was transparency. One also has to question his principal thesis that erudition and experience teach us how to read "difficult" poems. The "us" of his statement might be mistaken for some egalitarian notion of everyman but it is clear enough from the rest of the piece that Van Doren is addressing people like himself, or those he teaches. He does not state directly that a reader without experience as a literary sophisticate will never be able to make sense of poetry, let alone meet the new challenge of modernist poetry, but one suspects that by "how to read" he means "how to discuss and evaluate in an appropriately learned manner." This suspicion is confirmed by a comment by another academic 15 years after Van Doren when the apology for modernism was in full cry. Donald Stauffer promises to select "three poems by Pope, Herrick, and Burns for their apparent simplicity, and study … their actual poetic complexity." This should be paraphrased as, "you might *think* you understand these poems but, as I will show, erudite scrutiny brings out their true complexity." Aside from its patronizing subtext – that is, ordinary readers need help even if they believe they understand poems – it provides a cover-all formula in the rescue mission for modernism, contending that the apparently uncomplicated verse of the Imagists requires the assistance of the literati, just as much as the allusion-laden obscurities of *The Waste Land*.

In the work of apologists for modernism one finds persistent reference to an "audience" made up of "ordinary" or "general" readers but this already vague constituency disappears in a puff of smoke when closely scrutinized. Elizabeth Drew, for example, urges that Shakespeare is just as difficult to understand as the likes of Pound and Eliot. His complexities have too often gone unnoticed because "it is only because he appeals at so many different levels to so many different types of audience and reader[s] that his difficulty has escaped much comment" (Drew 1933, p. 82) Despite her commendable attempt at diplomacy, she obviously feels that Shakespeare's popularity among the common theatre-goer, or reader if that sort of person is literate, had hindered his recognition as a genuinely difficult writer, at least for those sufficiently clever and well-read to appreciate such a quality. The claim made by these critics to some knowledge of the "audience" or "readership" of poets such as Donne or Shakespeare in their own time is optimistic, verging upon fantastic. Even for the nineteenth century it is difficult for us to assemble an image of an "average reader" from the paucity of available evidence. I would contend that the oft-referred to audience of long dead poets was in fact a projection of something rather more tangible and concrete: the sort of person who during the 1920s and 1930s divided their tastes between cinema, radio, popular theatre, popular fiction, and, very rarely, poetry.

Harriet Monroe, as editor of *Poetry*, had in 1914 declared that the new poets should follow a dictum of Whitman's: "To have great poets there must be great audiences too." It is unlikely that Monroe deliberately intended to bewilder her readers but if she meant, as is generally assumed, that avant garde verse should be egalitarian in its appeal she might have chosen a less ambiguous motto. By "great audiences" did Whitman mean abundant or superior? Pound seems to have assumed the former, at least if his public letter of censure to Monroe, and by implication Whitman, is anything to go by.

> Had Dante the popular voice? He had his youthful companionship with Guido, and the correspondence with a man from Pistoja and with the latinist De Virgilio.
>   Must we restrict this question to poets? I ask the efficient man in any department of life. Can we have no great inventors without great audience for inventors? Had Curie a great audience? Had Ehrlich for his bacilli? Can we have no great financier without a great audience? Had the saviour of the world a great audience? Did he work on the magazine public? (Pound, 1914, p. 30)

Pound's opening question is not a rhetorical one. Most agree that Dante was perhaps the most challenging of the Renaissance poets but the idea that this alienated his work from a large audience of his contemporaries is preposterous. Readers of his poetry were composed entirely of his educated peers; in fifteenth century Italy the notion of a widely read book was a contradiction in terms. What really troubled Pound is evidenced in his closing sentence. The "magazine public" as he puts it was an unprecedented phenomenon. During the nineteenth century the novel had, for the first time, made literature a popular medium but by the early decades of the twentieth readers who did not belong to the intellectual and social elite were exercising new opportunities for diversion and entertainment via rapidly produced print media – "magazines" for example – or from words and images transmitted electronically. Literature had been swept into a new era of popular culture and it now had to compete for prominence with forms of recreation that were classed by the literary establishment as sub-cultural. It seemed like the advent of aesthetic democracy, in which the quality of literature might still be debated by the few while its relevance would gradually be eroded by the choice and tastes of the masses. Modernism was motivated, to a large degree, by aesthetic protectionism which involved two objectives: to cause literature to become sufficiently strange and incomprehensible so that the "magazine public" would reject it; to convince the cultural establishment to treat this as a favorable advance upon the status quo. These two would, thought Pound and others, wrest control of literature from the unedifying world of eminence-by-popularity and rebuild a cultural hierarchy with literature at its pinnacle, safely beyond the grasp of the ordinary reader.

In 1930 Mark Van Doren reflected upon how the previous decade had caused middlebrow readers such confusion and distress.

> A reader, then or now, who had been brought up on the poetry familiar to his parents, the household poetry, shall we say, of late nineteenth-century America, the poetry which millions of school children had memorized and politicians had quoted in their speeches, the poetry of Victorian England and of Victorian America, the poetry of Tennyson, Longfellow, and Swinburne (but chiefly of their innumerable and indistinguishable followers) – such a reader had every right to be bewildered a decade and a half ago … He frequently, indeed, resented the kind of poetry then coming upon the scene; or he refused to call it poetry at all. And no wonder. For the new poets were trying their best not to write like the new poets he had known; they were getting as far away from the usual thing as paper and ink could take them. They had declared war upon the current conceptions of poetry. (Van Doren 1930, p. 10).

Van Doren does his best, in a condescending way, to treat this kind of reader with respect. These people were content with the style of Victorian poetry which had become familiar, almost idiomatic. A jolt to routine expectations was, he contended, a necessity. Why? He does not make this clear but he implies a great deal. If we democratize taste it becomes stale. We must, therefore, cause it to become an aspirational ideal.

Joyce said of *Ulysses* "I've put in so many enigmas and puzzles that it will keep the professors busy for centuries arguing over what I meant, and that's the only way of insuring one's immortality." His observation has been quoted on numerous occasions in academic studies yet hardly ever commented on, which is an embarrassing acknowledgment of Joyce's prescience. He does not go quite so far as to state that he intended to put the book beyond the reach of the nonacademic reader but he does not need to. Despite the view of some academics that *Ulysses* dragged fiction from the hands of the nineteenth century bourgeoisie into the real world of its hero it is a fact that, as Joyce predicted, its status as a significant literary work would be sustained by academia. Without the assistance of careerist researchers and its unassailable position on the university canon of greats it would certainly not have endured, like Dickens's or Austen's novels, as a bestseller. One might contend that other indisputably superb works would be, if not forgotten, then read only by a tiny number of enthusiasts were it not for the protective arm of the educational and literary establishment: Milton's *Paradise Lost* is not most people's choice for holiday reading. As we have seen, some have argued that the major texts of modernism, not only *Ulysses*, are refreshingly egalitarian, inviting the ordinary reader to join more adventurous and erudite figures against the same intellectual challenge. Yet there is something about them that causes one to suspect that they neither expect nor would particularly welcome the interest of uncultured types.

Joyce is frequently praised for affording us by far the most comprehensive depiction ever of single fictional character. We witness Leopold Bloom's habits when he is visiting the lavatory, share his secrets, his half-formed speculations on everything from betting to God, look in on his erotic fantasies, are informed that he has not had sex with his wife Molly for 10 and a half years, since the death of their (on this we are even provided with an exact date) infant son, and we know his height, down to the half inch, and weight, to the nearest pound. We leave the book knowing Bloom as well as we know anyone outside it but we experience more than a catalog of details. We learn of him via the consistently shifting lens that Joyce employs to show him from a different perspective in every chapter. It has been said that Joyce chose, or invented, Bloom as the focus of his gargantuan enterprise because he was everyman, a figure who covered a spectrum from private tragedy to the utterly pointless and mundane. But let us reconsider this by asking the question of what sort of individual he would most certainly not have used as his principal character. Stephen Daedalus, the hero of *A Portrait of the Artist as a Young Man*, plays a secondary role in *Ulysses* but even if Joyce had pondered the idea of bringing him center stage the hypothesis would have folded immediately because a character such as Daedalus made him entirely unsuitable for the experiment that Joyce compels Bloom to undergo. Daedalus is a middle-class intellectual with high aesthetic ambitions. In the first episode we find Stephen reflecting on his mother's recent death.

> Stephen, an elbow rested on the jagged granite, leaned his palm against his brows and gazed at the fraying edge of his shiny black coatsleeve. Pain, that was not yet the pain of love, fretted his heart. Silently, in a dream she had come to him after her death, her wasted body within its loose brown grave-clothes giving off an odour of wax and rosewood, her breath, that has bent upon him, mute, reproachful, a faint odour of wetted ashes. Across the threadbare cuffedge he saw the sea hailed as a great sweet mother by the wellfed voice beside him. The ring of bay and skyline held a dull green mass of liquid. A bowl of white china had stood beside her deathbed holding the green sluggish bile which she had torn up from her rotting liver by fits and loud groaning vomiting.

Although this is related by a third person narrator it is Stephen's delicately nuanced intellect and sensibility that shapes the prose. It would have been quite possible of course to release this presence across the whole span of Dublin life that we encounter through the 24 hours of the book's duration, but Stephen's elevated mind-set would have dominated, or at least clashed with, the constellation of techniques employed by Joyce to refract and dissect the life of Bloom. To put it bluntly, Stephen is too clever to submit to such minute scrutiny. Joyce needed a man with an unambitious, suppliant mind-set, the kind who would not undermine an account of his eating habits such as found in "calypso."

> Mr. Leopold Bloom ate with relish the inner organs of beasts and fowls. He liked thick giblet soup, nutty gizzards, a stuffed roast heart, liver slices fried with crustcrumbs, fried hencod's roes. Most of all he liked grilled mutton kidneys which gave to his palate a fine tang of faintly scented urine.

Our thorough familiarity with every aspect of Bloom's existence, including his taste for foodstuffs redolent of "faintly scented urine," comes with a good deal of prurient attention to detail. It is not impossible that Stephen or others of his class and temperament enjoyed a faint whiff of urine with their food but such figures could not be portrayed in the way that Joyce deals with Bloom, from the outside like a specimen. Their intellect would short-circuit the procedure, probably enabling them to treat the odors of the food as the foundation for an unspoken meditative discourse on life and its transient nature.

In order to master the complexities of the novel a reader from the same class as Bloom, with the same limited cultural and educational background, would need to position themselves alongside the controlling hand of the book, to rise to Joyce's intellectual level and empathize with his daring experiment. At the same time, however, they would also adopt, like Joyce, a position of superiority over the man, Bloom, whose characteristics they once shared.

Virginia Woolf famously disparaged *Ulysses* for its "indecency." "Mr Joyce's indecency in *Ulysses* seems to me the conscious and calculated indecency of a desperate man who feels that in order to breathe he must break the windows" ("Mr Bennett and Mrs Brown"). Clearly, Woolf believes that Joyce deliberately lowered standards to increase the shock effect of his formal experiment but her ingrained snobbery causes her to overlook the fact that, despite appearances, his undertaking has a great deal in common with hers. Woolf's most frequently quoted comment, in defence of her own model of fiction is:

> Life is not a series of gig lamps symmetrically arranged; life is a luminous halo, a semi-transparent envelope surrounding us from the beginning of consciousness to the end. Is it not the task of the novelist to convey this varying, this unknown and uncircumscribed spirit, whatever aberration or complexity it may display, with as little mixture of the alien and external as possible?

Earlier in the same essay she attacks Arnold Bennett, the archetypical realist of the era, for his preoccupation with facts. He would, she argues, present a character by assembling details of what they wear, how they speak, and their body language but in doing so he would blind himself to a real understanding of this figure, their intangible inner presence: "I insubstantiate" she declares, "wilfully to some extent, distrusting reality – its cheapness." In *The Waves* we encounter insubstantiation in action. Each of its six monologists – Neville, Louis, Jinny, Rhoda, Susan, and Bernard – filters the "reality" of their life through a fabric of reflections on its fleeting or latent nature. Bernard is an artist whose vocation becomes the lens for his perception of the outside world. He states "I must make phrases and phrases and so interpose something hard between myself and the stare of the house-maids, the stare of clocks, staring faces, indifferent faces." Woolf's novel is routinely celebrated for revealing how each of the characters in it is, to the others, a passive agent, that they have, wilfully or otherwise, become "interposed" between what goes on in their minds and the network of emotions and feelings experienced by the others. It is, argue its champions, a meditation on the ineluctable tragedy of the human condition; we reach out to each other but experience something only partial or, even worse, a void.

I would disagree. At least the six intellectually mature, appropriately sensitive figures who inhabit the narrative are aware of their shared sense of distress and isolation. Persons such as the "housemaids" whose "stare" carries the same significance as that of "the clock" are thought unworthy, no doubt because of their limited intelligence, of taking part in such an exercise in mutual victimhood. Imagine what would have happened if Joyce had chosen to populate a novel with six versions of Stephen, moved them up to respectable middle class London and away from the mucky mercantile atmosphere of Dublin and expelled from the book – excepting occasional references to them as objects – figures such as Bloom or unnamed "housemaids": *The Waves* by James Joyce. Woolf objected to being obliged to share narrative space with the smells and habits of Bloom, but she misread the parallels between Joyce's technique and her own. We most certainly know more about Bloom than Bernard does of his "house-maids" but we don't really "know" him in the same way that the shared, and most certainly superior, background of aesthetic sensitivity burnished with erudition enables the six monologists to intuite something of each other. Bloom and the housemaids are virtual figures viewed from the outside, by their authors, by other characters, and by the readers. To become part of this third category, real life Blooms and housemaids would have to cease to be the kind of person that permitted them to appear in the novels in the first place.

John Carey describes the manner in which Woolf in *Mrs Dalloway* offers more than cursory attention to one of these low life figures. A beggar, singing for coppers, is generously allocated around 150 words but Woolf clearly runs out of patience with her continued presence and causes these same words to snuff out whatever claim to a personality she might have had. She turns her into a tree, a harrowing reminder of the countryside that once dominated the area around Regent's Park before urbanization and the Tube station entrance where people like her now stand.

Woolf might claim that the nineteenth century novel did little to dismantle the divisions by wealth and class that informed the society it represented, but modernist fiction was far more effective and sophisticated in cementing a hierarchy of the privileged and the excluded. It turned the latter into nonpersons and excluded them as readers.

Poetry was no more egalitarian. For most readers with an informed but unambitious interest in poetry *The Waste Land* was incomprehensible. The critics who confessed to varying degrees of puzzlement and infuriation were not so much inflexible conservatives as spokespersons for the then consensus of opinion. As we have seen in the previous chapter the consensus shifted in little more than a decade from a feeling of alienation to one of celebratory admiration. Nonetheless, the poem itself remained unaltered and there are certain parts of it that reward the sceptical reader with a revisit. Eliot, generously enough, offered the perplexed a hint at how they might comprehend and appreciate the poem's discontinuity and apparently ceaseless shifts of focus. In a note to the third section, he wrote:

> Tiresias, although a mere spectator and not indeed a "character," is yet the most important personage in the poem, uniting all the rest. Just as the one-eyed merchant, seller of currants, melts into the Phoenician Sailor, and the latter is not wholly distinct from Ferdinand Prince of Naples, so all the women are one woman, and the two sexes meet in Tiresias. What Tiresias *sees*, in fact, is the substance of the poem.

Clearly, Eliot wishes to avoid anything quite so simplistic as a speaker or persona. Tiresias is more a philosophical concept, a junction of nuances who defies any attempts to connect him, or indeed her, with what we would generally understand to be a recognizable human being. The note recalls Joyce's remark on how his legacy will at least provide professors with years of gainful employment. Tiresias too offers wondrous prospects for academics who would use him as a pretext for challenging exercises in intellectual improvement, without actually explaining what he is: that would injure the majestic profundity of the poem.

Yet the more closely one examines the work the more Eliot's enigmatic note betrays, perhaps unwittingly, the disagreeable function of Tiresias, and the equally unpalatable mind-set of his/her creator. One of the most famous passages of the poem occurs in "The Fire Sermon," the section to which

Eliot appended his note, involves the encounter between the typist and
"young man carbuncular"

> At the violet hour, when the eyes and back
> Turn upward from the desk, when the human engine waits
> Like a taxi throbbing waiting,
> I Tiresias, though blind, throbbing between two lives,
> Old man with wrinkled female breasts, can see
> At the violet hour, the evening hour that strives
> Homeward, and brings the sailor home from sea,
> The typist home at teatime, clears her breakfast, lights
> Her stove, and lays out food in tins.
> Out of the window perilously spread
> Her drying combinations touched by the sun's last rays,
> On the divan are piled (at night her bed)
> Stockings, slippers, camisoles and stays.
> I Tiresias, old man with wrinkled dugs
> Perceived the scene, and foretold the rest—
> I too awaited the expected guest.
> He, the young man carbuncular, arrives,
> A small house agent's clerk, with a bold stare,
> One of the low on whom assurance sits
> As a silk hat on a Bradford millionaire.
> The time is now propitious, as he guesses,
> The meal is ended, she is bored and tired.
> Endeavours to engage her in caresses
> Which still are unreproved, if undesired.
> Flushed and decided, he assaults at once;
> Exploring hands encounter no defence;
> His vanity requires no response,
> And makes a welcome of indifference.
> (And I Tiresias have foresuffered all
> Enacted on this same divan or bed;
> I who have sat by Thebes below the wall
> And walked among the lowest of the dead.)
> Bestows one final patronizing kiss,
> And gropes his way, finding the stairs unlit …

One cannot help wondering if Eliot's invention of Tiresias is a pre-emptive
not guilty plea against charges of rampant detestation of the lower orders.
By making him pitiable in his own right ("blind," "Old man with wrinkled

female breasts," and so on) Eliot assimilates him to the state of dreadfulness evoked everywhere else in the poem, and absolves himself of responsibility for Tiresias's observations. But one has to wonder: does Tiresias protest too much? After the minutely detailed description of how the couple have sex, apparently forced, in what was, up to 1922, the most meticulously seedy portrait of a room in literature, Tiresias proffers what seems a note of consolidation, almost sympathy: "I Tiresias have foresuffered all / Enacted on this same divan or bed;". The hint that they are all in this together is, however, soon dispersed. Tiresias continues: "I who have sat the by Thebes below the wall / And walked among the lowest of the dead." We have been told by Eliot that Tiresias transcends ordinary notions of time and space yet the obsessive concentration upon the shiftless, faintly unhygienic lifestyle of the couple leaves us in no doubt that this pair of philistines would be left dumbstruck by any reference to Thebes. Such classical tokens are, we suspect, Tiresias's solace against the world of commoners in which he has the misfortune to spend much of his time, as are his quotations from sixteenth century drama, Renaissance French poetry, and Hindu fable. If one requires further confirmation that, despite his plea, Eliot disguises himself as Tiresias consult the original draft which included the line that Eliot removed from the end of the passage above and replaced with the three dots: "And at the corner where the stable is, / Delays only to urinate, and spit." Along with the discarded lines is a comment from Pound who advised him to drop them. "[P]robably over the mark" remarked Eliot's co-pioneer in this new literary aesthetic. We certainly should not mistake Pound's observation as a token of his benevolence towards the couple. Quite the contrary. He is protecting his friend from possible accusations that he has gone "over the mark," and the fact that he seems content with the rest as within the bounds of fair representation further demonstrates that Eliot and Pound are part of the social and cultural elite to which Tiresias too belongs, and from which the young man and his girl are, by virtue of their foul ordinariness, most certainly excluded. The poem bears a close similarity to *Ulysses,* despite Joyce's bringing a little more humanity to his treatment of Bloom. In each case the complexities of the new literary enterprise become not only the preserve of an elite but also the means by which the text itself becomes an exercise in cultural and aesthetic apartheid.

We have already seen how supporters of modernism treated its difficulties, its self-evident inaccessibility, as a necessary antidote to the fearful prospect of a newly expanded cultural marketplace where popularity overturned aesthetic standards. The task of cultural and intellectual acclimatization demanded by these new works would improve the mind-set of the general reader. Yet there seems to be an anomalous relationship between this ideal and the inherent elitism of the works themselves, something that went far beyond their being difficult to comprehend. It is worth examining again some of the claims made about the improving capacities of modernism because beneath the reformist altruism something a little more sinister stirs. Gwendolyn Murphy compared the modernists with their immediate traditional predecessors, the Georgian poets, who are in her opinion "comparatively timid" (1938, p. xv). This evocation of strength and power features regularly in defences of the modernist project. Cleanth Brooks, one of the most influential academics of the mid-twentieth century, writes of the late, more complex verse of Yeats that "the average reader will balk ... at the amount of intellectual exercise demanded of him" (1939, pp. 63–4). Interestingly, Brooks leaves open to question the issue of whether such an "average" individual should be encouraged to work harder at their Yeats or, because of their innate laziness, be left outside the charmed circle of those prepared to engage in such an "exercise." The analogy between intellectual effort and physical exertion might simply be that, a convenient conceit, but it crops up so frequently that one begins to wonder about what really motivates these polemicists. Geoffrey Grigson, reviewing Pound's *Cantos* in 1933, wrote of it as "athletic writing, of a kind which has only been made possible by long severe training and dieting" (Grigson, 1972, p. 262); seven years later David Daiches reflected on how T.S. Eliot's "themes" exposed the "emptiness and flabbiness of modern life and thought, while in technique he employed every means he could to avoid that flabbiness which he was criticising" (Daiches, 1940, p. 115) while Marianne Moore exalted in verse "that is virile because galvanizes against inertia" (Moore, 1986, p. 397). Edith Sitwell did not quite allow the rhetoric of the gymnasium into her disparagement of ordinariness but she comes close to involving corporal punishment as a cure for lazy readers. Modernist poetry should "come as a shock to people who are used to taking their impressions second-hand – to people who want comfort and not the truth" (Sitwell, 1926, p. 22). Q.D. Leavis was not a wholehearted supporter of modernism but she felt that something ought to be done about "the reader – who spends his leisure in cinemas, looking through magazines and newspapers, listening to jazz music ... [which] does not merely fail him, it prevents him from normal development" (Leavis, 1932, p. 224). As another cultural reformist put it in the early 1930s, the "older ones are used up ... rotten to the marrow ... This is the heroic strength of youth. Out of it will come the creative man."

Certainly Adolf Hitler was no great litterateur, but his enthusiasm for the cathartic effects of effort and struggle and his preoccupation with a lean, virile state of mind finds an echo in a remarkable number of apologies for modernism. Hitler and Nazism were repugnant enough but there was an anomalous, indeed bizarre, sense of loathing for the ordinary citizen abroad among advocates of leftism. In a passage from David Lodge's *Nice Work* (1988), Vic – the no-nonsense self-made businessman – explains to Robyn Penrose, academic and fan of modernism, his reading preferences, or rather his lack of them. "'But reading is the opposite of work', says Vic. 'It's what you do when you come home from work to relax.' No, no, contends Robyn. 'Difficulty generates meaning. It makes the reader work harder.'" Lodge's portrait of the legacy of modernism – difficulty is good for us – is wryly amusing. For him, a senior professor of English and novelist, the institutionalization of modernism and its abiding educational benefits had become commonplaces of the literary and academic establishment. But his humor also enables him, and us, to overlook the murky ways in which all of this began half a century earlier. Eliot made it clear that the duty of the poet reached beyond a commitment to his genre. "Poets of our civilization, as it exists at present, should be difficult." The protection of civilization through the art of complexity sounds an honorable, if somewhat perverse, nostrum, but elsewhere in Eliot's writings on art and society it becomes clear he sees the danger as coming from a particular quarter. He is upset by the likely twofold consequences of the expanding education system, involving "lowering our standards" which, once lowered, will allow into hallowed cultural ground "barbarian nomads of the future" who will there "encamp in their mechanized caravans." We cannot help noticing that Eliot's snobbish observations are given an apocalyptic twist in Yeats's question on "what rough beast, its hour come round at last / Slouches towards Bethlehem to be born?" presumably without its caravan. Both images are vivid, hyperbolic, and faintly ludicrous, but if we work back through Eliot's pronouncements to his poetry we can discern a degree of continuity. The sort of persons whose recreational tastes involve "mechanized caravans" are close cousins to the "young man carbuncular" and his typist who Eliot only permits into his poem on the tacit understanding that their real counterparts will be discouraged from reading it because it is "difficult." José Ortega y Gasset, Spanish liberal philosopher, expressed the case more succinctly in *The Dehumanization of Art and Ideas about the Novel* (1925, trans 1968). Modernism, in his view, is a necessary "social agent" which cleaves from the dangerously amorphous notion of egalitarian society and popular culture "two different castes of men." Those who cannot appreciate, indeed make sense of, the new aesthetic will become the "inert matter of the historical process"; the rest, the justly "privileged minority," are the "illustrious," gifted with "fine senses." Marxism and Darwinism share a commitment to the inexorability of process, respectively economic/political and biological. Ortega y Gasset and many other modernists, right and left-leaning, offer us an aesthetic version of this model of history in which inert and superfluous matter, people included, is cast aside.

Those who advocated difficulty as remedy for social and cultural decay believed that to cause readers to question what a work means or even why they are reading it was a vital test of intellectual earnestness. Those who gave in would identify themselves as part of the encroaching temper of drab populism and could be left to their simple tastes. The pioneers, a minority, would forge ahead and master or at least savor the complexities of the text; they would form the new vanguard of discernment and erudition.

Literature before modernism had often courted the entitlements of High Art and with them the collaboration of selected readers but never before had it been quite so discriminatory in its nature. Ever since the invention of the printing press and the explosion of popular theatre in the sixteenth century the audience could decide on what type of book or spectacle best suited their tastes. But the modernists and their apologists seemed intent on excluding those who had swelled the tide of market-orientated reading by ensuring that the books, poems, and plays of the new age would alienate them. As shown, such a cultural and artistic program, coinciding as it did with the rise of tyrannical fascism and communism, appears monstrous, or it would were it not also utterly fatuous.

The first piece of writing to take a step outside the polarized critical debate on modernism was a short story by J.C. Squire, "The Man Who Wrote Free Verse." It appeared in 1924 in the *London Mercury* which Squire edited. At just over 20 000 readers the *Mercury* could claim to cover a whole spectrum of interests ranging from the new moving pictures and popular theatre to art exhibitions and contemporary poetry. Its readership was an index to the literary culture of the 1920s; it did not shun modernism and nor did it look down on those with an appetite for Bennett or crime fiction. Squire's story is one of the few documents that accompanied the emergence of modernism never to have been reprinted. It is absent from all of the anthologies published for academic study and despite the fact that it was read by an enormous number of people in the mid-1920s it has been consigned to virtual oblivion. The reason for this is straightforward: it provides an astonishingly accurate exposé of the egregious self-contradictions of modernist writing and as such poses questions regarding the now venerated status enjoyed by much of it.

The two principal characters are Adrian Roberts and Reggie Twyford, upper-middle class gents who evidently enjoy a private income and find themselves, while guests on the country estate of Lady Muriel, reflecting upon current literary fashions. Of the two Reggie is the more open minded, admitting that while he does not pretend to understand what is presently being talked of as a new regime in writing he is fascinated by why so many eminent figures are attracted to it – Lady Muriel herself has assembled an impressive collection of experimental novels and volumes of avant garde poetry – and what has motivated this generation of authors. Despite the Wodehousian tone of the opening the story soon mutates into a more serious engagement with the phenomenon of transformation, with Adrian taking on the role of Socratic sceptic, a foil to Reggie's puzzled musings. Eventually Reggie reaches something of a conclusion on the reasons for modernism. It is, he suspects, inspired by a much more extensive overturning of established ideas. "Scientific and social conceptions can't alter without modifying art; music changes and poetry may change; and I can conceive of new things being said in a new way." Against Adrian's objections he continues, and by illustration points to the correspondence between communist revolution, Dadaist verse, and Cubism, adding that it is "significant that when the Bolsheviks got into power in Russia they made all the Cubists … official artists" (Squire, 1924, p. 128). Reggie's formulation of the origins of modernism will seem familiar to us: Nietzsche, Darwin, Marx, and other ground-breaking nineteenth century thinkers altered conceptions of society and the human condition, and art, as a consequence, shifted away from its mimetic, representational complacencies. But we should remind ourselves that such cause-and-effect commonplaces were devised gradually from the 1940s onwards, largely by academics and with benefit of hindsight. In 1924, no one – and certainly not the modernists themselves – could offer a clear comprehensive explanation of what was happening. Bradbury and McFarlane's (1970) volume of essays by academics on the nature of modernism was the first major summation of scholarly wisdom on what it is and how it came about, and it is interesting to compare Richard Sheppard's chapter on "The Crisis of Language" with Reggie's postulations. Like Reggie, Sheppard treats modernist poetry as symptomatic of the demise of both the ruling classes and industrialized capitalism:

When poetry ceases to be a printed exercise in individual excellence ... art (if that term is not anachronistic in this context) becomes revolutionary gesture ... the right of everyone to practise poetry as he wishes becomes the equivalent of the right of everyone to political self-determination; the lowering of the status of language implies the rejection of all forms of elitism ... then the imaginative capacities of human nature must affirm themselves in what amounts to a social revolution. (Bradbury and McFarlane, 1970, p. 335)

Sheppard does not go quite so far as to endorse revolution as an ever-reliable cause for the improvement of humanity but he takes for granted the symbiotic relationship between aesthetic and political upheaval, and in this regard he represents the collective opinion of academia and much of the literary establishment half a century after the zenith of modernism: literature was conscripted as an index to an epoch of turbulence and change. In the 1970s Sheppard's thesis was the received wisdom and did not provoke objections, unlike that of his predecessor Reggie. Adrian replies that "I'm sure that highly elaborate nonsense means nothing whatever to the proletariat." In Adrian's opinion Bolsheviks sanctioned modernism as an insult to the bourgeoisie, the kind of lower middle class reader who would be appalled and perplexed by its "rape of language and the murder of ideas".

Adrian and Reggie embody the polarity of opinions on modernism during the 1920s but Squire, to his credit, does not advertise either as the more convincing advocate. Instead he provides a dramatic enactment of the debate and a means of drawing their exchanges towards some kind of conclusion. Adrian suggests that Reggie should embark on a career as a poet. If he does not succeed then his inability to match the quality of his peers will be a convincing endorsement of his enthusiasm for them as important literary pioneers; if, however, he is taken seriously, his own hoax, as a man who does not pretend to any talent, would expose the entire enterprise as fraudulent. Adrian takes the experiment seriously, instructing his friend in the essentials of a particular subgenre of modernist verse: "You must begin ... by emptying your mind completely and recording only disconnected impressions. You can work in the rebellion and work out the verbs later". He might seem facetious, even dismissive in his manner but no more so than Tristan Tzara in his manifesto "To Make a Dadaist Poem" published in the same year as Squire's story.

Take a newspaper.
Take some scissors.
Choose from this paper an article of the length you want to make your poem,
Cut out the article.
Next carefully cut out each of the words that make up this article and put them all in a bag.
Shake gently.
Next take our each cutting one after the other.
Copy conscientiously in the order in which they left the bag.
The poem will resemble you.
And there you are – an infinitely original author of charming sensibility,
even though unappreciated by the vulgar herd.

          (Tristan Tzara, "To Make a Dadaist Poem," 1924)

The two of them begin with an attempt to create a poem from an unrehearsed record of an actual but apparently inconsequential event, in this case Reggie hurrying to a lunch appointment.

> The chimney-cowls
> Gyrate
> In the wind
> There is a blot of ink
> On my paper.
> I am going to have lunch
> Before long
> And I am glad there is
> A
> Lobster.

This is not, as Adrian's comment on it makes clear, an attempt by Squire to parody Imagist-style verse. He gives it grudging approval as a first attempt but points out its faults: principally, that Reggie has redrafted what amounts to a passage of note-form prose on his thoughts about lunch. The flaw in this compositional method, Adrian contends, is that it preserves and, through the line breaks, give preposterous emphasis to Reggie's petty sensibilities: "you actually express, in one place, a genuine emotion: I mean when you refer to the lobster". Squire, via Adrian, is a perceptive analyst of the new poetic. If Pound had inserted a link-term such as "are like" or even "recall" between "The apparition of those faces in the crowd" and "Petals on a wet black bough," "In A Station of the Metro" would have suddenly become a little less abstract and impersonal and carried a slight trace of its author's involvement, like Reggie's first draft. Following Adrian's advice Reggie rewrites the piece and like Pound and the Imagists eradicates connectives and with them any hint of subjective input.

> Gyrating cowls.
> Ink.
> Oh God! A Lobster!

Imagist verse might seem an easy target in this respect but Adrian is equally alert to a counter-trend, pioneered by Eliot. "Don't forget the classical one and don't forget the one which is allowed to rhyme, by way of compensation for its especially polysyllabic obscurity." Again, Reggie follows Adrian's advice and comes up with a poem that goes beyond parody and is as close as is possible to a replica of Eliot's "Sweeney Among the Nightingales." Consider the following:

> Apocalyptic chimney cowls
> Squeak at the sergeant's velvet hat
> Donkeys and other paper fowls
> Disgorge decretals at the cat
>
> Gloomy Orion and the Day
> Are veiled; and hushed the shrunken seas
> The person in the Spanish Cape
> Tries to sit on Sweeney's Knees

If you are familiar with Eliot's poem you might recognize which of these stanzas comes from it, but, recollecting a passage is different from distinguishing it from the other by virtue of its intrinsic superiority or stylistic character.

Squire is not so much launching a polemic against modernism as pointing up a self-evident fact: that one of its largely overlooked features is its insistence upon stark disinterestedness. Most poets and novelists always shy away from blatant personal involvement – such an arrangement would blur the distinction between literature and autobiography – but they leave in place an intermediary, a storyteller or simply a voice, something that will maintain a bond, however slight, between the work and the world of feelings, fears, and dilemmas shared by the reader and the author. The most evident example of this presence is the author's stylistic signature; craftsmanship combined a trace of something more capricious and temperamental.

As Squire shrewdly discerned, modernism was set upon the depersonalization, indeed the dehumanization of literature.

His imitation of "Sweeney" testifies to much more than his skill as a mimic. He is able to replicate the poem so well because Eliot has displaced his private register – the most difficult feature of any work to convincingly reproduce – with a technique that turns in upon itself and remains untainted by the idiosyncrasies of self-determination.

Here we come upon the inherent paradox of modernism. The preoccupation of many of its practitioners with the growing and dangerous encroachment of popular culture, ordinariness, upon high art gave birth to poems, novels, and plays, which, by virtue of their complexity, would alienate the lazy or uninitiated. As a consequence, however, literary works that spurned evidence of individuality or personal involvement also became endlessly imitable. Squire, whether he knew it or not, was not only diagnosing a flaw in the works of Eliot and Pound, he was foretelling a quite dreadful legacy. We see it now throughout the cultural infrastructure that is the inheritance of modernism, in "installations" such as Tracey Emin's unmade bed. That too is horribly easy to imitate; some of us do it every morning. As art it is worthless.

One of the best-known poets of the past four decades remains a teenager. E.J. Thribb (17½) is the in-house versifier of the satirical magazine *Private Eye*. Thribb's particular metier is the poem upon an occasion, usually the death of eminent figure, done in the manner of early Pound or, as this style evolved, William Carlos Williams or Charles Olson. Thribb is a laughable institution yet he endures as a serious critique of modernism. His style is archly dreadful but consistently so and the fact that at least 30 individuals have been responsible for him should tell us something about our respect for the more "serious" practitioners of this form of writing. A Thribb poem of the mid-1970s will appear to have been written by the same person who produces the 2013 vintage. We associate the style with a name but only in the sense that the latter is appended to each poem; in truth technique has extinguished any proper notion of presence.

The following poem is called "Changing"

> unlike men must primary
> and swimming and the what she
> be served he meets Sophia
> startling that people could but she never
> – in keeping too much to pretend
> estranged him

It is an example of the school generally known as L=A=N=G=U=A=G=E poetry, which can trace its roots as far back as modernism – though most involved with it would decry anything so conventional as influence or affiliation. Two of its foremost champions and practitioners, Bruce Andrews (author of the above piece) and Charles Bernstein, preferred a cautionary account of what it involved in their preface to a 1984 collection of verse.

> Throughout, we have emphasized a spectrum of writing that places its attention primarily on language and ways of making meaning, that takes for granted neither vocabulary, grammar, process, shape, syntax, program, or subject matter. All of these remain at issue. Focussing on this range of poetic exploration, and on related aesthetic and political concerns, we have tried to open things up beyond correspondence and conversation: to break down some unnecessary self-encapsulation of writers (person from person, & scene from scene), and to develop more fully the latticework of those involved in aesthetically related activity. (Andrews and Bernstein 1984, p. ix)

Andrews and Bernstein are energized by the same objectives as the first modernists. They want to move ahead, distance themselves from precedent because precedent inhibits "aesthetic" advancement. I place inverted commas around their notion of the aesthetic because they are pursuing an agenda very different from that we would routinely associate with literary art. For them "language" is a laboratory for radical perceptions of existence while the notion of the artist is an "unnecessary self-encapsulation." Joyce's career as a novelist is exemplary in this regard. *Dubliners* carried traces of a break with the nineteenth century naturalist mode; literary impressionism had arrived. *A Portrait of the Artist as a Young man* explored the boundaries between the representational novel and the then uncharted territory of introspective fiction. *Ulysses* broke the link between fiction as it was previously known and what modernism could make it become. Like its predecessors *Finnegans Wake* polarized critics. Naysayers such as Richard Aldington (*Atlantic Monthly*, June 1939) ran out of patience – "Common honesty compels this reviewer to state that he is unable to explain either the subject or the meaning (if any) of Mr Joyce's book … Mr Joyce claims that he understands and can explain every syllable of the book. Doubtless, but who cares? Readers are not interested in what the author's words mean to him, but in what they mean to them." And in Aldington's view the 628 pages of the book are entirely devoid of meaning. Malcolm Muggeridge (*Time and Tide*, 20 May 1939) is equally confounded but a little less repulsed. He too finds it unreadable in any conventional sense yet allows for some metaphysical impulse behind the incoherence. "Words instead of straining to contain what has been dimly understood, to signify truth, strain to confuse. They desert experience and understanding, and signify only chaos, in the process inevitably disintegrating, ceasing to be words at all." French critics could generally be relied upon to defend modernist enterprises against Anglo-Saxon abhorrence and Georges Pelorson (*Aux Ecoutes*, 20 May 1939) goes further than Muggeridge and celebrates *Finnegans Wake* as a philosophical triumph. He concedes that the book involves no characters, no sense of place or narrative, but, he argues, that is the point. "We are not even in the presence of a semblance of a novel ... the master of the action , in this book, is in fact time, this enormous and cavernous belly where nothing is created which has not first been consumed, used up, submitted to endless digestions." Pelorson can claim to be one of the first to discern in the book a feature that has ensured its endurance as the archetype of pure experiment. It is not "about" anything in the sense that when we write about experience, or feelings, we rely both in literary and nonliterary language and relatively secure linkages between words and points in time and space.

Pelorson is excited because the book promotes literature to the elevated level of philosophy – beneath his florid image of "the cavernous belly" of time lurks the then very fashionable thesis of phenomenology explored in the work of Edmund Husserl – and once again we find that modernism is championed as setting a new agenda for poetry and fiction, causing us to confront the ways in which our easy presuppositions regarding experience and thought are being overturned. What must be recognized is that rather than animating a previously inert potential of literature this notion compromises its uniqueness. Although the parallels between Joyce's final novel and Duchamp's famous, and notorious, *Fountain* (1917) might seem tenuous – for one thing Joyce toiled over his piece for 16 years while Duchamp's is the definitive "found" work, comprising as it does a standard urinal basin, purchased locally – they have much in common. Duchamp is credited with initiating conceptual art, in which the intellectual gesture that underpins, and generally speaking precedes, the execution of the work takes precedence over conventional aesthetic concerns. This brings to mind Tzara's instructions on how to make a Dadaist poem and while much modernist literature involves a good deal of compositional input from the writer – Eliot's poems and Joyce's novels are clearly not "found" pieces – it shares with conceptual art something much more significant. The existential and intellectual questions generated by it are as significant as its self-contained aesthetic or thematic features. In short, what goes on outside it is as important as our recognition of its inherent qualities.

The following is a passage from Gertrude Stein's *The Making of Americans*:

> The boy stayed home, and the man said to him you must be clear in your wonder at the world around you, the place we share will not be that of later years when you have done many things and I am an old man. The boy put all he had in a bag and told the man that this is my world and the man looked at him and spoke, of a tree they had seen and stood beneath that day it rained. The boy took his bag outside and held it by the tree and soon the man, it was his father, touched the boy and the tree and then the boy said that he was interested and sad. He wanted all, but had not made the tree his own and now he would never do it. The father said the boy was bright and then they went back, to the home and other, other things.

Stein's novel should be treated as the prototype for the most innovative modernist fiction, *Finnegans Wake* included. Unlike the latter its manner is primitivist, marrying the words to the unambitious mind-set of a group of characters who never attach themselves to an enduring narrative. But, in common with *Finnegans Wake,* there is no story; in both we encounter a literary spectacle designed to be contemplated rather than experienced. It is the sort of book that one might open at random, do so again, and perhaps once more, without feeling that we have lost anything of its thematic coherence or narrative continuity. In the same way, we might visit a gallery containing a conceptualist installation the day after we first viewed it. Our ideas about its significance might have changed in the interim but this has more to do with us than with anything activated in us by the work in question.

At the end of "The Man Who Wrote Free Verse," Britain has become a Bolshevik republic and Reggie installed as "Poet Laureate of the Revolution," but we should not treat this as a diagnosis of modernism as essentially and exclusively leftist. Fascism was in its infancy in 1924 and Squire regarded the new aesthetic as sympathetic to all notions of exclusion and totalitarianism. The regime in Russia was a convenient example. Reggie's conditions of employment are that he serves the interests of the proletariat and his employers make it clear that "so long as [he] could not be understood they were quite satisfied with him." The "they" are the heads of the British Soviet, not the newly disburdened masses. What they feel about Reggie and his verse is never disclosed and despite its air of farcical hyperbole one aspect of Squire's closing scenario is extraordinarily prescient. Jump forward almost half a century to the posthumous publication of Theodor Adorno's

Aesthetic Theory. Adorno was a Marxist critical theorist who praised modernism, stating that "the task of aesthetics is not to comprehend artworks as hermeneutical objects [that is, things that might in a conventional sense be understood]; in the contemporary situation, it is their incomprehensibility that needs to be comprehended" (Adorno 1997, p. 118). Adorno contends that art should alienate itself from the discourses of bourgeois society and mass culture, which would otherwise co-opt it to a capitalist system that assigns a function, or meaning, to everything.

It is difficult to decide on whether this perception of modernism's cultural and social function is absurd or sinister. Historical evidence would encourage the former verdict given that the complexity, some might say the arbitrary meaninglessness of high modernism has endured largely as the preserve of the educated, usually left-leaning, bourgeoisie while mass culture has remained generally indifferent to it.

What is generally ignored by modern theoreticians and indeed those whose work litters the history of aesthetics since Aristotle is the simple issue of why we enjoy literature. I do not here refer to the notion of "enjoyment" as some form of psychoanalytical displacement, nor to any of the other intellectual or ideological states that only those not experiencing them claim to understand. No; my conception of enjoyment involves both a conscious apprehension of what makes us enjoy the book we are reading and a more visceral sense of pleasure: in short we like a book or a poem and we know also something of why we like it. It is possible, for example, to be enthralled or repulsed by a character in a novel by Austen, Dickens, or Waugh, caused to empathize with them, or hate them, as we might a real person, while at the same time remain conscious of the degree of craftsmanship that lies behind their creation. We may suspend disbelief, allow the story and its figures to draw us into the delusion, and also take a step back, side-line this personal inducement, and see the book as an artefact that raises questions about who we are and how we behave.

The advocates of modernist complexity wish to deny us this double perspective. The book or poem will become something that is assessed and analyzed in the same way that conceptualist art becomes the springboard for debate on the nature of representation, and my reference here to nonlinguistic art is purposive. Language is part of us. We can choose not to paint or we can elect to be uninterested in this year's winner of the Turner Prize but we cannot opt out of language, and language is the raw material of literature. All nonliterary art forms make use of dead matter – paint, wood, canvas, sounds generated from contact between objects, and so on – to construct artefacts, either representational or abstract. Literature is composed exclusively of language and language is what makes us human beings. For this reason we feel an empathetic, elemental closeness to literature, which sometimes, especially in novels, causes us to forget that the artwork is comprised of words alone. Some prefer pure escapism to what might be termed appreciative reading – and we look at this more closely in Chapter 7 on popular literature – but most of us enjoy a compromise, involving ourselves in the work while at the same time allowing for an objective perspective upon its form, its qualities, and the question of whether or how it reflects its author's state of mind.

In a much misunderstood passage the novelist Thomas Wolfe (1936) reflects upon the transformation over 15 years of *Ulysses* from an inaccessible conundrum to a classic.

> As people overcame their own inertia … became familiar with its whole design, they began to understand that the book was neither an obscene book nor an obscure book, certainly it was not a work of wilful dilettante caprice. It was, on the contrary, an orderly, densely constructed creation, whose greatest fault, it seems to me, so far from being a fault of caprice, was rather of almost Jesuitical logic which is essentially too dry and lifeless in its mechanics for a work of the imagination.

Wolfe's point is twofold: that *Ulysses* earned its eminence not through its intrinsic qualities but through a gradual process of persuasion and instruction by those who championed radicalism as something to be valued in its own right; that Joyce's self-conscious preoccupation with writing per se turned the book into an inert "lifeless" artefact. He did not mean by this that the reader is alienated from an involvement with its manifold allusions and structured complexities. Quite the opposite. It is a book that will require an infinite amount of attention and enquiry. That is his point: we will never really be able to stop reading it. It asks questions that lead us only to yet one more crossroads in a maze of dilemmas. Yet this perpetual game of intellectual scrutiny will never yield to the kind of intuitive involvement allowed by conventional novels. In the latter we often find ourselves hoping that a character gets away with something less than creditable, sympathizing with a figure whose crisis is otherwise intimate and internalized and hoping that what happens next compounds our own, inevitably biased, sense of sentimentality or empathy. As a consequence the text begins to fade into the background but crucially, if the book is any good, maintains a polite, mischievous presence.

The most conspicuous post World War II example of the enduring power of modernism to extinguish notions of character and presence was Samuel Beckett's *Waiting for Godot*. The first performance of its English language version was directed by Peter Hall at the Arts Theatre in London in 1955. Modernist fiction and poetry had become part of the furniture of British high culture, still disliked by some, particularly the loose affiliation of Robert Conquest's affiliates, yet indulged as a conspicuous legacy. But drama, at least in Britain, remained largely immune from the advances of the literary avant garde. Consequently, Beckett's play prompted early reviews that could have been written by those variously confounded and disgusted by the groundbreaking works of 1922. On this occasion the innovation enthusiasts took only a few days to upbraid recalcitrants and remind them of what they were missing. Harold Hobson first defended its qualities in *The Sunday Times* and more famously Kenneth Tynan praised it in *The Observer*. "*Waiting for Godot*" he declares, "has no plot, no climax, no denouement, no beginning, no middle and no end." It "jettisons everything by which we recognise theatre. It arrives at the custom house, as it were, with no luggage, no passport and nothing to declare: yet it gets through as might a pilgrim from Mars. It does this, I believe, by appealing to a definition of drama much more fundamental than any in the books" (7 August 1955). Hobson and Tynan raise without properly addressing a question that had dogged modernism since its arrival almost half a century earlier. The work might well undermine our complacent expectations of literature and shock us into a new level of apprehension, but in doing so does it cease to be something that we actually enjoy? As Hope-Wallace put in in *The Guardian* "the play bored some people acutely." In fact during the first performance almost half of those present left the theatre between the two acts, but Tynan does not regard this as a failing on Beckett's part. "Were we not in the theatre," he observes, "we should, like [Beckett's characters], be clowning and quarrelling, aimlessly bickering and aimlessly making up – all, as one of them says, to give the impression that we exist." Tynan's point is the premise for a large number of the more elaborate critical explorations of the play's significance (it punctures the delusion that life is meaningful) but it is no less ludicrous for that. It might well be the case that we spend much of our time "bickering" and "quarrelling" without reaching a satisfactory conclusion regarding the matters addressed but unless we have been visited by some horrific condition such as advanced Alzheimer's disease we do not sound remotely like Vladimir and Estragon.

One suspects that, despite himself, Tynan feels this too. He adds that the play will be "a conversational necessity for many years" or, as he might have put it, an event discussed at dinner parties by those proud enough to have endured two hours of ruthlessly unintelligible dialogue.

The performances in New York the following year were greeted even less indulgently than the Peter Hall production and the first audience to treat the English language version with seemingly unanimous approval saw it in San Francisco in November 1957. It was put on for one night only by members of the San Francisco Actors Workshop before an audience of 1400, a record number. All of the latter were inmates of San Quentin Prison and the stage was the defunct gallows in the now disused dungeons. There are few records of what the members of the audience actually felt about the play itself. Obviously, they did not, like their counterparts in London and New York, have the opportunity to walk out half way through and all we do know of the enthusiasm allegedly fostered by the performance comes from actors such as Alan Mandell who went on to direct the San Quentin Drama Workshop. However, I think it would be fair to surmise that the fascination of the San Quentin audience was inversely related to the spectrum of feelings, from unendurable boredom to intellectual snobbishness, that registered among those who could leave the theatre to go home or discuss the experience over a late meal with others. Most intellectuals and academics treat the San Quentin production as a testament to Beckett's greatness as a writer.

Martin Esslin in his widely celebrated study *The Theatre of the Absurd*, for example:

> Or perhaps they were unsophisticated enough to come to the theatre without any preconceived notions and ready-made expectations, so they avoided the mistake that trapped so many established critics who had condemned the play for its lack of plot, development, characterization, suspense, or plain common sense. Certainly the prisoners of San Quentin could not be suspected of the sin of intellectual snobbery, for which a sizable proportion of the audience of *Waiting for Godot* have often been reproached; of pretending to like a play they did not even begin to understand, just to appear in the know. (Esslin, 1969, p. 3)

Beckett had, argued Esslin, short-circuited the middle class taste for plays that involve plot or coherence, and those who knew the world as a visceral, unprotected experience – that is, convicts – appreciated the immensity of his achievement. With all due respect to the inmates of

San Quentin prison, circa 1957, it is unlikely that this one-night audience was equipped with the same range of erudite cultural reference points and interpretive skills that enabled Tynan and others compare it with conventional drama and celebrate its radicalism. What is more likely is that they found in it a brand of realism denied to all other audiences. The US legislature was, in the 1950s, even more ruthless in its use of consecutive sentences than today. Many inmates never expected to experience life outside the zoo-like cells in which they were confined and subjected to inhumanely routine inspection by guards for most of each day. For them, the sheer pointlessness of existence evinced by the inane pronouncements of Estragon, Vladimir, Lucky, Pozzo, and a Boy mirrored their own condition. It certainly did not enrich it or endow it with purpose – nothing could – but for the first time they found themselves witnessing a darkly farcical account of their lives written and acted by someone else. It would not have made them feel any better but, as countless defenders of modernism have preached, literature is not supposed to be an improvement on the world but rather a reminder that life cannot be improved upon; it is in fact more complicated and usually worse than we routinely persuade ourselves that it might be. Beckett had found his ideal audience: men who had given up hope, whose existences were as meaningless and futile as those of his characters, and this scenario involves an unsettling corollary. Those, such as Tynan, who promoted themselves as the intellectual vanguard because they had endured two hours of unintelligible drivel, would exist for the rest of their lives in a world where sentences have subjects and contexts, people have lives and histories, doors could be opened rather than persistently bolted, and the first night of Beckett's play would be treasured along with a collection of equally grand cultural prerequisites. Like Eliot, Woolf, and Joyce it is an example of art as hypocrisy and exclusivity. The only people who can properly appreciate its terrible pointlessness are members of the intellectual aristocracy and men serving life sentences. Those in between, the unenlightened who continue to regard it as a wearisome exercise in self-indulgence, will be regarded as philistines.

There is a story, perhaps apocryphal but instructive nonetheless, that some time after the launch of Tracey Emin's *My Bed* installation at the Tate in 1998 a new shift of cleaners was brought in to vacuum and tidy the gallery after closing time. Uninstructed that the empty bottles, stained knickers, used condoms, and other detritus surrounding the piece were part of its formal structure one cleaner decided to tidy it up. She was stopped before she changed the sheets, stained as they were with bodily secretions.

She was, she claimed, only doing her job but several weeks later two performance artists, Yuan Cai and Jian Jun Xi, decided that it was their job, or perhaps part of their vocation, to stage a pillow fight on the bed: it was, after all, a "living" installation. Other onlookers cheered. How should we treat these interventionists? I ask because their acts beg comparison with the only recorded comment from a member of the audience at the San Quentin performance. Asked if he would attend another play the unnamed convict answered "Maybe next month, or next year – or whenever ... Like the man said. Nothing happens!" (*San Quentin News,* 28 November 1957). Routinely the man's observation is seen as proof that when the "sin of intellectual snobbery" that dogged the play's reception by middle class audiences is swept away its significance can be *"immediately grasped"* (Esslin 1969, p. 1) but I am not certain of this. The response of the convict was very similar to that of the cleaner in that neither discerned a clear boundary between what were regarded by others as artworks and the dreary monotonous regime of their existences. The convict was not given the opportunity to expand on his comment and one wonders if by treating it as an astute insight into Beckett's Nietzchean vision theorists are, in effect, substituting their highbrow interpretation for his rather more literal response. Pretending that the convict is an idiot savant version of Esslin is the equivalent of conflating the act of the cleaner at the Tate with that of the two performance artists. His statement that "Nothing happens!" is in all likelyhood a reference to life in San Quentin rather than the philosophical implications of Beckett's work; at best, he was willing to put up with a slightly farcical two-hour enactment of his daily life in preference to being locked up for the same period. There is certainly no evidence to show that he expected any other play to be different from what he had just seen. It is of course pure hypothesis to speculate on how he would have responded to a performance of a play by, say, Eugene O'Neill; something that made sense and was, more significantly, based on a recognizable version of the world he recalled before incarceration, or is it?

What is reasonably certain is that he would not have felt, at least in his ongoing circumstances, as though the boundary between the world he would return to after the play and the play itself was virtually nonexistent. In this regard the convict and the cleaner have nothing in common with the performance artists. That the latter crossed the invisible boundary between the world and the installation self-consciously is a testament to *My Bed's* questionable status as art. On its own it is worthless; it requires a participating presence to grant it a veneer of significance. As we see in Chapter 4, the critic Stanley Fish performed a similar act with a random sequence of words; he encouraged postgraduate critics to interpret it as a poem. Once his Pavlovian interpreters had finished their work, however, it remained as it had always had been – a meaningless, insignificant accident.

If one strips a text, or a piece of plastic art, of the stylistic and formal intricacies that separate it from the detritus of the lived-in world or ordinary language, then participation by the viewer, reader, or spectator is encouraged and some might exalt in this as a leveling of the hierarchies of art: we feel that we are part of what in other cases seems remote. But does not the reader or viewer consequently lose any sense of respect for the artist as, in basic terms, a craftsman? Why admire a beautiful object if no apparent effort or skill has contributed to its formation?

Marina Abramović, an artist comparable with Emin, staged an event called *The Artist Is Present* in New York Museum of Modern Art (14 March – 31 May 2010). Abramovic spent 736 hours seated statically, silently, on one side of an unadorned wooden table, while a group of "sitters" booked places via Facebook to occupy the chair on the other side for short periods. An already vast exercise in mass fetishism was boosted by the participation, as a "sitter," of the singer Lady Gaga. Again, the cleaner, the convict, and the performance artists come to mind but we should remind ourselves that those who undertook acts of participation as a self-conscious gesture, became, as it were, part of the dynamic of the artefact; they did so with a sense of having joined the artist, becoming equal collaborators in an aesthetic enterprise. They are of course free to countenance such thoughts but they should be reminded that in doing so they are also cooperating with the artist in a process of aesthetic devaluation. If art can simply be made or contributed to without a collateral sense of effort or talent it is worthless. How do I know? Turn back in this chapter, to the extracts from a L=A=N=G=U=A=G=E poem and from Stein's *The Making of Americans*. Read them, consider your opinion on their value, and then turn forward to page 211 to the poems by Andrew Crozier.

Zadie Smith wrote an article for the *New York Times Review of Books* (20 November 2008) which, by virtue of the comments generated, must be regarded as diagnostic of the mood of the Anglo-American literati in the early twenty-first century. I have yet to encounter a respondent who goes against her general thesis. It is, ostensibly, a review article on two novels, *Netherland* by Joseph O'Neill and *Remainder* by Tom McCarthy, but this is the pretext for a 9000-word rumination on the state of contemporary fiction.

She begins with *Netherland*, a story about a transatlantic city trader whose mind-set reflects the traumas of post 9/11 Western culture. She does not judge it as in itself a bad piece of writing; it is much worse than that. It is, she reflects, the sort of book that might well grace the bedside table of President Obama and which can claim its place in the legacy of Balzac and Stendhal, scions of that old and powerful dynasty, "literary realism." Despairingly, she quotes one of its principal characters, "People want a story"; and replies: "But is this really what having a self feels like … Do they not sometimes want its opposite?" Which brings her to Tom McCarthy's *Remainder*, a novel whose first person narrator remains anonymous. Smith calls him "The Enactor" because, of course, without his participating presence the book would not exist. The opening 50 pages are puzzling because we learn little more than that he has been hit on the head by some enormous "thing." Eventually he receives a phone call from his lawyer. "I stood there for some time, I don't know how long, holding the dead receiver in my hand." His sense of shock comes from having learnt that whoever or whatever is responsible for the blow from the "thing" has agreed to £8.5 million in compensation. Thereafter we follow him and some equally vaguely sketched companions through an unpalatable London where self-absorption and nepotism predominate, at least for those not terminally destitute. It seems, so far, a parvenu nod towards the type of novel that Smith derided in her account of *Netherland*. But then we learn of what it is really "about." The "Enactor" has toyed with the idea of becoming a benefactor, using his newfound wealth to relieve the condition of dejected figures on the street who contrast so horribly with the pleasure-seeking lives of everyone else. "'What I want to know –' my homeless person asked." We never learn what the homeless person is about to ask because suddenly "the waiter" (who is referred to both as "he" and "she") first removes the tablecloth, then the table, and the Enactor observes "there wasn't any table. The truth is, I've been making all this up." Later the Enactor meets Nazrul Ram Vyas of Time Control UK who promises to relieve him of the burden of thinking and therefore creates the world on his behalf.

Fascinated as we might be by Smith's account of this game of metafictional smoke and mirrors ("impeccably written," as she puts it) she interrupts herself to tell of something that occurred in the "real" world, specifically the foundation of the International Necronautical Society (INS), before a small audience in New York on 25 September 2005, by its general secretary, Tom McCarthy, and its chief philosopher, Simon Critchley. I'll offer you a flavor of their manifesto:

> "We begin," announces General Secretary, "with the experience of failed transcendence, a failure that is at the core of the General Secretary's novels and the Chief Philosopher's tomes. Being is not full transcendence, the plenitude of the One cosmic abundance, but rather an ellipsis, an absence, an incomprehensibly vast lack scattered with debris and detritus. Philosophy as the thinking of Being has to begin from the experience of disappointment that is at once religious (God is dead, the One is gone), epistemic (we know very little, almost nothing; all knowledge claims have to begin from the experience of limitation) and political (blood is being spilt in the streets as though it were champagne)."

As Smith explains, the INS "freely admit ... to stealing openly from Blanchot, Bataille, Heidegger, Derrida and of course Robbe-Grillet." We consider the theoretical infrastructure created by these figures in Chapter 4 but let us observe for the moment that for those involved with literature since the 1990s this has become a fashionable intellectual accessary, rather in the way that anyone who cultivated anti-establishment credentials in the 1950s embraced existentialism.

Far more important are the parallels between this and documents of a century earlier. Glance through an anthology of creative manifestoes from about 1905 to the mid-1920s. Kandinsky (1912), Tzara (1918), Schwitters (1921), Grosz and Herzfelde (1925), Gan (1922), and Gropius (1919) among about a dozen more from literature, the visual arts, and music might have been writing extracts and appendices from the INS manifesto. True, not all the former idolize "debris and detritus" but such contraries are overwhelmed by an abundant harmony of gibberish, particularly on the nature of "form."

It does not matter if one agrees or otherwise with Smith, or the INS. What is difficult is to suppress a gasp of astonishment that someone who writes novels and, one assumes, knows about literature (a Cambridge graduate no less) should be so ignorant of what has happened to it. She observes that "'the received wisdom' of literary history is that *Finnegans Wake* did not fundamentally disturb realism's course as Duchamp's urinal disturbed realism in the visual arts ... metafiction that stood in opposition to Realism has been relegated to a safe corner of literary history, to be studied in postmodernity modules." The Duchamp mode of art-without-craftsmanship has over the past three decades generated vast amounts in auction houses (see for example Hirst and Emin). It is, by cost alone, far more elitist than the "representational" mode that, according to Smith, it undermined. *Finnegans Wake* has lagged behind in terms of sales – for the simple reason that few if any want to read it – but, as Smith concedes, its progeny survive as the aristocracy of high culture, "studied in postmodernity modules" in the kind of Ivy League universities that purchase Smith's services as writer in residence.

Smith seems not to realize that "literary history" as she puts it came to an end about a hundred years before she wrote her eulogy for modernism. Her cultural blindness is not an uncommon affliction; endemic would be a better term. Glance, if you will, at "Experimental fiction: is it making a comeback?" (W. Skidesky, *The Observer*, 1 August 2010). "Whatever happened to the literary avant garde" (Robert McCrum, *Telegraph*, 20 July 2009), "The end of the English novel" (Bill Buford, *Granta*, 4 August 1980, prompted by an article by Robert McCrum in *The Bookseller*), the introductions to *All Hail the New Puritans* (ed. Nicholas Blincoe and Matt Thorne) and *New Writing 13* (2005; ed. Ali Smith and Toby Litt) and Peter Ackroyd's *Notes For a New Culture* (1976). All are by practising writers but you will find their equivalent, albeit much more verbose, in academic volumes: John Sutherland's *Fiction and the Fiction Industry* (1978), Bernard Bergonzi's *The Situation of the Novel* (1970), and Jean Baudrillard's *Simulations* (1983). Each involves a defence of modernism just as staunch and resolute as those prompted by the conservatives and doubters at the beginning of the twentieth century.

Imagine that in 1900 or thereabouts advocates of the Romantic lyric and its aesthetic correlates were still battling against the view that such writings were, by degrees, self-indulgent and incomprehensible. Or, for that matter, envisage debates in the London journals of the late 1800s on what the new phenomenon the "romance" or "the novel" actually involves and whether it qualifies only as a minor province of literary writing. In each instance the hypothesis is ridiculous because radicalism or uncertainty had become part of a productive engagement with what had gone before; not absorbed or fragmented but rather incorporated as an element of a dialogue between the past and the present. Modernist innovation, by definition, cannot allow for this. It must involve an incessant forward movement that continually disavows both the past and the present and in this sense it has become a living paradox. Experiment is regarded as sacred because it exchanges the familiar for the unknown but experiment in literature will always repeat the formulae of the early modernists; radicalism must by its nature become a repetitive and fossilized procedure.

Modernism is the terminus of literary history, in that all subsequent and forthcoming attempts at innovation are versions of what has already been done. It is certainly the case that novels such as McCarthy's will continue to be written and published but as Smith points out they will by scions of the legacy of "Barth, Barthelme, Pynchon, Geddes, DeLillo, David Foster Wallace." Her list might include Samuel Beckett, Malcolm Lowry, B.S. Johnson, Christine Brooke-Rose, John Berger, David Caute, and Paul Auster, but in noting this I should also refer the reader to the colossal irony that underpins it. Experimentation maintains an addictive attraction among the literary intelligentsia yet no one seems courageous enough to admit that it is now also a key element of deeply entrenched tradition. The defining characteristic of the avant garde was its rejection of institutionalized practice so how can it be expected to overturn itself? The movement that promised to project literature forward from a condition of stagnation has now itself created a static, immutable impasse.

As I write, the vast majority of British reviewers for the weekly arts supplements of broadsheets and highbrow magazines are heaping praise upon Will Self's latest novel, *Shark* (2014). It is made up of a 480-page single paragraph, beginning and ending in mid-sentence. Within this collage of stream of consciousness technique and high cultural allusion (Freud, Kant, Robert Lowell, and T.S. Eliot are in there, among many other echoes) we can pick out about a dozen of Self's own creations, principally the anti-psychiatrist, Zack Busner. But as is usually the case with these multivocal cocktails it is difficult to locate the point at which one figure dominates the interior monologue and another takes over. Sometimes we can lock into something that resembles a theme or an event (Michael De'Ath – or maybe "Death" or "Dearth" – might well have witnessed the Hiroshima bomb) but overall Self succeeds in securing the novel against the simpleminded reader's search for coherence. Sam Leith in *The Observer* (7 September 2014) admires the way that Self's "superb writing" contributes to "something like a collective hallucination, a blurring of identity: the characters are gathered up into a narrative Gestalt." Which is all right then. *The Sunday Times*'s Theo Tait pronounces that the "ceaselessly inventive prose does an exceptional job of evoking consciousness" and concludes that "Self is creating something rather grand" (14 September 2014).

These reviews and many others are throwbacks to nearly a century ago, with a few adjustments. The defensive and/or pioneering subtext of the early defenders of the avant garde is superfluous these days, yet something like it endures. It is taken for granted that no one reading these upmarket newspapers would feel bored or infuriated by a novel that is devoid of a plot and convincing characters. This, the reviewers seem to be saying, is very high art *because* it does not tell you a story and instead demands of you a considerable, perhaps cathartically painful, intellectual investment. Quite a few of them refer to Self as the torchbearer for a number of grand antecedents (Tait treats his prose as an amalgam of Joyce, Eliot, and Celine) and it seems amazing that none is aware of the absurdity of an enterprise with which they, Self, and many other contemporary innovative novelists have involved themselves as practitioners and sponsors. Self's novel, like many similar pieces, is a case of retrograde cliché (even the broken sentence that opens and closes the book is a woeful nod towards *Finnegans Wake*). It is repeating a formula that was only radical three generations ago, one that has been reworked and mimicked so many times thereafter as to have become the equivalent of a religious ritual; it is comparable to the Roman Catholic mass – magically uplifting (allegedly) but in truth so routine as to have become little more than a banal habit. Imagine a cadre of modern novelists who offer their early twenty-first century readers replicas of the techniques and moods of George Eliot, Thomas Hardy, and Dickens. You can't. It is a foolish hypothesis because realism is a mutable entity, not easily reduced to abstract formulae. Most significantly it bears the imprint of its author; it is flexible enough to allow for writers to insinuate themselves between the various layers of description, dialogue, and narrative, make their mark, and then remove themselves into the background. Dickens' style died with his last novel but the openness and, crucially, the difficulty of writing realist fiction remains as a means of sorting the talent from the mediocrity. If there were contemporary imitators of Dickens – with appropriate updatings – they would be seen as just that, mimics offering no more than amusing curiosities. Yet with modernism we appear to have entered a version of the film *Groundhog Day*. Few of us are, like the hapless Bill Murray, conscious of history continually repeating itself with mindnumbing tedium. Most, like the rest of the film's characters, treat the endless circularity of events as revelations. On the same page as the *Observer* review of Self's novel we come upon another unctuous celebration of ossified radicalism, this time Elizabeth Day's assessment of Ali Smith's *How to Be Both*. The book has two narratives, one involving a present day character, a girl called George, who is trying to come to terms with the death of her mother, and the other the Italian Renaissance artist, Francesco del Cossa. In Day's opinion all of this amounts to "an eloquent challenge to the binary notions governing our existence," which reminds me of the sort of thing churned out in undergraduate essays on the philosophical significance of the avant garde, circa 1922. Day does concede that sometimes in the Francesco narrative we encounter poetic passages "so out of shape that … it is difficult to know what is going on." And she quotes: "down to / that thin-looking line / made of nothing / ground and grit and the / gather of dirt and earth and / the grains of stone…" These, she adds, are "undeniably beautiful, so does it matter if you can't work out what what's happening?" To which one might respond; no they are not and yes it does. The passage, like many others, reads like a piece by someone obsessed by William Carlos Williams but without the talent to produce even a pitiable imitation of his style. But because the book and its various compartments are self-evidently unorthodox Day adheres to the unspoken but prevailing evaluative mantra. If, like aristocrats of old, the book belongs within the same lineage of the modernist greats it is beyond criticism.

To return to my hypothesis of Victorian realism reborn in the work of 2014 novelists: few if any would take this seriously; at best it would be treated as an instance of postmodern drollery. Why then, are novels that recycle the same formulae that were celebrated when they were innovative – often a century ago – regarded automatically as immune from basic questions about their quality? It seems from the reviewers of Self and Smith that if a novel is fragmented in structure and as a story largely incomprehensible it must by its nature pose vital questions about the nature of existence; none of them even consider the possibility that the reader might be bored or dumbfounded or, God forbid, that the book shows evidence of lazy self-indulgence on the part of the writer. And as to the myth that formal originality is the guaranteed mainspring for aesthetic and intellectual exaltation it seems only fair to point out that Self is following the same dreary route charted by Gertrude Stein in *The Making of Americans* 80 years ago and that Smith's split narrative was already passé when the likes of B.S. Johnson, David Caute, Christine Brooke-Rose, Gabriel Josipovici, and others pitched camp during the 1960s on the site vacated by the modernist first generation.

On the page before the reviews of Self and Smith in the same culture supplement of the *Observer,* William Skidelsky reviews David Mitchell's *The Bone Clocks.* Mitchell is a curious hybrid, the offspring of an unlikely encounter between postmodern fiction and *The Reader's Digest*; his *Cloud Atlas* (2004) pulled off the remarkable double of being shortlisted for the Booker Prize and voted book of the month by viewers of Richard and Judy's afternoon chat show. He takes his creative cue from magic realism, in which the mundane aspects of existence are counterposed against factors such as the supernatural, time travel, and parallel universes. And again we find ourselves with a technique embalmed in history passing itself off as recherché: all of this was pioneered by South American writers 70 years ago. In *The Bone Clocks* a group of relatively believable figures (that is, characters who might not seem too out of place in realist fiction) are tracked through various points between 1984 and the mid twenty-first century, but alongside them we come across Horologists – reincarnated spirits – and Anchorites who secure their immortality by slaughtering children. I have yet to come across a reviewer who does not swoon in admiration for its greatness. None is willing to offer a straightforward account of what it is about but when faced with the apparently arbitrary avoidance of order and sense, intelligent people should, it is implied, treat such enquiries as vulgar, even philistine. Modernism's legacies are myriad and complex but the endurance of a purblind, pretentious respect for nonsense is grimly apparent.

Modernism, or postmodernism if you prefer, is in its own right a web of self-contradictions and it has caused an endemic bias within our conceptions of literature in general. Its intrinsic superiority to pre-1910 practices is seen as a foregone conclusion and as such we are reluctant to judge fairly the quality of work that in some way invokes the techniques of the former. Experiment has become a sine qua non for literary quality and as a consequence the notion of doing-it-differently has displaced more balanced, uncommitted notions of evaluation. In bringing literary history to a close modernism has also procured a widespread culture of evaluative paralysis.

3

Is Shakespeare Any Good?

Guests on *Desert Island Discs* are informed that three items can accompany them on their solitary exile, of which only one may be chosen by them; the other two, the Bible and *The Complete Works of Shakespeare,* are compulsory. Notably, never in the history of the program has a modern-day Crusoe stated that they have no interest in either. The two-book ordinance is as old as *Desert Island Discs* and during the 1940s the BBC no doubt thought protestations of atheism were unlikely during a politely civilized Sunday morning broadcast. But what of Shakespeare? Might intellectuals even pretend to indifference to or, God forbid, dislike of Shakespeare and expect to be taken seriously?

There are some recusants, notable both for their rarity and eminence and, to adapt Harold Bloom's theory that all writers fear and loathe their more admired predecessors, one has to wonder if their criticism of Shakespeare is really a form of attention seeking.

Voltaire and Tolstoy are the best known members of what Bloom calls the "School of Resentment" and Tolstoy in particular deserves attention because as a begrudger of Shakespeare's eminence he displays an almost farcical degree of desperation. In "Shakespeare and the Drama" (1906) he fidgets anxiously with ways of incubating distrust within Shakespeare's audience. According to Tolstoy, Shakespeare exalts in the "elevation of the lords" a "vulgar view of life" which by implication shows that he "despises

Is Shakespeare Any Good?: And Other Questions on How to Evaluate Literature,
First Edition. Richard Bradford.
© 2015 John Wiley & Sons, Ltd. Published 2015 by John Wiley & Sons, Ltd.

the crowd," "the genuine working class." It seems not to occur to him that the "genuine working class" did not feature in literature of any kind for at least 200 years after Shakespeare and even then these were inauthentic portraits by middle class or aristocratic writers, like Tolstoy, who knew nothing of their tastes or mind-set. Tolstoy goes on to claim that Shakespeare's fame "corresponded to the irreligious and immoral frame of mind of the upper classes of his time and ours." Even worse, Shakespeare's "trivial and immoral works" are aimed "merely at the recreation and amusement of the spectators" and therefore "cannot properly represent the teaching of life."

Tolstoy, contra Bloom, belongs not to the School of Resentment; rather he is a literary evangelist. He believed that literary writing should have a purpose and be judged on how effectively it executes it (in Tolstoy's view this involves despatching some kind of message to the audience on social injustice and moral propriety). Tolstoy dislikes Shakespeare because the playwright embodies an irritating rejoinder to his own credo of literature-as-power. He is an apologetic aristocrat yet he still feels it his duty to tell people, via his fictions, how to behave. This notion of literature as liturgy will be considered in more detail in Chapter 8, but for the moment consider this: Tolstoy raises several questions, which unite Shakespeare's admirers with his doubters. As a wordsmith, a poetic genius, a man who can form magnetic characters from agglomerations of conceits, he achieved more than had previously ever been conceived. But why? What was his objective? He is an ostentatiously literary writer yet he raises doubts about what literary writing is for. In my opinion, Shakespeare's enduring pre-eminence is ensured not by his attainments in relation to his competitors but because he was the first to place at the core of his work a dilemma that remains unresolved, an issue obscured during the perennial exchanges on how his work merits the devotional and fanatical attention heaped upon it. In short, a real estimation of his greatness, or otherwise, can only be undertaken if we accept that all of those who have, so far, debated his standing have remained ignorant of the true nature of his achievement. And what, you ask, does this amount to? Wait and see.

In much of Western society, at least in countries where English is the first language, Shakespeare has become an omnipresent and one might say oppressive figure. Unless one elects to completely eschew the title "educated" he cannot be avoided. In the United Kingdom it will soon be a necessary prerequisite that those who wish to continue their secondary schooling beyond the age of 16 (the only route to university) must attain a grade above "C" in GCSE Maths and English. Any grading lower than that will involve the pupil in resits, potentially incessant resits, throughout their period in the sixth form. Indeed some politicians have argued that the compulsory school-leaving age should be changed from 16 to 18. One assumes that no one has yet pondered the Kafkaesque consequences of these two interdependent ordinances: effectively those who persistently fail to reach "C" in the two key subjects will never be allowed to leave school at all. One also assumes that the farcical image of 60-year-olds filing into examination halls for their hundredth attempt at escape will cause whoever is in charge to repair this anomaly. However, while we ponder the image let us remind ourselves that one element of the procedure, even when amended, will endure. In the English examination Shakespeare will remain the dominant figure.

The hypothesis of the Bard as life-sentence is by parts laughable and horrific yet it involves only an extension of what our education system, indeed our culture, already asks us to endure. Familiarity with Shakespeare is not only the centerpiece of a formal education involving the arts and literature, his ghost permeates the supposedly more inconstant realm of casual cultural exchange: admit that you know, or care, nothing of Shakespeare and you immediately condemn yourself as a philistine. Routinely, Shakespeare's modern low cultural counterpart, at least in Britain, is taken to be the television soap opera. Their parallels point up their position at opposite ends of the aesthetic spectrum. Both involve a tripartite blend of dramatic performance, tragicomic characterization, and gripping plot lines, yet while Shakespeare uses poetry as a vehicle for the exploration of such universals as ambition, envy, love, despair, and death, the soap is the dramatic equivalent of a takeaway meal, unhealthily satiating but involving neither effort nor discernment on the part of the consumer. Or so we are customarily led to believe. Presently, however (Fall 2013), UK commercial television is running a publicity campaign for its two most popular soaps, *Emmerdale* and *Coronation Street*, in which 14 characters, seven from each show, appear in soliloquy mode, addressing the camera and audience with familiar parts of the set as background. Each is allocated a single pentameter line from a Shakespeare sonnet. The performance is teasingly ambiguous in that we are never certain if the soaps themselves are being marketed as today's equivalent of Elizabethan London's most popular playwright or if their actors are advertising their skills as twenty-first century Garricks, despite otherwise appearing three times a week as barmaids, car mechanics, adulterous taxi drivers, and so on. Either way it carries a resounding subtext: there is no escape from Shakespeare.

Suppose, then, you accept that his legacy has joined death and taxes as the only unavoidable aspects of existence and decide not only to familiarize yourself with his work (even if some of this intimacy is secondhand) but, more importantly, form an opinion on it: where do you begin? The obvious answer is: read his plays and poems. But let us also assume that you feel overwhelmed, humbled by the prospect of taking on what so many have already done, and written about, and prefer the company of a guide during your tours of his oeuvre. Your two best companions during such an undertaking are Harold Bloom and Gary Taylor, specifically in their respective books, *Shakespeare: The Invention of the Human* (Bloom, 1988) and *Reinventing Shakespeare. A Cultural History from the Restoration to the Present* (Taylor, 1990). These are not introductory guides but nor do they alienate the reader whose interest in the phenomenon of Shakespeare is genuine. The two authors have very little in common yet in their contrariness they exemplify the problems of dealing with Shakespeare, primarily the slippery issue of his greatness, or otherwise. Bloom returns us to an approach lost to criticism since the hyperventilating Romantics idolized Shakespeare as a creative deity. He is the erudite bull in a china shop, incautious regarding the sensibilities of his opponents and intent on proving that Shakespeare is indeed the greatest of all writers. His conclusion is implied in his subtitle: despite the advances made by Marx, Freud, and every philosopher from Descartes to Derrida on the nature of the human condition, Shakespeare did it first. Opinions differ on the soundness of Bloom's argument but his audacity is glorious. Taylor is more circumspect, examining treatments of Shakespeare from the inception of criticism in the seventeenth century to the present day. Unlike Bloom he takes the role of sardonic spectator marveling at the desperate, prodigiously diverse attempts made by virtually everyone who writes about literature to reach some conclusion on his significance. But rather than pick those that are, in his view, the most decisive and convincing he pronounces that Shakespeare and Shakespeare studies have combined to form a "black hole." This is an infinitely complex inversion of time and space where everything stated has its antithesis. Any new contributor, who, like Bloom, hopes to master its perversities, will be swallowed by it, never to return.

Even for those making tentative incursions into the industry of Shakespeare will feel, temperamentally, drawn to one or the other of the positions taken up by Bloom or Taylor. Taylor is not a jargon-wielding literary theorist. He writes with dry, sagacious clarity but he is resigned to the fact that he will never properly make sense of his feelings let alone justify to others his instinct that the man is unique. Bloom, on the other hand, feels that to indulge all other competing perceptions of Shakespeare's brilliance or his failings will postpone indefinitely his own impulse to make a decisive statement based on what Shakespeare says to him.

Space does not allow me to follow these two along all of their numerous tracks. Instead I will be ruthlessly selective regarding the material to be dealt with, and I will narrow the focus of the enquiry, the question, which informs their work and everyone else's dealings with Shakespeare, whether they write about him or not: to decide if he can be treated as the greatest of writers we must at the same time decide on what literary greatness involves.

Tolstoy and Voltaire can by no means be treated as the only eccentrics and recusants within the history of Shakespeare studies. They are in a minority, certainly, but it is a substantial minority. Wittgenstein judges him to have created worlds that are "all wrong, things *aren't like that.*" His creation operates according to "a law of its own"; he is "completely unrealistic (like a dream)." Goldsmith, similarly, found him drenched in an excess of "forced humour, far fetch'd conceit, and unnatural hyperbole" and Matthew Arnold condemned his style as the epitome of "detestable ... workmanship." These figures are certainly not a cabal with an agreed agenda. Their personal backgrounds and social contexts vary considerably but there is nonetheless a common base note in their chorus of complaints. None deny that Shakespeare is possessed of abundant talents as a poet. Indeed, their praise for his natural ability generally betrays a hint of condescension, a raised eyebrow that someone of such modest background could become a master of unbounded rhetoric, and this leads them comfortably to the crux of their reservations. Shakespeare, overwhelmed by his unearned gifts, over-indulged them; unable ever to satiate his appetite for greatness, he ignored and effectively suffocated his responsibilities to the higher objectives of literary writing. That avid fan of Stalin, George Bernard Shaw, cultivated a long-term abhorrence for Shakespeare's feckless misuse of his gift. "Shakespeare's weakness," he wrote, "lies in his complete deficiency in that highest sphere of thought [including] ... religion, philosophy, morality." In Shaw's view Shakespeare reveled in the presentation of life's varieties and extremities but failed to give his ideas, be they beneficent or evil, any salient function: "in all [his] fictions there is no leading thought or inspiration for which any man could conceivably risk the spoiling of his hat in a shower, much less his life."

Most Shakespeare critics treat these figures with tolerance. Comments upon them are rarely deprecating and the subtext seems to be that

Shakespeare spawned an ecumenical community which indulges mal-adjusted nonconformists. This, however, blinds us to an important though inadvertent message carried in their statements. Perversely, they have come to a conclusion on Shakespeare's importance that his admirers, in their awed perplexity, seem to overlook. Everything he has written is informed by pure literariness. His plays absorb us and make us re-examine our world but they refuse to instruct or illuminate; he magnifies, transfigures, the problems of existence but never attempts to resolve them. Examine closely the history of Shakespeare criticism and you will find that these same charges laid against him by the School of Resentment are echoed throughout the pro-Shakespeare camp. His first claim to uniqueness must be that the features of his work that catch the attention of those who resent his fame are precisely those that preoccupy his admirers. Both agree that Shakespeare is the most literary of writers but they differ on the intrinsic value of literariness.

His audiences and peers of the late sixteenth and early seventeenth centuries would certainly have spoken of him, but for the first printed records of a debate on his qualities we must go to the eighteenth century. Samuel Johnson is routinely cited as the most significant Shakespeare critic of the eighteenth century but his enduring eminence should not cause us to overlook the immense gallery of opinions published by his near contemporaries. Elizabeth Montagu was the leader of the so-called bluestockings, a group of women who during the mid-to-late eighteenth century propounded a range of theories on recent and contemporaneous developments in the arts and society. The following is from her *Essay on the Writings and Genius of Shakespeare* (1760).

> Shakespeare wrote at a time when learning was tinctured with pedantry, wit was unpolished and mirth ill-bred. The court of Elizabeth spoke a scientific jargon, and a certain obscurity of style was universally affected. James brought an addition of pedantry, accompanied by indecent and indelicate manners and language. By contagion, or from complaisance to the taste of the public, Shakespeare falls sometimes into the fashionable mode of writing.
>
> Shakespeare's plays were to be acted in a paltry tavern, to an unlettered audience just emerging from barbarity … The period when Sophocles and Euripides wrote was that in which the fine arts and polite literature were in a degree of perfection which succeeding ages have emulated in vain …
>
> Shakespeare was born in a rank of life in which men indulge themselves in a free expression of their passions, with little regard to exterior appearance. This perhaps made him more acquainted with the movements of the heart, and less knowing or observant of outward forms: against the one he often offends, he very rarely misrepresents the other …

> The hurley-burley of these plays recommended them to a rude illiterate audience, who, as he says, loved a noise of targets. His poverty and the low condition of the stage (which at that time was not frequented by persons of rank) obliged him to this complaisance; and unfortunately he had not been tutored by any rules of art.

It should first be noted that Montagu's notion of "pedantry" differs from the modern usage of overattention to detail and correctness. During the eighteenth century the term denoted an ostentatious and often unfocused display of knowledge: recklessly abundant erudition might serve as an accurate substitute. The passage quoted above goes against the predominantly laudatory mood of the essay but it is clear that Montagu feels it her duty to apologize for Shakespeare on his behalf. He was in her view a genius tainted by the uncouth cultural habits and conventions of his time. Her portrait of him as a flawed poet capable of holding up a mirror to the human condition ("[His] dramatic personae ... are actuated by human passions and are engaged in the common affairs of human life. We are interested in what they do or say by feeling every moment that they are of the same nature as ourselves") is not untypical of her time but what is most striking is her presentation of the theater of almost two centuries earlier as a brand of low-life revelry. Its subjects might often have been figures of epic or magisterial standing but these, she avers, were molded to suit the rough tastes of "an unlettered audience just emerging from barbarity." The exact status of the average late sixteenth century theatergoer will remain largely a matter for speculation but the work of recent cultural historians, sometimes assisted by archaeologists, lends substance to Montagu's disdainful presentation. That Tolstoy's notion of Shakespeare as a puppet of the aristocracy is made to look faintly preposterous by comparison might further tempt one to support her case.

Most importantly, Montagu suggests that the best known passages of Shakespeare, his poetic soliloquies, are magnificent but slightly damaged goods, sometimes veering toward luxuriant hyperbole in order to serve the tastes of those who prefer sound and linguistic game-playing to sense.

In an essay in the *British Magazine* (1762) the novelist Tobias Smollett is far less constrained. His subject is what must be the most quoted of all passages from Shakespeare's drama, Hamlet's ruminations on mortality and self-murder; and he opens:

> Over and above an excess of figures, a young author is apt to run into a confusion of mixed metaphors, which leave the sense disjointed, and distract the

imagination: Shakespeare himself is often guilty of these irregularities. The soliloquy in *Hamlet*, which we have so often heard extolled in terms of admiration, is, in our opinion, a heap of absurdities, whether we consider the situation, the sentiment, the argumentation, or the poetry.

The substance of Smollett's piece involves an exercise in petulant close reading, where he inspects Hamlet's speech line by line and points out the persistent injuries inflicted by Shakespeare upon the most liberal notions of coherence and logic. During the Restoration and the eighteenth century, poetry was expected to respect certain rules that prevented it from straying too far beyond the ideals of order and transparency exhibited in good prose. Metaphor and other conceits were, of course, approved of but their use fell somewhere between the purposive function of rhetoric and the well-documented allowances of literary decoration. Verse in which sense spiraled seemingly out of control was frowned upon but while virtually everyone agreed on what contemporary poets were supposed to do opinions differed on how to treat the work of their predecessors. Montagu regards Shakespeare as a primitivist genius, hinting that in a more civilized environment he might have tidied himself up, but Smollett is unforgiving. It is an essay very much worth reading not least because in its method it prefigures almost precisely the techniques evolved by the academic New Critics of the early mid-twentieth century (see Chapter 4). William Empson famously identified the deliberate, persistent use of ambiguity not as a calculated attempt to confuse or conceal meaning but as an arbitrary aesthetic gesture, as one of the defining features of verse. The following, from Smollett, might have been lifted verbatim from Empson's supposedly groundbreaking *Seven Types of Ambiguity* (1930).

> This soliloquy is not less unexceptionable in the propriety of expression, than in the chain of argumentation. – "To die, – to sleep – no more," contains an ambiguity which all the art of punctuation cannot remove; for it may signify that "to die, is to sleep no more"; or the expression "no more," may be considered as an abrupt apostrophe in thinking, as if he meant to say "no more of that reflection."

For Empson, ambiguity was one of the means by which poetry declared its independence from the conventions of nonliterary language. It did not so much rewrite the rules as engage in a ceaseless process of avoiding them. Smollett reaches a similar conclusion but judges Hamlet's soliloquy as an exercise in self-indulgence, artistically deficient and essentially meaningless. At one point he compares the passage with visual art and once more we find ourselves projected into the future, this time towards modernist painting, surrealism in particular.

> If the metaphors were reduced to painting, we should find it a very difficult task, if not altogether impracticable, to represent with any propriety, outrageous Fortune using her slings and arrows, between which indeed, there is no sort of analogy in nature. Neither can any figure be more ridiculously absurd than that of a man taking arms against a sea, exclusive of the incongruous medley of slings, arrows, and seas, jostled within the compass of one reflection. What follows is a strange rhapsody of broken images, of sleeping, dreaming, and shifting off a *coil*, which last conveys no idea that can be represented on canvas. A man may be exhibited shuffling off his garments or his chains: but how should he shuffle off a *coil*, which is another term for noise and tumult, we cannot comprehend. Then we have long-lived calamity, and time armed with whips and scorns; and patient merit spurned at by unworthiness; and misery with a bare bodkin going to make his own quietus, which at best, is but a mean metaphor.

One factor overlooked by Smollett, but which troubled a number of his contemporaries, was the question of who exactly is responsible for this cascade of imaginative excess. Obviously Shakespeare was its author, but did he intend that the effect of the soliloquy, as it registered for Smollett, should reflect Hamlet's slightly unhinged state of mind? The eighteenth century critics were not ignorant to the notion of poetic personae, both within and outside drama, and generally took against the tendency of the seventeenth century Metaphysical poets to allow into their verses speakers seemingly unable to curb their figurative immoderation. Shakespeare, however, confused them. On the one hand his singular energy and breadth as a writer seemed to override differences between his characters, the plays themselves becoming extended dramatic poems. This is Alexander Gerard in his *An Essay on Genius* (1774):

> A fertile imagination is apt to overload a work with a superfluity of ideas: an accurate judgement rejects all that are unnecessary. Shakespeare was not always able to keep the richness of his fancy from displaying itself in cases where judgement would have directed him to control it. That very exuberance of imagination which commands our admiration is sometimes indulged so far as necessarily to incur our censure.

Others found that poetic overexuberance was suitable when certain charac-
ters endured periods of irresolution and trepidation. William Richardson in
*A Philosophical Analysis and Illustration of Some of Shakespeare's Remarkable
Characters* (1774) writes,

> Shakespeare, is most eminently distinguished by imitating the passion in
> all its aspects, by pursuing it through all its windings and labyrinths, by
> moderating or accelerating its impetuosity according to the influence of
> other principles and of external events, and finally by combining it in a
> judicious manner with other passions and propensities, or by setting it aptly
> in opposition. He thus unites the two essential powers of dramatic invention,
> that of forming characters and that of imitating, in their natural expressions,
> the passions and affections of which they are composed.

Richardson and a few others made tentative steps toward a notion of language as symptomatic of forms of mental disturbance, but just after the turn
of the eighteenth century another critic went even further and pre-empted
modern psychoanalysis and psychology with his presentation of Hamlet
as the model of a split personality. It is now a commonplace that the
Romantics invented "Bardolatry," the unreserved adulation for Shakespeare
as a dramatic and poetic deity. Coleridge, Hazlitt, and the German poet and
critic, Schlegel, are cited as the prime movers in this enterprise and while
opinions differ on which of them was most influential and enduring
Coleridge's claim to Bardolater-in-chief is considerable. Chronologically,
Schlegel's work predates that of the other two but suspicions that Coleridge
might have "borrowed" some of his key ideas have been dispelled by recent
scholarship. Coleridge's lectures of 1811–1812, unpublished but containing
the kernel for the material that would later go into print, were delivered
2 years before Hazlitt's work appeared. Yet aside from the question of "who
got there first?" Coleridge stands out because of the sheer audaciousness of
his interpretations, particularly regarding Hamlet.

In 1811, Coleridge began a series of public lectures on Shakespeare which
drew enormous crowds and earned him almost unequivocal praise. The
greatest, by general consensus, was the lecture on *Hamlet* delivered on 2
January 1812. Hamlet had been routinely treated even by avid Shakespeare
enthusiasts as an aberration, his habits of speech, motives, and apparent
state of mind utterly inconsistent with what was understood as the human
condition. Coleridge concluded that his "wildness is but *half false*. O! that
subtle trick to *pretend* the acting when we are very near – what we act."
Coleridge's Hamlet shifts between two worlds, "The world within," an

interior life over which he maintains some control and "a perfect knowledge of his own character" and a state in which he "yields to the ... retiring from all reality," his bouts of mania.

Coleridge's interpretation of Hamlet's inner and outer states changed forever the way in which the play would be perceived and his lectures overall were a turning point in the history of Shakespeare criticism. He was the first to treat Shakespeare as a writer who not only represented humanity in extremis but who exposed hitherto unexplored complexities of the mind, and the most celebrated of these insights came in his examination of Hamlet.

Traces of Coleridge's thesis can be found within the fabric of numerous twentieth century readings of Shakespeare but while we should grant him a certain amount of credit as a pioneering thinker it is equally illuminating to digress slightly from Shakespeare himself and consider the origins of Coleridge's insights, which have as much to do with his own preoccupations as his interest in his predecessor.

During the 6 years before he began his 1811–1812 lectures Coleridge's obsession with Sara Hutchinson, Wordsworth's sister-in-law, had bordered upon the deranged. On the advice of her sister, Wordsworth's wife Mary, Sara – or "Asra" as Coleridge mythologized her – left Cumbria for good and one can appreciate Mary's concern for the well-being of her sibling. Wordsworth, 6 months earlier, had written to William Poole that their mutual friend was perpetually "frustrated by a derangement in his intellectual and moral constitution."

Wordsworth remained largely unaffected by this but Coleridge, stricken, retired to rooms in Hudson's hotel and filled pages of his *Notebooks* with what amounted to an exercise in psychological self-analysis. The document discloses Samuel Taylor Coleridge and his own presentation of Hamlet as indistinguishable. At some points he uses the first person, as if delivering a soliloquy, memorably in his declaration on his feelings for Asra.

> My love of Asra is not so much my Soul, as my Soul in it. It is my whole Being wrapt up in one Desire, all the Hopes and Fears, Joys and Sorrows, all the Powers, Vigour and Faculties of my Spirit abridged into one perpetual Inclination. To bid me not to love you were to bid me to annihilate myself – for to love you is all I know of Life, as far as my Life is an object of my Consciousness or my free will. (*Notebooks*, III, p. 3996)

This is a vivid example of Wordsworth's later description, in his *Memoirs*, of Coleridge in full flight with snatches of coherence and sense glimpsed and then swept away by the "majestic river of words," yet it also reminds one of Hamlet, perhaps addressing Ophelia, when as Coleridge puts it, "the prodigality of beautiful *words* … half [embody] … his thoughts." These, according to Coleridge, "retain a … shadowy … correspondence to the images and movements within." Coleridge too in his *Notebooks* is able to suspend his ravings and shift to a measured, third person reflective mode as if he is watching himself from the outside, just as he listens to and analyzes Hamlet. "Doubtless the fault must have been partly, perhaps chiefly, in myself. The want of reliability in the little things, the infliction of little pains, the trifling with hope, in short, all that renders the idea of a person recalls more pain than pleasure – these would account for the loss of Friendship" (*Notebooks*, III, p. 4072).

Coleridge's obsession with Asra and his consequent estrangement from Wordsworth certainly provided the impetus for his groundbreaking ideas on Hamlet yet even had he never encountered her it is likely he would have come to similar conclusions. Sara Hutchison only worsened endemic and enduring features of his temperament and his constitution as a literary artist. From his youth he was by parts perplexed and fascinated by the precipitate nature of the human condition, which seemed to him capable at any moment of informing him with its luminescence or immersing him in despair and many of his best known, most puzzling, poems both embody the innovative mood of the time and, more significantly, reveal a debt to Shakespeare. As we have seen, the principal, often repeated, objection to Shakespeare throughout the eighteenth century was that he was *too* poetic, that his imaginative exuberance inhibited sense and coherence. The same could be said of a number of Coleridge's poems, notably "Kubla Khan," and one cannot help but wonder if Wordsworth had this piece in mind when he offered a recollection of his late friend in his *Memoirs*. He compares him with a river:

> whose course you caught at intervals, which sometimes was concealed by forests, sometimes lost in sand, then came flashing out broad and distinct, then took a turn which your eye could not follow … in Coleridge's discourse [there was] always a connection between its parts and his own mind, though one not always perceptible to the mind of others.

It is a tribute, a compliment, but it would be difficult to find one more backhanded than this and it might easily be a quotation from a piece by one of Shakespeare's less tolerant eighteenth century commentators.

Coleridge initiated what might be termed the carte blanche school of Shakespeare criticism in which readers would exploit the abundance of his stylistic and representational gifts as opportunities to see themselves as versions of him. Coleridge himself is alleged to have commented years after the lectures that he saw elements of Hamlet in himself. His near contemporary, John Keats, left only fragmentary comments on Shakespeare, mainly in his letters. Writing to his brother in 1819 he stated that:

> A Man's life of any worth is a continual allegory – and very few eyes can see the mystery of his life – a life like the scriptures, figurative ... Shakespeare led a life of Allegory; his works are the comments on it.

For "Allegory" we might substitute Keats's better known concept of "negative capability," the poet's persistent state of "uncertainties, mysteries, doubts, without any irritable reaching after fact and reason [Being] content with half knowledge." Every statement, particularly in verse, carries only a trace of a deeper, immutable manifesto, closely resembling Coleridge's notion of an unsteady relationship between inner and outer worlds, and harnessed once more to Shakespeare as its supreme progenitor.

During the mid to late nineteenth century the enthusiasm of the Romantics was embalmed into cautious respect. Coleridge, Hazlitt, and others had led the revolution and the Victorians steadied the enterprise with uncontroversial scholarship. In 1874, Frederick James Furnivall composed the prospectus for the recently launched New Shakespeare Society and stated that the ultimate objective of its members would be to "get his plays as possible into the order in which he wrote them" and they would achieve this "by a very close study of [his] metrical and phraseological peculiarities." They then might feel able to give some attention to "the progress and meaning of Shakespeare's mind." The methodology described in the prospectus, indeed its mood, brings to mind the procedure of the postmortem examination but others could not quite resist the temptation of treating Shakespeare as a man much like themselves and Walter Bagehot sometimes comes across as a self-caricature of Coleridge and Keats, albeit an inadvertent one. Bagehot loved field sports, particularly the hunt, and from a careful close reading of *Venus and Adonis* he reached the conclusion that despite the poverty of indisputable biographical detail only a man who knew from experience that a "hare is apt to run among a flock of sheep [and] its so doing disconcerts the scent of hounds" could have written that poem; "mere imagination" played no part in it (Bagehot, 1853, p. 259).

Shakespeare, like Bagehot, was obviously a keen huntsman. In *The Economist* he argues that a man who marshals his abundant talents so well as to become "the popular author, the successful dramatist" was, in spirit at least, a quintessential entrepreneur and investor, a man who would thrive in the free-market economy of mid nineteenth century Britain (Bagehot, 1853, p. 301). Coleridge, Keats, Bagehot, and many others lend some support to Gary Taylor's ingenious notion of Shakespeare as a black hole. Taylor explains:

> If Shakespeare has a singularity, it is because he has become a black hole. Light, insight, intelligence, matter – all pour ceaselessly into him, as critics are drawn into the densening vortex of his reputation; they add their own weight to his increasing mass. The light from other stars – other poets, other dramatists – is wrenched and bent as it passes by him on its way to us. He warps cultural space-time; he distorts our view of the universe around him. As Emerson said, "now, literature, philosophy, and thought are Shakespearized. His mind is the horizon beyond which at present we do not see." (Taylor, 1990, p. 410)

The Shakespeare fixation spread beyond English Romantic poets. Throughout Europe during the late eighteenth and early nineteenth centuries, writers, philosophers, and aestheticians, all lit by the intellectual glow of the Enlightenment, were similarly entranced. Goethe, Herder, Guizot, Stendhal, Hegel, Müller, Tieck, and Victor Hugo, seem through their fascination to lose the faculty of discernment. Each relishes the challenge to their acumen as thinkers by taking on a figure at once panoramic in range yet as a man enigmatic and impersonal, and at some point all find themselves resorting to generalities and hyperbole; as Taylor put it "he distorts our view of the universe around him." This is Victor Hugo: "Like all lofty minds in full riot of omnipotence Shakespeare decants all nature, drinks it and makes you drink it … He does not stop, he doesn't feel fatigue … he is powerful." This, one might assume, is pardonably brief drift into grandiloquence but Hugo is merely warming up. A page later:

> Shakespeare … departs, arrives, starts again, mounts, descends, hovers, dives, sinks, rushes, plunges into the depths below, plunges into the depths above. He is one of those geniuses that God purposely leaves unbridled, so that they may go headlong and in full flight into the infinite.
>
> From time to time comes on this globe one of these spirits. Their passage, as we have said, renews art, science, philosophy, or society.

Not all of them lose focus to quite the same extent as Hugo, but there is a persistent tendency to follow a three-stage procedure. They will open with a combination of faux deference and an implied sense of duty: Shakespeare is an author of unique significance and only a person of accomplishment (i.e. "me") is up to the task of delineating his greatness. Soon, however, they find themselves, despite themselves, aghast at the nature of the undertaking. It is not that they are incapable of dealing with Shakespeare but they fear that to continue with the enterprise, and complete it satisfactorily, they might for the foreseeable future have to give up on everything else. Finally, refuge is sought, á la Hugo, in an egress of rapture. It is not insincere but there is nonetheless a whiff of desperation about it.

Following the Romantics and their complacent Victorian successors we come to the penultimate stage of Shakespeare's elevation to sovereign of the Western literary commonwealth: his adoption by academia. Prior to the mid nineteenth century the study of literature at university meant almost exclusively Greek or Latin. Once English was begrudgingly received as their modern counterpart a canon, a curriculum for study, had to be established and there is no record that any of this new generation of academics ever questioned the status of Shakespeare as the imperishable, steadfast leader of the team. An industry was established and a variety of figures – notably T.S. Eliot, John Dover Wilson, L.C. Knights, C.S. Lewis, and A.C. Bradley – applied themselves to the construction of a behemoth of scholarly texts and critical benchmarks that would effectively deter even the raising of the question of why Shakespeare was revered as the finest writer in English. Trudge through these early twentieth century editions and essays and you will search in vain for a commentator who seriously wonders if his veneration is justified. These critics sometimes argued. Notably, for example, Eliot took against Bradley's treatment of Hamlet as an exercise in mimesis, the representation of a real character; instead, contended Eliot, "he" was a poetic device, a reflection of Shakespeare's own troubled state of mind. But such exchanges always carried an implicit pretext: it was taken for granted that, irrespective of one's opinion on Shakespeare's particularities, his work was superior to that of all other writers in English. Aside from the fact that no one doubted his overall supremacy it was thought facile, indeed vulgar, to attempt to justify it.

The final juncture of Shakespeare studies, at least in academia, is persistent and durable for the simple reason that nothing like it will happen again. In Chapter 4 I examine in detail the damage done by Critical Theory to evaluative criticism in universities and to avoid spoiling your encounter with this sorry tale I will summarize only its more pertinent features.

The notion of the literary work as something definable and distinct from other discourses, and as a consequence our perception of the author as an artist or craftsman, was systematically eroded by Theory. Every Theorist, from the intellectually elitist votaries of Derrida to the Marxists and feminists, came to treat literature as either an adjunct to or a prerogative for something more significant, be this neophilosophical speculations on the nature of language and being or colloquies on our oppressive cultural legacy.

Gradually, Theory consumed all of literary history and the canon. Sometimes a touchingly humane whiff of preference or apathy was evident – the deconstructionists displayed a particular taste for Romanticism, for example – but overall the possibility that writers were in some way different from each other and therefore warranted particular scrutiny and evaluation was dispensed with.

Throughout the 1980s and 1990s, the heyday of Theory in the United Kingdom and the United States, triumphalism was the prevailing mood. In part this was fueled by a straightforward semi-juvenile appetite for insubordination, directed by academics against the supposedly orthodox views of their forebears. At the same time one can detect a barely suppressed pleasure in no longer being in awe of the book or the writer. Most Theory advocates had earned their credentials as specialists in a particular period or a given author, and for an intellectual egotist (generally a synonym for an ambitious academic) the thought of being in some way perpetually indebted to another, even someone dead for centuries, was execrable. No writer was exempt. Even early feminists such as Virginia Woolf were treated more as texts than artists.

It is impossible to calculate an exact date for the arrival of Theory in the United Kingdom and the United States but 1975 could be treated as a landmark year. Jonathan Culler, an American holding an academic post at Oxford, published *Structuralist Poetics*, the first comprehensive account of the cornerstone of Theory. It is a curious book because while it later featured as recommended reading on the first generation of Theory courses for students, it was at the time of its publication aimed primarily at academics. Within the English-speaking university system, word was out about the existence of this new, exciting phenomenon, especially among the ambitious younger dons, but hardly any of the primary texts were in English and even if some could understand Barthes in French a proper knowledge of what he represented would require research into 60 years of writing that preceded him, much of it in Russian, Czech, Hungarian, and German. So although *Structuralist Poetics* appears to be a pedagogic student guide, albeit an extremely demanding one, no students were ever expected to read it in 1975. It was designed as a lifebelt for those who would set up the courses on which it would later feature.

I mention this because it tells us much about the relationship between Shakespeare and Theory during the subsequent 10 years. Throughout this period the Theory industry went from inception to burly endurance, at least in terms of the number of elementary guides and self-consciously radical articles published, but there seemed nonetheless an ambivalence on what should be done with the monarch of the canon, the figure who embodied the contemptible establishment. The Theorists at first resembled faintly neurotic sharks circling their prey, their subcerebral instinct to strike short-circuited by something like unease, but in 1986 they began to move in.

Since the end of the 1970s, Routledge's "New Accents" had been providing short student-targeted accounts of the various branches of Theory but in 1984 an enterprising don with an eye for a market opening became general editor of Blackwell's "Rereading Literature" series. Despite Barthes' insistence that the author was dead and the general belief that the glorification of an individual artist involved connivance in bourgeois ideology each volume was devoted to a major presence in the literary canon and the series editor Terry Eagleton wrote the one on Shakespeare (1986). Typical of his approach is his contention that the three witches of *Macbeth* are the true "heroines of the piece." It remains unclear as to what particular "ism" is being marshaled in this instance but the claim exemplifies the working principle of the book: anything that shocks the reader into re-examining the complacent orthodoxies of the previous three centuries will do. Eagleton does not question Shakespeare's qualities, or otherwise, as a literary writer. Rather he ignores them completely, and in this respect he set the standard for all that would follow: Shakespeare is important not as a literary artist but as textual playground which provided the Theorist with the opportunity to pursue all manner of cultural, ideological, and political enquiries. Eagleton makes this point in his Foreword to the second edition of Malcolm Evan's *Signifying Nothing*, which shows Shakespeare to be a "textual fiction transformed into an equally fictive set of ideological images by a range of indubitably real political strategies" (Evans, 1989, p. x). It is difficult to summarize Evans's "approach," given that virtually all of the celebrities of European structuralism and poststructuralism are wheeled on as his confederates but in the Introduction he hints at a methodologic principle.

Such a project [as this] is hampered by the preponderance in Shakespeare studies of an idealist criticism which always purports to recover (at last) some hitherto inadequately revealed aspect of the test "as in itself it really is." (Evans, 1989, p. 9)

In other words whatever else happens hereafter I will studiously avoid anything that even implies that Shakespeare's work involves a particular meaning. At one point he contends that five words from *As You Like It* contain 172 different nuances but he is not attempting to outdo Empson as a collector of ambiguities, quite the contrary. Evans, citing Derrida as his counsel, is showing the traditionalist that any search for the true purpose and tenor of Shakespeare's writing is, by its nature, misguided, a delusion. A few months earlier parts of Evans's deconstructive onslaught had appeared as a chapter in *Alternative Shakespeares* (1985), a volume that might well endure as an embarrassing monument to the character of Theory. The title is both fitting and misleading in that each of the contributors does indeed offer a radical alternative to conventional Shakespeare criticism but what we are left with is a monument to his absence, something just as solidly enduring as the presence that the Theorists desperately and incessantly try to exterminate. As the editor John Drakakis states in the Introduction:

What follows firmly resists those strategies habitually mobilized by liberal humanism to draw into its historical aegis an infinite variety of interpretations generated by individual sensibilities, which it then permits to circulate around a stable and unchanging text. (Drakakis, 1985, p. 23)

According to Drakakis, not only is interpretation generated by the capricious or more likely ideologically hidebound sensibility of the given reader there is no such thing as a "stable and unchanging text" that might one day be scrutinized more rigorously for something closer to what Shakespeare hoped to achieve. Instead, the volume will yield up "a series of explorations of the ways in which historically specific readings are generated" which allow only for "the existence of structures within the text as devices for exclusion and repression"; the suspect notion of "'making sense' of a Shakespearian text is itself determined by a multiplicity of forces" (Drakakis, 1985, pp. 23–24). Even the phrase "Shakespearian text" is revealing. Nowhere in the volume do the contributors, in their phraseology, allow for the possibility that Shakespeare might have been a "writer" responsible for "literary works" let alone an artist of considerable standing and ability. Drakakis goes on to state that "the common objective to all these essays is the demystification of the 'myth' of Shakespeare" (Drakakis, 1985, p. 24). This would become the prevailing ordinance of Theorists-on-Shakespeare. As the figurehead, the leitmotif, of hegemonic–liberal–humanist culture Shakespeare's alleged greatness should not simply be challenged. Rather, all questions as to his significance are forbidden; he must become a nonperson. Drakakis recruits specialists from all brands of Theory to negotiate the structures of "exclusion and repression" and the "multiplicity of forces" generated by encounters with the "Shakespearian text" – and all scrupulously observe the mandate of refusing to treat Shakespeare as an author or regard his work as literature. Intriguingly, there would be *Alternative Shakespeares 2* (1996, ed. T. Hawkes) and *Alternative Shakespeares 3* (2008, ed. D.E. Henderson) and the series should be commended for its consistency. The recycled Theories are essentially unchanged and Shakespeare and his work endurably absent. Samuel Beckett would perhaps be amused by this exercise in perpetually discussing a person who each of the participants believes is nonexistent.

The Theorists shared out the Bardicidal tasks in a reasonably egalitarian manner but the coup de grâce was probably administered by the so-called New Historicists and their allies the Cultural Materialists. Stephen Greenblatt was the founder of the former and in his *Shakespearian Negotiations* (1988) he conducts an admirable smoke and mirrors exercise involving *The Tempest*. Greenblatt lines up, alongside the play, a sermon by one of Shakespeare's contemporaries, Hugh Latimer (while making it clear that there is no evidence that one knew anything of the other), a description of a botched public execution of 1603, an account of an expedition from England to Virginia in 1610, and he then jumps forward to H.M. Stanley's story of his encounter with indigenous central African tribesmen in 1877. Many commentators, from the nineteenth century onwards, had made use of the "context" of Shakespeare's plays as a means of pointing up their social and political relevance to contemporary audiences. Marxists took this a stage further by refusing to exempt him, as an "artist," from involvement in the ideological dynamic of his period. But none went so far as Greenblatt who in the opening chapter of *Shakespearian Negotiations* begins in a contritional manner, admitting that as a callow young scholar he was once entranced by the voice of the long dead Shakespeare and in those days he did not doubt that the magnificent plays "were in large part written by the supremely gifted alumnus of Stratford grammar school." Now he has grown up and realized that by separating Shakespeare from the other voices, some such as Stanley postdating him by a couple of centuries, he was deafening himself to the full chorus of discourses that properly illuminate our sense of what history and culture actually involve. At times one becomes uncertain as to whether he regards Latimer's sermon or Carleton's account of the execution as belonging, like many of Shakespeare's plays, in the broad genre of tragi-comedy or if, by contrast, Shakespeare's writing is just as "non-literary" as Latimer's or Carleton's. But this is by no means evidence of slovenliness; quite the contrary. It is part of Greenblatt's exercise in mystification. He invites us to compare Shakespeare's work with that of others – there are always tempting, self-evident parallels, such as the gallows as a stage – and then he blurs the boundaries between them so that Shakespeare himself becomes less an individual than a shady participant in a far more complex interwoven fabric of signs and forces.

Cultural Materialists such as Margolies and Sinfield bear a close family resemblance to Greenblatt. Both regard Shakespeare not as an author but rather as "an instrument of hegemony" (Margolies, 1988, p. 43) adopted by the cultural establishment and the education system to advance "capitalism and patriarchy" and "adjust young people to an unjust social order" (Sinfield and Dollimore, 1985, p. 135). Neither contend that a different way of teaching him might enlighten pupils to the improvements of socialism and feminism. Even if they could find in his plays some magically prescient traces of Marx or Woolf they would by implication surrender their role as superintendents of the ideological and cultural matrix of which Shakespeare is merely a symptom. They would then have to concede that as a literary writer he says something original and this would go against the maxim endemic to all practitioners of Theory. Each believes, often with zealous fanaticism, that they are in possession of the key to all human behavior. To allow that a writer speaks in a manner that is uniquely literary to an individual reader would be to gainsay this conviction, to undermine it. No authors were excluded from this exercise in aesthetic euthanasia, but perversely its progress has reinforced Shakespeare's status as the most prominent and enigmatic author in the Western canon.

There was, for example, a darkly comic incident during the 1985 World Shakespeare Conference held in West Berlin. The seminar on "Gender and Power" was one of the first major public forums in which feminist critics came together to share their opinions on Shakespeare, or so it was planned. What actually occurred was that delegates argued among themselves over the threat posed to feminist Shakespeare specialists by the emergent New Historicists who were, it was alleged, "more interested in power relations between men than between the sexes." This spat endured for a further 3 years as the New Historicists published replies and rebuttals. Both parties had lined up Shakespeare as their victim (and while they might object to this term, it is certainly the case that each wished to abolish him as an "author" in his own right) but so great was their appetite for the title of vanquisher of the canon's monarch, they turned their energies against each other.

Where are we now? Much of the zealotry that motivated Theorists endures only as a moribund obligation among students and academics and after the festival of Bardicide of the 1980s and early 1990s eminent traditionalists began again to make their presence felt. Typical of the restoration of relative sanity was Jonathan Bate's *The Genius of Shakespeare* (1997a). Bate does not bury his head in the sand. Fully aware of recent developments in academia, he despatches the Theorists with patrician economy and conducts himself as the mature successor to Hazlitt and Coleridge. It is a fine book but we soon realize that its title does not imply a question mark. In this, Bate belongs to the school of Eliot, Bradley, Wilson Knight: by attempting to estimate his greatness we will debase it.

Is there anything more to be said? I think there is and we should begin with the Theorist's preoccupation with extinguishing the notion of Shakespeare as an author. His mythologic role as sovereign of the Western canon presented a threat to their universal objective: remove its keystone and the edifice of literature as art would crumble. Most outside the Theoretical camp dismiss their work as self-evidently ridiculous and Brian Vickers in *Appropriating Shakespeare* (1993) was responsible for the most comprehensive exposure of their methodologic inconsistencies and aberrations, but Vickers and other Theory sceptics leave key issues unresolved. Principally, if Shakespeare's plays were crafted by a particular, superbly talented individual, what, beyond earning a living as an entertainer, was he endeavoring to achieve?

Measure for Measure is generally regarded as one of Shakespeare's "problem" plays. The principal problem for the reader or member of the audience is that is offers a series of questions that remain largely unanswered. It does not inscribe a reliable formula against which we can properly judge the violation of moral norms or the subversion of political, religious, or social absolutes. How should we judge Isabella's decision to preserve her own code of virginity and consequently to endanger her brother's life? Is Angelo merely a disagreeable individual or a symptom of a more widespread form of social and moral corruption? Is the Duke obliged to temporarily abdicate, disguise himself, and engage with the murky practices of his fiefdom because autocratic monarchy is no longer a practical institution?

Like many of Shakespeare's more tendentious dealings with the state and the individual, the context is shifted safely to a time and a place that are not early seventeenth century London. However, the questions of government and of administering the judicial system faced by the Duke bear a more than accidental resemblance to a number of ideas addressed by James I (before whom the play was first performed) in his tract *Basilicon Doron*. The image of Vienna as a city-state threatened by criminality and incipient moral anarchy could just as easily apply to the expanding capital of the new trading and mercantile powerhouse of England.

The play comprises partly prose and partly blank verse. Before Milton's *Paradise Lost* (1667) legitimized blank verse as a vehicle for nondramatic poetry, the form was treated by consensus as a hybrid. It was poetic in the sense that it adhered to the abstract template of the iambic pentameter and by custom its use was accompanied by an unprosaic abundance of rhetorical devices. The absence of rhyme and, in general, other sound patterns lent a little credibility to the speaker on stage, someone who, if they conversed with others or addressed the audience in couplets or stanzas, would seem ostentatiously unreal. We will never know if Shakespeare or his contemporaries succeeded in creating an authentic copy of the spoken improvised prose of the period, since no actual or vicarious record of the latter survives, but the evidence of the plays themselves, involving colloquialisms, slang, and casual syntax, indicates that this was their intention. What these plays provide, then, is a working model of the relationship, then perceived, between poetry and ordinary language. *Measure for Measure* and all Shakespeare's other plays confirm our expectation that poetry is, in general, the preserve of the mercantile classes, the gentry, and the aristocracy. Poetry was, irrespective of one's thoughts on its value, the badge of cultural sophistication. Nonpoetic language, then and today, is the pragmatic medium in which opinions are straightforwardly expressed and arrangements made, with priority given to the effective transference of the message rather than to the eloquence of the exchange; prose is the language of Shakespeare's lower orders. I should qualify the above with the term "predominantly" because while in most instances these two types of expression reinforce social stereotypes, there are also considerable overlaps, where people from one class borrow the linguistic garment of the other. It is even more intriguing when the two genres operate as part of the same dialogue. In these instances, Shakespeare provides a far more compelling and eloquent thesis on the relative capacities of poetry and ordinary language than will be found in any contemporary prose work that attempts to address the same topic.

In the following extract, Angelo, in the Duke's absence, is busily enforcing laws on public and private behavior, including sexual morality; his rationale being that a ruthlessly enforced code of personal ethics will result in a collective attendance to order and stability. Every member of Shakespeare's audience would have recognized parallels between this albeit largely secular ordinance and the programs endorsed by extreme branches of Protestantism, particularly in King James's home country, Scotland. Claudio, a young gentleman, tells Lucio, a resourceful opportunist of no obvious social rank, of his arrest for having had premarital sex with his fiancée:

Lucio	Why, how now, Claudio! Whence comes this restrait?
Claudio	From too much liberty, my Lucio, liberty:
	As surfeit is the father of much fast
	So every scope by the immoderate use
	Turns to restraint. our natures do pursue –
	Like rats that ravin down their proper bane –
	A thirsty evil, and when we drink we die.
Lucio	If I could speak so wisely under an arrest, I would send for certain of
	My creditors. And yet, to say the truth, I had as like have the foppery
	Of freedom as the morality of Imprisonment. What's thy offence,
	Claudio?

(Measure for Measure, Act I, Scene ii, 118–28)

Lucio's "Whence comes this restraint?" is a straightforward enquiry as to why Claudio has found himself in the custody of the Provost and his officers. But instead of answering him directly, as one might expect of someone detained, threatened with a death sentence, and for whom the actualities of life are all too tangible, Claudio launches into an extravagant melee of rhetorical flourishes, all of which involve profound observations on his existential state, while seeming to provide little useful information.

In purely rhetorical terms, Claudio's florid response involves a combination of euphuism (the extended use of balance and paradox), synoeciosis (expanded paradox), progressio (advancing by steps of a comparison), and syncrisis (comparing contrary elements in contrasting clauses), all interlaced with metaphor.

I document and specify these devices not because I see them as being much use in your social or intellectual life, dear twenty-first century reader, but because Shakespeare was offering the Claudios in his audience, and indeed the Lucios, something more than the next stage in his enthralling plot. For those with even a rudimentary grammar school education, Shakespeare included, Claudio's speech would have seemed very familiar, similar to the kind of exercise they were obliged to perform in the classroom. The basic textbooks for instruction on the devices and mechanisms of language were derived from Horace's *Ars Poetica*, translated into Italian and French in the fifteenth century and plagiarized in a variety of English manuals in the sixteenth century. Horace and his successors rarely reflected on the reason why people might write poetry or on its ultimate or even practical purpose; instead he and they offered voluminous instructions on its mechanics – meter, structure, rhetorical devices – and the potential effects of these upon the listener or hearer. Poetry was a means by which language could project you into another world, one where the actuality of everyday life was dispersed into various states of figurative speculation. In this regard it is not entirely implausible to see Shakespeare here as presenting poetry as a refuge from uncomfortable reality. Rather than face the blunt facts that he is under arrest and might soon be executed, he uses rhetoric, poetry, as a comforting, intellectually respectable escape. Lucio, replying, casts a somewhat sceptical eye upon his friend's performance: "If I could speak so wisely under an arrest, I would send for certain of my creditors." Such droll irony: verbal dexterity will not, he knows, undo reality.

As I have stated, many in Shakespeare's audience would recognize that the playwright has here annexed another agenda to his story of governance, love, and justice. Those who were literate might well have come upon Puttenham's *The Arte of English Poesie* (1589). This was the rough guide to everything that anyone might wish to know about verse. Puttenham even went so far as to "translate" the original Latin terms for rhetorical devices into what he deemed their familiar English equivalents, sometimes hilariously (*micterismus*, the "fleering frumpe"; *paradoxon*, "the wonderer"; *antitheton*, "the quarrelor," and so on). Readers of Puttenham and even of his more respectable high cultural competitors would have seen in Lucio something both familiar and disturbing, a man who has become an impressive rhetorician and versifier but who seems incapable of recognizing that his skills are but an avoidance of truth and contingent fact. Puttenham frequently assembles his lists of rhetorical devices as one might an armory of weapons:

> Mezozeugma, or the Middlemarcher
> Sillepsis, or the double supply
> Parison, or the figure of even
> Traductio, or the tranlacer
> Antitheton, or the quarreller
> Ploche, or the doubler
> Ironia, or the drie mock
> Meiosis, or the disabler

Micterismus, or the fleering frumpe
Charientismus, or the privie nippe
("These be souldiers to the figure *allgoria*
And fight under the banner of dissimulation.")
Paradoxon, or the wonderer
Synecdoche, or the figure of quick conceit
Noema, or the figure of close conceit
                    (Wimsatt and Brooks, 1957, p. 234)

One cannot help but notice the uncomfortable similarity between this marshaling of linguistic forces and Lucio's disciplined, and desperate, retreat from actuality into the apparent safety of rhetoric. Shakespeare's audience too would have observed this, and some might well have recalled Puttenam's remarks on what rhetoric and poetry achieve: "they deceive the ear and also the mind, drawing it from the plainness and simplicity to a certain double-ness, whereby our talk is more guileful and abusing." He continues: "And ye shall know that we dissemble, I mean speak otherwise than we think, in earnest and well as in sport, under covert and dark terms and in learned and apparent speeches." Claudio seems to be dutifully implementing Puttenham's directive on the creation of "doubleness," "dissembling," a deliberate "drawing" away from "plainness and simplicity." Puttenham, although willing to expand upon the immediate effects and consequences of poetry, never ventures a thesis on why exactly anyone might wish to use language in this way and nor indeed do many of his more elevated, high cultural contemporaries. Sir Philip Sidney's *The Defence of Poesie* (1595) is far more discursive and polemical than Puttenham, more a gentleman's essay than a textbook. Sidney parades his familiarity with his classical antecedents, Plato, Aristotle, and Horace, and attempts with languid unsuccess to reach some conclusion of his own on the value of poetry. Typically, he says:

> Poesy, therefore, is an art of imitation, for so Aristotle termeth it in his word mimesis, that is to say, a representing, counterfeiting or figuring forth; to speak metaphorically, a speaking picture, with this end, – to teach and delight.

Sidney not only distorts and misrepresents Aristotle's conception of mimesis, he also embarks upon an audacious perversion of logic, contending that representation, counterfeiting, and "figuring" (the use of metaphor) are but stages in the veritable process of truth telling and transparency. His so-called defense of poetry is a tissue of fabrications and self-contradictions. One cannot question his motive; he wishes to rescue verse from its status as a fickle testimony to the unreliability of language. But in attempting to argue that it is a vehicle for unalloyed fact and truth, he becomes the victim of his own flamboyant desperation. For a more honest account, go the Shakespeare's juxtaposition of the haplessly adventurous Claudio with the pragmatic Lucio and to Puttenham's description of verse as "guileful" and "abusing," the motor of "dissembling," "covert dark terms," and "dissimulation."

It is difficult to accept – but accept it we must – that the man ranked higher than any other in the field of English poetry perceived his medium as fickle and by its nature unreliable. There is a passage where Isabella, novitiate nun and sister of Claudio, argues with Angelo over the ethical and judicial validity of her sibling's death sentence. Lucio, at her shoulder, offers encouragement and guidance, rather in the manner of a theater director:

Isabella	We cannot weigh our brother with ourself:
	Great men may jest with saints; 'tis wit in them
	But in the less foul profanation.
Lucio	*(Aside to Isabella)* Thou'rt i' th' right girl: more o' that.
Isabella	That in the captain's but a choleric word
	Which the soldier is flat blasphemy.
Lucio	*(Aside to Isabella)* Art advis'd o' that? More on't.
Angelo	Why do you put these saying upon me?
Isabella	Because authority, though it err like others
	Hath yet a kind of medicine in itself
	That skins vice o' the top. Go to your bosom
	Knock there, and ask your heart what it doth know.

(Act II, Scene ii, 126–37)

Isabella and Angelo, as befits their social rank, converse in blank verse, marshaling orotund rhetoric devices to service their opposing arguments. Lucio, the pragmatist, commentates:

> Ay touch him; here's the vein (70)
> Ay well said (89)
> That's well said (109)
> O, to him to him, wench! He will relent: (124)

Wryly, Shakespeare leaves us uncertain as to what aspect of Isabella's performance Lucio feels is deserving of such unreserved commendation. He might of course admire her intellectual gravitas and linguistic versatility but it eventually becomes evident that he senses that these are actually of little practical use in the world of instinct and contingency. He suspects that Angelo is not so much persuaded by her argument as entranced by her physical presence and, because of her vocation, her elusiveness. And Lucio is correct. Angelo, supposedly guardian of high principles, does indeed offer Isabella a reprieve for her brother, provided that she has sex with him. The Duke, in disguise, arranges a "bed trick" when Angelo's ex-fiancée Marina is substituted for Isabella and Angelo becomes entrapped by his own hypocrisies.

It would be misleading and do a grave injustice to Shakespeare's superlative intellect to treat *Measure for Measure* as a play that addresses itself only to the intractable problems of morality, justice, and governance. It has a second agenda, not unrelated to its more conspicuous themes, but which establishes it as a work of beguiling originality. It is about writing, specifically the difference between poetry and everything else. The plot's engine, its motivating force, is the dynamic relationship between contingency, desire, and action. Ideas, abstract principles, and beliefs are continually invoked but rendered laughably ineffectual by the power of actuality. Ideals and their intellectual and spiritual appendices are always addressed in verse, while events, the opportunity to do something or effect change, are occasioned exclusively by prose.

Act III, Scene i is a wonderful composite of the play as a whole. Its two most memorable passages involve Claudio alone in his cell contemplating the nature of death:

> Ay, but to die, and go we know not where;
> To Lie in cold obstruction and to rot;
> This sensible warm motion to become
> A kneaded clod; and the delighted spirit
> To bathe in fiery floods, or to reside
> In thrilling region of thick-ribbed ice;
> (Act III, Scene i, 116–21)

Removed from the context of the play, this could, credibly, be offered as a lyric poem on mortality – plenty of similar ones were being written at the time. Figurative excursions and lurid imagery become substitutes for grisly unalterable fact. Shortly after this, in the same scene, the Duke explains how he intends to effectively entrap, indeed blackmail, Angelo with the bed trick:

Duke	Have you not heard speak of Mariana, the sister of Frederick the great soldier who miscarried at sea?
Isabella	I have heard of the lady, and good words went with her name.
Duke	She should this Angelo have married; was affianced to her by oath, and the nuptial appointed.

(Act III, Scene i, 215–17)

The exchange between the Duke and Isabella, in prose, if governed entirely by the nostrum that facts, some of them distasteful, are what determine our lives and prospects; language enables us to acknowledge them, particularize our intention to deal with them, but they, rather than it, set the agenda for what we can be and do. Poetry, however, both in exchanges and in such monologues as Claudio's, is by its nature delusional. We can build metaphoric universes from simple ideas, but in the end all we have produced is a piece of language; entrancing, wonderful, beguiling, even persuasive, but in the end absolutely futile.

Measure for Measure was certainly not the only play in which Shakespeare made writing as much the subject of his work as its vehicle. Examples abound of slippages between the extraordinary worlds conjured by verse and the mundane particulars rendered in prose. A rare comic exchange takes place between Prince Henry (verse) and Falstaff (prose) in *Henry IV Part I* where the latter seems to be engaged in a flat translation of the aristocrat's elegy over the seemingly lifeless body of his old drinking partner. More significantly, we encounter this same tension in the play that most regard as his goodbye note to the trade. Nearly all of Act I, Scene i of *The Tempest* is in prose, as the Boatswain, his crew and passengers desperately attempt to keep their vessel afloat in the storm. Prose seems appropriate, given that their world is now composed exclusively of contingent, unpredictable, and deadly facts – there is little opportunity for imaginative speculation.

They do not, of course, die but find themselves on the Prospero's island, a place just as fantastic and hypothetical as the Afterlife. On the island, everyone apart from the seamen and the ordinary passengers speaks in blank verse. Even Caliban, a figure able to acquire aspects of the human but originating from a much lower point in the chain of being, is comfortable with the sophisticated nuances of the form. At one point, he plots with Stephano, the drunken butler, and Trinculo, a jester, an assault on his master Prospero. They speak in prose, while he declaims, elegantly, in the high cultural idiom taught to him by Prospero. Indeed, he knows no other form of speech:

Trinculo	I did not give thee the lie: Out o' your wits and hearing too? A pox o' your bottle! This can sack and drinking do. A murrain on your monster, and the devil take you fingers!
Caliban	Ha, Ha, Ha!
Stephano	Now forward with your tale – Prithee stand further off.
Caliban	Beat him enough: after a little time I'll beat him too.
Stephano	Stand further – Come, proceed.
Caliban	Why, as I told thee, 'tis a custom with him I' the afternoon to sleep: there thou may'st brain him Having first seiz'd his books; or with a log Batter his skull

(Act III, Scene ii, 88–101)

The concluding enjambment reminds one of the counterpoint between improvisation and design in Donne's "The Flea." The syntax cuts across the two pentameters but the slight pause at the line ending preserves their formal architecture. Caliban hesitates and in that brief moment reflects, perhaps savors, the exact nature of his intent. There is, of course, something superbly incongruous about the refinement, the pure artistry, of the passage and its content:

> with a log [he pauses and reflects]
> Batter his skull…

What sort of creature is this who has become so well assimilated to the conventions of high art while being still, essentially, subhuman? He is, at least in part, the creation of Prospero, the ultimate autocrat who not only governs his domain but within it enjoys a sense of other-worldliness, controlling creatures who are not quite real but who nonetheless converse admirably in the idiom allotted to them by their master. Prospero's closest counterpart in the real world is the literary writer, the playwright, and poet.

Shakespeare, aside from his designated status as the greatest writer in English, was also, albeit obliquely, an immensely shrewd critic. In his plays he continually raised questions regarding the nature and function of poetry and, most astutely, left them unanswered.

Greenblatt, in arguing that Shakespeare and his work are part of the vortex of discourses that erodes the boundaries between literature and everything else, is not merely offering a challenging theoretical model. He is pretending not to hear a message from Shakespeare directed unambiguously to him and everyone else: on how literature – or more specifically poetry – is intrinsically different from nonliterary language. In *Measure for Measure* the characters themselves are self-consciously aware of how poetry distorts the otherwise transparent nature of language, of how extended conceits disrupt any rational correspondence between words and truth.

One reason why Greenblatt might have overlooked something whose relevance to his thesis is striking is that it raises serious questions about the validity of his project and those of his fellow New Historicists and their close allies the Cultural Materialists. First of all, it is understandable that in his plays Shakespeare incorporates a significant number of self-referential engagements with the status of poetry, particularly regarding its relationship with the more pragmatic function of ordinary language. Lucio's sardonic comments, in prose, on how Claudio, speaking in verse, seems unable to offer a coherent, transparent account of his predicament is a case in point. What Shakespeare is doing here is replicating in miniature the contemporaneous state of uncertainty – evidenced in the prose writings of Puttenham and Sidney – regarding the significance and character of poetry. This would be troubling for Greenblatt to acknowledge because, on the one hand, it brings our attention back to Shakespeare the individual, the specific creator of a text that declares its independence from Greenblatt's model of the dynamic kasbah of competing discourses. Moreover, we encounter Shakespeare speaking to us – that voice from the dead that Greenblatt dismissed as a delusion – of the essential difference between poetry and everything else, proclaiming that the former is a unique and special discourse, operating in a self-consciously inventive realm of its own. Hearing the voice once sought and then dismissed as a foolish caprice is bad enough but listening as it undermines the premise upon which your methodology is founded would, for Greenblatt, have been unendurable.

Yet, does proof that Shakespeare suffocated the intellectual pretentions of the Theorists four centuries before their birth render him the greatest? To address this we should turn again to the noisiest, most Falstaffian, of Shakespeare's modern advocates, Harold Bloom. According to Bloom, Shakespeare "invented the human as we continue to know it" (Bloom, 1998, p. xviii). Specifically Hamlet, both as an individual and a work – in Bloom's opinion the two are inextricably interwoven – is the most important literary invention of all time, which is not to say that the rest of Shakespeare's creations are correspondingly diminished. Rather they are versions of what he compresses into Hamlet's anguished dilemma. He is the first to explore in language the tension between our "inner and outer worlds." Luther questioned the division and buried it with theology. Montaigne blinded himself to its irresolvable horrors, as did Nietzsche, and Freud turned it into a professional assignment. Shakespeare was the only one who accepted and enacted it as an irrevocable dilemma. He was not a nihilist; Falstaff was a version of Hamlet:

> Whether we are male or female, old or young, Falstaff and Hamlet speak most urgently for us and to us. Hamlet can be transcendent or ironic; in either mode his inventiveness is absolute. Falstaff, at his funniest or at his most reflective, retains a vitalism that renders him alive beyond belief. When we are wholly human, and know ourselves, we become most like either Hamlet or Falstaff. (Bloom, 1998, p. 745)

Bloom's case is far more compelling than Bate's poised fastidiousness yet it raises another question. Even if Shakespeare does outrank Nietzsche, Wittgenstein, and Freud as a diagnostician of the human condition what, as a consequence, does he also become? Is he a man who uses literature as a more rhetorically convincing medium than philosophical prose? If so, does he diminish the status of literary writing, marshal its resources as a populist alternative to the dullness of intellectual discourse? Look at Bloom again and the suspicion grows that if we accept his argument ad hoc Shakespeare the literary writer becomes Shakespeare the frustrated philosopher, channeling these repressed ambitions into his more profitable job as playwright and impresario.

I find myself in only partial agreement with Bloom. Shakespeare did do something unprecedented and unsurpassable but he did not deploy his literary talents as a means of inventing, or disclosing, "the human." Rather, he invented literature.

Literature since the Renaissance has been marked by a persistent sense of discontentment. Periods of stability and formal consistency have been disrupted by subcurrents of perceptible anxiety. Even in the the eighteenth century, when poetry in particular became governed by prescriptive regulations and conventions, the collective desire to make literature conform was driven by a fear that at some point a maverick trend would cause it to become discontinuous and incoherent: the pressurized anxieties of the Augustans were in an important sense the cause of Romanticism.

Frequently, change was anticipated by individual moments of enquiry, even of dissatisfaction. Sterne is famous for writing a novel whose only discernable theme is the strangeness of writing novels and Fielding, in an albeit less ostentatious manner, displayed in his fiction a similar fascination with the nature of his genre. Both pointed up the organic evolutionary nature of fiction, its rootlessness as a form with no specified function. They predicted what would happen to the novel during the nineteenth and early twentieth centuries, a repeat of Romantic poetry's revolt against Augustanism.

We routinely treat the self-referential novel, the work that questions its status as language and art, as modernism's challenge to the complacencies of classical realism, forgetting as we do so that Shakespeare laid down this same challenge in his plays when he had his characters speak to one another in what seemed different languages; had them, as a consequence, inhabit different worlds while conducting a dialogue.

Continually, writers will explore the boundaries and possibilities of received convention and eventually the dam of convention will be broken by the pressure of enquiry. Bloom is correct to state that Shakespeare created in his characters and their language complex existential issues that we more routinely associate with Wordsworth, Coleridge, Proust, Joyce, Ibsen, Beckett, but he did more than that. For the first time he caused literature to question its function and nature, a state of perplexity that would energize literary history thereafter.

Consider again Tobias Smollett's condemnation of Hamlet's soliloquy as a "confusion of mixed metaphors, which leave the sense disjointed ... a heap of absurdities." In a more detailed, sober estimation of Shakespeare's verse style Smollett's contemporary Lord Kames, in his *Elements of Criticism* (1762), found that sometimes Shakespeare's seeming fixation with figurative originality took on a life of its own, with invention renouncing accountability to sense.

> To draw consequences from a figure of speech, as if the word were to be understood literally, is a gross absurdity, for it is confounding truth with fiction:
>
> > Be Moubray's sins so heavy in his boson,
> > That they may break his foaming courser's back,
> > And throw the rider headlong in the lists,
> > A caitiff recreant to my cousin Hereford.
> > [*Richard II, 1.2.50ff.*]
>
> Sin may be imagined heavy in a figurative sense, but weight in a proper sense belongs to the accessory only, and therefore to describe the effects of weight is to desert the principal subject and to convert the accessory into a principal.

It would be too easy to dismiss such figures as purblind reactionaries. They represent a solid consensus with more indulgent critics such as Johnson in the minority. More importantly, however, we should not ascribe their reservations regarding Shakespeare simply to the prevailing mood of Augustanism. Shakespeare was, they knew, exceptional but they could not quite reconcile his extraordinary achievements with their sense of confusion. It was not so much that his verse was carelessly overwritten; more that no one had done this before. But quite soon they would. Once the likes of Blake, Coleridge, and Keats had established "sense disjointed" as part of the lexicon of poetic writing there were no further complaints about Shakespeare. At the same time, however, there seemed a collective forgetting that Shakespeare stood alone for two centuries as a figure who had tested not only the limits of metaphor but had made us think again of what literature could do and as a consequence what it is.

Case proved? It is time, I think, to descend from the universal to the particular. In 1996 Al Pacino directed and starred in a film called *Looking for Richard* in which Pacino and Frederic Kimball visit Stratford in search of an epiphany. As "A" list members of the Hollywood-based film industry they realize that despite their efforts it will be difficult to close the gap between the man who clothed himself in the densely embroidered garb of Puttenham's rhetoric and their forthcoming attempt to stage *Richard III* in the United States. They adopt a direct approach by standing before Shakespeare's alleged "bed of birth" in the hope that they will in some way absorb a sense of his presence. Instead they accidentally set off an alarm, summoning a small army of security officers appointed to ensure that the embalmed pastoral monument of Stratford remains undisturbed by those who dare to treat it as real. The film is a wry, amusing essay on high and popular culture yet it also carries an apposite message on what Shakespeare has become. The managerial apparatus of Stratford is supposed to guard its tourist cash cow against reckless visitors but it is but one branch of a vast multifaceted industry – including academia, the cultural establishment, and the cautiously protected high arts strand of the media – which stands between Shakespeare and us as individuals. In short, the one-to-one interaction that enabled Coleridge to feel he knew Shakespeare intimately, albeit in his case as a perverse, deluded fantasy, is now forbidden.

Few would now be so naïve, or egotistical, as to claim knowledge of Shakespeare's private sensibility but even if we attempt to make sense of his work as a footstep toward forming an opinion on its value we find that we first have to bypass, more often surpass, the vast reams of solidified opinion within which his plays are entombed. The process is exhausting, forbidding, but most significantly it desensitizes us. One of the most appealing moments in the vast network of transactions that reading now involves comes when we pick up a book, probably a novel, with little knowledge of its author or content. By about page 5 a number of questions will compete for our attention. Do we want to know what happens next? Is a particular character charismatic enough for us to suspend disbelief? And, most significantly, are we growing to admire or question, perhaps even love or hate, the figure responsible for putting the words on the page? These opening impressions are tentative but they are not ephemeral. As we proceed they expand and contract in significance and our shifting relationship with each of them will continue until the closing page, unless of course we decide that the book is unendurable and replace it unfinished on the shelf. It is possible, just, to envisage such a rendezvous even with such eminences as Dickens, Austen, Henry James, or Hardy; some people only begin to discover the so-called canon after managing to exempt themselves from its attractions at school. It is difficult, however, to conceive of such an innocent encounter with Shakespeare and in this respect Pacino's farcical attempt to bypass the accretions of learning and intuit something directly from the bed seems horribly accurate.

Yet at some point each of us must have felt something about Shakespeare, even perhaps when first obliged to study him, that is visceral and instinctive. The problem is of course that if we attempt to make this the foundation for a judgment on his importance as a literary artist we will eventually find, or more likely have it pointed out to us, that someone else got there first. To adapt Taylor's analogy, we are not so much swallowed by a "black hole" as silenced by louder, more authoritative voices saying what we might wish to say but well before we have the chance to do so.

What opportunities remain for those of us who wish to speak our minds, express our opinions on the Bard? The commentators discussed fall into three categories: a small body of vituperative competitors who decry him; the vast majority who argue over the nature of his qualities; and the recent wave of Theory zealots who set out to assassinate him. Is it possible to like or dislike him without becoming affiliated to one part of this triumvirate?

My answer to this question must be partial because I can only conceptualize what it means to enjoy Shakespeare. I cannot speak of this from experience. If I could hereafter avoid any further contact with his work I would happily do so. I shall here state that this does not align me with Tolstoy, who did not question his qualities as an artist but despised him for misusing his talents. I dislike him at a much more rudimentary level and to close this chapter I will attach myself to the evaluative equivalent of a lie detector, ask myself why I feel as I do and answer honestly.

Shakespeare is a magnificent verbal craftsman, but there is a problem with this. It is certainly the case that no one can be too good at what they do, yet to encounter someone who never ceases to be, by degrees, magnetic, forbidding, and addictively ambiguous prompts a complaint that goes beyond aesthetic appreciation: he never leaves us alone. A well wrung-out cliché has it that we cannot have too much of a good thing. In my view, we can. We require periods of release, intellectual leave of absence, but Shakespeare, even when he shifts to prose, is like the waiter standing at our shoulder with yet one more outrageously fine concoction, just when the customer craves rest.

Many of us, sometimes despite ourselves, enjoy those moments when a writer begins to reveal their weaknesses, their sense of doubt or uncertainty about the task undertaken, and allow aspects of their personality – just as flawed and defective as our own – to inform the work. The tear in the fabric testifies to a sense of humanity, even humility, in an author. The work does not as a consequence become a curiosity; rather it allows us to see, simultaneously, the unfinished product and the artist struggling to complete it. More often than not it is at such moments we feel a sense of empathy with an author, not a diminution of their standing as an artist but a supplementary portrait of them as real, imperfect, and vulnerable. One will search in vain for the personality of Shakespeare in his work. True, his plays are rated, by consensus, in terms of their significance. Some, *Hamlet* in particular, are routinely classified to a level above, say, *Coriolanus* or his less problematic history plays, but these fluctuations are treated as artistic modalities and not fallings away from perfection; it is assumed that the master will turn his attention to some issues less challenging than others. Occasionally there are hints of misogyny and antisemitism but in this respect, at least by sixteenth century standards, he was unexceptional.

His near contemporaries such as Jonson and Marlowe are ranked lower than him because their work carries, allegedly, an imprint of their individual perversities. Shakespeare, in my opinion, marries perfection and anonymity in a way that is disturbing.

But these are but minor displeasures compared with a particular brand of loathing that has enduring since my youth and will, I am convinced, continue until my death. When in David Lodge's *Changing Places* (1975) the odious Howard Ringbaum declares that he has never read *Hamlet* we find ourselves with a wonderful working model of the relationship between Shakespeare and intellectual elitism. Ringbaum is egregiously ambitious and narcissistic and his determination to win the drink-fueled game of Humiliation, whose victor will be the player who proves himself the most woefully ill read, mirrors his desire to outrank all of his academic peers. He knows that an unapologetic ignorance of Shakespeare's greatest work is an act of heresy that will deter other competitors. He lies but he does so with ruthless calculation, sensing that no one else in the game will dare even to pretend to such a state of ghastly philistinism. He wins the game but as a consequence loses tenure. We have to ask: is this an accurate reflection of Shakespeare's status as the deity of the chattering classes? The answer is yes, for the simple reason that we will never be able to test Lodge's comic scenario in the real world. Neither an academic nor anyone with a serious claim to intellectual respectability would confess to this, at least without later allowing themselves the option of claiming it had been a joke.

Shakespeareanism – by which I mean an ability to engage with his work – has become the all-encompassing prerequisite for entry level intellectualism. In their endeavor to extinguish the "myth" of Shakespeare the artist even the Bardicidal Theorists buttressed the notion of untouchability that has surrounded him for three centuries. Not once during their various attempts to undermine his cultural pre-eminence do we find evaluative disquiet, an expression of doubt regarding his skills as a thinker or writer. This is understandable given that judgment of any kind runs against their belief that intrinsic quality, or the lack of it, is a bourgeois delusion. Yet as a consequence they succeed in rendering him even more immune from critical censure than even his most rhapsodic devotees. Moreover, their obsessive concern with Shakespeare as the ultimate challenge serves to reinforce the solidly conservative notion of him as the mandatory element of cultural wholeness.

For further confirmation that Shakespeare is securely guarded by intractable elitism we should consider parodies of him and popularized commentaries on his life and work. This list sometimes seems interminable but there are consistencies. Richard Curtis, writer and director of *Four Weddings and A Funeral* and many similarly patronizing reflections on middle-class angst, once took time off from films to present *Skinhead Hamlet* in which the Prince, entering Gertrude's bedchamber, addresses her as "Oi Slag!" and she replies with "Watch your fucking mouth, kid!" On the face of things he is pointing up the radical difference between the vernacular of people who today attend the cinema – the modern equivalent, he implies, of

Shakespeare's audience – and Shakespeare's abstruse poetic flourishes. In truth, however, he is offering the educated Shakespearian a freemason's handshake of superiority: only those who do not speak like his working class Hamlet will get the joke.

Similarly, the first episodes of the long-running *Blackadder* television series (1983) involve a tragi-comic rewriting of *Richard III* in which instead of dying on Bosworth Field Richard is accidently beheaded by his son Edmund (aka Blackadder) whose incompetence has a catastrophic domino effect on all the major, disastrous events of British history. The parody is not aimed at Shakespeare himself but rather at those Shakespeareans who appropriate and misread him for their own chauvinistic purposes. It takes two things for granted: that the average viewer is someone with an elementary knowledge of *Richard III* (and by association *Henry V, King Lear,* and *Macbeth*) and that this viewer will uncritically sympathize with the program's left-wing agenda. Thus, the person who one assumes would benefit from all of this – the "ordinary" individual, routinely indoctrinated by right-wing historical propaganda – will need the equivalent of a degree in English (Shakespeare and New Historicism included) in order to understand it.

A better known parody involves the hazy territory of Shakespeare's biography. The film *Shakespeare in Love* (1999) was co-written by Tom Stoppard, who many would regard as at least a claimant upon Shakespeare's legacy: he is contemporary Britain's most intellectually challenging popular playwright. The film is largely invention interwoven with more credible elements, notably Will's rivalry with Marlowe and *Romeo and Juliet* as a version of Shakespeare's on-screen relationship with the fictitious Viola. Again, a form of cultural apartheid is at work, given that while a filmgoer who knows of Shakespeare only vaguely, by name and reputation, would follow the engaging story well enough (the film was immensely popular) the dense fabric of allusions to his plays and poetry will, for others, shift the experience to a rather more elevated level of amusement. Stoppard and his co-screenwriter, Marc Norman, succeed brilliantly in their work yet they also surreptitiously secure Shakespeare the intellectual from the vulgar attentions of those who seek simple entertainment.

I could continue but I will instead assure you that in every instance of Shakespearean appropriation or seeming caricature the author and his plays remain both sacrosanct and, less palatably, the preserve of the social and intellectual elite. The latter tendency carries a good deal of involuntary irony given that those involved are both middle class and sanctimoniously left-leaning.

To summarize, it is now impossible to regard oneself as culturally and intellectually sufficient without first having a thorough knowledge of Shakespeare's works along with an implicit affirmation of their uniqueness, or often their invulnerability. This is the essential cause of my unease with Shakespeare. It is difficult to apportion blame either to the man himself or to the cultural establishment for this situation, though one would tend to exonerate the former since it is preposterous to imagine that he could deliberately engineer let alone foresee the future. But at the same time one must appreciate that its consequences are corrosive and malign, reaching far beyond the questions raised by this single author. I confess to feeling an empathy with Tobias Smollett. In part I sympathize with his case. Substitute the names of, say, Dylan Thomas, Gerard Manley Hopkins, or Robert Browning in the instance of his notoriously self-indulgent *Sordello,* or Charles Tomlinson, for that of Shakespeare, and the contention that intelligibility is sacrificed for "sense disjointed," "a heap of absurdities" stands. Some would treat Smollett as overcensorious, unable to properly appreciate Shakespeare's superlative imagination and radical style, but it could equally be argued that Shakespeare was responsible for licensing a brand of impenetrability that would fester in the margin of mainstream poetry and eventually, with modernism, infect its core. But there is something much worse abroad. Smollett and his like have now become nonpersons. The instinct that mobilized his critique might in some persist but it will persist silently. Smollett might have gone on to state that he found Shakespeare unendurable and was able only to sample his material before casting it aside, prefiguring Lodge's Ringbaum but basing his refusal to read *Hamlet* on an honest declaration of evaluative distaste. Again, such persons might well exist but we will never learn of their identity, with one very notable exception. I stated earlier that one of the more unsettling aspects of the Shakespeare myth is his forbidding anonymity, fostered in part by a dearth of biographical facts and by his own tendency to hide personal quiddities or biases beneath a monolith of conceits. I should revise this assertion because on one occasion we do encounter William Shakespeare speaking to us incautiously about the work of William Shakespeare. No, I do not claim to have discovered a ludic manuscript. The text has been in the public sphere since the end of the sixteenth century and its authorship is largely undisputed. Few would doubt that Shakespeare composed *Titus Andronicus* but an equally small number attempt to justify or excuse his involvement. During the eighteenth century the more sensitive members of the audience were made nauseous and later plagued by nightmares; this in a time when attendance at public executions was deemed neither vulgar nor unseemly. In the nineteenth century it was hardly performed at all; not banned in a formal sense, but treated by consensus as the ghastly family secret of which no one spoke. Only in the later twentieth century have more daring, or maladjusted, critics seen it as worthy of comparison with his most celebrated plays. Their governing thesis is that Shakespeare, being a genius, was attuned to the true depths of evil long before its manifestations in the Holocaust, Rwanda, and Bosnia. It is made up of a full gallery of horrors – incorporating rape, murder, dismemberment, cannibalism, and arbitrary cruelty – and it offers no explanation for these acts of barbarity. It could indeed be advertised as the first instance of sado-prurience disguised as literature, in that if you do not derive some perverse satisfaction from the foul activities depicted there is little else to claim your attention.

It caused Bloom to become apoplectic, calling it "a poetic atrocity," citing the 1955 production – directed by Peter Brook and starring Laurence Olivier – as evidence as its failure as a tragedy. Apparently the audience laughed several times during scenes that were supposed to be tragic, notably when Lavinia is instructed to carry Titus's severed hand in her mouth. What is lacking from Bloom's account is any attempt to explain why Shakespeare had become so unShakespearean and in this respect he exemplifies a general mood of embarrassment-by-silence, with the exception of those, such as Jan Kott, who saw it as a prediction of the worst that the twentieth century could provide in terms of terror and cruelty.

In my view it can make no claims to being a work of moral prescience. If it predicts anything it is the viewpoint of Smollett because its true subject is literary writing. The passage that for most typifies the peculiarity of the play is Marcus's speech on finding the dismembered Lavinia after her rape (Act II, Scene iv, 11–57). Even in Brook's adventurous 1955 production the speech was cut completely. Bloom saw it as slightly deranged parody of Marlowe, and others such as Bate and Vickers have wrestled with its perversities and attempted to wring from it some deep cultural essences, all of them very modern.

Read it and then read the better-known tragic soliloquies, especially that of Hamlet. There are, you will find, parallels that are enlightening and disquieting. In Marcus's speech there is a continuous mismatch between his apparent addiction to poetic discourse and its subject.

> what stern ungentle hands
> Hath lapped, and hewed and made thy body bare

Of her two branches, those sweet ornaments,
Whose circling shadows, kings have sought to sleep in

There is nothing wrong with this conceit, in its own right. Indeed, the image of the hacked tree as involving "sweet ornaments" with "complex shadows" soon to be removed by "ungentle hands" is one that Wordsworth might have formulated two centuries later. But something tells us that the actualities of rape and dismemberment should not be the foundation for such stylistic exuberance. The true subject of the passage, indeed the play, is the relationship between what can be done in language and what exists outside language. Sometimes, this play shows us, there are unsuitable matches; sometimes, it implies, writing about things too terrible for verse is inappropriate. It raises questions about the vast, often ridiculous, philosophical arena that has now been built around *Hamlet* and his other "great" works. In this respect Shakespeare is remarkably prescient in caricaturing and questioning the cultural legacy he would spawn – "serious" literature – and for this reason the play is shuffled into the margins of literary studies. It is Shakespeare's self-inflicted Achilles heel but does it therefore undermine my earlier assertion that he is the most coldly impersonal of all literary writers? No, because it also involves an extraordinary act of hubris. He leaves it as the booby trap that will frustrate his interpretors' attempts to reach a final conclusion on his achievements, but not as a gesture of humility. Quite the contrary. Imagine if Turner could be brought back from the dead to speak with a carefully chosen assembly of art historians and critics in a gallery filled with the former's finest works. Turner answers questions from the excited assembly with stunning predictability, telling them nothing they do not already know, and then before leaving unveils another work that is unquestionably his own, beautifully executed, and seemingly designed to satisfy only the most barbarous and prurient tastes. He smiles, chuckles, and departs after refusing to take further questions. Shakespeare's *Titus Andronicus* was calculated to deliver the same message: I am too great for you to properly comprehend my character or my work.

Bardolatry, even in its bizarre contemporary manifestation, fosters an endemic reluctance to evaluate literature. Those in the canon ranked just below Shakespeare benefit from his secure position but this notion of a meritocracy frustrates rather than encourages broader inclinations to judge the intrinsic quality of works. We might assess other writers in comparison with Shakespeare but since we cannot decide on why Shakespeare is the best the very notion of evaluation is eroded. More specifically, while there are various causes for the endemic failure to address the notion of evaluation in schools and universities the invulnerability of Shakespeare must be regarded as one reason for this stifling of debate. Despite the institutionalization of Theory, now moribund yet permanently resident, Shakespeare is still acknowledged as the pre-eminent figure in the Western canon. If evaluative assessment of the center is forbidden then as a consequence ripples of inhibition spread outward through the inner circles to the periphery.

4

Mad Theories

The history of English as a university discipline has been well documented and it is tempting to conclude that Theory became so fashionable with academics themselves because it offered a respectable, if borrowed, lifebelt for a subject about to drown in a sea of amateurish vagueness and delusion. However, the true cause of the problems endured by academic English is its undoubted but unacknowledged status as a pariah. No other field of study involves such an uncomfortable, incestuous relationship with its subject as does English (and here you may substitute French or Chinese, provided that the subject is literature). Historians and sociologists create narratives from all types of evidence – most of it is recorded in language but rarely if ever is it intended as art. Historians seek to disclose authenticity from the material at hand; no more and no less. Aesthetics-focused subjects such as art history or music involve themselves in the dangerously fickle activity of evaluation but crucially their medium, language, is not the one they share with their subject. With English it is, and this is one of the reasons that Theory has taken an addictive hold upon the discipline. It is in its various manifestations an annexation of other fields – politics, sociology, ideology, linguistics, philosophy, and so on – all of which allow their practitioners to treat their subjects with the condescending superiority of the anthropologist or the clinical indifference of the pure scientist.

Is Shakespeare Any Good?: And Other Questions on How to Evaluate Literature,
First Edition. Richard Bradford.
© 2015 John Wiley & Sons, Ltd. Published 2015 by John Wiley & Sons, Ltd.

A number, notably Marxists and cultural materialists, have argued that the sacred grand aesthetic of literary writing should be exposed as a charade and literature treated as but one strand of a broader weave of discourses and sociohistorical symptoms. Some of them are I suspect resolute and secure in their convictions – sad though this is – but most Theory advocates are in truth attracted to the separation of Theory from its subject because it secures them against a dreaded fear of embarrassment. Amazingly, in the long, tortuous history of the academic study of English no one has reflected at length upon the fact that when you write about writers you are, of necessity, entering the unforgiving competitive realm in which they have already achieved eminence. If their work is good, perhaps spectacularly good – and why else would you be writing about it – then it demands a correlative tribute in the quality of the writing that attends it.

Some have risen to the challenge. Bradley and Saintsbury (albeit more than a century ago) were erudite, fickle, and amusing; more recently figures such as Carey and Ricks have produced criticism that involves a stylish exchange between the interpreter and the artist. But in the vast majority of academic writing in English over the past three decades isolationism and inwardness are buttressed by Theory.

Theory is fed to undergraduates largely via a system of introductory guides. Students with sufficient time and courage can be persuaded to sample the core material but their perception of the broad panorama of Theory, its history and character, is shaped by secondary texts – a level of dependency which far outranks that of the old fashioned relationship between the novel or poem and concomitant guidebooks. All of these introductions are partisan and biased – some outspokenly, others only by implication – and the standard for this brainwashing process was set by Terry Eagleton's *Literary Theory*, now in print for more than three decades. Some studies treat the Formalists and the New Critics with apparent impartiality, but grudging acknowledgments of their qualities are overridden by a consensus that everything they attempted to do was shown by their successors, the real Theoreticians, to be mere delusion and fantasy. They are treated as curiosities, historical footnotes, because in their somewhat disorganized, idiosyncratic way they were pledged to a single objective, one that is anathema to the doctrines of Theory that have prevailed for almost 40 years. They perceived literature as being characterized by intrinsic defining features, which set it apart from other linguistic practices and which made it art. It goes without saying that the various brands of post-Formalist, post-New Critical thinking would not indulge such an outrage. Art is, depending on your branch of Theory, an assembly of bourgeois falsifications, a sign system no better or more significant than advertising, or a refuge for xenophobic bias or male exclusivity.

The Theory wars are over, not because either faction has achieved supremacy or admitted defeat, but because any subsequent exchanges will be familiar and predictable. There is nothing new to be said. The effect of this state of stagnation upon Theory in universities, however, is less straightforward. Whatever else might have occurred had Theory not emerged 40 years ago as the fashionable shibboleth for all those looking for tenure and promotion is a matter for speculation. What has happened is that Theory has taken up residence in academia and become an obligatory feature of virtually all that is published – particularly pedagogic pieces – but with no obvious focus or function. In doing so it has effectively suffocated the one opportunity for university English to claim for itself an intrinsic sense of purpose and value. Theory has immunized criticism from that most contentious subjective feature of talking or writing about literature: an inclination to offer an opinion on whether or not the book or the author is any good. The reasons for this are many and various, but most obviously the Theoreticians' perception of the reader and author as the subjects or constructs of specific ideological conditions and discourses undermines the notion of their being able to recognize aesthetic value or quality as intrinsic features of anything. This has, however, completely separated academic criticism – and by implication its reflection in teaching – from that broader fabric of exchanges involving, for example, newspaper critics and readers, or even two people arguing over a drink, where evaluation – the recognition of what is or is not literature of quality – is the central issue.

I am not of the opinion that "good taste" can be taught or that even if students were made aware of why and how they prefer one poem to another graduates in English would be better people or more able to cope with the world beyond university. But if English and indeed other arts and humanities subjects can claim any sense of purpose or justification they must, I would aver, be able to offer students a means of framing their instincts, enable them to articulate them and to better examine their relationship with more fundamental systems or states of mind. A starting point for this, in the albeit rarefied sphere of literary aesthetics, is the confidence and ability to evaluate, judge, and assess the quality of texts, and this over the past

30 years has been forbidden in a quietly Stalinesque manner by all advocates of Theory and many of their predecessors.

Even among the Anglo-American Traditionalists – that is, those whose affliliations predate the influx of Theory – evaluation was treated with suspicion, mainly because it was associated with the undisciplined realm of the literary marketplace. John Crowe Ransom's "Criticism Inc" (1937) is taken by many to be the mission statement of the more influential US academic critics of the 1920s and 1930s, and it is a very curious document. It comprises a list of interpretive predilections that should be excluded from any professional encounter with a literary work.

- "Personal registrations" (tears, humour, desire, excitement) can be procured by the chemist or the Broadway producer.
- "Synopsis and paraphrase" are the stuff of "high school classes and women's clubs."
- "Historical studies" tell us about the poet and his circumstances but are of not necessary relevance to the particular effect of the poem.
- "Linguistic studies" might assist with a "perfectly logical" understanding of "content," but not with a proper understanding of the poem.
- "Moral studies": "moral content is not the *whole* content" (Ransom, 1937, p. 236).

On the face of things this might seem an attempt to isolate purely aesthetic qualities from dangerous distractions but whatever Ransom's objective the result was disastrous. By striving to turn literary appreciation into something like a religious epiphany Ransom effectively paralyzes the reader. Certainly it would not be wise to allow our estimation of a book's quality to rest exclusively upon "personal registrations," "synopsis or paraphrase," "historical studies," or even a combination of the three but by eliminating them completely from the complicated experience of reading we narrow the focus of appreciation to a point of almost robotic detachment.

It is absurd to pretend that most people do not indeed read literary works, novels in particular, because they can "procure" from them, "tears, humor, desire, excitement," and even worse to treat such enjoyments as inferior and expendable. Yet Ransom is incapable of allowing that these factors might play some part in the broader spectrum of effects that constitute a full appreciation of a book. His mind-set typified the collective anxiety of his profession, desperate to protect its subject, literature, both from the claims of other disciplines and from the tarnished realm of popular entertainment, and aspects of his defensive manner shadow the landmark manifestoes of New Criticism. W.K. Wimsatt and M. Beardsley's "The Intentional Fallacy" (1946) is based on the same premise as Ransom's list of exclusions. Their particular concern is that readers might in some way treat the effects generated by a poem or novel as a reflection of its author's state of mind. They wished to ensure that critics and students did not fall prey to the simplistic delusion that a poet was speaking to them through their lyrics and again we find that paranoia overrules discretion. At all costs, they contend, do not assume that you are listening to the author via the work because in doing so your attention will be distracted from its purely literary qualities. The danger here, they felt, was that the borderline between literature and autobiography, or simply truth-telling, would be blurred. As a consequence, however, they took a further step towards an institutional ban on finding connections between literature and the real world, including that part of it occupied by the author. Their "The Affective Fallacy" (1949) is a detailed, systematic reinforcement of Ransom's exclusion of "personal registrations" from the orbit of serious critical interpretation.

In their two essays, Wimsatt and Beardsley draw a line between what we might encounter in the literary text and our collateral desire to telescope this into an assumption about real emotional factors that might have influenced the author. In general, the idea that the text allows us access to a living individual and their preoccupations is disallowed. Similarly, I.A. Richards of the Cambridge English Faculty argued in *Principles of Literary Criticism* (1924) that while literature might rehearse or reconstruct the emotional tensions that crowd our existence "the question of belief, or disbelief, never arises" (Richards, 1966, p. 277) by which he means that the issue of authenticity or of whether the text is an accurate index to the author's mental condition is irrelevant.

William Empson's *Seven Types of Ambiguity* (1930) and Cleanth Brooks's *The Well Wrought Urn* (1947) consider, respectively, ambiguity and paradox as inherent, even definitive characteristics of poetry. However, they also make it clear that while in nonliterary exchange these effects are generally the result and cause of uncertainty, fraud, deliberate falsification, misapprehension, or indecision, in literature they are purely aesthetic and stylistic devices, unincriminated by the cause and effect relations of the actual world. Though not necessarily intended as such both books contributed significantly to the working maxim in academic criticism that while the author exists, his/her preoccupations and experiences should not be allowed to intrude upon the exclusively scholarly and evaluative domain of textual scrutiny.

The insistence by these critics that we must detach literary works from an apparent origin, an assumed context, or a particular content as sanctioned by a given writer, was a desperate attempt to isolate literature from everything else and secure for it a purely aesthetic dimension. Disastrously, it had completely the opposite effect. In basic terms, if the author as an individual is excluded from the experience of critical scrutiny then we suffer a correlate difficulty in evaluating him or her as an artist. Many of the New Critics did try to articulate their views on what is, and what is not, high quality literature but in each instance we find them caught between an instinct to voice an opinion and a more powerful, sometimes unspoken, ordinance that to do so will in some way cheapen the whole enterprise. There is an almost comic passage at the opening of chapter 1 of Empson's *Seven Types of Ambiguity* where he appears to be laying out a prefatory thesis for his account of "ambiguity of the first type" but finds it impossible to suppress a rant against a group of writers he clearly finds pitiable. He reserves a particularly low opinion for poets of the nineteenth century who he treats as more concerned with the "atmosphere" of verse than with the particulars of device and effect. "They found themselves," he contends, "living in an intellectual framework with which it was very difficult to write poetry, in which poetry was rather improper, or was irrelevant to business."

> Almost all of them, therefore, exploited a sort of tap-root into the world of their childhood, where they were able to conceive things poetically, and whatever they might be writing about they would suck up from this limited and perverted world an unvarying sap which was their poetical inspiration. Mr Harold Nicolson has written excellently about Swinburne's fixation on to the excitements of his early reading and experience, and about the unique position in the life of Tennyson occupied by the moaning of cold wind round a child frightened for its identity upon the fens. Wordsworth frankly had no inspiration other than his use, when a boy, of the mountains as a totem or father-substitute, and Byron only at the end of his life, in the first cantos of *Don Juan* in particular, escaped from the infantile incest-fixation upon his sister which was till then all that he had got to say. As for Keats's desire for death and his mother, it has become a byword among the learned. Shelley, perhaps does not strike one as keeping so sharp a distinction between the world he considered real and the world from which he wrote poetry, but this did not in his case improve either of them; while Browning and Meredith, who did write from the world they lived in, affect me as novel-writers of merit

with no lyrical inspiration at all. Coleridge, it is true, relied on opium rather than the nursery. But of all these men an imposed excitement, a sense of uncaused warmth, achievement, gratification, a sense of hugging to oneself a private dream-world, is the main interest and material. (Lodge, 1972, p. 151)

Irrespective of whether you agree with it, this is bracing criticism. And here I should correct myself: it is bracing because of the likelihood that many *will* disagree with it, might indeed find it profoundly misguided, even offensive, feeling that it does a grave injustice to poets they hold in affectionate regard. Empson knew that he was straying into dangerous territory. He was treating individual poets as artists who, albeit because of circumstances beyond their control, were poor writers, especially compared with those who preceded them. "Before the Romantic Revival the possibilities of not growing up had never been exploited, so far as to become a subject for popular anxiety." It is a rousing, controversial polemic; but, he realizes, it simply will not do. He must resign himself to dealing with the dry mechanics of the literary artefact. "This introduction has grown too long and too portentous; it is time I settled down to the little I can do in this chapter, which is to list examples of ambiguity of the first type." One can detect a sigh of resignation here because he never again allows himself license to explore the reasons for the use by poets of ambiguity – or abstinence in the case of Victorians – and from that build a case of his own for the work of some being of more significance, even displaying a greater sufficiency of skill, than others. Instead he adopts a lateral movement from poem to poem, acknowledging the presence of their authors but not asking questions about their specific abilities or the reasons for their technical superiority, or otherwise.

Cleanth Brooks in his discussion of paradox in *The Well Wrought Urn* faces, without acknowledging, a similar dilemma. He discusses John Donne's "The Canonizaton" and he asks,

And how necessary are the paradoxes? Donne might have said directly, "Love in a cottage is enough." *The Canonization* contains this admirable thesis, but it contains a great deal more. He might have been as forthright as a later lyricist who wrote, "We'll build a sweet little nest, / Somewhere out in the West, / And let the rest of the world go by." He might even have imitated that more metaphysical lyric, which maintains. "You're the cream in my coffee." *The Canonization* touches on all these observations, but it goes beyond them, not merely in dignity, but in precision.

> I submit that the only way by which the poet could say what *The
> Canonization* says is by paradox. More direct methods may be tempting, but
> all of them enfeeble and distort what is to be said ... Deprived of the character
> of paradox with its twin concomitants of irony and wonder, the matter of
> Donne's poem unravels into "facts," biological, sociological, and economic.
> (Lodge, 1972, p. 300)

Brooks is so desperate to establish that poetry is comprised of uniquely
complex devices which transform "facts" into art that he overlooks key
questions latent in his account. He contends that "The Canonization" is
superior in "dignity" and "precision" to a matinee lyric by Buddy DeSylva
and Lew Brown ("You're the cream in my coffee") but the difference appears
to involve Donne's choice, and by implication ability, to set himself a more
taxing technical challenge than that faced by "song and dance librettists."
The criterion of self-imposed compositional difficulty is suitable enough
when dealing with the distinction between high art and popular culture but
becomes more problematic when we consider an issue that Brooks
cautiously avoids. Why is Donne deserving of more detailed attention than,
say, his near contemporary William Habington, whose stylistic signature is
comparable but who is held to be of slight significance by comparison? If
paradox could be measured and documented in terms of its density and
collateral challenge to the technical and intellectual skills of the poet,
then Habington would rank as Donne's equal. Yet Sir Herbert Grierson
(1921), who edited the first major anthology of seventeenth century lyric
poems, refers to Habington in the preface as writing with "tedious thin-
bloodied seriousness"; sufficient justification, one assumes, for the inclusion
of only two of his pieces. Donne outnumbers his contemporaries with 34
entries. Grierson's brief dismissive estimation of Habington is not entirely
ungrounded. He believes Donne sets the exemplary standard with his
juggling act of passion and self-deprecation, but is he therefore suggesting
that this should be a general evaluative principle? If so, does it apply only to
the subgenre of the late Renaissance lyric or should all poetry in some way
be measured against it? Grierson, a freelance belle lettrist with no academic
affiliations, does not trouble himself with such pedantry but Brooks and
Empson cannot allow themselves the same indulgence. As a consequence
they shy away from treating ambiguity and paradox as an index to the
essential feature of a poet's particular quality. The borderline between
the nascent "science" of academic criticism and the dangerously fluid zone
of taste – so partial and emotionally weighted – was too narrow to tread.

T.S. Eliot was not employed by a university but his influence upon the progress of academic criticism from the 1920s onwards was immense. In "Tradition and the Individual Talent" (1919) we come across the theoretical mantra which, while not acknowledged, informs and frequently paralyzes the work of the New Critics. Eliot appears to regard a poet's willingness to absorb themselves in the traditions and precedents of the past as a precondition for competence and esteem. Yet alongside this apparent requirement for erudition runs a doctrine at once more gnomic and sinister. "The progress of an artist is a continual self-sacrifice, a continual extinction of personality ... It is in this depersonalization that art may be said to approach the condition of science" (Lodge, 1972, p. 73). Eliot was concerned that those aspects of our world not accountable to the predictability of science or the discipline of the intellect – corollaries of the "personality" – might blur the distinction between art and passion. Crucially, he extends this model of creativity to include interpretation.

> Honest criticism and sensitive appreciation are directed not upon the poet but upon the poetry. If we attend to the confused cries of the newspaper critics and the susurrus of popular repetition that follows, we shall hear the names of poets in great numbers; if we seek not Blue-book knowledge but the enjoyment of poetry, and ask for a poem, we shall seldom find it. I have tried to point out the importance of the relation of the poem to other poems by other authors, and suggested the conception of poetry as a living whole of all the poetry that has ever been written. The other aspect of this Impersonal theory of poetry is the relation of the poem to its author. And I hinted, by an analogy, that the mind of the mature poet differs from that of the immature one not precisely in any valuation of "personality," not being necessarily more interesting, or having "more to say," but rather by being a more finely perfected medium in which special, or varied, feelings are at liberty to enter into new combinations. (Lodge, 1972, p. 73)

While Eliot stops short of stating it bluntly, what he actually asks of the reader is to treat the "mind" and "personality" of the poet as inventions, features of the poem that are as patently depersonalized as meter and metaphor. There are obvious parallels between Eliot's model and the preoccupations of Wimsatt and Beardsley with intentionalism and affect and Empson's and Brooks's uncomfortable attempts to distinguish the defining characteristics of poetry from the question of which poets make best use of them.

Once the author is treated as a figure with a greater degree of technical skill or as being possessed of a more forbidding intellectual presence than his/her peers or predecessors then all manner of disquieting issues emerge. The worst is frighteningly straightforward. If we can prove that one poem is better than another, and that its author is the superior craftsman, then the essential notion of aesthetic appreciation, criticism, as a discipline in its own right is compromised. All it can do is discover what an author, with all his/her foibles and capricious personal affiliations, has brought into being. It can record greatness, or mediocrity, but is correspondingly subordinate to the pre-existing variables of authorial talent and skill. As a result, the notion of the author as an active constituent of the work and its effect upon the reader was systematically excised from the protocols of academic criticism even before the arrival of Theory.

In "The Function of Criticism" (1923) Eliot ponders the ideas of his near contemporary Middleton Murry on individuals who give "allegiance to something outside themselves" (Lodge, 1972, p. 79), which in Murry's view will always be an artificial restraint against the more powerful influence of the "inner voice." Eliot's real concern emerges as literary appreciation. The "inner voice," at least in Eliot's view, involves the licensing of ill-disciplined preference:

> The inner voice, in fact, sounds remarkably like an old principle which has been formulated by an elder critic in the now familiar phrase of "doing as one likes." The possessors of the inner voice ride ten in a compartment to a football match at Swansea, listening to the inner voice, which breathes the eternal message of vanity, fear, and lust. (Lodge, 1972, pp. 79–80)

He is reinforcing the point made in "Tradition and the Individual Talent." Individuality is by its nature poorly managed and if we allow it to influence taste our cultural infrastructure will be overrun by the intellectual counterparts of the football supporter; fractious, partial, and impassioned. His solution was to imbue the critical process with the truism of depersonalization, to make readers surrender instinct to the discipline of textual analysis and learning.

According to most historians of criticism, Theory systematically undermined the elitism of New Criticism but while the former ushered in a good deal of political radicalism it faithfully maintained the determination of its predecessors to eradicate individual response and the notion of the author from all acts of interpretation. As I will argue, in order to evaluate the quality of any artefact we must perform the simple teleological exercise of treating it as the product of an artist. Even if we have little reliable evidence as to the actual circumstances and life of that figure we should be able to regard evidence of literary craftsmanship as a guarantee of their presence. To disclaim any sense of the author's existence, as the New Critics insist, disables us as readers. In very basic terms, in order to fully appreciate and articulate our sense of a work's value we must have some collateral image of an artist whose skills, ideas, and indeed emotions brought such qualities to life. Cutting the thread between the work and its originator diminishes our faculties of appreciation.

Routinely, the New Critics are portrayed by historians of criticism as the *ancien régime*, a coterie of figures who dominated Anglo-American academic thinking in Britain and the United States until the end of the 1960s when theories evolved mainly in Continental Europe began to find advocates in the United Kingdom and the United States. There is some truth in this, particularly in that many of the *arriviste* Theorists shifted the focus away from the New Critical preoccupation with the literary work as an inviolable object of scrutiny toward issues such as literature as one of many forms of communication and representation and the very nature of interpretation. But despite their myriad differences the New Critics and their more fashionable and allegedly radical successors had one thing in common; a determination to dispossess the author of their role as communicator and creator. Roland Barthes' famous essay "The Death of the Author" (1967) amply demonstrates the endurance of this aversion.

> The Author, when believed in, is always conceived of as the past of his own book: book and author stand automatically on a single line divided into a *before* and an *after*. The Author is thought to *nourish* the book, which is to say that he exists before it, thinks, suffers, lives for it, is in the same relation of antecedence to his work as a father to his child. In complete contrast, the modern scriptor is born simultaneously with the text, is in no way equipped with a being preceding or exceeding the writing, is not the subject with the book as predicate; there is no other time than that of the enunciation and every text is eternally written *here and now...*
>
> We know now that a text is not a line of words releasing a single "theological" meaning (the "message" of the Author-God) but a multi-dimensional space in which a variety of writings, none of them original, blend and clash. The text is tissue of quotations drawn from the innumerable centres of culture ...
>
> Once the Author is removed, the claim to decipher a text becomes quite futile. To give a text an Author is to impose a limit on that text, to furnish it with a final signified, to close the writing. Such a conception suits criticism very well, the latter then allotting itself the important task of discovering the

Author (or its hypostases: society, history, psyche, liberty) beneath the work: when the Author has been found, the text is "explained" – victory to the critic. Hence there is no surprise in the fact that, historically, the reign of the Author has also been that of the Critic, nor again in the fact that criticism (be it New) is today undermined along with the Author. In the multiplicity of writing, everything is to be *disentangled*, nothing *deciphered*; the structure can be followed, "run" (like the thread of a stocking) at every point and at every level, but there is nothing beneath: the space of writing is to be ranged over, not pierced; writing ceaselessly posits meaning ceaselessly to evaporate it, carrying out a systematic exemption of meaning. (Lodge, 1988, p. 283)

Barthes is credited with moving structuralism beyond its status as a framework for analysis towards the more dysfunctional realm of poststructuralism but his essay demonstrates that the author's status as a nonperson was not a product of the transition. It all began with the Swiss linguist, Ferdinand de Saussure (1857–1913), whose lecture notes were published posthumously by his peers and pupils as the *Course in General Linguistics* (English translation, 1959). Crucial to Saussure's influence upon structuralism and poststructuralism is his distinction between *langue* and *parole*.

The *langue* is the system of rules and conventions that governs the operation of a language, at its most elementary a combination of grammar and semantics. The *parole* is a particular instance of linguistic usage, generally with self-defining parameters. We can ask for a telephone number in a single sentence which would constitute a *parole*, as would a far more gigantic sequence of sentences all of which are in some way interconnected, and in this respect a novel also could be seen as a *parole*.

One of the most contentious issues to emerge from the various uses and investigations of the *langue–parole* or structure–event formula is in the threat it presents to the notion of originality, individuality, or, in current phraseology, the autonomy of the subject. If, when using language, we need to draw upon the vast impersonal structure of the system in order to be understood, then it would seem that what we say or write is by no means unique to our personal, prelinguistic experience or perceptions; rather it is something made available from a shared system of enabling conventions which constitute and delimit the varieties of discourse. The implications of this model of language are disturbing to say the least because ultimately we must accept that everything said or written can never be truly original. Each individual *parole* can only constitute a statement made available by an impersonal system, the *langue*, rather than, as we might like to believe, the expression of something deeply personal, ranging from an extreme emotional outburst to the declaration of an immutable truth. The model became the working predicate for structuralists such as Claude Levi-Strauss and the early Barthes who averred that every act of signification, from the painting to the advertisement or road sign, should be read as the product of an overarching system of signs. The person allegedly responsible for such acts, in literary terms the author, was effectively a function of the process by which the system makes the statement available. Michel Foucault's *What is An Author?* was translated into English in 1977 and its question mark is disingenuous. Foucault is certain of what an author is, or rather is not.

> One can say that the author is an ideological product, since we represent him as the opposite of his historically real function. (When a historically given function is represented in a figure that inverts it, one has an ideological production.) The author is therefore the ideological figure by which one marks the manner in which we fear the proliferation of meaning … I think that, as our society changes, at the very moment when it is in the process of changing, the author-function will disappear. (from reprint in Lodge, 1988, p. 372)

The disappearance of the author brings about, inevitably, the abolition of quality as a feature of the literary work. Even if we know hardly anything of the author of a work – and here Shakespeare springs to mind – or even if the former is little more than a name on a title page, their total eradication short-circuits any attempt at evaluation. We feel foolish, indeed self-deluded, when affirming that a particular work without a specific human origin is of greater value than another. How can it be "better written" if it was not formulated and executed by a specific individual?

Michael Riffaterre was the first structuralist to examine the full consequences of the demise of the author for literature and the act of reading. With tongue firmly in cheek he invented the terms "Superpoem" and "Superreader." The former is his cold-blooded specification of what sort of work we would be left with if we took seriously the vast fusion of attempts during the twentieth century to define literature, in particular the poem. Aside from Brooks' notion of "paradox" and Empson's various grades of "ambiguity," US based critics, influenced by European linguistics and Formalism, had come up with immensely complex formulae that specified the poetic function as an intrinsic defining element of the text. Harry Levin and Roman Jakobson were the most prominent and influential figures in this field. Riffaterre did not go quite so far as to dispute their findings, but rather he put on display the kind of work, the "Superpoem," that would confront us if all of these formal minutiae were taken into account. In short we would, he contended, be able to comprehend only a tiny percentage of its dense interrelated patterns. It might exist, but only as something that we can understand as we do an ordinance survey map; in parts but nowhere near as a whole. Appreciating the parts and the whole as constituent elements of single moments of enjoyment would be an unreal hypothesis, only conceivable as an all-consuming non-human function created by the world of IT. The principal target of Riffaterre's piece is the practice known as "close reading," instituted by the New Critics as yet another attempt to distinguish serious analysis from the transitory experiences of pleasure and entertainment. Close reading is by its nature an exercise riddled with contradictions and inconsistencies. The poem, or the novel, is turned into a static artefact while the critical scrutineer takes advantage of this immobile space to locate thematic and stylistic patterns that resemble a scene of the crime investigation. Time and movement are frozen to enable the investigator to locate connections between objects and clues, and as Riffaterre demonstrates the entire procedure is a preposterous falsification of what actually happens when we read poems and novels. No one would deny that what Brooks and Empson claim to find in poems are actually there, but a question arises when one considers the kind of attention required for all of their findings to become comprehensible, let alone enjoyable. The author meanwhile has been dispatched even further into the hinterland beyond interpretation, a figure whose qualities as an artist have been side-lined completely by the busy complexities of textual scrutiny.

Barthes picked up where Riffaterre left off with *S/Z* (1970). The subject of his work is, ostensibly, Balzac's novella *Sarrasine* though it gradually becomes evident that he might have chosen a car repair manual or travel guide to Argentina as the target for his exhaustive analysis. In 1970, structuralism was in its heyday as an intellectual powerhouse and Barthes, though still little known in Britain and the United States, was its most esteemed and charismatic practitioner. However, he had come to suspect that it had become an activity overwhelmed by its own seemingly limitless powers of analysis. Everything from advertisements to symphonies could be subjected to all-consuming systems of classification and scrutiny;

existence, it seemed, had been turned into a sequence of predictable indices. Barthes divides *Sarrasine* into 561 irreducible units of prose, which he calls lexies, and goes on to examine how these combine in Balzac's work to produce five categories of effect and response: hermeneutic, semic, symbolic, proairetic, and cultural codes. Each would register with fans and advocates of structuralism as familiar systems of analyzing the world, but such readers would gradually become more uneasy as Barthes leads them into what is promised as a realm of clarity and stratification but turns out to be a labyrinth. Barthes' 561 lexies can comprise anything from a single word to a lengthy series of sentences and he justifies this seemingly random division by claiming that each lexie foregrounds a particular engagement with one or more of his five codes. At the same time he brings his method into question, often by digressing on the kind of reader who might be especially absorbed by the operation of particular codes. Digression number LXXI focuses on lexie 414 in which Sarrasine embraces a castrato in the mistaken belief that he is a woman and Barthes acknowledges that the code in operation here will depend on the disposition and tempera-ment of the reader: one might embody the proairetic (narrative) code and be primarily concerned with what happens next; another might promote the cultural code in their preoccupation with the moment's relation to their own experience of sexuality and its cultural context. Barthes' performance in *S/Z* involves an attempt to overturn the all-consuming claims of struc-turalism, and indeed less ambitious systems of analysis, to a comprehensive understanding of literature and its effects on the reader. As such it has much to recommend it, not least because it allows for the reader to operate capriciously, outside impersonal protocols of interpretation. Yet at the same time he further displaces the author from any role in all of this, and as a consequence the author's skill as a literary craftsman becomes a matter of complete insignificance.

Barthes' hypothetical reader is a projection of a Francocentric myth – an enigmatic and instinctive ideal – and to an extent he acknowledges this. it is the objective of *S/Z* to undermine the expectations of real readers, the vast majority, who enjoy the comforts of predictability. The implica-tions of Barthes' piece are fully explored in a work by a US critic, Stanley Fish: "How to Recognise a Poem when You See One" (1980). Fish describes how, when teaching a course on the religious lyric, he asked his class to interpret a modern lyric chalked on the classroom blackboard. This "text" was actually a list of surnames left over from the previous class on linguistics (to add a sardonic edge the names are those of major US literary-linguists of the 1960s and 1970s):

> Jacobs – Rosenbaum
> Levin
> Thorne
> Hayes
> Ohman (?)

His students demonstrated an apparent literary competence:

> The first line of the poem (the very order of events assumed the already constituted status of the object) received the most attention: Jacobs was explicated as a reference to Jacob's ladder, traditionally allegorized as a figure for the Christian ascent to heaven. In this poem, however, or so my students told me, the means of ascent is not a ladder but a tree, a rose tree or rosenbaum. This was seen as an obvious reference to the Virgin Mary who was often characterized as a rose without thorns, itself an emblem of the immaculate conception. (Fish, 1980, p. 324)

Fish's description of their analysis continues for a further 500 words. This experiment, which Fish claims to have performed with similar results in "9 or 10 universities in 3 countries," supports his claim that "acts of recognition, rather than being triggered by formal characteristics, are their source" (Fish, 1980, p. 326).

Fish's thesis is that his students have been programmed to interpret the tensions and paradoxes allegedly inherent in verse but that this procedure is in truth something that they impose upon the text once key signals – specifically line divisions – prompt them to accept that what they encounter is a poem.

His exercise is sardonic, almost convincing, yet it is also deeply fraudulent. He informs them that the text on the blackboard is a poem and its typographic structure might indeed invite comparisons with more radical pieces by Cyd Corman, Robert Creeley, even e.e. cummings. What he does not do, however, is to ask them to express an opinion upon this "poem", that is, to offer an account of what the poet is attempting to achieve and an evaluation of his/her success. Had he done so it is possible – given his students' self-evident familiarity with modernist technique and its offshoots – that someone might well have contended that the anonymous blackboard poet was clearly inferior to a figure such as William Carlos Williams. What had this person achieved by abandoning anything resembling syntax when Williams, in pieces such as "Spring and All", had shown how to challenge the regularities of syntax and line structure by making use of them radically and not by leaving them out? This might well have prompted another of Fish's precocious charges to wonder how anyone might enjoy, admire, or even be stimulated by a "poem" that apparently required not even linguistic, let alone creative, competence to write. Warming to this theme another might suggest that they go through the New York telephone directory, throw it in the air several times, and on each occasion select at random a surname from the opened page. It is likely, they could aver, that in six "lines" one could assemble a richly laden trajectory of social, ethnic, cultural, and religious reference points. But if anyone can do this, is the resulting text worthy of being called a "poem?"

We will never know why Fish did not invite his students to go beyond recognition and cold interpretation to evaluation but there is a good deal of circumstantial evidence to allow for conjecture. Literary Theory in this period did not allow for evaluation. Its prevailing doctrine was that poetry is one of many discourses and that its claim to aesthetic pre-eminence is a delusion: therefore how could one literary text be aesthetically superior to another if the independence of poetry as an art form was itself a bourgeois fantasy.

Terry Eagleton in *Literary Theory: An Introduction* contends that the ideal of separating poetry from other modes of expression, defining it, leads to a dangerously apolitical brand of literary criticism. The textualist notion of poetic style as nonpragmatic, self-referential language causes us to detach the literary text from the real world of political and ideological discourse. A pre-occupation with aesthetics prevents us from recognizing that what we might value as good verse is effectively a reflection of the ideological prejudices and preconditions of a particular society or period. He states: "Literature, in the sense of a set of works of assured and endurable values, distinguished by certain shared inherent properties, does not exist" (Eagleton, 1983, p. 11).

Eagleton goes about proving its nonexistence by employing the same teleology as Fish: by "disclosing" intrinsically poetic features of language in texts that are self-evidently nonpoetic. In one instance he fixes upon the Formalist notion of estrangement as elicited by language that is perversely unusual, specifically the effects of ambiguity or paradox which Empson and Brooks, respectively, identified as the persistent defining features of verse.

Consider a prosaic, quite unambiguous statement like the one sometimes seen in the London underground system: "Dogs must be carried on the escalator." This is not perhaps quite an unambiguous as it seems at first sight: does it mean that you *must* carry a dog on the escalator? Are you likely to be banned from the escalator unless you can find some stray mongrel to clutch in your arms on the way up? Many apparently straightforward notices contain such ambiguities: "Refuse to be put in this basket," for instance, or the British road-sign "Way Out" as read by a Californian. But even leaving such troubling ambiguities aside, it is surely obvious that the underground notice could be read as literature … Imagine a late-night drunk doubled over the escalator handrail who reads the notice with laborious attentiveness for several minutes and then mutters to himself "How true!" What kind of mistake is occurring here? What the drunk is doing, in fact, is taking the sign as some statement of general, even cosmic significance. By applying certain conventions of reading to its words, he prises them loose from their immediate context and generalizes them beyond their pragmatic purpose to something of wider and probably deeper import.

His thesis is as flawed, and as calculatedly fraudulent, as Fish's. Certainly one might "find" effects and devices customarily ranked as poetic almost anywhere, but the fact that they are notable for their rarity, exceptions to the general condition of nonpoetic writing, testifies to their status as accidents or curiosities. In poems they form a consistent element of the stylistic fabric of the text, something deliberately and calculatedly fashioned by the poet and which distinguishes the poem from the sphere of nonpoetic discourse. Unwittingly, Eagleton's invention of a drunken close reader undermines both his own and Fish's arguments. In both instances the reader is a faintly absurd hypothesis. Fish's students are erudite, commendably articulate versions of Pavlov's dogs while Eagleton's drunk is, one assumes, someone no longer able to discriminate between something that was intended as a literary text and a sign on the underground. This raises the question of why neither of these theorists themselves admits to being unable to distinguish "real" poetry from accidents or randomly assembled groups of words. If, as they contend, poetry is to a large extent a construction of the sociocultural conditions in which it is apprehended then where does this leave professors of English? They seem intent upon rejecting their predecessors' maxim that poetry is definable and recognizable in terms of its intrinsic features yet they appear equally reluctant to place themselves in the position of the hypothetical readers of their exercises who are incapable of making a rational distinction between what is and what is not poetry.

The exercises undertaken by Culler, Fish, and Eagleton became, during the 1970s and 1980s, the equivalent of a fraternal nod of recognition; an acknowledgement of shared affiliation to a new program of perceiving and classifying poetry. Along with his "interpretation" of a piece of prose as the equivalent of a close-reading of a sonnet, Jonathan Culler redrafted a sentence from W.V. Quine's philosophical treatise *From a Logical Point of View* as a free verse poem to show how the iconic foregrounding of words gives the – false – impression that "intrinsic irony or paradox," characteristically poetic features, are its presiding template. Hence: "We are dealing less with a property of language than with a strategy of reading" (Culler, 1975, p. 163). Veronica Forrest-Thompson (1978) redrafted a *Times* leader article on the new chairman of the BBC as a Poundian lyric and interpreted it accordingly. Hawkes (1977, pp. 139–140), reversed this procedure, albeit with the same objective, and repeated Culler's submission that William Carlos Williams's "This is Just To Say" has only been interpreted as a poem because critics are prompted to impose such readings in response to its shape and the prestigious status of its author. I deal in detail with this last poem in Chapter 6 but at this point it is enough to observe that the critics who make use of it to bolster their thesis that literature in abstract definable terms does not exist have deliberately anesthetized themselves to any notion of pleasure or for that matter distaste. By a bizarre twist of logic, they have, in order to promote the notion of interpretation above an autonomous author and text, extinguished themselves as intelligent interpreters.

Moreover, each of these theorists projects their strategies of reading onto putative figures who are, if not quite as tangible as the students or the drunk, certainly not the theorists themselves. Again, this enables the theorist to operate in a vacuum, or to be more accurate from a position of omniscient security: better informed than their delusional predecessors but at the same time able to stand outside the deluge of competing discourses which denies poetry the right, as Eagleton puts it, to "exist."

The premise upon which these exercises were based is now accepted dogma, never challenged, and this is both a disgrace to the academic profession and a disaster for its prospects. Fish's point in his comment that he has tried his same experiment in at least nine universities, with the same results from his Pavlovian charges, is that cultural registers per se are programmed by a collective consensus of expectations and have nothing to do with the intrinsic qualities of the object. In truth, he showed himself either incapable or unwilling to allow his students to think for themselves.

I have asked my own students to perform similar exercises, insisting that they not only conduct a dry critical analysis – based upon their encounters with other similarly costive and oblique modernist pieces – but also that they incorporate comments on the quality of the work and express their opinions on the accomplishments of the poet. I have used early examples of the work of that acclaimed practitioner of the Westernized haiku, E.J. Thribb, resident versifier of *Private Eye* (having checked in advance that none of the group are readers of *Private Eye* – a confirmation that saddened me greatly), a free verse piece enjambed and shaped by myself with the words borrowed from an article on truffles in a magazine belonging to my wife, and a classic early William Carlos Williams poem which I calculated and hoped that none of them had previously encountered. We talked of how small temperamental fissures could be discerned in the cutting or the isolation of a phrase, of how the language shaped its own poetic currency, province, and its particular emotional domain: this bespoke something unique and special – a combination of the poet's private register with his consummate skill as an artist. I should add that this was the response to the poem by Williams. The E.J. Thribb piece and the redistributed sentences from the article on truffles were dismissed as "crap," "infantile," "self-caricature," and "laughably incompetent."

I would not go as far as to argue that my students are intellectually superior to Fish's or the putative victims of Eagleton's and Culler's dogma but I would claim that Theory exercises a dreadful stranglehold upon English Studies. Its presence discourages the expression of opinion on the quality, even the enjoyability, of works. I encouraged them to open up. Being asked to evaluate literary art, to identify and estimate its qualities, means that you are obliged to conduct a private exercise; self-scrutiny. If after hours of close reading you can recognize that one poet is a genius and another a buffoon then you can move to the next stage, take a step back and look at how such judgments are made. They are your judgments and estimations but will you stand by them, defend them against opposing views? If you can, you are on the way to achieving some kind of balance between the quixotic preserve of individuality and the forum of argument and debate where subjectivity must be balanced against a system governed by abstract rules and conventions. Distinguishing good writing from rubbish – an activity outlawed by Theory – is in truth the keystone to English Studies' claim upon relevance.

At the 2005 annual conference of the Modern Languages Association of America, playwright and novelist, Ariel Dorfman, offered a beguiling paper, based, he claimed, on personal experience. He told of how CIA agents had recently detained him in a windowless room in Washington DC airport. One of his interrogators, the silent one, bore a disturbing resemblance to Trotsky, while the other, more loquacious, agent tortured him with endless questions and accusations designed to at once depress and unsettle him. Dorfman quoted from memory the interrogator's verbal assaults, comprising the kind of syntactic contusions and lexical hieroglyphics made fashionable by the likes of Derrida, Lacan, Lyotard, Foucault, Irigaray, and their like, and taken on as a routine critical dialect by many literary academics in the United States and the United Kingdom. Disturbingly, most of Dorfman's audience failed to appreciate the joke and appeared confused by being offered a discourse that they recognized as their own within a most unusual context. The darkly comic image of intellectual inaccessibility allied with isolation from the world at large seemed beyond their comprehension.

Dorfman was not just playing games. His escape from Pinochet's Chile, under fear of imprisonment, and his grandparents' experience of the European pogroms testify to his commitment to the duty of writers as witnesses to the actualities of the world in which they live. What irritated him and prompted him to deliver his lecture was the apparent disjunction between the extensive fabric of what we might term literary culture – comprising writers, reader, publishers, and so on – and the institutions, universities, wherein literature is studied intensively. He later commented that what shocked and depressed him most was the fact that he had become the victim of his own politically charged game of subterfuge. After being pursued through his hotel by academics and graduate students who seemed in a state of near nervous breakdown he gave up trying to lighten the mood in explaining that he had put on an act, and retreated to his room. There he pondered the unedifying fact that the professionals committed to discussing the kind of work he produced appeared to exist in a different universe. He was prepared for the occasional bad review of his fiction or the tangible mood of disdain that sometimes spreads through a theater audience but it seemed that academics had removed themselves completely from the realm where opinions might be expressed. He had encountered, in real life, embodiments of the brand of Theory promulgated in the work of Eagleton, Culler, and Hawkes, figures whose solipsistic preoccupations had nothing to do with making genuine judgments on authors and books.

The lexicon, mannerisms, and intellectual hauteur of literary theory are now endemic features of the critical writing of all but a small minority of academics. As a quasi-discipline in its own right Theory has some things to recommend it – challenging as it does routine preconceptions regarding issues such as identity, language, race, and gender – but at the same time its own preoccupations have effectively alienated it both from its alleged subject, literature, and the body of individuals who are that subject's lifeblood, intelligent ordinary readers.

Caught somewhere in the middle is the hapless undergraduate, often seduced by the thrills of Theory and its albeit somewhat shop-soiled reputation as a hive of radicalism – virtually all of it is now standardized and dogmatic – yet puzzled by what exactly it has to do with the rest of their degree, let alone their personal inclinations as readers and their prospects as graduates. English as a university subject has never had much of a reputation as a discipline that encourages intellectual, let alone evaluative, endeavor but since the arrival of Theory we now seem committed to suffocating opinion even as a reflex. The first book to call itself *After Theory* (by Thomas Docherty) appeared as early as 1990, with Eagleton following with a piece carrying the same name in 2004 and many more working some reference to cessation into their titles (such as *Life.After.Theory* and *The Novel After Theory*). Rarely can the world of academic publishing have been bombarded with so many misnomers. As each of these tomes reveals, their authors are not reflecting on the death of Theory. Their true preoccupation is a blend of faux disappointment and poorly disguised ambition. None dispute the overall benefits of Theory per se; what they are trying to do is to aggrandize a particular, and refreshed, element of it above all others – usually that upon which they have built their reputation. "After" can be read as "new prospects for me" – reformulated Marxist, post New Historicist, Queer Theorist, Radical Green Theorist, and so on. What endures from the heyday of Theory is a determination to extinguish literature as a recognizable and different art form and the author as the person exclusively responsible for the qualities and flaws of the book. To allow either back into the forum of criticism would license the validity of concepts such as literary autonomy and aesthetic quality in an activity that has for some time treated them as an irrelevance.

The most depressing aspect of the PMLA farce was its illustration of how ideologically inflexible Theory had become. Evidently no one was capable of accepting Dorfman's image of CIA foot soldiers – no doubt to a man agents of the neocon hegemony – using as blind noise a discourse that they recognized and had come to treat with intuitive sympathy; suddenly Derrida et al. were presented as architects of a dreadful extension of waterboarding in which the brain is bombarded by a string of limitless, densely packed units of gibberish. It many ways it was inevitable that Dorfman's delegates should blind themselves to the irony of his exercise. They themselves had become the mirror image of the horrible brainwashers he depicted in his story, which returns us to the ghastly consequences of the enduring influence of Theory in universities. Does it matter that most academics now deliver papers and write books that most intelligent people regard as incomprehensible? This question too carries a good deal of, albeit unintended, irony given that higher education, particularly in the United Kingdom, is becoming more and more a privatized degree showroom, with a well-paid vocational outcome the principal attraction. Perhaps prospective English graduates have ambitions to become journalists. If so they might read those media dons who grab space in the weeklies. All are hypocrites who attempt with varying degrees of success to write normal prose, in which books and authors are referred to as though they exist, for the general reader. Thus, we have the image of the English graduate as a bipolar individual; either thrust into the real world with a rapidly growing awareness that what they have had to endure is an imbecilic ritual, or sucked back into the system as graduate students, with any suspicion that Theory might be irrelevant to their research stifled at the outset. Regarding this last: I write having just scrutinized the introductory courses for a postgraduate degree in English at a UK institution. Theory is all pervasive, like some North Korean version of post-Maoism. The running subtext is: don't even *think* about evaluation.

Two years before Dorfman's "joke" incident Alan Sockal and Jean Bricmont published *Intellectual Impostures* (2003), a scathing revelation of their fellow cultural theorists – including all of the second generation, from Derrida to Lyotard – as fraudsters, figures who had built global reputations on their hiding of fatuities and contradictions beneath jargon. They were inspired, in part, by Andrew C. Bulhak of Monash University who in the late 1990s created a computer program that recycled key terms and syntactic structures from a mainframe of poststructuralist writings, a procedure that mimicked a sequence while at the same time revealing it as random and incoherent. All of this is in itself instructive but it is even more intriguing to consider the parallels between key aspects of the avant-garde – Dadaist verse, Dylan Thomas's fondly treasured incoherence, and Stein's fiction, for example – and the mesmerizing illusions of high Theory. In both instances we are caught in a treble bluff: we pride ourselves on our appreciation of what is nonsense; we blind ourselves to its status as nonsense; we are unwilling or unable to accept that little effort has been involved in its construction. Once more, evaluation is the principal victim. Most significantly, the experiment showed that if you are prepared to hide within a discourse that is essentially meaningless and consequently incomprehensible to other, normal, human beings, your own sense of discrimination, your skill as an evaluator, is diminished almost to the point of zero.

Out of respect for the long-deceased Author, and their work, I feel I should make it clear that both were despatched to the interpretive afterlife by two groups of executioners. In Britain the vast majority of those who became advocates for Theory in the 1960s and 1970s saw it as a vehicle for their radical, generally left wing political affiliations. The LTP (Literature Teaching Politics), for example, was formed in the early 1980s as an inter-campus focus group which concentrated on how the political principles of most of its members could be harnessed to a somewhat chaotic influx of new ideas from Continental Europe. Similar groups from around the same period included NETWORK (feminist and women only), Oxford English Limited (with "Limited" referring to the state of the English Faculty curriculum), the Marxist Feminist Literature Collective, and the Association of Cultural Studies. John Barrell (Sussex), Catherine Belsey and Terry Hawkes (Cardiff), Nicole Ward Jouve (York), Lisa Jardine and Jacqueline Rose (London), Janet Todd (East Anglia), Antony Easthope (Manchester Metropolitan), Peter Widdowson (Middlesex), Raman Selden (Sunderland), and of course Terry Eagleton (then Oxford), amongst many others, organized conferences, set up undergraduate courses, and published student-targeted books. All groups and individuals shared the same objective: how to fashion a radically left wing plan for English Studies from the medley of theses formed during the previous 80 years across the channel. And all reached a similar conclusion: focus on theories that in various ways subsume subjectivity and individuality beneath systems and all-inclusive concepts. "Literature" could then be treated as one of many launch pads for the study of more significant issues such as ideology and politics. None of them offered any original ideas; they made do with politicized versions of Barthes, Derrida, and others desperately retuned to suit a specific ideological agenda. Essentially, the British branch of Theory was made up of intellectual egotists posing as left wing agitators. Their successors – circa 2015 – find themselves with an infrastructure of practices, ideas, and forms of writing that are useless and, especially for the non-academic, alienating, but too deeply entrenched to permit for serious criticism.

In the United States, Theory developed rather differently. The following is an example of American Theory in its heyday; deconstruction employed by one of its most esteemed evangelists, J. Hillis Miller.

It is possible to distinguish chains of connection which are material elements in the text, like the real things; or metaphors, like the figures of grafting or of writing; or covert, often etymological associations, like the connection of grafting with writing or cutting; or thematic elements like sexuality or murder; or conceptual elements, like the question of cause or the theory of history; or quasi-mythological elements, like the association of Tess with the harvest or the personification of the sun as a benign god. None of these claims has priority over the others as the true explanation of the meaning of the novel ... Taken together, the elements form a system of mutually defining motifs, each of which exists as in relation to the others. The reader must execute a lateral dance of interpretation to explicate any given passage, without ever reaching, in this sideways movement, a passage which is chief, original, or originating; a sovereign principle of explanation. The meaning, rather, is suspended within the interaction among the elements. It is immanent rather than transcendent ... This does not exempt the reader from seeking answers to the question of why Tess is compelled to repeat herself and others and then suffer through those repetitions. The answers, rather, must lie in the sequence itself. (Hillis Miller, 1982, pp. 126–127)

Commendably, Hillis Miller is rather light with the gibberish and abstruse vocabulary that has clogged most Theory-infused writing since the 1980s – perhaps an Ivy League background is difficult to shrug off – but nonetheless he does a magnificent job of dumbfounding the hapless reader who expects him to say something about Hardy's novel, let alone comment on its qualities. Deconstruction is the top of the range intellectual counterpart to *fin de siècle* cultural decadence: a license to fondle ideas, enjoy their corrupt vacuousness, and then lounge in dissipated contemplation of nothing very much. Which is fine, for those paid and disposed to enjoy such opportunities, but in truth – and this was Dorfman's shrewd subtext – there is and always has been a disturbing similarity between Theory and those brands of thinking and writing that are in their manner elitist and impenetrable and in their character totalitarian.

Paul de Man has called attention to the closing line of Yeats's "Among School Children": "How can we know the dancer from the dance?" De Man argued that practically all readings perceive this as a figurative or rhetorical question. We already know that we cannot distinguish dancer from dance; this playful inter-animation of object and experience is the central theme of the poem. He went on to argue that it is just as valid to regard this question as literal and non-figurative:

In which the final line is read literally as meaning that, since the dancer and the dance are not the same, it might be useful, perhaps even desperately necessary – for the question can be given a ring of urgency, "Please tell me, how *can* I know the dancer from the dance" – to tell them apart. (de Man, 1979, p. 12)

De Man argues that either interpretation – figurative or literal – involves a procedure that brings the poem into line with what we think it is trying to do. Instead of choosing one or the other, he urges us to accept that both are vital to a proper critical engagement with the text: in Derrida's terms an acknowledgement that neither we nor the poet can "command" the text's shifts between an apparent desire for an answer and its implications that an answer is inappropriate, unnecessary, or impossible.

Does this mean that deconstructive criticism should simply respond to, perhaps rejoice in, the indecipherable complexities of the poem? Geoffrey Hartman (1980), a deconstructor, seems to think so: "literary commentary may cross the line and become as demanding as literature: it is an unpredictable or unstable genre that cannot be subordinated, a priori, to its referential or commentating function."

The critics who seized upon deconstruction as a literary critical strategy in the 1960s and 1970s (notably Geoffrey Hartman, J. Hillis Miller, and Paul de Man) saw it as offering a new, untested avenue for literary studies. For the New Critics, the process of bringing literary criticism into line with the more respectable disciplines of the social sciences and humanities had involved a difficult and apparently unresolvable conflict between treating poetry as one of the many historical, political, or philosophic discourses and maintaining that it is intrinsically different from all these. Deconstruction offered the possibility of doing both: interpreting literature, particularly poetry, as a nexus, a forum of tensions between what we seem or want to know, and the means (language) by which we investigate, disseminate, and celebrate this knowledge. This is Hartman on "indeterminacy":

> Indeterminacy does not merely *delay* the determination of meaning, that is, suspend premature judgements and allow greater thoughtfulness. The delay is not … [merely] a device to slow the act of reading till we appreciate … its complexity. The delay is intrinsic: from a certain point of view, it is thoughtfulness itself, Keats's "negative capability", a labor that aims not to overcome the … indeterminate but to stay within it as long as is necessary. (Hartman, 1980, p. 270)

The reason for the enthusiastic annexation of deconstruction by a generation of US literary academics who had inherited the grand but rather untidy legacy of New Criticism is indicated in Hartman's term "thoughtfulness itself." He perceives poems, very conventionally, as the record or trace of a "process" of mediation. All other discourses are shackled to the collateral objective of making sense of their subject or, at a more complex level, reaching some conclusion as to its state. Poetry, according to Hartman, "labor[s] ... not to overcome the ... indeterminate." The critic should not attempt to resolve the ambiguities and uncertainties of the poem or propose an answer to the questions raised by it; they should instead become one half of a dialogic relationship with the poem's irresolvable state of indeterminancy. On the face of things the intellectually detached mood of the deconstructionists had little in common with the politically inspired gallery of largely UK based theorists, yet there is a crucial and depressing similarity between them. The former are so preoccupied with the activity of criticism that they rule out such crude and vulgar correlates as reaching any kind of conclusion on whether the text is any good. The notion of "naturalization" – specifically using criticism to translate a self-consciously complex literary work into evaluative language – is regarded as graceless and boorish. It is, they argue, the *process* of involving oneself with the text's uncertainties that makes criticism and indeed literature worthy activities. It has, as I have stated, an air of the *fin de siècle*, art-for-arts sake era about it, but this is misleading. The more often one reads de Man's solemn musings on Yeats's closing line the more we wonder if the former has lost his sense of proportion. In these words Yeats casts an intriguing glance on how the lazy routines of language can undermine our sense of a straightforward match between what is said and what is seen. But do they merit the status granted to them by de Man as a nexus of interpretive, even philosophic issues? A curmudgeonly reader might take Yeats's enquiry at face value and come up with an answer, such as: "Wait until the dance stops (it can't go on for ever). The dancer will still be present but the dance will no longer exist. That's how to tell the difference." Of course, de Man, or even the average comprehensive school teacher, would probably treat such a respondent as a philistine, an intellectual vandal who shows insufficient respect for one of our classic poems. But such would be a knee jerk reaction, because neither would pause to consider why it is so easy to come up with a literal solution to Yeats's existential dilemma. In my view "Among School Children" is a vastly overrated poem, a vehicle for poorly disguised self-regard and intellectual solipsism. As the "sixty year old smiling public man," makes his way through the class of children (note "public"; surely ordinary infants recognize me, he seems to say) he carefully tops up his lexicon of conceits with very bare, rudimentary images, perhaps just to show that he too is of the people. And then he turns these into metaphors and compressed philosophical issues that attempt to be profound in an ordinary way but often come across as fatuous and simplistic, and he completes this exercise with the much quoted final line. This is of course my own opinion, with which you are entitled to disagree vehemently. My point is that de Man short-circuits such evaluative opportunities. He involves himself in an "indeterminate" engagement with the poem and while he does not soil the delights of this experience by drawing a conclusion from Yeats's piece he takes it for granted that the poem is of a sufficiently elevated aesthetic and intellectual status to merit his attention. And he does so without commenting on how or why it has attained this status. The same can be said of Hillis Miller, Hartman, and the rest in their deconstructive enterprises. Like the politicized Theorists – though for different reasons – they disconnect the activity of criticism from the sense of a triangular encounter between reader, text, and writer, one that involves a continuous questioning by the reader of whether what the writer has done is any good.

There are close parallels between Hartman's notion of criticism and J. Hillis Miller's "The Critic as Host" (1995):

> Take, for example, Shelley's "The Triumph of Life." It is inhabited, as its critics have shown, by a long chain of parasitical presences, echoes, allusions, guests, ghosts of previous texts. These are present within the domicile of the poem in that curious phantasmal way, affirmed, negated, sublimated, twisted, straightened out, travestied, which Harold Bloom has begun to study and which it is one major task of literary interpretation today to investigate further and to define. The previous text is both the ground of the new one and something the new poem must annihilate by incorporating it, turning it into ghostly insubstantiality, so that it may perform its possible-impossible task of becoming its own ground. The new poem both needs the old texts and must destroy them. It is both parasitical on them, feeding ungraciously on their substance, and at the same time it is the sinister host which unmans them by inviting them into its home, as the Green Knight invites Gawain. Each previous link in the chain, in its turn, played the same role, as host and parasite, in relation to its predecessors. From the Old to the New Testament, from Wordsworth and Coleridge, the chain leads ultimately to "The Triumph of Life." That poem, in its turn, or Shelley's work generally, is present within the work of Hardy or Yeats or Stevens and forms part of a sequence in the major texts of Romantic nihilism including Nietzsche, Freud, Heidegger, and Blanchot, in a perpetual re-expression of the relation of host and parasite which forms itself again today in current criticism. It is present, for example, in the relation between "univocal" and "deconstruc-tionist" readings of "The Abrams" reading of "The Triumph of Life" and the

one I have implicitly proposed here, or, in a perhaps more problematic way, between Harold Bloom and Jacques Derrida, or between Jacques Derrida and Paul de Man, or within the work of each one of these critics taken separately. (Lodge and Wood, 2008, p. 408)

This goes some way to explain the premise upon which de Man and others treat the actual text and its author as irrelevances in comparison with the procedure of deconstructive/poststructuralist reading. The critic, along with presences such as Heidegger and Freud, are "links in a chain." Certainly many individuals, indeed literary authors, are mentioned by name but it is clear that this is a matter of economy and convenience; they exist by virtue of the text that might well bear their name but beyond that they are of no significance. The activity of writing, literary, nonliterary and critical, involves only the interactive relationship between texts themselves. All of this begs the question of how and why Wordsworth, Coleridge, Hardy, Stevens, and so on – or to be more accurate their textual proxies – deserve their place on the chain. Who put them there and on what criteria? Which raises another question. If, as the deconstructionists insist, matters such as the evaluation of literature and by implication its status as an art form are irrelevant, why did not Hillis Miller include as "links in the chain" a 1956 Hotpoint washing machine service manual or the scribblings from a semi-literate 8-year-old's primary school workbook?

The presiding mantra of deconstruction is the denial to the reader of any hope that a particular interpretation of the literary work will predominate and therefore enable them to admire the act of crafts-manship undertaken by a given author. Aside from its contribution to self-indulgence and inaccessibility deconstruction was determined to undermine anything that resembled an evaluative faculty, whether grounded only in instinct or supplemented by erudition. Certainly, the history of Theory has seen occasional clashes between its branches that might suggest a healthy indulgence of dissent. During the 1980s for example, the deconstructive purists of the high-powered US Ivy League institutions had an amusing set-to with the emerging so-called New Historicists, who seemed to aver that the sociohistorical contexts of literary and other texts might, just, be discernable entities. But these were sideshows, distractions from an overarching unity of purpose that has suffocated all aberrations. I'll give this a name: cultural relativism. Irrespective of the seemingly inherent disparities within Theory – and the Queer Theorists, the poststructuralists, the feminists, and the Marxists and such newcomers as the ecotheorists sometimes appear to have little in common – a single, common agenda unites it: an utter contempt for the idea that a particular piece of writing or a writer might be superior to others.

We have already considered Greenblatt's studied indifference to the distinction between verse and prose in Shakespeare and it should be noted that verse features only in the margins of groundbreaking New Historicist writings, which causes one to suspect that they, by this omission, recognize that a discourse so belligerently different from all others in its character and with no given function will, at the very least, prove to be a subversive aberration from their notion of textual interdependence; its peculiarity proclaims its autonomy. This suspicion is borne out in Bennett and Royle's lauded, student-targeted *An Introduction to Literature, Criticism and Theory* (1995), in which the authors embark upon a New Historicist interpretation of Wordsworth's "Alice Fell, or Poverty." As they point out, a poem whose ostensible subject is poverty and deprivation invites comparison with con- temporaneous texts that deal with related topics, such as Adam Smith's *The Wealth of Nations* (1776), and, at a more impressionistic level, they consider a passage from Wordsworth's sister Dorothy's journal in which she offers what we can assume to be an authentic account of the dire, impecunious condition of a real woman called Alice Fell. This "join the dots" exercise, where correspondences are located between the poem and other discourses, is fascinating, but it skews a number of New Historicist claims. What we are offered is a conventional, biographical, and empirical account of how Wordsworth's poem might well have borrowed details from a real experience and an equally orthodox comparison between the way the poet Wordsworth deals with economic inequality and its treatment by political philosophers such as Smith. Bennett and Royle undo their own exercise and, unwittingly, the branch of Theory, New Historicism, they are attempting to illustrate and defend. They move, with confident agility, between the three texts – Wordsworth's, Dorothy's, and Smith's – without even considering that poetry is not simply another discourse but rather one governed by arbitrary conventions in which the responsibilities to notions of truth or sincerity, perceived or privately intuited, which inform Dorothy's journal and Smith's pamphlet, no longer obtain.

For all their apparent differences, deconstruction and New Historicism have something fundamental in common. For each, the author, as a real figure with talent and a sense of artistic purpose, is absorbed into various impersonal notions of discourse and intertextuality. Discrimination, an inclination to rank an author or a work as in some way superior to another is abolished. As I have already stated this has created the somewhat bizarre situation whereby Theory is ever present in academia but incompatible with anything resembling a workable schedule for the appreciation of literature. The influence of Theory among academics has destroyed, or at best shackled, any inclination to discuss with students matters such as value, skill, talent, or beauty. Read reviews and review articles in the best broadsheets and weeklies and you will find writers who, when encountering something worthy of celebration or disdain, will raise their game stylistically and intellectually, recognize that when making such judgments, criteria have to be both established and practiced. The ultimate question, "Is this any good?" is attended by the correlative demand: I must show that I am good enough to make such an assessment. To indicate how far the universities have distanced themselves from the real world of books and readers try to find a similar ordinance of demands either acknowledged or practiced in a piece of academic writing. You will not.

The New Critics and the Formalists are the poor relations of Theory; treated with varying degrees of condescension and indulgence but in general ostracized because they committed the cardinal offense of attempting to define literature, to specify how it differs from all other uses of language and types of representation. This was unpardonable because once the rules of the game generally known as literary writing are established it might be possible to pass judgment on how well, or otherwise, it is played. And the idea of innate superiority or inadequacy was anathema, albeit for different ideological reasons, to all branches of post-1960s Theory.

The connection between cultural relativism and the politics of post-1970s academia, particularly in the arts, is self-evident: the instinct and practice that prompts us to rank some literary works as superior to others corresponds with the dreadful ideologies of class, race, and gender discrimination, and in this regard Theory is not just self-indulgent gibberish. It is dangerous. Until we re-establish an agenda that acknowledges that literature is intrinsically different from pop music, soap opera, and the sign systems of advertising, recognize its cultural superiority and begin to apply judgmental criteria to different literary works, then English studies will continue to play its part in the maintenance of an all-encompassing inflexible dogma which forbids the affirmation that some cultures, beliefs, social systems are intrinsically preferable, superior, to others.

I recall listening to coverage of the twentieth anniversary of the Enniskillen Remembrance Day bombing on the *Today Programme* on Radio 4. In November 1987 the IRA murdered 11 people who were attending the wreath-laying ceremony in Enniskillen to commemorate the dead of, mostly, the two world wars. On the anniversary the BBC interviewed an academic – humanities based – who contended that the Enniskillen bomb would be differently interpreted, be subject to the various ideologies and narratives that make up the various perceptions of the Troubles. In 2007 the latter could be confidently consigned to the past tense. Aside from the activities of a few recalcitrant psychopaths of both traditions mainstream terrorists had retired and become part of the political infrastructure.

It goes without saying that the subject of his discussion had little in common with literature, but there is a remarkable similarity between the structure of his argument and that of legions of literary theorists. The text, or in the case of Enniskillen the act, is subordinate, a dependent, mutating subject of a fabric of hermeneutic perceptions and states of mind. Stephen Greenblatt has built a successful academic career upon replacing the notion of plays as particular works of art created by specific authors with the captivating idea of social energy constantly circulating; nothing is fixed or certain and all is subject to a dynamic of competing forces. This is part of the fashion parade of contemporary literary Theory, labyrinthine but generally harmless. However, the logic – if such activities can be dignified by such a term – of his writing has now permeated the world in which bombs, not plays, are debated. It is relativism at work, apparently unchallenged as the model for how society operates and how people think. The academic interviewed by Radio 4 presented the Enniskillen bombing, Greenblatt style, as something indeterminate and fluid. He did not doubt that it had occurred – and nor did Greenblatt question the fact that plays were performed – but he questioned its essential *difference*. Instead he argued that its nature, the motive behind it and the emotional registers that it stirred, were flexible, subject to Ireland's complex ideological fabric, the constantly circulating energy of tribalism. The relatives of the victims must have felt greatly consoled.

What he did not do was to venture an opinion on whether the people murdered were more or less deserving of their fate than others who have died over the past 40 years – some killed when assembling their own explosive devices, for example. The parallel between Greenblatt's model of Renaissance culture and society and the formula with which academia and other branches of the intelligentsia frame the Troubles is striking and unsettling. As I write, another clash between act and interpretation has shown how Theory plays a part in the way that many of us think. The individuals who murdered journalists and police at the Paris offices of *Charlie Hebdo* magazine and customers in a nearby kosher supermarket were unambiguous regarding their motives and, as they saw it, the justification for their actions. They were exacting revenge against those who had disparaged Mohammed in images or acted against his superiority by their mere existence (in this last case, Jews, Judaism, and the State of Israel). Religious and political spokespersons of all kinds denounced these acts and their perpetrators, and all accompanied their condemnations with codicils. The general opinion was: they were not acting on behalf of true Islam. The question of what true Islam amounts to was left open, though there is an unspoken consensus: it is exemplified by Muslims who have reconciled their religious affiliation with the liberal, indulgent mood of free expression that prevails in most Western democracies. Few would deny that such persons exist but the notion of all non-violent Muslims as embodying this ideal is questionable to say the least.

The vast majority of Muslims in non-Islamic states did not openly endorse the Paris killers but there is a gray area between endorsement and empathy: all spokesmen for the Muslim faith made it clear, and expected others to accept, that the creation of images of the Prophet amounted to a criminal offense, or it would do if Sharia law were in place. The only major UK figure to suggest that Islam per se is retrogressive, inflexible, and incompatible with largely secular liberal societies was fully aware that he was an outsider, the only one willing to speak his mind, and while he did not expect his opinions to be accepted without dispute he offered an explanation for his isolation as the public spokesman for views that many others shared: multiculturalism. Multiculturalism evolved from the expansion of Humanities and Social Sciences in UK universities from the 1960s onwards and has since become a fundamental tenet of political discourse and policy. Its relationship with Theory is self-evident: it is the political and ideological embodiment of cultural relativism. No set of beliefs or practices should be treated as superior, or inferior, to others – despite the fact that some religious and behavioral ordinances might be seen by many as primitive, even tyrannical.

The mantra seems to be: stand back and contemplate this fascinating assembly of forces – cultural, historical, visceral, but do not dare make judgments of your own. The prohibition against evaluation within literary studies is a collateral result of the more powerful ideological embargo on the treatment of poems, plays, and novels as an independent stratum of language. It might seem perverse to compare this calamity of academe with the acts of murderous fanatics. Structuralism and poststructuralism did not foment terrorism, inadvertently or otherwise, yet the dialogues that follow terrorist acts in developed Western societies are riven with the same ideological inhibitions and conjugates that disallow the making of decisions on significance and value in university Arts faculties. Theory entraps; it claims to offer unfettered radicalism while chaining its converts to an inflexible regime of what can and cannot be thought and said. The intellectual mechanism that eradicates discernment and evaluation from our encounters with cultural objects is identical to that which excludes moral judgment from political killing. It is almost as though the act of laying a bomb at a war memorial, shooting cartoonists who dare to depict the Prophet, or issuing a death sentence against those who depict the latter in a novel (see Chapter 8) have now become the equivalent of a textual gesture; all part of an interpretive fabric from which such simplistic notions of guilt, responsibility, and unalloyed hatred have been dispatched to the hungry maw of sign systems and ideological apparatuses. We are forbidden from telescoping blame from the murderers themselves to the communities and ideals they claim to represent. That would involve judgment and as a consequence discrimination – the presentation, if only by implication, of some beliefs and cultures as superior to others. The person who feels that we should no longer indulge the practices of, say, religions that seem to them intrinsically authoritarian faces the same problem as the undergraduate who regards the prescribed author as self-indulgent and overrated. Both are effectively prevented from testing their opinions: the notion of "discrimination" as involving prejudice and subordination has swallowed up its other designation as a rational act of insight and discernment.

Despite the seeming incompatibility between the intellectually abstruse French and US poststructuralists and the various branches of political radicalism that informed advocates of Theory in Britain, the two groups were committed to the dismantling of Formalism, and for that matter any other kind of critical practice that treated literature as an art form distinguishable from other kinds of speech and writing. To allow such practices to flourish would have been to open a door upon questions that both factions wished to suffocate. If we read something and feel confident about how its defining constituent features work we then have the ability to consider, with confidence, how a particular author makes use of these devices and compare their work with that of their competitors. We move beyond simply visceral impressions such as suspense, enjoyment, horror, emotional engagement, even boredom, to a contemplation of the figure, the artist, who is responsible for the text that invites these sensations. Our ability to distinguish between the various components of a novel or a poem and our sense of how each segues into another enables us to assess the ability of the person who choreographs these nuances and interfaces.

5

Defining Literature:
The Bête Noir of Academia

As we have seen in the previous chapter, only the New Critics and the Formalists have attempted a definition of literature. The former, though commendably inspired, were haphazard and unfocused in terms of methodology. The Formalists have been more scientific in their approach, often adapting the findings of advanced linguistics to their studies, but both are treated with equal contempt by avatars of structuralist and poststructuralist Theory and its various ideological offshoots. Eagleton in his student-targeted *How To Read A Poem*:

> Formalism … is a negative aesthetics – one that defines poetry not by any features that it might exhibit, but by its difference or deviation from something else. The poetic is constituted by what it bounces off against and so is dependent on the alienated reality to which it is a response … It also implies questionably, that creativity is nowhere to be found in everyday language and experience; it is, rather, the privileged preserve of whatever resists them. There is a smack of elitism about this doctrine, even though several of the Formalists were Bolshevik fellow travellers. This "radical" scepticism of the common life has raised its head again in our own time, in the postmodern assumption that the creative is to be found only in margins and minorities, in the deviant and anti-consensual. (Eagleton, 2006, p. 50)

Is Shakespeare Any Good?: And Other Questions on How to Evaluate Literature,
First Edition. Richard Bradford.
© 2015 John Wiley & Sons, Ltd. Published 2015 by John Wiley & Sons, Ltd.

Eagleton either assumes that his pre-eminence as a literary theorist will overrule potential objections to his account or he is basing it on a very slipshod acquaintance with Formalist writing. It is true that many of the Formalists were "Bolshevik fellow travellers" but it was their naïve faith that the new political environment would allow ordinary citizens access to all literary culture that alienated them from the hardline Marxists of the 1930s. The Formalist notion of literature as an aesthetic and intellectual opportunity was at first treated by the Communist regime as consistent with the overall vision of a utopian redistribution of wealth, including cultural resources. But it became evident to many Bolsheviks that their conception of writing as a craft had much in common with the guild-based phenomenon of entrepreneurialism, one of the forces behind the early industrial revolution. In short, the Formalist model of literary artist and reader as free agents was soon treated as anathema to a society organized according to doctrine. They were criticized in Trotsky's *Literature and Revolution* (1924), written when its author was still regarded as Lenin's heir apparent, and in the 1930s Stalin's censors outlawed their theories. They did not advocate "a negative aesthetics," as Eagleton puts it; quite the contrary. Their aesthetic principles were positive in that they encouraged interpretive individuality and their basic premise was that in order to voice our opinions on the quality of a book or the talents of an author we need to have a basic sense of their tools and their raw material; we need to know what literature is. They were revolutionaries certainly but their ideals did not suit the authoritarian revolution of Bolshevism. By the early 1930s most of the formative members of the group had left for mid and Western Europe. By World War ll many of these same exiles, notably Roman Jakobson, had set off for the United States – 90% of the most influential Formalists were Jewish. It is sad, unjust, that they have also been displaced by the more self-absorbed and ideologically inflexible branches of criticism and to a degree the chapter that follows is a memorial to their enterprises, but only to a degree. The spirit of their work deserves unreserved acclaim but they were not faultless in its execution. They will, then, be made use of as the backbone for this chapter but I will go much further than they did in terms of arriving at a definition of literature. We will begin with poetry.

Poetry is the most versatile, ambidextrous, and omnipotent of all types of speech or writing yet, paradoxically, it is the only one that is unified by a single exclusive feature, which enables us to identify it as the most ostentatious literary genre of them all. This element is the double pattern; as an example of it in operation consider John Donne's poem "The Flea."

Mark but this flea, and mark in this,
How little that which thou deny'st me is;
Me it sucked first, and now sucks thee,
And in this flea, our two bloods mingled be;
Confess it, this cannot be said
A sin, or shame, or loss of maidenhead,
    Yet this enjoys before it woo,
        And pampered swells with one blood made of two,
        And this, alas, is more than we would do.

Oh stay, three lives in one flea spare,
Where we almost, nay more than married are:
This flea is you and I, and this
Our marriage bed, and marriage temple is;
Though parents grudge, and you, we're met,
And cloistered in these living walls of jet.
    Though use make thee apt to kill me,
        Let not to this, self murder added be,
        And sacrilege, three sins in killing three.

Cruel and sudden, hast thou since
Purpled thy nail, in blood of innocence?
In what could this flea guilty be,
Except in that drop which it sucked from thee?
Yet thou triumph'st and say'st that thou
Find'st not thyself, nor me the weaker now;
    'Tis true, then learn how false, fears be;
        Just so much honour, when thou yield'st to me,
        Will waste, as this flea's death took life from thee.

We cannot see the speaker but we know from circumstantial evidence that he is male. In the opening stanza he argues that his silent companion's apparent reluctance to have sex with him is unfounded. Sex, he contends, is no more distressing or immoral than an insect bite. Moreover, just as the flea has "enjoyed" both of them so, he implies, might they delight in a comparable mixing of fluids. The flea, he observes, swells and feels pampered by its harmless and pleasurable act – so why shouldn't they?

We can infer from his words in the second stanza that the woman has rejected his argument. She has indeed attempted to swat the flea, to destroy the active feature – in technical terms the vehicle – of his metaphor. She fails, at least in her first attempt, and he pleads for restraint: "Oh stay," he begs, don't kill it. The man is thinking and speaking in response to the unpredictable, he is improvising, and as he readjusts his trope to suit new circumstances he begins to contradict himself. In the first stanza he stated that the fleabite, like sex, involved no great moral consequences. Now he compares the mingling of their blood in the insect with the physical and spiritual union of marriage, and the flea is promoted to the status of a religious icon: it is a temple, whose "living walls" sanctify their union. The conceit seems almost to have acquired a hungry momentum of its own and the man even begins to speak to her as if they were already married. "Though use make thee apt to kill me" he concedes, meaning that the routines of coexistence might well breed bitterness, the destruction of that symbol of their potential union, the flea, would amount to the violation of some higher covenant involving them and it: "A sacrilege, three sins in killing three."

His grand hyperbole, inspired as it is, appears to have left the woman unconvinced, since between the second and third stanza she succeeds in dispatching the insect. "Cruel and sudden hast thou since / Purpled thy nail in blood of innocence," he observes, marshaling his mental resources for yet another twist upon the original figure. He begins with a mild rebuke and next returns to his initial presentation of the flea as a harmless, innocent, agent of pleasure. Then, still thinking and speaking on the spot, he refashions this image to renew his strategy of seduction. Neither of them, he informs her, is the "weaker now" and this is a measure of the "false fears" behind her reluctance to accept his argument and his advances.

One could argue that Donne has in "The Flea" conducted an exercise in mimesis. We have no record of how people spoke to each other in the early seventeenth century but evidence suggests that it would not be entirely implausible for an educated intelligent individual to telescope his thoughts into extended metaphors – if characters in contemporaneous drama in any way resembled members of the audience then flamboyant figurative language was something of a fashion statement. Significantly, Donne informs the piece with a special claim upon credulity and believability by creating a dialogue, albeit with one party remaining silent. He contends, she responds, and he makes further use of his sophistication – by degrees suave and suspect – to offer yet another version of his original proposition. Exchange the early seventeenth century informal idiom and vocabulary for its early twenty-first century counterpart and play down the figurative excesses and religious imagery and it could be an exchange overheard last week in a restaurant, albeit one with a somewhat unappealing tolerance of insects. "The Flea" seems at one level a wonderfully plausible, authentic rendering of actuality yet at another we are made aware that both of its characters are patently unreal, that they do not exist, and could never have existed.

It is unlikely though not entirely unthinkable that a person could be so flamboyantly inventive for so long – leaving aside the listener who, four centuries past and today, would be more likely to feel impatient than impressed – but it is impossible to conceive of him doing so while fitting his speech into three identical stanzas, each rhyming aa bb cc ddd; three couplets and a triplet. The meticulous baroque design is further complicated by the fact that each couplet is comprised first of an octosyllabic line, followed by a pentameter, with the triplet made up of an octosyllable and then two pentameters. Moreover, each line is iambic, in that with very slight exceptions every even syllable is stressed more emphatically than the two syllables that precede and follow it.

What we encounter in every component part of "The Flea," from individual syllables to complex rhyme schemes and a perpetual metaphor, is a tension between immediacy – it is in the present tense and the speaker appears continually to adjust his words to changing reponses – and a structure so self-evidently arbitrary and complex that it completely undermines any claim upon spontaneity and verisimilitude.

This is the double pattern in action. One half of it is made up of devices, effects, habits, and frames of reference that poetry shares with all other linguistic discourses; as I have indicated "The Flea" could, just, be a record of a conversation overheard in a bar. The other half of the pattern pulls against this: it announces the text as a poem by compelling aspects of language into patterns that serve no purpose elsewhere in speech and writing.

The metaphor seems heedlessly adaptable to whatever is required of it while admitting of such tortuous layerings of rhetoric and imagery as to defy any credible sense of spontaneity. The complexity of each stanza seems to betoken a desire by Donne to test himself, to see if he has the skill to sustain at least the impression of immediacy while fitting his words into a determinedly complex design, repeated three times. He even sews into the texture of the poem a secondary sound pattern which on a brief reading beguiles like a distantly heard snatch of music but on closer attention involves an exercise in acoustic brainwashing. The flea, the bite, the man, and the woman are drawn into a chain of semantic and phonetic associations: "this flea," "in this," "me is," "Me," "Thee," "be," "This flea," "and this," "temple is," "kill me," "added be," "killing three," "guilty be," "from thee," "fears be," "to me," "from thee." Critics have for centuries debated the effect of repetitive sound patterns – predominantly, rhyme, assonance, and alliteration – upon our standard cognitive mechanisms. No firm conclusions have been reached but by consensus it is accepted that they interfere with our ability to make sense of language. They create a layer of echoes that runs as a counter-current to the conventional relationship between phonetics and semantics, sound and meaning. One might argue that Donne's dense fabric of internal and external rhymes creates a beguiling musical accompaniment to the speaker's sophistry, something that might plausibly be a reflection of his personal manner, indeed his temperament. However, this impression of guileless charm is undermined by evidence of planning and calculation. Continually, the swirling sound patterns return us to the five predominant themes of his argument: "this flea," "is," "Thee," "be," "me." We cannot be certain if this would have some subliminal effect upon the listener, an almost hypnotic counterpart to the twisted logic of the argument, but the effort that went in to organizing this effect testifies to the fact that it was preplanned and not spontaneous.

There is a portrait of Henry VIII by Holbein that is famed for its ability to beguile, often unnerve, onlookers. Practically everyone who sees it is stunned by its unusual authenticity. It is not that Holbein has captured something exclusive to the notorious monarch, more that the face in the frame appears to acquire a mobility; from different perspectives his expression seems to alter and his eyes, infamously, seem capable of following you around the room. The effect is powerful and because of this transient. We quickly withdraw from our state of transfixed credulity and remind ourselves that what we are looking at is an assembly of paint and canvas put into operation by an immensely talented craftsman.

The experience is peculiar and magnetic. We almost simultaneously apprehend a flicker of pure reality alongside a complex act of representation. Our struggle to reconcile a sense of unmediated perception and our admiration for the processes that make this available is comparable to our encounter with Donne's "The Flea." At one level the poem is engagingly transparent; we feel that we are listening to an encounter between two living human beings and we become sufficiently persuaded and intrigued to form opinions about what sort of man he is – his background, the reason for his showy ostentatious manner – and to wonder about his silent addressee; is she impressed, anxious, fearful, bored? At the same time Donne embeds these two individuals so deeply in a network of sound patterns and figurative devices that they become functions of language; not figures who use and respond to words but creations of words.

Richard Wollheim evolved a general theory on the nature and effects of the visual arts which he called the "twofold thesis," using Holbein's portrait of Henry VIII as a paradigmatic example of this.

> If I look at a representation as a representation, then it is not just permitted, but required of me, that I attend simultaneously to object and medium. So if I look at Holbein's portrait, the standards of correctness require me to see Henry VIII there; but additionally I must – not only may but must – be visually aware of an unrestricted range of features of Holbein's panel if my perception of the representation is to be appropriate. (Wollheim, 1980, p. 213)

There are obvious parallels between Wollheim's twofold thesis and the double pattern in the sense that in both the poem and the painting we are aware almost simultaneously of the object and the medium that makes the object available. However, there is a significant difference. The medium of the visual arts is a metalanguage, a representational system in its own right with generic habits and conventions and comprised of material such as paint, stone, canvas, and wood. The medium of poetry is words, the same words that we use throughout our conscious existence. Poetry does not reinvent language; it can only use what is already available. What it does is to create unusual relationships between words, relationships that persist for the duration of a single statement, the poem. In the visual arts the relationship between the medium and the object, and by object we effectively mean reality, is infinitely flexible. Up to the mid nineteenth century virtually all art was representational in the sense that the perceiver did not need to understand the history or conventions of painting to recognize the thing in the picture. Since then, however, artists have pioneered a variety of unprecedented techniques which explore the very nature of perception and existence. Often their paintings do not attempt simply to imitate physical objects but rather employ shapes, colors, and juxtapositions in order to raise questions regarding our relationship with what we complacently term reality. So while Holbein was a traditional representational painter Wollheim's twofold thesis is relevant also to pictures by figures such as Jackson Pollock, many of whose best known works involve blocks of color divided by geometric designs. Pollock's object might not be immediately recognizable to the perceiver but, as Wollheim states, our recognition of that fact that his painting exists in the same extended generic field as Holbein's causes us to engage in a process of interpretation, a contemplation of its object, albeit one that is an abstract fabric of ideas rather than a human being.

The fact that the compositional and interpretative conventions of painting can accommodate the radical differences between Holbein and Pollock illustrates the dissimilarity between the twofold thesis and the double pattern and in turn the uniqueness of poetry both as a literary genre and a means of expression and representation.

It would be impossible for a poet to create the equivalent of a Pollock painting for the simple reason that the only source for a poet's medium, his raw material, is language. Certainly one could, if so inclined, create something that in formal terms resembles a poem but is so purposively incoherent, sometimes ungrammatical, as to disrupt any clear sense of what it means – and as we will see poems that come close to this formula have been produced by esteemed practitioners of the genre. However, even though the relationship between the constituent parts of the piece creates a sense of opacity and confusion the fact that poetry draws exclusively upon language for its components means that verse can never obtain a level of abstraction or incomprehensibility comparable with Pollock. Its fundamental indivisible building blocks are words and, however haphazardly one assembles a string of individual words, they will interact to create broader strands of meaning, albeit sometimes unorthodox and semi-coherent. Painting can make worlds of its own, revise and refresh its own conventions of design and signification. But poetry is tied to the medium that does not merely reconstruct perceived reality; it is part of perceived, and lived, reality. We, as human beings, can neither think nor function without language; language is inseparable from our existential condition. Poetry appropriates and refashions aspects of language according to its own conventions. These are seemingly arbitrary and purposeless given that in all nonpoetic uses of language the abstract regulations that allow us to assemble and decode messages serve a self-evident purpose: the organizational principles of the medium – predominantly grammar – are designed to occasion the most efficient and unambivalent delivery of the message. Poetic devices such as the stanza, rhyme schemes, alliterative and assonantal patterns, metrical form, and the persistent use of metaphor make no obvious contribution to the principles of clarity and pre-cision that underpin virtually all uses of language. The occurrence of rhyme in ordinary speech is usually accidental. It is the cause of embarrassment and is guarded against because the repetition of sound will draw the listener's attention away from the logic of the statement. Similarly, if someone held a conversation, delivered an address, or wrote an article while adhering to a strictly iambic pattern most witnesses would pay less attention to the mes-sage than to the curiosity of the spectacle. Metaphor does of course feature frequently in ordinary language but tacit customs are maintained to regulate its effects. Were you to reply to your general practitioner's enquiry on how you felt with the declaration that you were "lonely as a cloud that floats on high o'er vales and hills" the GP would, with some justification regard this either as facetious gesture or evidence of a burgeoning nervous breakdown.

More significantly, metaphor in everyday language is, by habit, the exception to the predominating literal, transparent mood of the rest of the text. It is used with indulgent caution to underscore a particular point but it never becomes a persistent, extended feature of the text. Donne maintains and refashions his metaphor of the flea bite for the entirety of the poem, and in verse – particularly during Donne's period of the Renaissance – such exercises in figurative endurance are as much the custom as the exception.

For poems that have the least in common with Donne's we should go to the early twentieth century, to the work of those who advocated and practiced the aesthetics of modernism. Modernist poetry developed into a number of distinct sometimes antithetical subgenres but its originating tenets focused upon a desire to unshackle the writer and the poem from what were seen as the restraints of conventional writing, specifically traditional meter and rhyme scheme and the characteristic accessories of orotund diction and portentous metaphor. Free verse, or vers libre, was born and one if its most celebrated practitioners was William Carlos Williams. The following is Williams's "Spring and All":

> By the road to the contagious hospital
> under the surge of the blue
> mottled clouds driven from the
> northeast – a cold wind. Beyond the
> waste of broad, muddy fields
> brown with dried weeds, standing and fallen
>
> patches of standing water
> the scattering of tall trees
>
> All along the road the reddish
> purplish, forked, upstanding, twiggy
> stuff of bushes and small trees
> with dead, brown leaves under them
> leafless vines –
>
> Lifeless in appearance, sluggish,
> dazed spring approaches –

This poem has, it seems, purged itself of every device and technique that we customarily associate with poetic writing. There are no metaphors and the closest Williams comes to a figurative gesture is in the phrase "dazed spring." The adverb "dazed" is usually associated with a living creature rather than a season, but we are likely to encounter many similar usages in informal speech: "the dead of night," "lazy days," "happy places" are, strictly speaking, rhetorical figures but they are taken for granted by most as the routines of verbal exchange.

The only apparent concession to conventional verse is the use of poetic lines but these do not attend to any abstract formal structure; there is nothing that resembles meter and there are no sound patterns or rhymes. The lines seem improvised, random, the kind of sequence that one might find in a notebook. Indeed, the syntax itself is casual, sometimes haphazard and heedless. There is a verb phrase at the beginning of the poem – the speaker seems to have picked out a thought in mid-sentence – and we are left to wonder what exactly *is* "By the road to the ..." One might assume that he means "I am standing by the road" or "I was looking down the road" but neither of these oblique possibilities is thereafter confirmed or reinforced. The sentence structure of the poem as a whole is paratactic; unfocused, apparently improvised, and composed guilelessly at the moment of inspiration or perception. Prior to modernism this effect was never encountered in literary writing and rarely if ever in any other species of formal discourse, being found only in the rambling hesitations of casual speech or in the letters and notebooks of the ill-educated. The overall impression is of an attempt to preserve for posterity the moment at which prelingusitic perception becomes language. The passage,

> All along the road the reddish
> purplish, forked, upstanding, twiggy
> stuff of bushes and small trees

seems a record of the speaker attempting to match what he sees with a satisfactory description, trying out various words from his mental lexicon in the hope of coming upon the right one. The "reddish / purplish, forked, upstanding, twiggy / stuff," he states, hoping that eventually he'll find the phrase he is searching for.

In this respect there are parallels with "The Flea." Both speakers are busily adjusting their verbal output in accordance with unfolding circumstances, in one case the responses of the listener and in the other the cumulative impression of a passive scene. At the same time, while Donne's poem involves a persistent counterpoint between artifice and improvisation, Williams's attempts to rid itself completely of the former. It is as though Holbein's Henry VIII has walked out of the wall and become as real as his onlookers, no longer a compound of paint, canvas, and self-evident painterly devices.

It is difficult to imagine how an equivalent to Williams's poem could be executed in the visual arts, given that a distinction between object and medium, the twofold thesis, is a basic requirement for works of painting and sculpture. There is, of course, Damian Hirst's *A Thousand Years,* involving a rotting cow's head assisted in its process of decay by regiments of hungry maggots and flies.

If there are indeed parallels between "Spring and All" and *A Thousand Years* a significant question is raised regarding craftsmanship and technique. Irrespective of any alleged cultural or ideological subtext that might attach to Mr Hirst's piece it is self-evidently the case that as an artwork in its own right it required of its producer no effort, skill, or intellectual engagement. Even if we had no interest in art or in the general state of contemporary culture any of us could produce something which, as a medium, was possessed of comparable qualities. Since Williams appears to have achieved a similar level of transparency, a transcendence of the devices and conventions of verse, has he too produced a "poem" that makes no claims to be a meticulously crafted work of art, that is in truth something that any one of us, given the inclination, might jot down?

To address this question we must consider the fact that Williams, while rejecting the traditional poetic line – that is, the unit that pays heed to some abstract notion of a given length or metrical structure – does not abjure the line as a de facto token of poetic design. Williams's lines do not conform to any predictable or consistent pattern but they exist, tangibly, as supplements to the standard building blocks of words, clauses and sentences. As a consequence he has invoked the tension between the two aspects of the double pattern, a gesture that both pays allegiance to the defining characteristics of poetry and places before an author a fundamental test of skill. Consider lines 2–5:

> under the surge of the blue
> mottled clouds driven from the
> northeast – a cold wind. Beyond the
> waste of broad, muddy fields

Is there any logic or apparent purpose in Williams's breaking up of the already casual sentences into arbitrary structures? Intriguingly the line ending at "blue" could have been a complete, conclusive statement. Metonymy, logical metaphor, is found frequently in ordinary speech: "wheels" has long served a colloquial substitute for car, as has "the crown" for the royal family. It would not involve a strenuous imaginative effort for Williams's speaker to settle upon "the blue" as an alternative to sky. Suddenly, however, we swing around the line ending to find that "blue" has been returned to its traditional adjectival role. Why we wonder does he leave "the" dangling at the end of the subsequent two lines? Is he mocking the decorum of traditional versification where custom would discourage such ungainly constructions? Perhaps, but when we consider the manner of the poem as a whole we begin to discern an intention at once more radical and commendable. In grammar there is no device that accommodates the pauses and hesitations that are an inevitable feature of unrehearsed speech but the curious, unclassifiable gap between "the" and "northeast" imitates the moment that it takes for the speaker to synchronize his perception of the cloud with his intuitive sense of the compass. Similarly "Beyond the" stops syntax, briefly, while the speaker's mind searches for a means of describing a featureless landscape.

In traditional verse, enjambment is indulged by critics and used by poets with a certain amount of caution, given that it undermines the ordinance that coherence is paramount. The standard defense for it is that it sets up a pseudo musical counterpoint between syntax and meter, but since Williams has abandoned all concessions to the latter he seems to be both invoking and rewriting the regulations of conventional verse. The

<blockquote>
small trees
with dead brown leaves under them
leafless vines
</blockquote>

is in appearance guilelessly unplanned – it seems as unostentatious as a snatch of conversation – but in fact it incorporates two very different levels of meaning. The small trees could well be perceived as having "dead brown leaves under them," with the pause allowing the perceiver to gather his thoughts into a more succinct, almost tragic summary: "leafless vines." Alternatively, the relaxed demotic manner of the poem might encourage one to close the gap at the line ending and read "under them leafless vines" as an unbroken albeit ungrammatical sequence.

There is no evidence, either within the poem or implied by its apparent context, that enables us to reach a conclusion on which of these interpretations is correct. That Williams sews into the same sequence of words two simultaneously present but distinct trajectories of sense testifies to the fact that despite the considerable differences between the two poems "Spring and All" and "The Flea" belong within the same corpus of texts and that their creators are attuned to a single uniquely poetic feature of composition, the double pattern. Williams rejects the traditional orthodoxies of meter, rhyme scheme, and figurative devices yet still makes use of the tactile materiality of language to create counterpoints between the progress of his syntax and a fabric of pauses and hesitations. He employs features of language that have no designated function outside poetry to create multiple layers of sense.

Donne's and Williams's poems belong at opposing ends of the broad spectrum of texts that incorporate the double pattern as their generic keynote. With Donne we encounter verse that involves a thickening and foregrounding of purely conventional poetic devices to the extent that univocal single registers of meaning are at every level disrupted or supplemented. Williams uses conventional, self-evidently poetic devices and conventions sparingly, yet the fact that they are present at all, sometimes in unprecedented unorthodox manifestations, is sufficient to create a conspicuous relationship between the two halves of the double pattern.

In *The Republic* Plato has much to say about poetry. In Book 10 an exchange takes place regarding the nature of imitation and representation: the subject is ostensibly art, but the primary motive is as usual to determine the nature of truth. By the end of the dialogue Socrates has established a parallel hierarchy of media and physical activities. The carpenter makes the actual bed, but the idea or concept behind this act of creation is the demiurge's. The painter is placed at the next stage down in this creative hierarchy: he can observe the carpenter making the bed and dutifully record this process. The poet, it seems, exists in a somewhat ambiguous relation to this column of originators, makers, and imitators.

> Perhaps they [poets] may have come across imitators and been deceived by them; they may not have remembered when they saw their works that these were but imitations thrice removed from the truth, and could easily be made without any knowledge of the truth, because they are appearances only and not realities. (Plato, 1888, p. 312)

In short, the poet is capable of unsettling the hierarchy that sustains the clear relation between appearance and reality. Poets, as Aristotle and Plato recognized, are pure rhetoricians: they work within a kind of metalanguage which draws continuously upon the devices of rhetoric but which is not primarily involved in the practical activities of argument and persuasion. As the above quote suggests, they move disconcertingly through the various levels of creation, imitation, and deception, and as Plato made clear, such fickle mediators were not the most welcome inhabitants in a Republic founded upon a clear and unitary correspondence between representation and truth.

While Plato's stern indictment of poetry has never been officially sanctioned his sense of it as a dissolute aberration from the conventions of nonpoetic discourse has endured. He was the first commentator to note that poetry was a law unto itself, capable of creating trajectories of signification that transgressed the consensually agreed contract between reality and language. He had postulated a forerunner to the double pattern. A more recent critic was more precise on how poetry achieves its aberrant status:

> The poetic function projects the principle of equivalence from the axis of selection into the axis of combination. (Jakobson, 1960, p. 39)

Jakobson's notion of "equivalence" corresponds closely with Plato's contract between linguistic representation and truth. In nonpoetic discourse this is dominated by the "axis of selection." When we use language we choose individual words from the axis of selection and assemble them according to the conventions of the "axis of combination" or, in basic terms, grammar. It is possible to create a nonsensical yet grammatically correct sentence:

> I am song but a shameful sea must soon be inside the pastry.

The pronouns, connectives, adjectives, verbs, and nouns follow the abstract rules for grammatical coherence but because the relationship between key individual words bears no resemblance to the rational and logical connectedness between their equivalents in the prelinguistic world the sentence appears absurd and incoherent. The axis of selection refers to the choice that we make when we select each consecutive word in the construction of a sentence. We know we have to use a verb or a noun or a pronoun, but which one? Our decision is influenced primarily by the general principles of clarity and coherence, so we opt for a word that corresponds as closely as possible to the idea or fact that we wish to communicate; we attempt to close the gap between language and reality. The poet, however, chooses words not according to a sense of duty to an extrinsic frame of reference. Instead, the chain of meanings and connections becomes possessed of its own internalized anti-logic; the poem is a law unto itself with the relationship between images and ideas within the text superseding any responsibility to notions of order and reason that prevail outside it. This is what Jakobson means when he refers to the "principle of equivalence" shifting from the axis of selection to that of combination. The selective axis is the mechanism that anchors specific linguistic utterances or writings to a broader consensus on what word is appropriate in the context or apparent intention of the statement. When we write, or indeed read, a text we focus both upon how each word reacts with others in the same syntactic chain and also on how the expanding image or fabric of ideas corresponds with some precedent drawn from our general sense of the real and the plausible. In Jakobson's model of poetic writing this second register, anchoring the text to an extrinsic frame of reference, is subordinated to a more powerful mechanism where words and images shed their allegiance to the normative conventions outside the poem and create their own internalized dynamic.

Poetry, through the double pattern, enables the poet to engage with the standard public conventions of language while undermining their authority. The poet controls separate levels of linguistic organization, some peculiar to verse and the others common both to verse and all other nonpoetic discourses, and is as a consequence able to create a limitless number of permutations upon effect and meaning through their interaction. For both its creator and reader the poem obtains an ultimate state of expressive freedom.

Novels shift us much closer than poems to the linguistic raw material – written, spoken, and indeterminate – that we will find, and use, in everyday life. Open a novel at random and it is likely that somewhere on the page you will come across a passage remarkably similar to something you have recently read or heard, written, or spoken. In a traditional work of fiction dialogue or reported speech will very often seem interchangeable with conversations overheard in a bar or the street or even exchanges we have been involved in only hours before we picked up the book. Between such passages the narrator's account of what is going on in first or third person could be all but indistinguishable from a journalist's report on their encounter with a living person and actual events, the diary of a real person recounting their relationships with or impressions of other authentic uninvented figures, or even a story told to us by a friend, an amusing raconteur, about what happened to them at work on the previous day. So, we might ask, if fiction is a hybridized compound of every known kind of nonliterary discourse, how can it be literature? The simple answer to this question is that while the building blocks of fiction can be located in the world, their relationships with each other outside the novel are random and unpredictable; the novelist puts them together, and adjusts them, in a manner that is self-evidently crafted and mechanical. Each relates to the other like the components of a machine. The double pattern in fiction is as definitive and evident as in poetry, with a difference. The distinction between the literary and nonliterary features of a poem is in most instances clearly drawn while in fiction there is a constant sense of interaction and blurring.

Jane Austen's narrator in *Northanger Abbey* (1818) describes the main character of the novel in its opening sentences: "No one who had ever seen Catherine Morland in her infancy, would have supposed her born to be a heroine. Her situation in life, the character of her father and mother, her own person and disposition, were all equally against her." Throughout the novel the narrator never discloses any personal, social, or familiar relation with the characters, but the opening is not consistent with this impression of objectivity. How can he, or she, know as much about Catherine as she does of herself? Chapter 9 begins:

> The progress of Catherine's happiness from the events of the evening, was as follows. It appeared first in a general dissatisfaction with everybody about her, while she remained in the rooms, which speedily brought on considerable weariness and a violent desire to go home. This, on arriving in Pulteney Street, took the direction of extraordinary hunger.

We have to assume from this either that the narrator accompanied Catherine from the rooms to Pulteney Street and when there spoke to her about her mood or that he/she assembled this information from conversations with Catherine's acquaintances. But if we read on we will find that neither of these assumptions is plausible because later in the passage we are told how long Catherine slept and of her "first wish" on awakening. This last piece of information would remain unobtainable to anyone not possessed of clairvoyant powers. Sometimes the narrator discloses Catherine's thoughts and feelings in a way that Catherine herself is incapable of doing: "'My dear Eleanor' cried Catherine, suppressing her feelings as well as she could" (Chapter 26).

The picture of Catherine Morland that emerges from the detailed considerations of her acts, thoughts, motives, and ambitions is comfortingly authentic, in that as the novel proceeds we gradually get to know her in much the same way that we form impressions about people we meet and spend time with in the real world. Yet at the same time unnerving questions are raised when we consider how we are able to do so. In this respect the narrator of Austen's novel is as bizarre and unreal a presence as the speaker in Donne's "The Flea." In both instances we make sense of the work by reading through it to a set of images, a story, which are engaging and realistic, while at the same time we are aware these effects are related to us by figures who cannot properly exist, are assembled largely from uniquely literary devices. The double pattern informs all aspects of each work.

As shown, even a poem so different from Donne's as Williams's "Spring and All" exemplifies the enduring, and defining, qualities of the double pattern and with this in mind let us compare Austen's *Northanger Abbey* with Joyce's *A Portrait of the Artist as a Young Man*. Joyce subtly erodes the conventions that enable Austen to maintain a distinction between the narrator and Catherine in that we are often uncertain of the point when Stephen or the narrator takes control of the story. In chapter 4 Stephen contemplates a girl on the beach:

> Her slate blue skirts were kilted boldly about her waist and dovetailed behind her. Her bosom was as a bird's, soft and slight, slight and soft as the breast of some dark-plumaged dove. But her long fair hair was girlish, and touched with the wonder of mortal beauty, her face.

The description is hyperbolic in two senses. There are disclosures of clumsy eroticism, which is consistent enough with what we know of Stephen's notion of decadence as a necessary attribute of the artist, and aside from what the girl actually provokes in him sexually she also prompts him to rehearse his writerly ambitions, embarrassingly. Joyce achieves via his elusive, ghostly narrator what would be impossible with a conventional first or third-person storyteller. We learn a great deal about Stephen but, unlike Catherine, we are never certain of whether he is deliberately betraying confidences or if by various means the novel shows us aspects of his character that he might otherwise withhold.

Austen's and Joyce's novels differ greatly in their employment of the devices and methods of fiction yet in another sense they declare their similarities as a separate species of writing. It is a truism that modernist writing both undermines and emphasizes the mechanisms that realism conceals. But look closely at Austen and Joyce and this mantra opens itself to questions. Joyce blurs the boundary between the narrative and the mind-set of the character and some have argued that his exercise is as a consequence more significant intellectually than the practices of the realists: it makes us think about the fundamental issues of representation, language, and existence rather than entertains us with stories that involve us emotionally without challenging our conceptions of art and life. Really? It might, conversely, be argued that the peculiar relationship between Catherine and her narrator is more problematic than what we encounter in Joyce. For one thing Joyce persistently reminds us that he is playing tricks with the conventions of fiction. He never leaves alone the expectations of his reader, of 1908 vintage, more attuned to the legacies of Austen. His use of the double pattern comes close to exhibitionism. Austen, on the other hand, presents the relationship between the teller and the tale as far less problematic, or so we are led to believe. But is she attempting to disguise her techniques or is she offering the more astute and inquisitive reader cautious clues, invitations to look more closely at the peculiar mannerisms of novels such as *Northanger Abbey* where, after several readings we begin to wonder more about the mind-set of the narrator than his/her subject, Catherine.

Viktor Shklovsky evolved a model of fiction that invites comparison with Jakobson's theory of verse. Shklovsky (1917) reduced fictional struc-tures to two opposing and interactive dimensions: *syuzhet* and *fabula*. *Fabula* refers to the actuality and the chronologic sequence of the events that make up the narrative; and *syuzhet* to the order, manner, and style in which they are presented in the novel in question. The *fabula* of Dickens's *Great Expectations* (1861) concerns the experiences, in and around London, from the early childhood to the adulthood of Pip. Its *syuzhet* involves the presentation of these events in Pip's first-person account of their temporal, spatial, and emotional registers.

In Dickens's novel the first-person manner of the *syuzhet* has the effect of personalizing the *fabula*; Pip's description of Miss Havisham and of his relationship with Estella is necessarily influenced by factors such as his own emotional affiliations, his stylistic habits, and his singular perspective on spatio-temporal sequences and conditions. If *Great Expectations* had an omniscient, third-person narrator we might learn more about the events that contributed to Miss Havisham's condition and we might be offered a more impartial multidimensional perspective on the relationship between Pip and Estella. In short, the *syuzhet* can effectively alter our perceptions of the *fabula*. Shklovsky showed a particular taste for novels that self-consciously foreground the interaction of these two elements, and his essay (1921) on Laurence Sterne's *Tristram Shandy* (1759–1767) is frequently cited as an archetype of Formalist method. Throughout the novel the eponymous narrator maintains an interplay between his story (the *fabula)*, and the activity and conditions of telling it *(syuzhet)*. Despite the general view that Sterne's work is a premodernist aberration from the evolving convention of realism – and consequently worthy of esteem – Austen's *Northanger Abbey* has much in common with it. The *fabula* seems at first to be a depersonalized impartial account of what happens to Catherine but look closer and we find that the narrator's cautious omniscience raises questions about who is telling the story. Is the narrator Catherine's surrogate or Austen's? Playfully, this uncertainty shifts us between what we think we know and what we are allowed to know, and as a consequence tests Austen's skill as a choreographer of perspectives. She proves to be a magnificent craftswoman.

Joyce's *A Portrait of the Artist as a Young Man* is Sterne's first modern counterpart. Joyce too erodes the boundary between the narrative and the narrator's state of mind, and here a question arises. He was foregrounding an element of Austen's novel that was implicit and persistent. So one has to ask: is literature that is self-consciously about writing more significant than that which questions, without constantly reinforcing, our notion of literature as art rather than representation?

Gerard Genette's *Figures III* (1972, first published in English in *Narrative Discourse*, 1980) follows up where Shklovsky left off with a complete and comprehensive typology of narrators and narrative techniques. Genette classifies narrators by borrowing a term from Plato's *Republic*: diegesis. Plato distinguishes between diegesis (the story constructed by the narrator) and mimesis (speech and dialogue as a mimetic record of someone's thought and opinions). Genette uses diegesis as a much more comprehensive formula, which incorporates the narrator's control over the novel's characters who apparently speak or converse independently of the story. Genette's principal distinction is between what he calls the extradiegetic and the autodiegetic narrator. The extradiegetic narrator remains distant from the story, and the most obvious signal of distancing is the continuous use of the third-person account, while the exemplary autodiegetic narrator uses the first-person pronoun and tells the story as an element of his/her own experience.

Compare Austen's use of the extradiegetic narrator with the following passages from D.H. Lawrence's *The Rainbow*. Chapter VI begins

> Will Brangwen had some weeks of holiday after his marriage, so the two took their honeymoon in full hands, alone in their cottage together.

Apart from the quasi-sexual conceit of "full hands," this seems a dry impartial description of the couple's activities immediately after their wedding. A page later, however:

> Here at the centre the great wheel was motionless, centred upon itself. Here was a poised, unflawed stillness that way beyond time, because it remained the same, inexhaustible, unchanging, unexhausted.

> As they lay close together, complete and beyond the touch of time or change, it was as if they were at the very centre of all the slow wheeling of space and the rapid agitation of life, deep, deep inside them all, at the centre where there is utter radiance, and eternal being, and the silence absorbed in praise: the steady core of all movements, the unawakened sleep of all wakefulness.

One has to wonder if we are expected to treat this as a reliable account of how they felt. If so, further questions arise. If "they" are at the "centre of all the slow wheeling of space" does each of them feel exactly the same way about this moment of transcendence, as the narrator implies? Often in Austen's novels we find that the narrator and the main character involve themselves almost in dialogue, the one supplementing, even questioning, what the other implies. Lawrence's narrator, here and in other novels, becomes something of an autocrat. If Catherine was a little more sagacious or was more inclined towards honesty she might sound like her extradiegetic counterpart but it is difficult to take seriously the hypothesis of Will enquiring of his bride, "Are you enjoying this rapid agitation of life, deep, deep, inside us both?" and Anna replying, "Yes indeed and I'm especially pleased by the utter radiance, and eternal being, and the silence absorbed in praise." Lawrence's narrator is determined to inform the world of the novel with complex philosophical speculations of which, for all we know, its inhabitants might remain ignorant. He is as much like an anthropologist as a cautiously unobtrusive choreographer of events and emotions. I say more of Lawrence's didactic manner in Chapter 8 but for the time being it is sufficient to note that he presses the self-defining boundaries of fiction to their limits. The Brangwens are his, Lawrence's, instruments for a thesis on the human spirit and sexuality but *The Rainbow* does not quite exchange its status as a work of fiction for that of an existentialist textbook. Certainly, the Brangwens are manipulated as exemplars of concepts and abstractions yet at the same time the narrator depends on them for his own existence. If they were not present he too would be extinguished. In order to make his opinions on life and being seem convincing he has to take on the role of observer and without the interplay between his observations (*syuzhet*) and the events observed (*fabula*) his enterprise would collapse. Lawrence ruthlessly misuses fiction, employs art as propaganda, but *The Rainbow* is for all that still a novel.

Genette's typology of narrators is underpinned by the general principle of focalization: the mental image generated by the words (Jakobson uses the term "referential" to account for the same process). In the novel the status of the narrator (autodiegetic, extradiegetic, first person, third person) will often determine the manner and level of focalization, but, as we have seen from *Northanger Abbey*, there is not always a predictable and parallel relation between narrator and focalizing agent. At one level Catherine herself is the focalizer, in that the spatio-temporal dimensions of the narrative correspond with her experiences. At another level the unidentified narrator will disclose Catherine's thoughts and feelings in a way that Catherine herself is either incapable of doing or unwilling to do in speech. Conversely, Lawrence's narrator uses focalization as a means to an end, treating the focalizing agents as specimens, illustrations of his visionary (some would say fascistic) notions of the human spirit. Nonetheless, Austen and Lawrence make use of the mechanisms of fiction to construct a world that is separate from the one that we, outside their novels, inhabit. It is a world where all aspects of existence depend upon the relationship between forms of writing.

Anthony Powell's *The Acceptance World* (1955) opens as follows.

> Once in a way, perhaps as often as every eighteen months, an invitation to Sunday afternoon tea at the Ufford would arrive on a postcard addressed in Uncle Giles's neat, constricted handwriting. This private hotel in Bayswater, where he stayed during comparatively rare visits to London, occupied two corners in a latent, almost impenetrable region west of the Queen's Road.

The manner is unaffected, comfortable with itself and without great ostentation, yet it raises an abundance of questions, first about the narrator and more profoundly about the nature of the story that will follow – its characters, prevailing themes, and its sense of an ending. It is not for a further 500 words that we encounter the pronoun "I" and throughout this opening passage it is clear that the narrator has taken great care to postpone any clear recognition of him as first or third person. Uncle Giles could be his, the narrator's, uncle but it is often the habit of a family or even a loose social group to refer to a particular member in such a way irrespective of their actual relationship, by blood or marriage, to the rest. There is no initial confirmation that the narrator is related to or even knows Uncle Giles, an uncertainty sustained by the otherwise unremarkable comment that the invitation would arrive on a postcard. Generally speaking, third-person narrators, at least in conventional novels, disclose the content of sealed correspondence only when the envelope has been opened and the letter read by a character. The public status of the postcard, showing Uncle Giles's handwriting as "neat, constricted" to anyone inclined to glance at it, again allows the narrator to appear uninvolved.

The opening is a deliberately contrived strategy of narrational reticence on Powell's part but what, if anything, does it portend regarding the rest of the novel? Once the game of hide and seek concludes it cannot be returned to. The narrator begins to mix with the characters he describes – indeed he has an affair with one of them – and becomes subject to the same sequence of events and actions that, subsequently, none of them can alter. At the same time, seemingly inconsequential observations accrue as an assembly of questions about his personality, questions that absorb us just as much as his own portraits of his fellow participants.

Powell is telling us two stories. One involves a Bayswater region once genteel and now in the mid 1950s as shabbily ill-kempt as the assembly of middle and upper class figures for whom it has become a time capsule. This story is told by Nick who also, sometimes negligently, provides us with another; this one about himself. He is protective, often costive, about how he really feels, allowing his talents as a choreographer to cause the other figures to move into the foreground, but he sometimes allows us a glimpse into what he would, we know, prefer to keep to himself. Again, the double pattern is at work, informing all aspects of the novel, from slight, apparently unimportant phrases to the figures who appear, depart, return again, and gradually evolve as individuals. And Nick also is part of it; Nick, to whom every word of the text belongs. He is an autodiegetic narrator with profoundly extradiegetic tendencies. He speaks for himself, speaks apparently openly of people he knows and observes, yet hides and obscures a great deal. We come to regard him, wonder about him, in much the same way that we would of people we know, or think we know. Yet throughout this period of acquaintanceship a question must continuously be asked. What other person – on the page or in life – will affect us in the same way as Nick? And the answer is straightforward: no one. He is coterminous with the novel. Without the world that he creates, following that reticent, costive opening passage, he would not exist. It is certainly the case that we will read accounts of their lives, of wars, politics, cooking, or car maintenance, by very real individuals who exist independently of their writing. But none of them will use the devices and architecture of fiction as the grounding for their existence on the pages in the same way as Nick does.

Powell's strength in this novel is exhibited in his ability to cause its two dimensions to interact, from every word chosen by Nick to each of the enduring impressions of failure, despair, and comic resignation that the characters leave with us after the closing page. Novels, or at least novels worthy of esteem, are autonomous works whose constituent features cooperate to create imaginative worlds between their covers, worlds that exist independently of nonfictional experience and discourse.

Shklovsky's and Genette's theories of fiction have much in common with Jakobson's model of the poem. Fiction is made up of a far more disparate array of borrowings from nonliterary language than verse and therefore involves a more complex gallery of framing devices, but for both genres we can see how the double pattern enables the writer to draw upon and reorganize common features of language. There are, for example, close parallels between the speaker in Donne's "The Flea" and the dynamic relationship between Catherine Morland and her narrator. The former's speech is at once spontaneous and unpremeditated and subject to the complex baroque structure of the three stanzas while Catherine is someone both convincing and unreal. We come to know her as we might do a figure who we encounter socially, yet via her narrator we learn more of her than is possible in a real life encounter. Both are naturalistic presences, characters who come close to transcending their purely literary functions but at the same time they invite us to inspect the devices and procedures that are responsible for their existence.

Conversely, William Carlos William's speaker closely resembles the voices that populate modernist fiction. In both instances the boundary between the devices and conceits of writing – literary and nonliterary – and an unbounded presence, speech, shift continuously; sometimes they appear to be erased and on other occasions we are reminded, self-consciously, of what is happening in the text, of its artificiality and perverse arbitrary nature.

For those who might remain sceptical about the Formalists' definition of fiction I would ask them to consider the following passage written in the early 1850s:

> In the present volume where dialogues are written down which the reporter could by no possibility have heard, and where motives are detected which the persons actuated by them certainly never confided to the writer, the public must once for all be warned that the author's individual fancy very likely supplies much of the narrative; and that he forms it as best he may out of stray papers, conversations reported to him, and his knowledge, right or wrong, of the characters of the persons engaged. And, as is the case with most orthodox histories, the writer's own guesses or conjectures are printed in exactly the same type as the most ascertained patent facts.

This is not, strictly speaking, literary criticism but it is more insightful than most pieces that purport to be. The author is William Makepeace Thackeray, or to be be more accurate the narrator of his novel *The Newcomes* (1853) who has taken a short break from his role in the book to reflect on his curious range of activities. If you regarded the author-in-the-text as a habit of postmodernism – foreshadowed by Sterne – think again. But this is more than merely a self-referential gesture on Thackeray's part. He prefigures not only late twentieth century avant-garde novelists but also offers a concise account of the Formalist notion of what fiction writing involves. He, the narrator, (i.e. Thackeray's proxy for the duration of the novel) is an almost superhuman figure. He states that many "dialogues" written down by him are exchanges he could never have heard and that he is able to report on the thoughts of individuals without ever having spoken to them. He admits that "much of" the narrative is determined by his "fancy" – leaving open the mischievous question of where the rest comes from – and declares that along with his own inventions he collects material from the world of "ascertained patent facts." He rejoices in his role as chameleon and puppeteer, at once the orchestrator of the novel's mechanisms and devices and a ghostly presence capable of disguising himself among the machinery of the work. He revels in shifting across the spectrum between extradiegetic and autodiegetic modes, activating characters anonymously while allowing his "fancy" to determine their fate. He confesses gladly to being the focalizer while his characters, his "stray papers and conversations," his focalizing agents, often appear to come from "the most orthodox histories," records of the real world. As a novelist writing of his trade Thackeray gives playful animation to what the Formalists coldly classify. Most significantly, he shows how the novelist is unlike any other kind of prose writer, at once the choreographer of the book's movements and devices yet uniquely unreal, a figure who reports the unheard and unspoken and whose "guesses and conjectures" are always present and forever hidden. Barbara Herrnstein Smith, a post-Formalist, echoes Thackeray, albeit in the lumpish manner of modern critical writing: "In a novel or tale, it is the act of reporting events, the act of describing persons and referring to places that is fictive. The novel represents the verbal action of a man reporting, describing, and referring [but who is] pretending to be *writing* a biography while actually *fabricating* one" (Smith, 1978, pp. 29–30). Or in Thackeray's terms, the author, or rather the narrator, of a novel, has two roles simultaneously – as one who tells a story as though it was fact but who shows himself to be the cause of, and part of, an act of pure invention.

In 1850 Charlotte Bronte attached a "Biographical Note" to the second edition of her sister Emily's *Wuthering Heights* and asked a question:

Whether it is right or advisable to create beings like Heathcliff, I do not know: I scarcely think it is. But this I know; the writer who possesses the

creative gift owns something of which he is not always master – something
that at times strangely wills and works for itself.

She does not contend that creativity is some form of alchemy, causing the
magical birth of "beings" with their own sense of purpose and independence;
not quite. She concedes, as a fellow novelist, that the enterprise of fiction
involves "rules and principles" (which later the Formalists would conscientiously document) but Bronte is fascinated by the tension between those
rules and principles that the author may select and "lay down" and those
which "for years lie in subjection." She is referring here to the way in which
the forms and devices of fiction are in a constant state of evolution, and
more specifically to how her sister caused Heathcliff to seem at once charismatic and malevolent. Emily's use of different narrative foci was built upon
previous novels yet was unprecedented in its effects, and Heathcliff's ambiguous status is due to a triumph of technical craftsmanship and originality.
Charlotte Bronte is, like Thackeray, a Formalist before her time. She recognized that her sister turned the standard conventions of *syuzhet* and *fabula*,
extradiegesis, autodiegesis, and focalization against each other, while, crucially, concealing her method from the reader. Hence, her claim that Emily
was in possession of something that "strangely … wills and works for itself"
was a compliment to her sister's ability to make this *appear* to be an autonomous agency. In truth she was praising Emily as an artist who could manip-
ulate and refashion the defining techniques of fiction writing.

The best way to test Thackeray's and Bronte's formulae – and those of their
successors – is to apply them to works that walk a fine line between the novel
and nonfiction. Orwell's *Homage to Catalonia* (1938) and Isherwood's *Mr
Norris Changes Trains* (1935) appear to have a great deal in common. Both
are gripping first-person stories about their narrators' adventures in Europe
during the years before World War II. However, few would dispute that
Isherwood's book is a novel, albeit involving a fair amount of autobiographical context lifted from the author's experiences in 1930s Berlin, while
Orwell's is a reasonably trustworthy documentary account of his involvement in the Spanish Civil War. Our knowledge of the authors' lives reinforces our notion of the books belonging to different genres, but without that
how would we go about proving the distinction from the words on the page?

The books open in a remarkably similar manner, with each narrator
telling of his meeting with a stranger. Isherwood: "My first impression
was that the stranger's eyes were of an unusually light blue. They met
mine for several blank seconds, vacant, unmistakably scared. Startled and

innocently naughty, they half reminded me of an incident I couldn't quite place ... They were the eyes of a schoolboy surprised in the act of breaking one of the rules." Orwell: "In the Lenin Barracks in Barcelona, the day before I joined the militia, I saw an Italian militiaman standing in front of the officers' table ... His peaked leather cap was pulled fiercely over one eye ... Something in his face deeply moved me. It was the face of a man who would commit murder and throw away his life for a friend." Both make use of the same familiar lexicon of tricks and nuances that characterize first-person narration in fiction; physical cues become the building blocks for private impressions, hypotheses, and speculations as to the what the two strangers are like, or are capable of.

If both writers had continued in this manner it would indeed be difficult in terms of form and style to distinguish between them, and Orwell's work would, technically, qualify as fiction. But they do not. Certainly we can sometimes pick out the kind of stylistic signatures that dominate Orwell's novels but these are self-consciously minimized to allow more space for Orwell to report military actions and political developments in terms of unadorned facts, and also for him to comment on what he saw much in the manner of a news reporter, though not a particularly impartial one. He is enabling the *fabula* to suffocate the *syuzhet*; which might raise the question of why a novel cannot be written which is so overpoweringly literal and naturalistic that we forget that it is fiction – the prose version of "found" art where the sheer authenticity of the text appears to have displaced literary artifice. Perhaps it can; but we should also recognize that one aspect of the book that cannot be treated either as an element of the *fabula* or the *syuzhet* is the narrator himself, who neither attempts to hide within the text nor impose himself on it. The narrator – Orwell – always makes room for the specifics of his story and numbs himself to its curiosities and elemental horrors; all of that is handed to the reader largely unmolested. It is not impossible that a book like this could be published, marketed, and sold as a novel but surely most readers would treat it as identical to Johnson's *Journey to the Western Isles of Scotland* or Lawrence's *Twilight in Italy and other Essays,* yet pretending to be something else.

Such cross-genre ruses are not entirely unknown. The so-called prose poem comes to mind but the fact that a collection of the most notable of these items would be little more than 20 pages in length testifies to the significance of a genre pretending to retain its character while giving up any serious claim to it. Few if any would treat a *fabula*-exclusive "novel" as anything more than a curiosity for the simple reason that fiction, as

Thackeray pointed out, is possessed of key self-defining features that attract the reader to it. In Isherwood's book the narrator is ever-present and mischievously elusive, apparently relating the truth as he observed and experienced it but sewing his account with doubts. He makes us wonder about facts and certainty, turns other characters into figures we think we know, yet, as we leave the novel, causing them to remain as mysteries. And he himself is both convincing and shifty, a good teller of a story who is able to become an unreliable part of the fiction. These are the bald technicalities but distinguishing between fiction and nonfiction is a small matter when we wonder about a bigger question. Which would you rather read? Fiction when it plays its tricks, displays its complex gallery of manners and representational figures, or fiction that is indistinguishable from nonfiction? Most significantly, does not the former show us a real literary artist at work?

The Formalists disclose the elementary tools of literary writing, the means by which an able craftsman displays his/her skill. Technical dexterity does not guarantee greatness but without it the poem or the novel will never be able even to make a claim upon enduring significance. Craftsmanship, the control of the double pattern, is a prerequisite for excellence, and with this in mind let us consider literary evaluation.

6

Evaluation

Each of the critical issues and debates discussed so far carries with it a subtext which is rarely if ever acknowledged let alone canvassed: evaluation. Aside from such involuntary functions as breathing, everything that we encounter causes us to judge it. Look at a building, a landscape, a chair, or indeed another human being and somewhere among the spectrum of registers and distractions that attends the experience will feature an elementary, sometimes embarrassing, reflex; whether or not we like it. This could involve all manner of judgments and instincts, from the aesthetic to the visceral, and the same heedless impulsive sensation accompanies our first reading of a poem or a novel. For some of us dissatisfaction, boredom, or perplexity might constitute our conclusive experience of the work, but most will press ahead, read it again, and question their initial response. This next, measured stage of scrutiny – perhaps involving a comparison of the work with others we know – is the doorway between subjective impression and the complex procedure of putting our thoughts into words, talking to others about the piece, and the more formal activity of recording our observations on the page. The latter constitutes the activity of literary criticism.

In what follows I want to examine the question of how much of our initial evaluative judgments we leave behind when we pass through that doorway and whether literary criticism, with its various rules and conventions, permits

Is Shakespeare Any Good?: And Other Questions on How to Evaluate Literature,
First Edition. Richard Bradford.
© 2015 John Wiley & Sons, Ltd. Published 2015 by John Wiley & Sons, Ltd.

us to make judgments regarding the quality of literary writing. I shall not promote ill-considered caprice as a substitute for learning and sophisticated scrutiny; rather it will be my intention to consider how various formal and aesthetic concepts might be used as a prism for discriminatory judgments on the relative value of literary works.

Abstract principles such as excellence only become tenable through their exemplification in specific texts, and further verification of prestige will be found when these are contrasted with texts that are demonstrably inadequate. Evaluation therefore entails comparison and in what follows I attempt an impartial estimation of the relative qualities of a number of works. I begin with poems by Philip Larkin and William McGonagall. My choice of the latter might seem to question my premise of impartiality given that his name has become synonymous with laughable incompetence. He is treated with indulgent condescension by everyone within, and indeed outside, the literary establishment and the *Oxford Companion to English Literature* (Drabble, 2000) cursorily refers to him as "the world's worst poet." However, it is impossible to locate detailed, measured assessments of his work upon which such judgments could be founded. He is, then, ranked by all-comers as an incompetent poet but this in effect amounts to condemnation without trial.

There is an intriguing article by Paul Werth, "Roman Jakobson's Verbal Analysis of Poetry" (1976), which presents Jakobson's methods as embodying the flaws and failed objectives of conventional criticism. Werth claims, correctly, that the application of Jakobson's exhaustive stylistic methodology to a poem by McGonagall discloses levels of complexity and sophistication comparable with those that Jakobson and Jones found in a Shakespeare sonnet. Werth's point is that there is no predictable relationship between "linguistic evidence and critical instinct" and that it is impossible to prove the general opinion that "the value of [McGonagall's poem] is ... abysmally low." It is true that Jakobson does not supplement his analyses with evaluative comments – he leaves that to the reader – but such an omission does not disprove the contention that knowledge of the primary, formal features of the poem properly enables us to substantiate our judgment of its quality. This is McGonagall's poem:

> All hail to the Rev. George Gilfillan of Dundee,
> He is the greatest preacher I did ever hear or see.
> He is a man of genius bright,
> And in him his congregation does delight,
> Because they find him to be honest and plain,

Affable in temper, and seldom known to complain.
He preaches in a plain straightforward way,
The people flock to hear him night and day,
And hundreds from the doors are often turn'd away,
Because he is the greatest preacher of the present day.
He has written the life of Sir Walter Scott,
And while he lives he will never be forgot,
Nor when he is dead,
Because by his admirers it will be often read;
And fill their minds with wonder and delight,
And wile away the tedious hours on a cold winter's night.

McGonagall uses irregular rhythm and line lengths, but so did Coleridge in "Christabel" and Blake and Whitman in their most celebrated work. His rhyme scheme – aa bb cc dd – juxtaposes a note of regularity against an otherwise flexible formal pattern and one might even contend that his piece is a modest forerunner to modernism, particularly since he eschews metaphor and ostentatious imagery; he could almost be cited as an early quasi-Imagist. So far, then, McGonagall appears to be an engaging, innovative writer but his failure as a poet is due to his apparent unwillingness or inability to decide whether he is writing poetry or prose. The rhymes interfere with the progress of the syntax, but not in a way that creates a purposive, let alone elegant, tension between the two dimensions of the double pattern, the poetic and referential registers. The rhymes are found and dumped at line endings as a duty to poetic custom, and syntax is altered only as a concession to this convention. Consequently, we encounter embarrassing sequences of non-sequitors. The line "He has written the life of Sir Walter Scott" is not in itself clumsy or awkward but one senses that once McGonagall has launched himself into the next one his desperate search for a rhyme – or perhaps his predecision regarding the rhyme word he intends to use; "forgot" – blinds him to the ponderous unintentionally droll character of the resulting couplet. Then we encounter the inept coda:

Nor when he is dead.

Again one must assume that in his frantic attempts to find matching rhyme words for each unwieldy chunk of syntax he has lost any cognizance of the terrible effects than can be caused when the two halves of the double pattern are unskilfully coordinated.

McGonagall, in his chaotic, mildly endearing way, poses a serious question for evaluative criticism. We may judge him to be a bad poet because his failure to control and command the poetic stratum of the work compromises his ability to absorb its nonliterary dimension and to offer the reader an unexpected and possibly enlightening perspective on the relation between language and perceived reality. If he had written a prose essay about the activities and characteristics of the Reverend Gilfillan and told us roughly the same as he does in his poem, stylistic evaluation would be suspended. But because he uses a form in which the structural dimensions of the text constantly interfere with its communicative purpose, we begin to ask questions about how, and how well, he deals with this provocative merger of style and function. In effect making sense of the poem becomes an evaluative rather than a purely practical procedure. McGonagall, by writing a poem, provokes our wish to understand the text, only to leave us disappointed. His literary style is an encumbrance, an irritation, rather than a medium that transforms or even constructs the message.

Despite being loathed by the more sanctimonious among the literary and academic establishment for his alleged personal shortcomings, Philip Larkin, unlike McGonagall, is treated by most as an accomplished poet. Few, if any, have doubted the quality of his "An Arundel Tomb," but what justifies its ranking as a first rate poem? The following are the opening and closing stanzas:

> Side by side, their faces blurred,
> The earl and countess lie in stone,
> Their proper habits vaguely shown
> As jointed armour, stiffened pleat,
> And that faint hint of the absurd –
> The little dogs under their feet. ...
>
> Time has transfigured them into
> Untruth. The stone fidelity
> They hardly meant has come to be
> Their final blazon, and to prove
> Our almost-instinct almost true:
> What will survive of us is love.

The poem adheres to the complex stanzaic formula of iambic, octosyllabic lines, rhyming abbcac, but the syntax maintains the unforced accumulation of detail and reflection that one might expect in a private journal. The first three stanzas are dominated by the speaker's description of the details of the tomb and among the diction and syntax is found a light distribution of registers which are, if not quite anachronistic, self-consciously unusual. "Proper habits vaguely shown" carries a hint of the naughty ambiguity of the Renaissance lyricist, and the words "lie in stone" would if found in a poem three centuries older than this prompt a suspicion that the verb "lie" is playing beyond its apparent reference to a recumbent final posture. The poetry that engages most with the brutal contrariness of life as brief, nasty, and pointless while pretending to be something else is that of the seventeenth century lyricists, the Metaphysicals, and "An Arundel Tomb" seems to nod sardonically towards that tradition. This suspicion is further encouraged in the final stanza, in which we learn that

> Time has transfigured them into
> Untruth.

The enjambment is meticulously disingenuous, in that he hesitates but only to delay the acceptance of a grim certainty hinted at throughout the poem.

Many commentators upon the poem have failed to recognize that its speaker is robustly unpersuaded by everything he apprehends, that the poem is in actuality an affirmation of cynical disbelief both in the significance of love as anything beyond the emblematic and the possibility of there being anything after death. Such misreadings testify to the brilliance of Larkin's counterpointing of the deferential manner of the poem against what it actually says. The final stanza comes close to being a triumphant celebration of love's abiding power but the deceptively innocuous modifiers, "hardly," and, twice, "almost" assassinate this optimistic motif; an "almost true" will always be a lie. Larkin's achievement here is threefold. His orchestration of a demanding stanzaic formula with a relaxed yet shrewd manner is exemplary; the two parts of the double pattern, by their nature incompatible, are elegantly amalgamated. If this were his only accomplishment then the poem might be classed as a fine example of technical proficiency, but Larkin's meshing of poetic devices with ordinary language serves as the perfect vehicle for an effect at once beguiling and unimprovable. As we follow the eye and the reflections of the speaker he appears fascinated yet uncertain about the significance of the tomb, but gradually – particularly when we read the poem two or three times and consider more closely its delicate nuances of meaning – it becomes apparent that the speaker's polite esteem for this tribute to the endurance of love and the spirit is simply that; in truth he has no illusions regarding anything beyond lived experience. The double pattern frames and orchestrates an interplay between routine and elemental states of mind.

In the nonliterary world there is a consensus on the appropriateness and suitability of idiom or vocabulary. We would not, for example, reply to an email from a boyfriend with "Your manner of linking the consciousness of deviation to translatability in fact condemns what one wants at least to describe" when "Are we meeting later, or what" would do. And nor would we begin a job application or complaint to a council official with a phrase such as "My dearest Johnny-boy, I wish so much…" In general we have an intuitive alertness to what is required by the context of the statement but in verse this is complicated by the formal architecture of the poem, capable as this is of throwing into bold incongruous relief phrases or habits of speech that outside the poem might be more cautiously or appropriately situated. Philip Hobsbaum's "A Lesson in Love" is a brief narrative piece in which an academic tells of how he seduced one of his students, apparently during a tutorial. These are the closing stanzas:

> Which is the truer? I, speaking of Donne,
> Calling the act a means and not an end,
> Or at your sweet pudenda, sleeking you down:
> Was there no other way to be your friend?
>
> None, none. The awkward pauses when we talk,
> The literary phrases, are a lie.
> It was for this your teacher ran amok:
> Truth lies between your legs, and so do I.

Hobsbaum, unlike McGonagall, earned himself a respectable level of esteem within the literary establishment but there is, at least in my view, something about this poem that recalls the latter's work. One can observe, without comment, that it is comprised of regular pentameter quatrains, is in tone conversational and reflective with hardly any recourse to figurative language, with the exception of that memorably vivid closing line. Some poems telescope their substance into a brief phrase which is often recalled or quoted as a condensation of the themes addressed. (Yeats's "A terrible beauty is born" from "Easter, 1916" is a prime example.) The final line of "A Lesson in Love" has a comparable though lamentable effect. From the first line onwards one begins to detect an uneasy relationship between the personal idiosyncratic tone of the piece and the dry formality of its structure. If, in a novel, a somewhat condescending pretentious Lothario were to use the term "modest Irish miss" (stanza 1), then go on to revel in his recollection of her "full mouth" and in due course "legs thrashing" (stanza 2), "stocking tops" and "tight blue pants bursting to be off" the author might be commended for a grating blend of caricature and candor – especially if that author was male. In a poem as formally painstaking as this, however, the contrast between the locutionary manner and its containing framework seems, to put it lightly, inappropriate. The speaker who, in a novel or even in the real world, would appear in his own right a blend of the odious and the absurd is here a constituent controlling element of the text and his presence does considerable damage to the quality of the latter as a work of literature. The dreadful counterpoint between his pompous erudition – "speaking of Donne" – and his visceral intent, including the prurient phrasing of "your sweet pudenda, sleeking you down," would in any context cause one to recoil (or if male perhaps issue an apology on behalf of one's gender). But when framed within the cool exactness of a regular quatrain the presence seems anomalous and embarrassing. One even recalls the tragi-comic spectacle of McGonagall as he seeks desperately to cram his unwieldy syntax into a rhyme scheme. Here the execution is more controlled and the effect all the worse for it. Consider the rhymes. In purely technical terms they are correctly disposed but the parallelisms of sound point up the grotesque transposition of the speaker's lexicon with his state of mind. "I knew" – "your eyes gave me a clue" (stanza 1); "your tight blue pants" – "our romance" (stanza 2). The closing line exemplifies the speaker's, and it must said the poet's, blindness to stylistic malapropisms. It is a conceit that defies any attempt to make sense of it it but not because of its complexity; critical analysis does not immunize one from unendurable disquiet.

It is not too difficult to identify incompetent writing in regular verse in the sense that a poet's inability to properly reconcile the twin demands of the double pattern will become painfully evident. But with free verse there are no particular syntactic or metrical rules that the reader might invoke to judge the quality of a poem. Jonathan Culler can turn a prose discourse into a free verse poem by visually foregrounding parts of its syntactic framework, and Stanley Fish claims to have distilled impressive interpretations from his students in response to a poetically "shaped" list of surnames on the blackboard (see Chapter 4). At the less serious end of the aesthetic spectrum *Private Eye*'s resident free versifier, E.J. Thribb ("a poet, 17 and a half," though by now probably 57) has produced absurd and amusing examples of "occasional" free verse.

Erratum
In my last poem
"Lines on the
100th Anniversary
Of the Birth of
W. Somerset
Maugham"

The word "Yorkshire"
Appeared as
"Workshire."

Keith's mum
Spotted it
Immediately though
I confess I did
Not when I read
The proofs.

I regret the
Inconvenience this
May have caused to readers.

One mispelt word
Like this can
Completely destroy
A poem
                    (8 February 1974)

Thribb has established himself as a comic institution (four of his works feature in D.J. Enright's *Penguin Book of Light Verse*, 1980) because we, his amused readers, are still uncertain about what the writing and interpretation of free verse actually involve. The import of the piece is clear enough: an erratum by an unselfconsciously adolescent poet ("Keith's mum spotted it immediately"). As a prose note this text would function as an engaging, even charming, example of ingenuousness, but it becomes comic because its division into lines projects it into the "serious" sphere of the poetic. But why do we not find William Carlos Williams's "This Is Just To Say" (1934) equally laughable?

          This Is Just To Say
          I have eaten
          the plums
          that were in

the icebox
and which
you were probably
saving
for breakfast

Forgive me
they were delicious
so sweet
and so cold.

Culler proposes that the only reason that we interpret this as a poem is because we have become accustomed to the typographic design of free verse, and that once this signal of high-cultural intent registers we bring to it a lexicon of interpretative and evaluative responses.

> Given the opposition between the eating of plums and the social rules which this violates, we may say that the poem as note becomes a mediating force, recognizing the priority of rules by asking forgiveness but also affirming, by the thrust of the last few words, that immediate sensuous experience also has its claims and that the order of personal relations (the relationship between the "I" and the "you") must make a place for such experience. (Culler, 1975, p. 175)

He reprints the poem as if it were a note left on the fridge to demonstrate that the two texts differ only in terms of the reader's programmed response; in short, we would not, if sane, interpret a similar message from whoever else uses our kitchen as a solemn reflection on "immediate sensuous experience" and the "order of personal relations."

One suspects, however, that Culler has allowed the bulldozer of Reception Theory to crush any nascent, personal register of aesthetic cognizance. His model of interpretation depends upon the assumption that Williams assembled the poem almost at random from a piece of prosaic, raw material; the sentence containing the note on the icebox is the text that he actually "wrote" while the poetic structure, comprised of three free verse paragraphs is the equivalent of Andy Warhol's famous framing of a soup tin or the positioning of Damien Hirst's decaying cow's head in an art gallery as an "installation." I would contend that when Williams wrote the poem he was fully alert to how the lines would play the predominant part in the poem's demonstration of how the mind can, in no more than 30 words, begin to intuit something subtle and transcendent in the otherwise commonplace. The free verse lines attend to no abstract pattern but they maintain a degree of consistency, never allowing a significant syntactic sequence to overrun their governance of the text. They separate, even mobilize and counterpoint brief noun and verb phrases (which surely, is evidence more of planning than, as Culler avers, the random redistribution of a pre-existing sentence). This design is immensely effective. The first and the third verse paragraphs are structurally almost identical, yet the latter unfolds the moments of pleasure in such a way that we forget the banality of the opening and are entranced by a speaking presence seemingly preoccupied with his own guilty indulgences. As a poem that coopts the two dimensions of the double pattern to create a portrait of a sentient mind at work it begs comparison with Larkin's, despite their superficial stylistic differences.

What then of E.J. Thribb? Thribb is, of course, the creation of several talented satirists, but his self-evident incompetence, his role as a postmodern McGonagall, raises significant questions with regard to quality and evaluation. Specifically, if Thribb's creators are capable of making conspicuous stylistic abominations in a free verse poem then there must, by implication, be ways in which an accomplished poet can create quite the opposite effect. Clearly, Thribb's piece invokes the twentieth century sub-genre of the "found" poem, pioneered by the Imagists, and exemplified in Williams's "This is Just to Say", a poem whose manner and diction seem to have more in common with casual, unalloyed moments of thought or expression than with the self-conscious stylization of much literary writing. Thribb is guilty of the very compositional bungling of which Culler falsely accused Williams. His poem does indeed, when reprinted as prose, seem as though it was originally intended as an erratum on one of his previous poems. The line breaks point up, give absurd prominence to, domestic banalities:

> Keith's mum
> Spotted it
> Immediately

They also testify to the fact that if the writer of this piece had intended it as a poem and, more significantly, was far more technically proficient than Thribb, he would not first have written it as prose and then redistributed it typographically. He would instead have given attention to the continuous interaction between the line and syntax.

Thribb demonstrates, fortnightly in his appearances in *Private Eye,* the pitfalls and dire consequences of misusing the deceptively simple form of free verse. Williams in "To A Poor Old Woman" (1934) shows how its potentialities can be handsomely realized:

> *To A Poor Old Woman*
> munching a plum on
> the street a paper bag
> of them in her hand
>
> They taste good to her
> They taste good
> to her. They taste
> good to her.
>
> You can see it by
> the way she gives herself
> to the one half
> sucked out in her hand
>
> Comforted
> a solace of ripe plums
> seeming to fill the air
> They taste so good to her.

How, then, do I justify my claim that Thribb's and Williams's poem belong at different ends of the aesthetic spectrum?

The subject of Williams's poem is an episode of unadorned unremarkable simplicity – a woman eating plums on the street – yet he invests the moment with vividness by allowing his language to become a mimetic index to an image which, visually, the reader can never apprehend. The movement of the woman's hand from the bag to her mouth and the apparent sense of satisfaction she derives from the experience is telescoped by Williams into his own similar fascination, perhaps even delight, at the shape and texture of the very ordinary phrase, "They taste good to her." Just as the woman derives pleasure from "the way she gives herself / to the one half / sucked out in her hand" so Williams savors the texture of five words, the meaning of which – "the taste" – is altered slightly with each reshaping.

In terms purely of skill and technique, good poets are those who create a fertile contrapuntal relationship between the two dimensions of the double pattern, and in this respect Larkin and Williams are exemplary. McGonagall's, Hobsbaum's, and Thribb's work involves clumsy and often embarrassing mismatches between these two dimensions. More significantly, the quality of a poem is concomitant with the poet's success in creating from the double pattern a perspective upon a theme, idea, experience, or object that cannot be obtained via nonpoetic language. Larkin, without reaching any manifest conclusions, shows how complementary and sometimes competing, emotional and intellectual impressions attend an encounter with a sculpted tribute to life beyond death; he does so, moreover, in a manner that belies the normative logic of prose. Williams crystallizes a moment of apparent insignificance as a model of how perception, empathy, and language interact, and again he demonstrates how poetry is not merely an autonomous genre but one that is possessed of unique expressive capacities.

Given that McGonagall and Thribb are patently incapable of orchestrating the two dimensions of the double pattern the reader is preoccupied almost exclusively with the spectacle of a poet failing to master the fundamentals of his vocation and as a consequence any indulgent questions regarding what the poet might be attempting to achieve become immaterial. Hobsbaum is not so much technically inept as guilty of the gauche mismatching of two stylistic registers. The effect is not entirely dissimilar to that caused by Thribb but, since it was unintentional, more likely to cause embarrassment than amusement.

Consider Roland Barthes' distinction in *S/Z* between works *scriptible* (writerly) and *lisible* (readerly). Roughly summarized, a scriptible text demands the participation of the reader in the production of meaning while its lisible counterpart involves a straightforward transference of effects to a more passive reader. One could argue that Wordsworth's "The Idiot Boy" is far more lisible than scriptible in the sense that we are fully informed of who the characters are, and what they do; and there is an uncomplicated correspondence between these details and the emotive effects of the poem. Eliot's "Prufrock" is scriptible in that we remain constantly uncertain about the nature of the speaker and the context of their incoherent account, and we are consequently obliged to speculate on how the text works and what it means – in Barthes' terms we become the co-writers of the text.

One issue rarely addressed in critical debates is this: are lisible poems of higher quality than their scriptable counterparts or vice versa? I ask it because Barthes and everyone else implies, without specifically stating, that the realm of the scriptable – largely though not exclusively modernist writing – is far more worthy of intellectual engagement than literature that is easier to comprehend.

The following is the opening stanza of Dylan Thomas's "When, Like a Running Grave":

When like a running grave, time tracks you down,
Your calm and cuddled is a scythe of hairs,

Love in her gear is slowly through the house,
Up naked stairs, a turtle in a hearse,
Hauled to the dome.

The relative adverb "When" introduces the complex explanatory clause of
the first line, and we are uncertain if the unfolding situation will involve the
specific circumstances of when time will track you down like a running
grave or whether time will always track you down like a running grave. This
uncertainty is not resolved; rather it is further complicated by a montage
of syntactic and semantic discontinuities. What exactly is your "calm and
cuddled"? The semantic pattern of a "scythe of hairs," "Love in her gear,"
"naked," "hearse," suggests perhaps a tension between sensual, physical
images and death. The poem extends Eliot's precedent in "Prufrock," and
takes it beyond any acceptable balance between intrinsic and imposed
coherence. Read the rest of the poem and if you can intuit continuities between random patterns of sound and sense and what is intelligible you are,
I believe, deceiving yourself. The potential for self-deceit is provided by a
complex and admirably precise formal pattern. Each stanza consists of four
roughly iambic decasyllabic lines, followed by a quattro-syllabic coda. These
are held together by a system of alliterative–assonantal off-rhymes, binding
each stanza into a discernable pattern of a bbb a. Without this concession to
regularity the poem would be meaningless. The reader is bounced from one
point of metrical and phonic foregrounding to the next and at a subliminal
level something like continuity is discernible; in truth the poetic dimension
of the double pattern has replaced and overridden intelligibility.

We are not dealing with the shambolic utterance of the semi-literate
infant or of the heroically inept non-native speaker, something that we
feel it is our polite duty to "correct." Nor are we indulging the stylistic
incompetence of a poet such as McGonagall. Thomas's command of both
dimensions of the double pattern is self-evident; but he has chosen deliberately to allow the poetic to subordinate the cognitive features of the poem.
On the one hand Thomas has proved himself to be a versatile craftsman –
his abundant provision and dextrous control of the standard lexicon of
poetic devices matches that of any Renaissance poet – yet at the same time
he has posed a question for the reader for which there is no simple answer.
His poem is as difficult to understand as the most radical modernist or
postmodern text yet in all other respects it is self-consciously conventional.
Is he therefore practicing a form of self-indulgence, protecting a poem
that says very little behind the façade of orthodoxy; or is he challenging
the routine expectations of what the double pattern can tell us about the

arbitrariness of language? The question is not a matter for impartial scrutiny because it raises a supplementary enquiry. Can we enjoy – by which I mean appreciate both aesthetically and intuitively – what we can never properly comprehend? Or should we set aside such subjective idiosyncratic inclinations and give attention to overarching intellectual and ideological aspects of poetic writing? If your reply to the former is no, then you are more likely to prefer poems that fall into the category of the lisible; and if your response to the latter is in the affirmative your favored territory is mostly likely scriptible verse.

Within academic criticism there is a perhaps understandable predilection for the scriptible poem. Since the 1960s literary theory has been dominated by the premise that language or discourse shapes and determines all brands of belief and experience, so poems that voraciously resist any affiliation to nonliterary language – that is, refuse to be made sense of – are sound material for the academic industry. By creating a language that is self-referentially poetic, which hints at coherence and continuity and then forecloses the offer, they point up the arbitrariness of all linguistic systems.

There are only three book-length collections concerned exclusively with the relationship between poetry and Theory (Murray, 1989; Easthope and Thompson, 1991; and Acheson and Huk, 1996) and in each more than three-quarters of the essays are concerned with the kind of radical avant-garde verse that lends itself to such Theory-orientated questions on the nature of signification and the unsteady connection between subjectivity and textuality. Each book indicates that from the perspective of a Theory-dominated academic world scriptible poems are by their nature accorded a higher status than their more conservative, accessible counterparts, a consensus that sidelines such questions as authorial skill and craftsmanship in favor of a hierarchy in which the posing of complex intellectual and interpretive questions is the principal criterion. In this regard J.H. Prynne, one of those who have kept the flame of Poundian modernism alight, is a particular favorite (he is for example accorded an entire chapter in Easthope and Thompson). Peter Ackroyd contends that Prynne's poetry "does not have any extrinsic reference. There is only a marginal denotative potential since the language aspires towards completeness and self-sufficiency" (Ackroyd, 1976, p. 130). Veronica Forrest-Thomson cites Prynne as an exemplar of what she terms the "disconnected image complex," which is a concept, a nuance, even a nominative reference to a person or thing, whose thematic frame of reference is distributed almost exclusively through the poem itself, while maintaining no coherent relationship with the world outside it. The following are passages from Prynne's "Of Sanguine Fire" followed by Forrest-Thomson's engagement with it.

> wait for it, Pie
> conceives a whiff of apple, even short crust, wait for
>   it, like the bold face too many, pyloric mill
> racing; yet Outwash runs on for the cloud –
>   *but are always Fresh,*
>   *Vigorous and Bright, like the life and*
>   *quickness of the Morning, and rejoyce like*
>   *the Sun to run their Course –*
>
>   and
>
> makes it through zero gravity, he too on the
>   verge of deep narcosis. He slides his face
> down three stairs, skipping the treads; he merely
> thinks abruptly of a red sexy pudding.

Pie and Outwash inhabit a familiar world of apple-pies, stairwells, taxis, but they are not themselves entirely part of this world. Each of them sums up a complex idea of how the physical world may appear in a poem. Pie stands for the disillusioned imagination facing its own inadequacies while Outwash stresses rather the robust physical world asserting its independence. These two figures are the main image-complexes of the lines. It is difficult to distinguish others since the constant movement from one implied external context to another does not allow consistent development of image-complexes over several lines; they appear momentarily only to disappear again. This disappearing quality in the image-complexes brings the conventional and the thematic levels closer together as the thematic contrast between the angels and the physical world is seen in the contrast between the rhythm of the italicised lines and the rhythm of the long descriptive lines. Yet the very obtrusiveness of the formal differences make these into image-complexes in themselves; each different rhythm has its different theme. (Forrest-Thomson, 1978, pp. 142–145)

Forrest-Thomson also offers her own criteria for evaluation. The most worthy poems are, in her view, those that challenge the routine relationship between the intrinsic features of the text and its extrinsic frame of reference. Such poems resist what she calls "Bad Naturalization." Naturalization is a term used by Theorists to describe what happens when we create what amounts to a summary of a literary text, either as part of the procedure of reading or as a more formalized written discourse such as an essay or a review. Why more routine terms such as "making sense of" are now deemed insufficient to account for this is part of the mystery of Theory. But to return to Forrest-Thomson: some naturalizations are "Bad" because the poem allows the balance of power to shift toward the critic and the normative field of logic and explanation. "Of Sanguine Fire" incites "Good Naturalization." It "restores both the resources of lyric and the resources of thinking in poetry." The key phrase here is "thinking in poetry," meaning that the best poetry, that which restores "Good Naturalization," obliges, or rather enables, us to suspend our instinct to "make sense" of whatever we read or hear. By this she does not mean that we should aspire to some pre-cognizant quasi-mystical state, but rather to treat the poem's shifts between flickers of extrinsic meaning and internalized patterns of syntax, semantics, and image complexes as an ongoing experience rather than interpretation. She contends that poems that aspire to a state of poetic autonomy, unreliant upon the regimen of coherence, order, and common sense endemic to all other modes of communication, are accordingly the best. The following is one of the most well-known, most widely discussed poems in English.

> *Anecdote of the Jar*
> I placed a jar in Tennessee,
> And round it was, upon a hill.
> It made the slovenly wilderness
> Surround that hill.
>
> The wilderness rose up to it,
> And sprawled around, no longer wild.
> The jar was round upon the ground
> And tall and of a port in air.
>
> It took dominion every where.
> The jar was gray and bare.
> It did not give of bird or bush,
> Like nothing else in Tennessee.

In Forrest-Thomson's view this is a poem meditating on the relation between art and nature, between human and natural reality.

The process of interpretation involves accepting the world of ordinary experience as given, finding in it various already-known attitudes to the problem of which the poem speaks, and clarifying the poem by relating it to these attitudes. In a sense the interpreters are right: the poem is written in

complicity with these assumptions; it demands this type of reading. This is
not to say that Stevens is a bad poet; he is not. But he is not an original poet
in the sense of questioning what his readers require of him, or the reality
they require him to reproduce. (Forrest-Thomson, 1978, pp. 51–52)

Stevens, then, is a competent but unoriginal poet, producing work that is
"complicit" with the predominantly rationalist and empiricist expectations
of nonpoetic discourse. Certainly, "Anecdote of the Jar" is far more orthodox
than the work of Prynne or indeed much of the verse of Eliot and Pound –
all of whom Forrest-Thomson regards as "original" by her definition of the
term – but I would profess that it transcends her strict criteria regarding
Good and Bad Naturalizations. It enables us to combine both in a single
reading and in doing so presents itself as a far more "original" and indeed
subtle example of poetry at its best. One could indeed argue that it is a
meditation "on the relation between art and nature," but not in the sense
that one might expect such reflections to manifest themselves in language.
Stevens' syntax achieves what the orthodoxies of language would seem to
prohibit, in that he maintains, simultaneously, two registers or nuances of
intention, and he does so not simply as a gesture to some aesthetic or
philosophical conceit but as a uniquely poetic fulfilment of mimesis. We
will never know if the phrase "And round it was" is a coordinate clause
prompted by the feeling of petty omniscience that comes with standing
upon a promontory, or if it is an, equally inconclusive, reflection on the jar's
roundness. This moment of irresolution informs the remainder of the poem,
the sentences reach toward some possible, often intimated conclusion, but
always turn back upon themselves, and this beguiling effect of strands of
meaning opening, pausing, and diversifying is grounded upon the speaker's
vacillation as to what exactly is the focus of his thoughts and his discourse:
the jar, the hill, the surrounding countryside, the unfixed relationship between all three? Had a comparable effect been discharged via a naturalistic
record of hesitant speech, perhaps even the interior monologue, then the
speaker and the writer would be disjoined; the former would be as much the
imitative creation of the latter as his language. But Stevens achieves both a
wonderfully authentic model of improvisation alongside a residue of
something more elegant and calculated. The lines move between a relaxed
iambic pattern and the abandonment of rhythm, and the competing thematic
foci submerge and resurface persistently yet unpredictably in semantic and
phonemic echoes: "round it was," "Surround the hill," "sprawled around,"
"round upon the ground," "a port in air," "everywhere," "gray and bare."

The poem can indeed lend itself to a Bad Naturalization in that critics have built around it abundant theories on Stevens' preoccupations regarding art and nature, intellectualism and primitivism; but this is the fault of the critics, not Stevens. Such naturalizations are, in truth, unappreciative misreadings. "Anecdote of a Jar" involves "thinking in poetry" in the sense that its oscillations between up to four predominant foci are too subtle to document precisely. There is never, for example, a single point at which one theme is immune from the nuanced presence of others: the musical equivalent would be counterpoint in which melodic phrases overlap to the extent that their interaction negates any clear perception of their separateness. We are aware, when we read it, that this multi-layered effect is occurring but to describe it in terms of, say, degrees of paradox or ambiguity or as a realization of a profound tension between contrary philosophical issues does a grave injustice to the operation of the poem as a work of art. The fact that it provokes such responses in critics testifies to its quality and indeed its superiority to the self-referential poetic work of Prynne and others of his ilk. It catches the reader between a desire to make sense of it – it is relatively speaking accessible and coherent – and the difficulty of doing so without ruining its immediate and manifest effects. It is a poem that we can enjoy, can indeed at a cursory level understand, but one that at the same time confounds our ability to describe precisely how our understanding of it conditions our enjoyment.

Forrest-Thomson was an exceptional and daring critic in that she at least ventured a rationale for the discernment of importance and significance in poems. At the same time, however, the limitations of her technique were depressingly prescient. She was writing in the late 1970s, the beginning of the assault by literary Theory upon the redoubt of traditional belle lettrism, New Criticism. The lexicon, mannerisms, and intellectual premises of Theory are now endemic features of the critical writing of all but a small number of academics and as a result academic criticism is to a large extent immunized from that most contentious, subjective feature of talking and writing about verse: whether or not the poet is possessed of talent. Forrest-Thomson indicated that the fact that Stevens is a good poet – by which she means a skilled literary craftsman – is irrelevant. The reasons for this viewpoint – by now the overwhelming consensus – are various, but most significantly they stem from the perception of the reader and poet as subjects or constructs of specific ideological conditions and discourses, which in turn undermines our notion of being able to recognize aesthetic value or quality as intrinsic features of anything. Talent and refinement have not been completely eliminated from perceptions of a poet's character but their importance is now deemed negligible.

I would aver that the very best poems are not those that make naturalization difficult. That would be to equate significance with some putative intellectual transaction between poet and critic: the latter's training and experience will equip them fully to deal with the poem's refusal to release a seam of intelligibility and to treat this as part of a broader discourse involving matters such as authority, subjectivity, signification. In my opinion, excellence is apparent when naturalization appears unproblematic but where it is equally evident that the skills employed by the poet to achieve this seeming state of transparency will test and sometimes exceed the capacities of the critic to describe how they do so. It is here that critical analysis becomes both symptomatic of the acumen of its practitioner and a diagnostic indicator of true poetic quality.

With this in mind consider these two poems by Andrew Crozier.

> Five quarters duck lofty club bar rubbish
> With a short but sound composition – secure.
> It's from the oldest opera. As a wise precaution
> Ten cat-men break the laws of pain
> In an old man's stride. As first offenders
> A portly body of nurses is detailed fast
> In a gross Roman style of wrestling.

> A dozen boas flailing cheesecake sweet
> And rare. Though spoiled and forward
> Made to last. Not his term – yet.
> If you came to assert they move it slowly
> Use an edge and turn. My mother sat and
> A goitered ream of waltzers all in blue
> Held and clear a Turkish Bath for use.

In both, compound images and flickers of continuity are present, but stubbornly resistant to intelligibility. A determination to evade the predatory attention of the interpreter informs both pieces and in this respect they belong in a tradition that began with Pound and has since manifested itself in the work of postmodern writers. Depending upon one's cultural and indeed temperamental predisposition it is possible to be enthralled by such pieces, perceive them even as both aesthetic and political refusals to conform. Our incurious and complacent expectations are threatened and we are reminded that art can be thrillingly incitive. Both seem to involve the poet's stylistic signature, specifically a tendency to connect resonant noun and verb phrases, such as "goitered ream of waltzers," "Roman style of wrestling," "My mother sat," "an old man's stride" in a manner that both disrupts any internal thread of continuity and refuses to correspond with any logical sequence in the world outside the poem.

Some might contend that Crozier's breathless disdain for coherence, his creation of a world of signifiers that eludes the normative sphere of order and familiarity is to his credit. In both pieces he achieves an extraordinary almost magical chiascuro of impressions, never allowing the reader to steady themselves even with an intimation of what might happen next.

Others might well feel that poems so consistently impenetrable are little more than prompters to equally abstruse discourses, in prose, on the nature of signification and truth and that as works of art their intrinsic qualities are negligible; they have substituted the traditional responsibility to literary craftsmanship for a role in a much broader discourse – involving critics and theorists – where aesthetics and culture are seen as subdivisions of ideology. At a more elemental level one might feel that poems that refuse to make sense are both displeasing and predictable.

Both points of view are founded upon subjective predispositions ranging from one's accustomed intellectual outlook to straightforward matters of taste. How do we go about reconciling these variables with a measure of quality that is more objective?

At this point I should make a confession. Only one of these pieces is by Crozier. If you know his work you might be able to identify it, but if you do not, can you tell, from your scrutiny of both, which was composed by a respected avant-garde poet and which put together in roughly 30 minutes by me, Richard Bradford? You might compare your response to each with your engagements with poems that stir a comparable feeling of disorientation. In this respect you could consider Dylan Thomas as their conventional precursor (in the sense that his use of meter and rhyme is incongruously orthodox) and John Ashbery's "Sortes Virgilianae" as achieving in narrative verse what these distil into a lyric. Their closest relatives would probably be found within the so-called L=A=N=G=U=A=G=E school of poetry (see Nicholls in Easthope and Thompson, 1991) especially in the work of Steve McCaffery. As you subject both "poems" to various modes of scrutiny and comparison other questions will arise. Principally, if the dissimilarities between them are so slight have we not come upon a simple test of quality? A poem whose effects can so easily be reproduced must be of questionable value.

Choose a poem by an anthologized, mid twentieth to early twenty-first century poet and subject it to an exercise in imitation (I suggest the use of a piece from recent literary history because it will draw upon our own idioms, vocabulary, and accustomed frames of reference; the reproduction of archaisms, involving sufficient background reading, can result in ventriloquism).

You will first need to familiarize yourself with the most telling formal characteristics of the work. Impersonal stylistic features such as the use of a given stanzaic formula, rhyme scheme, or metrical pattern are fairly easy to assimilate and reproduce. Less straightforward is the feigning of, say, a preponderance or avoidance of figurative or nuanced language and the original text's level of engagement with an external frame of reference. The final stage, where you attempt to write not simply "in the manner of" the poet in question but to capture the quintessence of their achievement, is where the exercise in imitation offers a new perspective upon the ways in which we understand and appreciate poetry. To build a poem of any sort requires a thorough knowledge of the mechanics of verse and of the range of choices available within the vast but recognizably autonomous zone of the poetic. As a consequence the re-creation of the formal particulars of your chosen poem will further extend your awareness of what happens in poems per se. However, it is the shift from stylistic impersonation to the capturing of the poem's uniqueness that involves a collateral move from the mechanics of form to the tendentious issue of excellence. If you are able to re-create, to your own satisfaction, a piece that is identical in its nature, effect, and significance to the original poem then you are either an enormously gifted poet manqué or the chosen poem is of slight importance. If on the other hand you are capable of identifying the minutiae of the poet's technique but defeated by the task of achieving a comparable fabric of effects then you have come upon a vital clue in the search for that feature of verse that is manifest yet difficult to define: inimitable superiority. I have already performed this exercise with Crozier, with self-evident results, and if you would care to turn back to Chapter 2, you will find a prose passage by Gertrude Stein and another quotation from a L=A=N=G=U=A=G=E poet which are also forgeries, though not acknowledged at that point. Did you see through my acts of fakery? If not, you might think again about the level of esteem granted to high modernism.

The following is a short piece by Philip Larkin.

As Bad As a Mile
Watching the shied core

> Striking the basket, skidding across the floor,
> Shows less and less of luck, and more and more
>
> Of failure, speeding back up the arm
> Earlier and earlier, the unraised hand calm,
> The apple unbitten in the palm.

The poem is a brief meditation upon a feeling that all of us experience, involving by degrees irritation, pessimism, and a sense of failure. No cause or circumstances are attributed to the sensation and indeed any intimation of presence is almost displaced by the image of the thrown apple core. It is an uncomplicated and transparent piece and my synopsis seems in this regard superfluous. However, the striking feature of the poem is the complex yet almost imperceptible interchanges between pictorial images and equally powerful abstractions. In the first two lines the syntax seems synchronized exactly with the unfolding sequence. The movement of the apple core to the basket and then to the floor is played out in an almost cinematic manner. But at the verb "Shows" the register shifts suddenly from the visual to the figurative, at least until after "failure," when we encounter a curious blend of the two. There is a subliminal sense of watching the film played backwards, with the object returned via the basket to the hand, but this is attended by an equally powerful abstraction – "failure," resignation, the certainty of unsuccess – which follows the core literally and metaphorically to a point prior to the beginning of the poem, "the apple unbitten the palm."

The internal sound pattern is interwoven with shifts between the visual and the abstract. In the first stanza "s" and "c" alliterations predominate; "shied," "striking," "basket," "core," "skidding," "shows," "luck." It is rare to encounter sound pattern employed so effectively as a supplement to sense but Larkin here makes use of alliteration as a coupling device, a means of counterpointing the syntax against the progress of images. Significantly, the last word in this alliterative sequence is "luck," the point at which the unemotive sequence of objects is exchanged for a concept. Thereafter only two drifting echoes of a previously dense sequence remain – "spreading" and "unraised" – a magnificently delicate deployment of artifice as mimesis; the sense of acceptance that loss is part of his ineluctable state is accompanied by the speaker's exchange of technique and design for uncluttered transparency.

My account of how the formal apparatuses of the poem contribute to its effects is I think accurate and insufficient. There are so many delicately nuanced shifts between the visual and the reflective, the concrete and the abstract, motion and stillness, observation and rumination – all executed within six short lines – that it is impossible to document their order or precedence. On the one hand it speaks eloquently to the reader who is neither obliged nor inclined to describe its operations while for those who attempt to do so, primarily critics, it outpaces efforts to impose upon it a formula or explanation. It does not, like Thomas, Prynne, or Crozier, create complex images that detach it from the world outside the text but at the same time it makes use of a spectrum of devices and creates a fabric of impressions that are exclusively poetic. This achievement, in my estimation, testifies to its exceptional quality and it is for this reason that I shall not attempt to create a poem of comparable merit. I can catalog its mechanisms but there is a significant difference between describing what a poet does and being able to replicate their accomplishment, and this I aver is the most reliable measure of excellence.

I will conclude this section on poetry with a brief glance at a pernicious aspect of our cultural ethos that endures, embarrassingly, like the proverbial elephant in the sitting room. I shall call it "protectionist condescension." It is protectionist in the sense that the poems involved make use of the mechanisms, often the labels, of verse technique as an attempt to claim some aesthetic status that they do not deserve. At the same time a considerable number of people within the cultural establishment connive in this with an act of evaluative blindness because they believe that such verse appeals to the kind of people who might not be routinely drawn to the writings of Pound or Eliot. I have chosen to discuss it here rather than in Chapter 7 on popular literature because its protected status shows it to be as much the property of the highbrow intelligentsia as a sub-genre which appeals to a mass audience; it thus raises questions about evaluation and politically correct cultural tokenism. The best known examples are the so-called Liverpool Poets of the 1960s, who claimed some allegiance to the American Beat movement of the previous decade but were in truth part of a robust sociocultural confidence trick. Adrian Henri, Roger McGough, Brian Patten, and others offered a confection of working class primitivism – lovably and calculatedly unaffected – and an undemanding, seemingly spontaneous stylistic packaging that proved irresistible to a considerable number of the largely left-leaning middle class literary hierarchy. Typical of the trend is McGough's "Bucket."

> every evening after tea
> grandad would take his bucket for a walk
>
> An empty bucket
>
> When i asked him why

he said it was easier to carry
than a full one

grandad always had
an answer
for everything

The free verse technique carries a slight token of avant-garde adornment – it casts a knowing glance towards Williams – but this is offset by the easy, unpunctuated account of grandad, with his apparent eccentricities and unpretentious wisdom, the kind wrought from a life where carrying buckets was a grim necessity and no one took "dinner" or "supper" – "tea" was the evening meal.

The problem with this type of verse was that it became a cliché, with as many self-defining rules and conventions as the erudite, bourgeois writing it was supposedly an attempt to escape from. McGough's poem is almost as ludicrous as the fortnightly offerings of Thribb. It and many like it have been made exempt from the ridicule deliberately prompted by Thribb because notions such as the "vernacular," "regional verse," and "working class naturalism" are its keynotes; criticize these factors, even by implication, and you open yourself to charges of elitism and class-based disdain-fulness. But while such elements offer this kind of writing protection they also severely restrict it in terms of range. The double pattern is present but both elements involve a conformist element of simplicity, which sometimes borders on the simplistic. Abstruseness and intellectual exhibitionism are easy enough to detect and censure but at the other end of the spectrum an apparent inability to shift beyond homespun minimalism leads to creative stagnation and on the reader's part, weariness.

The trend begun in Liverpool would spread beyond the North West and its two best known women representatives are Pam Ayres and Wendy Cope. Ayres is a twentieth century version of Wordsworth's "The Mad Mother"; demonstrably very sane, eccentric, and wry rather than demented, but equally proud of her provincial country background and lack of a formal education beyond school. She is the living embodiment of the people's poet in that she does not so much write *to* her audience as *like* them, were any inclined to take up pen or word processor and compose verses. The closing stanza of her "Poem for the Diamond Jubilee" is terrifyingly memorable.

I wish our Queen a genuinely joyful Jubilee,
Secure in the affection of the mute majority,

> I hope she hears our voices as we thank her now as one,
> Sixty years a Queen. A job immaculately done.

One at first begins to wonder if McGonagall has been reincarnated as Poet Laureate but soon enough we suspect more complex motives on Ayres' part. Is it perhaps an exercise in self-caricature, maybe a gesture of creative humility in honor of the monarch's long service? It is not completely unlike her other work, while being almost self-consciously much, much worse. Alternatively, it is not entirely impossible that Ayres has achieved something undreamt of even by Barthes and his peers: a seamless blending of author, text, and reader. It sounds like a poem composed by the most affectless, artlessly sincere member of the "mute majority," its egregious incompetence a testament to their affection for the Queen. But surely, one might then ask, would Ayres stoop to such a patronizing act? Perhaps not, but the same question must also be addressed to a more recent star who has galvanized critics in the worlds of popular music and mainstream verse, Kate Tempest.

Tempest is a white, working class, rap performer who has also taken to publishing volumes of poetry, her third and most recent being *Hold Your Own* (2014). A few commentators have expressed reservations about her work but the vast majority are beguiled and awestruck. *The Guardian* (30 October 2014), typically, praises the way "she picks up the fabulous, familiar characters [from classical literature and mythology] dusts them down and hauls them into the present." In this instance the character is the transsexual Tiresias who Tempest updates and transfers to inner-city London.

> Shuffling, lonesome, sipping black lager,
> Park-drunk. Spouting maniacal laughter
> Hard up. Head down. Scarf, gloves, parka…
>
> He spits brown phlegm at the oncoming darkness.

The language is self-consciously unliterary, so much so that it obtains the level of rough transparency that we normally expect in the writings of teenagers encouraged to "creatively" utilize their thoughts and experiences. The benefits for the writer are a matter for debate – depending on how much credit we give to the notion of writing as a form of catharsis – but for the reader there is a sense of having encountered a curious variation on "found" art, in which the guileless, untutored speaker and the controlling presence of the artist are indistinguishable. The latter does of course deliver the irregular sound-pattern, the rap-style undertow and the off-rhymes. But these too – the poetic elements of the double pattern – beg questions regarding purpose and quality. Frequently, they seem to combine a cultural gesture towards conventional "high-art" verse with an act of vandalism against it. We have to ask ourselves: is the relentless stylistic clumsiness deliberate, and if so why? We leave Tiresias as an old man alone in a foul café, mumbling to himself about the state of the world: "Buzzwords everywhere. Progress. Freedom / He picks his teeth with a dirty needle / And kicks his feet to the latest jingles. / Ain't got time to be dating singles. / Far too busy trying to make things simple." One is faced with a problem similar to that raised by Ayres. Few, if any, would dispute that this is quite dreadful poetry, but what is the cause of its insufficiency? Has Tempest simply overreached her abilities, assumed that rap/performance techniques automatically qualify her as a poet? Or has she created not only Tiresias but also deliberately presented Tiresias's author as a protest against all things orthodox and elitist, including good writing? The latter seems unlikely at least if we take seriously the prevailing opinion of the literary establishment. In 2013 she was presented with the Ted Hughes Award for which the principal criterion is "innovation" rather than heroic self-caricature.

In truth, Tempest's admirers within the cultural hierarchy are seizing the opportunity for a moment of conscience-salving. They have admitted a fully fledged outsider into their exalted ranks: that she is art school rather than university educated (the same alma mater as Ms Emin, as many note) and has served her creative apprenticeship in an area of popular performance pioneered by people of color helps to maintain the principle that "highbrow" literary culture can become an open, equitable ethos. The fact that in order to praise her they must also blind themselves to her inability to write good poetry is an example of purposive hypocrisy and self-delusion. Also, it tells us something about the status of poetry. Imagine if the Booker Panel decided to award their exalted Prize to E.L. James, author of the *Fifty Shades of Grey* series of novels, and indeed that these same novels were exalted in the review columns of the serious weeklies as radical masterpieces. It is, of course, an absurd hypothesis. Why? Because they are poorly written populist trash (see Chapter 7). The evidence that they appeal to a vast number of "ordinary" readers would be treated as irrelevant since their qualities as "literary" fiction are negligible, yet Tempest is lauded as someone who has bridged the gap between popular and highbrow culture (irrespective of the fact that her abilities as a poet are comparable with James's as a novelist). Tempest is feted not because she is any good but because her work puts into reverse the model of aesthetic hegemony promoted by Pierre Bourdieu in *La Distinction* (1979).

Bourdieu claimed that the governing classes used high art as a means of appropriating images, ideas, and most crucially a language of appreciation from which the less well-educated proletariat was excluded. He did not regard high culture as necessarily superior to its low cultural counterpart but through a conspiracy involving the cultural establishment and the education system it appeared to be so: it seemed to ordinary people to be discouragingly difficult to understand and discuss. Thus, Tempest's use of poetic technique as subordinate to a combination of angry vernacular discourse and popular art forms is seen as a revolution against the aesthetic, and indeed social, hegemony documented by Bourdieu. However, the possibility that a considerable amount of mainstream, conventional poetry is not merely different from popular culture but superior to it, and that it therefore involves a greater demand on the intellectual and stylistic acumen of the writer is ignored; as is the collateral possibility that the random imposition of a poetic framework upon a repetitive, crudely political rant might result in something as flawed as *Hold Your Own*. There is a grim irony in the insistence by many academics that only dense, scriptible, poetic writing is worthy of intellectual engagement while the same constituency offers unstinting praise to simplistic, lisible verse as serving the appetites of the ordinary reader.

Poetry is still regarded as the most exalted, self-evidently literary of literary genres – the top-shelf of the cultural hegemony in Bourdieu's model – and by grafting on to it the media-generated baggage of performance poetry, popular music, and rap, Tempest has joined a tradition initiated by Duchamp and perpetuated by the likes of Emin and Hirst. The contextual preconditions for art are acknowledged (in Tempest's case in a careless nod towards poetic structure) but thereafter any sense of respect for intrinsic notions of craftsmanship or an implied competitive dialogue with acknowledged greats is abandoned. For poetry to still be regarded as the final bastion of high art – as the ultimate challenge to popular nonliterary forms – is, I suppose, a backhanded tribute to its enduring status. Somewhat depressing, however, is the prevailing impression that while it continues to be recognized as a genre per se, many within the critical hierarchy appear willing to exchange its once elevated status as an art form for a means of bargaining in a world where relativism seems to have replaced evaluation.

Let us now turn out attention to fiction, and begin with a question. Are there fiction writers who can match McGonagall regarding the numbingly incompetent misuse of the double pattern? There are many. Their work is sanctioned by the commissioning editors of major publishers and it goes into print without being improved by copyeditors. These are, however, the authors of popular fiction, work that appeals more to the escapist than the literary connoisseur. It would be unfair both to them and to their "literary" counterparts to deal with them here. The contest is one-sided, its result a foregone conclusion, and some of these pitiable figures will be scrutinized in the next chapter. Our search for the subnormal among those classed as "literary" becomes more arduous. Generally speaking, mainstream publishers provide an evaluative filter for what deserves to be in print. Certainly, stories abound of how good authors receive dozens of rejection slips before finding someone who will take them on, but these only illustrate the fact that, eventually, quality will be recognized. Yet there are exceptions. Edmund Wilson can claim to be one of the most important literary critics of the mid twentieth century. His *Axel's Castle* can justly be regarded as the first comprehensive account of what modernist literature was and did. These days he is less famous as a fiction writer but during the 1930s and 1940s he was ranked alongside Hemingway. One of his earliest, most successful works is, technically, a novella but would qualify as a full-length piece of fiction if published separately. His first person narrator is an East Coast US intellectual and one of the most striking episodes is his account of a sexual encounter with a young semi-literature immigrant girl of middle-European origin.

> But what struck and astonished me most was that not only were her thighs perfect columns but all that lay between them was impressively beautiful too, with an ideal aesthetic value that I had never found there before. The mount was of a classical femininity: round and smooth and plump; the fleece, if not quite golden, was blond and curly and soft; and the portals were a deep tender rose, like the petals of some fleshly flower. And they were doing their feminine work of making things easy for the entrant with a honeysweet sleek profusion that showed I had quite misjudged her in suspecting as I had sometimes done that she was really unresponsive to caresses. She became, in fact, so smooth and open that after a moment I would hardly feel her. Her little bud was so deeply embedded that it was hardly involved in the play, and she made me arrest my movement while she did something special and gentle that did not, however, press on this point, rubbing herself somehow against me – and then consummated, with a self-excited tremor that appeared to me curiously mild for a women of her positive energy. I went on and had a certain disappointment, for, with the brimming of female fluid, I felt even less sensation; but – gently enough – I came, too.

Simon Karlinsky, editor of the letters between Wilson and Nabokov, observed that "the prosecution and banning of Wilson's … *Memoirs of Hecate County* contributed to the collapse of the Victorian moralistic censorship that has persisted in western countries till the end of the 1950s." Perhaps, but it was in this case a contribution to freedom bought at a severe cost to good taste.

Imagine, if you can, a version of Donne's speaker who unshackles himself from the impersonal structure of verse and goes on to give voice to an obsessive puerile preoccupation with genitalia. He has eschewed the literary dimension of the double pattern. If he could be treated as a caricature of aspects of maleness or a sub-Beckettian exercise in presence subsumed by speech then some balance might be restored. Unfortunately, Wilson's narrator is horribly uncontrived and embarrassment in listening to him is not a proxy response; we want him to go away. It is the prose equivalent of Hobsbaum's poem.

Ghastly ingenuousness had replaced the balance between individuality and art. It is bad writing, but one has to wonder if a work at the other end of the spectrum, where all is foregrounded contrivance, is just as egregious.

Joyce's *Ulysses* has generated a cultural infrastructure of its own, with the remaining landmarks of the 24-hour Dublin odyssey attracting groups of dedicated fans every 16 June, "Bloomsday." Some are academics and many others first encountered the book via its status as one of the most prestigious works in the literary canon, enshrined in the university curriculum since the mid twentieth century. One has to wonder if the affectionate nostalgia that envelopes buildings such as the Martello Tower, on the pretty coastline south of Dublin where the novel opens, is inversely related to the actual experience of reading it?; if a summer day out in the friendly environs of Dublin is some kind of guilty compensation for what is denied to us in the book: to put it bluntly, enjoyment.

The best known passage is probably Molly Bloom's interior monologue which offers us a combination of her inner and outer worlds, respectively thought and language, but the substance of the novel is more complex and varied than this. It shifts us unpredictably between the inner states of Bloom, Molly, and Stephen, through more conventional narrative techniques, journalistic reportage, a potted history of English prose style, and operatic collage to theatrical dialogue; and these are only the more ostentatious variations. For example, the following four passages are but a handful of the stylistic repackagings of the thoughts and activities of Leopold Bloom.

He entered Davy Byrne's. Moral pub. He doesn't chat. Stands a drink now and then. But in leapyear once in four. Cashed a cheque for me once.

What will I take now? He drew his watch.

Bloom mur: best references. But Henry wrote it: it will excite me. You know now. In haste. Henry. Geek ee. Better and postscript. What is he playing now. In haste.

BLOOM: (*Behind his hand*) She's drunk. The woman is inebriated. (*He murmers vaguely the past of Ephraim*) Shitbroleeeth.

What caused him irritation in his sitting posture? Inhibitory pressure of collar (size 17) and waistcoat (5 buttons), two articles of clothing superfluous in the costume of mature makes and inelastic to alterations of mass by expansion.

Novels before *Ulysses* had filtered the narrative through a variety of perspectives, as in Emily Brontë's *Wuthering Heights*, but none had incorporated anywhere near so many diverse and apparently unrelated stylistic and generic modes as are found in Joyce. *Ulysses* seems determined never to come to rest upon a single persistent method of balancing the method of narration against the events narrated, continually subverting any attempt by a reliable narrator to control the work and instead offering the reader a kaleidoscopic medley of linguistic media. David Lodge summed up the effect: "The reader of *Ulysses* is never allowed to sink into the comfortable assurance of an interpretation guaranteed by the narrator, but must himself produce the meaning of the text by opening himself fully to the play of its diverse and contradictory discourses." Lodge addresses himself specifically to Joyce's novel but his theoretical, interpretive model is borrowed from Barthes.

> The space of writing is to be ranged over, not pierced; writing ceaselessly posits meaning ceaselessly to evaporate it, carrying out a systematic exemption of meaning ... a text is made of multiple writings, drawn from many cultures and entering into mutual relations of dialogue, parody, contestation ... The reader is the space on which all the quotations that make up a writing are inscribed without any of them being lost; a text's unity lies not in its origin but in its destination. (Barthes, *Image – Music – Text*, 1977; reprinted in Lodge, 1988, p. 171)

It could be argued, as we have seen in Chapter 2, that modernist exemplars such as *Ulysses* are improvements on their forebears, artistically and intellectually, in that few would maintain that the world can be properly understood from a single perspective; that by exposing the relativism and diversities of linguistic representation *Ulysses* implements literary art for a higher instructive, existential purpose. We not only admire

Joyce's achievement; our standard conceptions of what novels and indeed language can do are challenged.

Lodge and Barthes propose that Joyce and like-minded writers are responsible for showing us what, in fiction, their realist predecessors denied or obscured, that "realism" in its routine usage is a misnomer: the "real" is, as Joyce demonstrates, far more complex and unsettling. Perhaps, but this mantra raises two questions that the prevailing eminences of the literary establishment and academia either overlook or conceal. First of all, even if we concede that *Ulysses* had a role in the revolution of ideas that shaped the twentieth century, is this, we should also ask, what fiction is supposed to do? Next, and more significantly, if we accept Lodge's and Barthes' theses without question are we deliberately misrepresenting the qualities and complexities of Joyce's predecessors?

Dickens, in writing *Great Expectations* (1861), faced the problem of reconciling 30 years of recollected events, experiences, and their emotional effects with their reconstruction in a single retrospective narrative. At the beginning of his story, Pip tells of his first meeting with Magwitch and of his theft of the pork pie:

> The mist was heavier yet when I got out upon the marshes, so that instead of my running at everything, everything seemed to run at me. This was very disagreeable to a guilty mind. The gates and dykes and banks came bursting at me through the mist, as if they cried as plainly as could be, "A body with Somebody-else's pork pie! Stop him!" The cattle came upon me with like suddenness, staring out of their eyes, and steaming out of their nostrils, "Halloa, young thief!" One black ox, with a white cravat on – who even had to my awakened conscience something of a clerical air – fixed me so obstinately with his eyes, and moved his blunt head around in such an accusatory manner as I moved round, that I blubbered out to him, "I couldn't help it, sir! It wasn't for myself I took it!" (Chapter 3)

Dickens creates a subtle balance between Pip the adult narrator and Pip the child, the subject of the narrative. The passage sustains a single figurative device: the younger Pip's surroundings are variously mobilized and personified as agents of justice and retribution, which works well in situating the reader in the experience of the youngster. The gates, dykes, banks, and cattle combine as pursuers and accusers in an image that one might expect to visit a mind already beset by ingenuous tension and unsophisticated guilt. At the same time the perceptions of the youngster are assimilated to the stylistic and rationative maturity of the adult narrator. The black ox whose markings resemble a "cravat" might, just, register subliminally for a nervous boy, but only an adult could put together the resonant figurative image of a creature "who even had to my awakened conscience something of a clerical air." We have to ask ourselves: is it really plausible that the elder Pip's memory of these occurrences involves an authentic recollection of how, 30 years before, the ox assumed the "accusatory manner" of a clergyman, the symbolic index to a society's moral code, and prompted in him the panicked, contrite explanation of his act. The incidents of the passage are consistent with the rest of the unfolding narrative but the polished manner in which they are orchestrated causes us to wonder if this very accomplished adult portrait retains anything of what actually went on in the mind of the adolescent, let alone the order of the events.

The whole novel describes the experiences of Pip from childhood to maturity and throughout we are aware that the older Pip is persistently selecting and refining elements of his past. He is constantly battling to integrate recollected moments and emotions with his current temperamental state, allowing for the former – sometimes involving the acts and reported speech of Magwitch, Estella, and Miss Havisham – a degree of autonomy and therefore authenticity while weaving them together into a story that, for him, Pip, provides a cause-and-effect explanation for the constituent features of his life so far and their effects on him. Often, in line with the precedent set in the above passage, cracks begin to show and we are prompted to wonder: can we trust him? Is he telling us the truth? We do not, of course, extend such questions to the status of Pip as an actual individual. We know he is made up entirely of words; an invention of Charles Dickens. Yet, at the same time, along with telling us an engaging story this compelling device draws us into a contemplative private debate on the nature of truth and memory, on whether we deceive ourselves involuntarily, perhaps to protect ourselves against what we would rather not admit, perhaps to secure our sense of sanity.

With this in mind let us return to Joyce. Leo Bersani offers the model of "realist" fiction – a genre that Dickens typifies – peddled by academics and members of the literary establishment who treat modernism as by its nature superior:

> The formal and psychological reticence of most realistic fiction makes for a secret complicity between the novelist and his society's illusions about its own order. Realistic fiction serves nineteenth century society by providing it with strategies for containing (and repressing) its disorder within significantly structured stories about itself. (Bersani, 1978, 63.2)

What Bersani means is that the stylistic mannerisms of novels such as *Great Expectations* enable the writer to impose a formal and aesthetic order upon their source material. In short, realism amounts to a conspiracy of falsehoods, enabling the author to smooth over the incongruent, sometimes incomprehensible nature of their world and enlisting the reader in the same state of self-deluding security. Modernism, according to Lodge and Barthes, exposes this collective chimera by causing the reader to confront the splintered, sometimes antagonistic nature of representation and it is unlikely that anyone today would challenge Bersani's conception of how modernism improved literary history. It has become an immutable truism, in the same sense that we accept that the Enlightenment opened the door to what would eventually emerge as tolerant secularism and liberal democracy. Yet it is riddled with inconsistencies and falsifications.

Lodge echoes the nostrums of the apologists for Joyce who rescued his work from the pre 1940s consensus of opinion: the latter held that he was fascinating, the apogee of self-conscious experiment, but beyond that no more than a temporary curiosity. Within decades this consensus had been overtaken, or more accurately overruled, by the view that we must reassess the relationship between literary art and entertainment. The latter was downgraded by the new alliance between academia and high culture because of the threat it posed to the overarching doctrine of aesthetic elitism: why bother discussing in seminars what the vast majority of the literate public talked about in their sitting rooms (and the classic case here was Dickens)? Their case was that literature at its most elevated should involve the reader in an intellectual challenge, ask questions about their level of erudition, their abilities to engage with the continual shifts from one representational register to another and to treat the work not in the vulgar sense of a story with a beginning, a middle, and an end, but rather as celebration of discontinuity and inconclusiveness.

Their point is valid, particularly with Joyce, but what they overlook is the fact that such effects had already been achieved, not least by Dickens, and by far less ostentatious means.

The evaluative model applied to the poems discussed is easily adaptable to fiction. Dickens and Joyce combine overtly literary and nonliterary registers in a manner that both challenges and confirms our notion of fiction as a definable genre. Every element of Dickens's book is informed by the presence of Pip; he impresses his temperament upon its structure and minutiae, determines its tempo, decides upon what is and what is not disclosed. He embodies the narrative yet the one thing that he or Dickens never concedes is that he is entirely and exclusively a literary device. Conversely, Joyce's characters, principally Bloom, Stephen, and Molly, are exercises in the arbitrariness and diversity of language, unrelenting reminders – or insistencies, depending on your point of view – that language and knowledge are interdependent. Dickens does not hide the incongruities between literary and nonliterary language but nor does he draw our attention to them. Joyce on the other hand rarely ceases to do anything else.

The two novels belong at opposing ends of the generic spectrum but before we treat them as the equivalents of Prynne and Larkin we should consider how the processes of naturalization and evaluation are complicated by what the novel, as a genre, demands and allows. It is routinely argued that the conventional realist novel makes the reader's role in the process of naturalization virtually redundant. We allow the story to evolve without too much interpretive participation and accumulate a composite knowledge of each character's foibles, motives, private histories, and so on, in accordance with the author's generous provision of nuance and guidance. There are, of course, commendably demanding tasks performed by the novelist in the achievement of such effects but it is largely a matter of choice as to whether we notice them, let alone admire the skills required in their execution. Barbara Hardy observes in the introduction to her edition of George Eliot's *Daniel Deronda* that the villain, Grandcourt, seems one of the most authentic characters in fiction because Eliot provides us with such a variety of perspectives on his character, including those of his wife, mistress, accomplice, children, competitor, and indeed the author herself. We have views of him that are,

> Impressed, wary, intimately horrified, ambitious, cowed, right, wrong, serious, frivolous, dismissive, contemptuous, and deeply critical.

Even if, at the end of the novel, we feel we know him as well as we do our closest acquaintance in real life, will we take account of how we acquire this level of intimacy?

It is unlikely that even a person who purchases a novel in an airport bookshop as a diversion from the boredom of 13 hours in economy class (true, *Daniel Deronda* would be a somewhat improbable choice, but bear with the scenario) would treat it exclusively as a parallel universe; the words on the page can never be a transparent medium. The reader will, instead, apprehend the book in two ways: read through it and quietly exult in the spectacle of Grandcourt's nastiness in the same way that revelations on innate villainy attract us to lurid tabloid accounts of murder trials, and at the same time take some account of how George Eliot and her narrator choreograph the activities of Grandcourt, Alcharisi, Gwendoline, and Daniel himself. Conversely, the brand of experiment typified by *Ulysses* does not allow us this double perspective – to admire Joyce's technical accomplishments while conceiving of Stephen, Bloom, and Molly as actual people. If our primary concern is an engrossing story that lasts as long as the flight then we are much less likely to choose Joyce as our companion than George Eliot. The same could be said of Christine Brooke-Rose's *Such* (1966) which concerns itself with the 3 minutes between the main protagonist's heart failure and his return to full consciousness, with flashbacks to his randomly recalled past. Perhaps, for the more intellectually adventurous flyer, David Caute's *The Confrontation* (1969–1971) might appeal in that its characters are self-evidently less important than the notion of representation. It is made up of three texts: a play, a critical essay by one of the characters from the play, and a short novel. Sometimes individuals wander from one work to another but rarely hold our attention for long enough for us to ask what they are really like or what they are up to. More recent works in the same vein include the fashionable novels of the American writer Tao Lin. In many ways he recalls the late B.S. Johnson (self-memorialized in *The Unfortunates*, 1969, a novel that incorporates 25 unbound chapters which can be read in any order we wish) but while Johnson did interesting things with the physical make-up of his books Lin makes it difficult to dissociate his material in print with an online persona willing to engage with readers on message boards and discuss their ongoing experience of his fiction. The hoary old postmodern device of the author-in-the-work has now become author-on-internet or even Twitter. His *Richard Yates* is an affectless, deadpan account of a writer's relationship with a girl he met online. Most recently he has offered us *Taipei* (2013) in which nothing much happens. Characters narrate themselves, but not in the manner of Dickens's Pip who generally shows concern for the reader's attention span and their affection for language. Rather, Lin's creations describe themselves as if they are third person narrators in some way locked out of the narrative itself but always trying to get in. An engaging experiment, one might think, except that their story, indeed the world that incorporates them without really containing them, involves only events and people that are disconnected, unamusing, and unremittingly tedious. It is possible to treat the novel as a skilfully executed exposé of the inadequacies of language alongside a reminder that the devices and gimmicks of realist fiction are but a shoddy mimetic delusion, insufficient and irrelevant to the true challenges that art should confront. James Joyce is back, now equipped with WiFi and Twitter.

The double pattern informs, and defines, all works of fiction just as it does all poems, but the two genres differ in one important sense. From its commencement the novel appealed to readers because it was both mimetic and fantastic. It trod a fine line between an authentic representation of life and a reconfiguring of life's chaotic, unpredictable, and for some meaning-less, nature, as a story in which the role of each character became more clearly defined and the sequence of events that we generally regard as fate acquired a reassuring logic. All of this was supplemented by the thrill of wanting to know, and then being shown, what happens next. But even the originators of the English novel, Fielding and Richardson in particular, were sufficiently fascinated, and puzzled, by the resources they commanded to make them conspicuous and to open a second line of communication with the reader on the very nature of the task in hand. In this respect Sterne's *Tristram Shandy* was not so much a protest against orthodoxy as a some-what quixotic, ostentatious reminder of what all eighteenth century fiction writers and readers already knew.

At the other end of the spectrum the modernists and postmodernists can only practice their trade in recognition and acknowledgement of the alternate mannerisms of realism.

Does the fact that few fliers on their way to the intercontinental departure gates would purchase a work by Lin – assuming they know what to expect from it – tell us anything of its intrinsic qualities, in comparison with a more conventional novel? It does. Certainly, escapism should not be allowed completely to displace aesthetic evaluation and while there are some readers who might choose to read Dickens simply for the thrill of the plot (indeed his popularity during his lifetime was treated by some of his high-minded contemporaries as vulgar populism), he at least presents us with the choice between appreciation and diversion. Pip is a skilful narra-tor yet he is also vulnerable, allowing slight inconsistencies in his account to make us wonder about his trustworthiness. We are engaged, enter-tained, by his story but at the same time we contemplate the spectacle of a man anxiously crafting a linguistic monument to his own sense of assurance, even his sanity. We can, just, detect the manner in which the threads of this entirely artificial fabric are woven together, and we have to ask ourselves: is this novel "about" the story narrated by Pip or is it about Pip himself, an embodiment of the untrustworthy character of language, memory, and truth?

Here, we come upon the essential difference between the two modes of writing. Writers within the Joycean legacy secure their status by a persistent strategy of avoidance and refusal, continually searching for ways in which traditional techniques can be eluded or undermined. The traditionalists, however, can make use of, draw in, experimental, self-referential strategies without completely abandoning their affiliations to the telling of a good story. In my view, the latter presents for the novelist by far the greater challenge to imaginative breath and stylistic craftsmanship, and offers for the reader a much broader range of aesthetic and intellectual questions. Which produces the better kind of fiction? The one that commits itself fully to a self-conscious exploration of telling stories, or the one that tells a story while splitting our perspective, sustaining our interest in what happens while enabling us to treat the work as a challenge to what we too often take for granted about the nature of fiction and, ultimately, language and existence? The question, I believe, answers itself. The latter is self-evidently far more demanding of the writer and the reader. The novelist must cause the two texts to work in harmony while retaining nuanced elements of their integrity and allowing neither to completely obscure or undermine the other. For the reader, there is the engrossing combination of being drawn into the realm of suspended disbelief, where characters and their dilemmas often seem disturbingly authentic, while contemplating the spectacle of the artefact in construction and the artist at work. With this in mind it is instructive to recall the passage in the preceding chapter, from Thackeray's *The Newcomes*, where the novelist interrupts himself to reflect on the nature of his task, in a cogent and remarkably accurate anticipation of the Formalists' definition of fiction. Almost a century earlier Fielding did something similar in *Tom Jones*.

> For as I am, in reality, the founder of a new province of writing, so I am at liberty to make what laws I please therein. And these laws, my readers, whom I consider as my subjects, are bound to believe in and to obey; with which that they may readily and cheerfully comply, I do hereby assure them, that I shall principally regard their ease and advantage in all such instructions: for I do not, like a *jure divino* tyrant, imagine that they are my slaves, or my commodity. I am, indeed set over them for their own good only, and was created for their own use, and not they for mine.

As was his wont, Fielding appears to be composing this with a wry smile, presenting himself as the omnipotent creator of the new universe of fiction, but beneath the self-caricature is a subtly contrived model of how the novelist and his proxy the narrator interact with the book and the reader. Once more, postmodernists should wonder about the originality of their enterprises. Fielding's readers are, he states, inconstant entities. He might be "set over them" yet he was "created for their own use" allowing here for at least as much interpretive range as licensed by Barthes' death of the author. Throughout he breaks down the boundary between the novelist as adjudicator, creator of "laws," and the reader's sense of fiction as a shifting, potentially lawless realm. In short he is offering a model of fiction where the conspicuous relationship between the plan, intention, for the book and a sense of energized uncertainty is the principal criterion for quality. It could be argued that I am overgenerous in my provision of conventional fiction with the capacity to meet this criterion and I will return to that later.

For the time being, and to conclude this chapter, I look at and evaluate five novels that self-evidently blur the distinction between the lisible and the scriptible text. Each incorporates both, but in very different ways, and their relative qualities point up several common misperceptions regarding the nature of fiction and how it should be judged. They are John Fowles' *The French Lieutenant's Woman* (1969), Anthony Burgess's *Inside Mr Enderby* (1963), Kingsley Amis's *The Green Man* (1969), Martin Amis's *Money* (1984), and Muriel Spark's *The Only Problem* (1984).

The French Lieutenant's Woman is generally seen as a testament to the arrival of modernism as a fully accredited partner in the literary mainstream: conventional fiction was no longer treated as belonging to the enduring hierarchy but rather as a purblind subordinate. For much of the work Fowles conducts an exercise in literary ventriloquism, recreating the styles and mannerisms of Victorian novelists in a story of alleged moral delinquency and obsession that in the nineteenth century would have been subject to routine strategies of evasion and displacement. Fowles does a creditable job of reinventing the mood and tempo of certain kinds of mid nineteenth century fiction. He is far less flamboyant than Dickens and avoids the edge of mischief sometimes evident in Thackeray: his style could best be described as a blend of the restrained pomposity of Trollope and George Eliot's judgmental poise. All the time, however, the performance is undermined by hints at self-caricature, almost self-loathing. Because, apart from telling us the story of Charles, Sarah, and Sam, the narrator is also providing the reader with a course of instruction on the true nature of nineteenth century society and the shameful untruths propounded in its fiction. Superficially, the novel has little in common with the high-modernist techniques of Joyce, but it is ranked as part of the same innovative current. Both involve the self-conscious foregrounding of the mechanisms and devices of the novel and Fowles's most notable contribution to this trend is his use of the narrator – in effect himself, the author – as an active partici pant in the text. Unlike the standard third or first person narrator, who tells the story while rarely acknowledging their role as storyteller, Fowles never tires of reminding the reader that he and we are witnessing an almost farcical act of deception. Famously, Fowles steps into the novel towards the end to announce that there will be two very different endings. It will not, he informs us, simply be a matter of us choosing which of them we enjoy the most or which, in our view, seems the most suitable conclusion, given the impression already formed by our encounters with the various charac-ters. No, it will not be as straightforward as that. Instead, our sense of com-pletion will be compromised by the necessity of having to read both before we decide on which we prefer, so even though we might be pleased more by one than the other we will be troubled by the knowledge that the other still exists. Fowles performs this task of instruction, or rather he warns us of what is about to happen, in chapter 55 by boarding the same train as Charles and sitting next to him in the same compartment. During this Charles is asleep and does not therefore have to witness his fate being discussed by the man who is also his creator. How convenient, we might feel, and then remind ourselves that it is not a matter of chance or convenience at all. Given that the narrator, Fowles, is exclusively respon-sible for this whole exercise in suspended disbelief he has ensured that Charles, his creation, is asleep while he reflects upon the nature of fiction and fact, explaining in particular that he is obliging us to experience two endings because the conventions of Victorian fiction were too simplistic and normative, allowing us to assume that most, if not all, the dilemmas addressed in the novel can be brought to some conclusion. This, assumes Fowles, demonstrates the levels of dishonesty plumbed by his Victorian forebears. He puts his character to sleep to ensure that he, Fowles, can plan the direction of his life without interruption, but instead of neatly, if fraudulently, tying the threads of the narrative together he obliges us to confront the existential verity of "the open, the inconclusive ending," to everything. All of this is intellectually high minded but compared with the coverage of such matters in philosophic treatises by those with a specialization in the discipline, is it not also somewhat amateurish and pretentious? Do we need to have lessons in epistemology disguised as works of fiction, and even if the answer to this is in the affirmative another question is raised: should the novel be a didactic tool employed to make Wittgenstein less painful?

It goes without saying that Fowles accomplishes all of this with an admirable degree of aplomb. The novel is treated as a minor modern classic and rarely will such levels of esteem be allowed to endure if there are fundamental flaws at the basic level of literary craftsmanship. What, however, does Fowles expect to achieve by invoking and then fastidiously undoing our expectations as largely passive readers? Is there a generic purpose which underpins the otherwise arbitrary modernist preoccupation with innovation?

Most commentators treat the book as exercise in worthy self-scrutiny, a novel that entertains while exploring, as might a literary theorist, the very nature of writing and entertainment. Perhaps it is, but there is something else about it that recalls the kind of novelist whose presumptions and ideals it sets out to undermine: an inflexible assurance in his own conception of writing that comes close to evangelism.

Aside from the narrator's walk-on role, even during the long passages when he pretends to a degree of balanced, impartial reporting of events, he persistently reminds the reader of how much has changed since the 1860s. Specifically, he contrasts what the characters think of themselves and the way they perceive and treat each other with the momentous historical landmarks that separate us from them. We are given to suspect that Charles's apparent interest in Darwinism is more bourgeois pretension than a reflection of his anti-establishment mind-set. The narrator takes care to present him as demonstrably more stupid than most of his supposed social inferiors, notably Sarah and Sam, and reminds us that while he has heard of Darwin he, and his like, have blinded themselves to currents that will within a century sweep their class from its complacent position of superiority. Charles has certainly never heard of a certain "German Jew" then toiling away in the British Library on the founding documents of socialism.

Mrs Poultney and Mrs Fairley run the kitchens, we are told, in the manner of "incipient sadists," displaying all the "crassly arrogant" traits of "British Imperialism" and who would, 80 years hence, have found "a place …

in the Gestapo." Mrs Poultney is never given to doubt her moral position, her "fear of hell" assuaged by the promise of "God's reward."

Few would doubt that nineteenth century society was riven with self-moralizing hypocrisy but the assumption, which the novel both takes for granted and expounds, that the more radical elements of late 1960s thinking had reached the summit of political intellectual and cultural enlightenment is arrogant and some might say delusional. Fowles's narrator, in fact Fowles, is just as guilty of the charge of complacent ethical self-fulfillment that he lays against his nineteenth century predecessors. The use of literature to promote an ideological or religious conviction – righteous, obnoxious, or otherwise – is, as I argue in the concluding chapter, the basis for flawed, bad, and mendacious writing. Fowles does worse than this by not only using his novel to mount an assault on the assumed defects of Victorian society and culture, but also to imply that modernist technique, by its nature, is morally superior to traditional writing.

In chapter 13 the narrator pauses to prepare the reader for a jolt in their expectations and to make it clear that feels he his role goes beyond that of scourge of outdated beliefs and systems; he also embodies a mode of writing more suitable for an improved political zeitgeist.

> If I have pretended until now to know my characters' minds and innermost thoughts, it is because I am writing (just as I have assumed some of the vocabulary and "voice" of) a convention universally accepted at the time of my story: that the novelist stands next to God. He may not know it all, yet he tries to pretend that he does. But I live in the age of Alain Robbe-Grillet and Roland Barthes; if this is a novel it cannot be a novel in the modern sense of the word. (p. 97)

This, one assumes, is intended both to caricature and ridicule the predispositions of the realists but both Fielding and Thackeray, to name but two, allow themselves into their novels to confess that they are not properly in control of the minds and acts of their characters and adopt far more charismatic and amusing approaches to the enigma of storytelling and verisimilitude.

Fowles's book is cleverly executed, an ingenious meditation on literary devices and literary history, but it is a bad novel. The reader is treated in a manner that can only be described as patronizing. First we are invited to revel in our self-confidence as bright connoisseurs who appreciate the intellectual demands of the avant-garde. At the same time Fowles assumes that we will be both his pupils and affiliates, willing to follow the track of historicist re-education and radical aesthetics charted by his narrator.

Fowles's technique is not necessarily well-suited to his proselytizing purposes, as Martin Amis demonstrates in *Money* (1984). Amis too appears in his own novel but his relationship with its narrator becomes an exercise in brilliant comedy, the antithesis of Fowles's earnest sanctimony.

John Self, narrator of his own story and producer of self-evidently crass TV commercials, is a literary paradox. His life is composed of sordid excess, involving sex (purchased, pornographically witnessed, or forcibly obtained), cigarettes (60-a-day), alcohol consumed by the gallon, drugs selected and self-administered with impressive versatility, topped by an unassuageable appetite for artery-clogging junk food. Self's taste for low-life hedonism would be equalled by his unconditional philistinism, if only he had some remote notion of the cultural landscape that exists somewhere other than world he shares with his fellow narcissists and deadbeats. He has a vague recollection of Orwell's *Animal Farm* from school days, without any accompanying conception of its status as a literary work. This is the sum of his cultural estate. The paradox is that as a first person narrator he is a genius. How, we ask ourselves, can a man with no sense of what literature is invest his account of his own vile, grotesque existence with such wry humor and time his prose so beautifully? His account, for example, of his brief excursion to a New York live pornography emporium is symphonic in the way that strata of humiliation and degradation are segued towards a triumphantly masochistic apogee.

> Finally I devoted twenty-eight tokens' worth of my time to a relatively straight item, in which a slack-jawed cowboy got the lot, everything from soup to nuts, at the expense of the talented Juanita de Pablo. Just before the male's climax the couple separated with jittery haste. Then she knelt in front of him. One thing was clear: the cowboy must have spent at least six chaste months on a yoghurt ranch eating nothing but ice-cream and buttermilk, and with a water-tight no-hand job clause in his contract. By the time he was through, Juanita looked like the patsy in the custard-pie joke, which I suppose is what she was. The camera proudly lingered as she spat and blinked and coughed ... Hard to tell, really, who was the biggest loser in this complicated transaction – her, him, them, me. (Amis, *Money*, 1985, p. 47)

Self is a reply to Fowles's insistence that the bourgeois narrator – first or third person – is by its nature inauthentic. Self, the sub-cultural yob, is a far more accomplished, and amusing, prose stylist than any of Fowles's representatives and he is more than that. Fowles's narrator plays two roles, first as the embodiment of the tradition he persistently censures and also as unbidden counsel for the reader on what novels should be and do in the radical late twentieth century. Self hires Martin Amis to help him out with the screenplay for a film and aside from their business relationship the novelist finds it necessary to offer his new acquaintance some thoughts on contemporary fiction.

> The distance between the author and narrator corresponds to the degree to which the author finds the narrator wicked, deluded, pitiful or ridiculous [...] the further down the scale he is, the more liberties you can take with him. You can do what you like with him really. This creates an appetite for punishment. The author is not free of sadistic impulses. I suppose it's the –
> (Amis, 1985, pp. 246–247)

At this point he is interrupted by Self (who finds the subject tedious and is more concerned with his toothache), but the impact of their exchange is clear enough. Martin Amis seems a self-absorbed bore, so preoccupied with the nature of fiction writing that he is unable to raise his conversation to the level of his edgy, mercurial associate. All of this reinforces our fascination with Self, a man who is far more engaging than the figure who created him, despite the former's aversion to anything resembling literary culture.

Amis encourages us to take an unfavorable glance toward *The French Lieutenant's Woman* and the aesthetic preconceptions that surround it, but to treat *Money* solely as a satirical gesture would reduce it to the status of Fielding's *Shamela,* a fine novel but one whose status depends on its role as a nagging appendix to another. Amis's achievement transcends his rejoinder to Fowles because Self is both a bravura performance, an entertainment, and an exemplar of something unique to fiction writing. We are continually fascinated as much by the fact that he should not be able to deliver his story so brilliantly as we are by the story itself. Most significantly, Amis succeeds for more than 400 pages in causing us to forget that Self is not a sub-cultural vandal, that he is Martin Amis disguised as a sub-cultural vandal, never allowing the mask to slip. Fowles offers us a solemn lecture on social and cultural history, while Amis does something remarkable with literary language that is neither instructive nor patronizing. Which is the better novel?

In the end it is your decision, but in my view those who appreciate literature for its quality as a discourse without an earnest purpose will favor Amis.

Burgess's *Inside Mr Enderby* does not play host to its author, in the sense that Burgess refrains from entering the story alongside Enderby and the other rather grotesque inmates of the narrative. Yet the narrator – third person, but Burgess in all but name – obtains the same effect by gradually and incessantly drawing our attention away from what actually happens to Enderby and towards the question of how exactly such a peculiar and ostentatiously unconvincing story could have been conceived.

It begins with the narrator's representation of Enderby's fart – "Perrrrp" – and continues:

> A posterior riposte from Mr Enderby. Do not touch, Priscilla. Mr Enderby is not a *thing* to be prodded; he is a great poet sleeping. Your grubby finger out of his mouth, please Alberta …

Who are Priscilla and Alberta, we ask, but the question remains unanswered. They are certainly not characters in the novel but they could, just, be conceits for Enderby's lurid fantasies, figures who might be interested in him as a poet and a man.

Francis Xavier Enderby composes poetry on the loo. His bath is the filing cabinet for his work in progress and we learn more of his rather distasteful physical characteristics and his habits than we would wish. He has published some of his work but his life seems to involve little more than a dyspeptic postponement of oblivion. The narrator, however, is showily present throughout, imposing himself as an erudite impresario on the otherwise morbid details of Enderby's existence. Even when describing the mundane particulars of Enderby's day he cannot help but publically ransack his thesaurus of literary history for allusions: "Johnson's scrofula, Swift's scataphobia, or Keats's gallop of death-warrant blood." Eventually his orotund self-absorption threatens to displace the story itself and as if to compensate he seems to resort to increasingly implausible developments in an otherwise uneventful plot. For example, Enderby decides send to the editor of *Fem*, a women's magazine, a complaint about a recent recipe but by accident places one of his poems in the envelope instead. He and the editor correspond, meet, begin a relationship, and eventually marry. The marriage is brief and Enderby, alone, attempts suicide and the novel ends with him confined in a mental home.

If asked for a brief description of what the novel is "about" the reader's first instinct would be to summarize the rather bizarre episodes that transport

Enderby from his bohemian and insanitary existence in a Brighton flat to a mental institution. But most readers would also be aware that the story is more than a challenge to credibility. It seems carelessly, lazily, put together; not so much the product of an overactive imagination as a distraction from other concerns. It is the narrator who is the principal character. He does not actually feature in the narrative itself, and indeed we know nothing of his background. He remains anonymous, but his verbosity, his obsession with what he can do with the abundance of myths, cultural registers, and conceits that constitute his personality, relegates the eponymous subject to a subordinate role. The narrator puts up with his duty to Enderby while continually performing for the reader. He does not, like Fowles or Amis, appear in the novel; he does not need to since he dominates it in every other respect.

As a contribution to the middle brow avant-garde, Burgess's novel is original and mildly satirical but at the same time it does not allow for sustained enjoyment. Just as Enderby seems an unfortunate obligation for a narrator preoccupied with his own personality so we become rather weary of the enduring presence of the latter.

Maurice Allington, the narrator of Kingsley Amis's *The Green Man* (1969), owns and runs a hotel and restaurant called the Green Man, 40 miles from London and within easy reach for the culinary sophisticates of Cambridge. Maurice begins:

> The point about white Burgundies is that I hate them myself. I take whatever my wine supplier will let me have at a good price (which I would never dream of doing with any other drinkable). I enjoyed seeing those glasses of Chablis or Pouilly Fuissé, so closely resembling a blend of cold chalk soup and alum cordial with an additive or two to bring the colour of children's pee being peered and sniffed at, rolled around the shrinking tongue and forced down somehow by parties of young technology dons from Cambridge or junior television producers and their girls. Minor, harmless compensations of this sort are all too rare in a modern innkeeper's day.

The mixture of gossipy candor and detail sets the standard for the next five pages of Maurice's introduction to his world. He tells of his family: his wife Joyce; Amy his 13-year-old daughter from his first marriage; his 80-year-old father. He confides in the reader: he drinks a bottle of whisky a day and he intends to have sex with "tall, blond and full-breasted Diana," the wife of his closest friend. All of this is shot through with asides on the varying qualities of his port and salmon dishes, the gullish philistinism of his clientele and the "hypocrisy" of having *sauce vinaigrette* with avocado pears. Depending on our disposition we soon form an opinion on Maurice Allington, usually either aversion or fraternal affiliation, and our visceral response testifies to his disarmingly real presence.

Maurice seems to feel the need to confess, unapologetically, while embedding his confidences in meticulous detail and a question soon arises as to the reason for this. It is almost as though he has to reassure himself that his story is true. He is given to entertaining his guests, particularly Americans, with the tale of Thomas Underhill, who owned the inn in the seventeenth century, made a pact with the devil, sacrificed his wife, and monitored the murderous activities of a wood creature from whom the pub takes its name. Gradually, but with remarkable credibility, Maurice works another story into the account of his life: the legend is true and Underhill has returned. Maurice has seen him several times, most vividly in the lane behind the house soon after he has seduced Diana.

Given the chaos of his domestic life, the recent death of his father and his increasing consumption of drink we might be forgiven for treating his visions of the demon as evidence of a psychological breakdown, at least until chapter 4. From his sitting-room Maurice witnesses the freezing of time and space. "Down to the left, forty or fifty yards away across the grass, a couple of waxworks cast their shadows, the seated one with a hand stuck out in the direction of something, probably a cup of tea, that the standing one was offering it, and were Lucy and Nick," his daughter-in-law and son. In his sitting-room is a young man, whom Maurice describes with customary attention to detail: about 28, clean-shaven, good teeth, silver-grey suit, black knitted tie, humorous but not very trustworthy face. The young man is God.

> "Are you a messenger?" I asked.
> "No. I decided to come uh … in person."
> "I see. Can I offer you a drink?"
> "Yes thank you. I'm fully corporeal. I was going to warn you against making the mistake of supposing that I came from inside your mind, but you've saved me that trouble. I'll join you in a little Scotch, if I may."

Maurice achieves a remarkable balance between the cool verisimilitude of his account and its totally implausible subject. He passes God a glass of Scotch.

> The hand that came up and took it, and the wrist and lower forearm that disappeared into the silver-grey shirt cuff were by no means complete, so that

the fingers clicked against the glass, and at the same time I caught a whiff of that worst odour in the world, which I had not smelt since accompanying a party of Free French through the Falaise Gap in 1944. In a moment it was gone, and fingers, hand and everything else were as they had been before.
"That was unnecessary," I said, sitting down again.
"Don't believe it, old boy. Puts things on the right footing between us. This isn't just a social call, you know. Cheers."

The quality of this passage exists in its combination of empirical detail and something that Maurice cannot describe. The hand and are arm "by no means complete," but the precise nature of this phenomenon is registered only in allusions that Maurice can share with the reader: the fingers click against the glass as if the nails from Christ's crucifixion are still there, and the "worst odour" recalls equally indescribable events from the last war. God, it seems, is quite capable of incorporating the most distressing aspects of the human condition.

The only other occasion where God and an agent of Satan appear as characters in a literary text is in Milton's *Paradise Lost*, which was a poetic rewriting of the Book of Genesis and not a solidly realist story set in the England of the late 1960s. Milton's contemporaries would have treated the narrative and figures of his poem as indisputable truths, albeit made more vivid in language that resembled that of Shakespeare's drama. It is unlikely that Amis himself – like Allington, an atheist – would have expected a similarly unquestioning response from his readers, yet irrespective of our faith, or lack of it, we are unsettled by Allington. He is not mad and he has no reason to falsify the incident in which his teenage daughter also witnesses the creature. He presents, I would contend, far more troubling questions regarding the nature of fiction and truth than either Fowles's or Amis junior's exercises in metafiction. The rationale for causing the author to appear in his own work has some credence as a means of exposing the myth of realism yet at the same time it is implicitly patronizing: it begs the question of how stupid or gullible we would expect a reader to be when we feel the need to remind them that fiction is not really true. Amis succeeds primarily in sustaining the presence of Maurice Allington as a figure by parts magnetic, unbecoming, and thoroughly believable; so believable that those episodes in his story that should defy credibility do not do so. We take them as seriously as he does. In terms of the double pattern the novel begs comparison with paintings by Maurits Escher, particularly his staircase that both ascends and descends simultaneously, catching us between what our rational faculty treats as impossible and what our less rational but equally powerful instinct tells us is undeniably the case. Yet Amis surpasses Escher. The latter's work is static, available for lengthy undisturbed scrutiny and as a consequence tending to yield up the devices and tricks that lie behind its effects. *The Green Man* is made up of a single fluid voice, capable of drawing us into his world, obliging us to share his experiences, his feelings of disbelief, and his absolute certainty that what happened is the truth. And, unlike Escher, and for that matter Fowles and Martin Amis, the cracks or deliberately contrived fissures do not show.

Burgess's narrator merits comparison with Muriel Spark's third person presence in *The Only Problem* (1984). The principal character of the novel is Harvey Gotham, whose private income enables him to retire to France and give full attention to his monograph on the Book of Job. Gotham discloses no academic ambitions. Indeed, he is reclusive, eschewing any form of public scrutiny. He is preoccupied with issues of purpose and cause, particularly the question faced by Judaeo-Christians on how to reconcile the notion of creation and divine benevolence with a world that seems beset with suffering. At the same time Gotham has to deal with the distraction of a police investigation involving his estranged wife Effie who is suspected of being an active member of a terrorist group and responsible for several armed robberies. Gotham's self-enclosed universe is regularly invaded, by the police, his sister-in-law Ruth, his closest friend from England, Edward, and several others who are obliged, without much enthusiasm, to endure his company.

It turns out, eventually, that Effie has indeed been an active terrorist. The police inform him, with due concern and decorum, that she has been killed during an exchange of fire in Paris. The story is bizarre and improbable, a blend of subdued eccentricity and something quite terrible. Its parts and thematic foci are incongruous; they ought not to be contained in the same work of fiction. What makes the novel work is the narrator, a figure who combines for all concerned, particularly though not exclusively Gotham, disbelief and indifference, with just a hint of sympathy.

Edward, visiting Gotham in his chateau, has just listened to his friend's account of his most recent thoughts on Job.

> Edward had always maintained that the link – or should he say fetter? – that first bound him to Harvey was their deep old love of marvellous Job, their studies, their analyses, their theories. Harvey used to lie on his back on the grass, one leg stretched out, the other bent at the knee, while Edward sat by

his side sunning his face and contemplating the old castle, while he listened with another part of his mind to Harvey's talk. "It is the only problem. It all boils down to that."

"Did you know," Edward remembered saying, "that when Job was finally restored to prosperity and family abundance, one of his daughters was called Box of Eye-paint? Can we really imagine our tormented hero enjoying his actual reward?" (Spark, *The Only Problem,* 1984, p. 29)

We suspect, but can never be certain, that Edward treats such memories in much the way that adults recall the enthusiasms of early childhood; with embarrassment but not without affection. But what of Gotham himself? Should we pity him, even see him as ludicrous?

In the end it is up to us, because the narrator does an excellent job of being both present as the action unfolds yet seemingly disinterested regarding any knowledge of why anything occurs or, more significantly, what the characters really think or feel.

The narrator invites us into the peculiar world of Gotham, Edward, Ruth, and the rest, dresses it, makes it all the more fascinating, but then denies us an invitation to go any further. We know the characters well, become the more fascinated by them as the narrative proceeds yet along with the trail of clues toward something particular there is a concomitant, thickening gallery of enigmas and unanswered questions.

Throughout the book we are faced with versions of this same state of uncertainty and in the end it remains unclear if the overriding theme of the work is the profound philosophical questions that preoccupy Gotham or the, albeit blurred, portrait of the man himself: a faintly absurd, hubristic figure whose wealth enables him to insulate himself from the day-to-day obligations and problems faced by everyone else. Indeed, we even begin to wonder if the clues sewn into the work regarding Effie's decision to leave him indicate a series of causal relationships far more gruesome than anything contemplated by Gotham in his abstruse theological speculations: that is, his self-absorption and conceited eccentricity drove her to become a terrorist.

By causing her narrator to appear both indifferent to and bemused by the characters and incidents of the book Spark succeeds in telling us two versions of the same story. It is the equivalent in fiction of Wollheim's twofold thesis. Like the Holbein painting of the monarch, the portrait of Harvey Gotham is disconcerting, created with considerable skill by a narrator who vacillates between his subject's tragic state and his absurdity and never allows us to arrive at a final conclusion on either. Some readers will find this perplexing, even infuriating, while others will treat it as a suitably challenging exercise in mimesis, a reminder that our knowledge of other is always beset by qualifications and uncertainties. I would contend that Spark's achievement in literary craftsmanship is something that we cannot help but admire, irrespective of whether or not the novel suits our temperament.

At this point, then, the shortlist is reduced to two, Kinglsey Amis and Muriel Spark. Both step effortlessly between the two dimensions of the double pattern, causing us to watch the narrative unfold almost as if we are part of it while continually reminding us that this world is suspensive, arbitrary. But in my view *The Green Man* is a finer work than *The Only Problem* and the best of the five. It is magic realism without that subgenre's ostentatious crudeness and as a novel that makes God so credible that even an atheist will question his kindness it has exceptional qualities. Gotham, Enderby, Self, and Charles are ingenious creations, devices that mobilize the works that contain them. But in each instance it requires some effort to respond to them in the way that we would to a real person, loved or hated. With Allingham an equal amount of effort is required to resist joining him in his sitting room, with God. The route between actuality and invention is the same in both cases. We are conscious of taking it but with Kingsley Amis we do not naturalize the work, it captures us.

7

Popular Literature

The most widely quoted account of how popular fiction differs from its "serious" or "literary" counterpart is Henry James's essay "The Future of the Novel" (1899). James makes it clear that while the novel began life in the eighteenth century it had reached a form of maturity during the 99 years prior to his drafting of the essay. As to the future of the form James seems haunted by a fear that something quite dreadful might imperil its already precarious status as the newest literary genre; so dreadful in fact that he cannot quite bring himself to describe it let alone give examples of its manifestation. Instead he opts for a sketch of the social and cultural environment that encourages the mutation of this fearful virus:

> We are ... demonstrably in the presence of millions for whom taste is but an obscure, confused, immediate instinct. In the flare of railway bookstalls, in the shop-fronts of most booksellers, especially the provincial, in the advertisements of weekly newspapers, and in fifty places besides, this testimony to the general preference triumphs. (James, 1899, pp. 48–49)

Most of the readers of James's essay, who were probably also devotees of his novels, would have recognized the subject of his coy deliberations: popular fiction, particularly the kind of sensationalist novel or crime

Is Shakespeare Any Good?: And Other Questions on How to Evaluate Literature,
First Edition. Richard Bradford.
© 2015 John Wiley & Sons, Ltd. Published 2015 by John Wiley & Sons, Ltd.

writing that outsold even the work of figures such as Dickens. The image of the shop window and the overlit railway carriage or station had a terrifying quality for those who feared that the tastes of the masses might someday, perhaps quite soon, begin to encroach upon the sublime territories of the cultural elite. James seems to have borrowed this, unapologetically, from Matthew Arnold who had contemplated "tawdry novels ... produced for the use of our middle class ... designed for people with a low standard of life." Such books would, according to Arnold, "flare in the bookshelves of our railway stations." Thirty years after James, Q.D. Leavis shuddered at the prospect of literary culture as a marketplace, subject to the taste of those who spend their "leisure in cinemas, looking through magazines and newspapers, listening to jazz music."

James, and for that matter most others who find popular fiction distasteful, tend towards a certain vagueness regarding the actual nature of the books that sate the rapacious appetites of the consumer. Perhaps they feel it beneath them to engage directly with sub-cultural products and take it as a given that their readers will be sufficiently elevated to do without illustrations of the dreaded material. James allows himself but a brief engagement with the cause of his distress. "When society was frank, was free about the accidents and incidents of the human constitution, the novel took the same robust ease as society." He speaks of the eighteenth century. "The young men then were so young that they were not table high. But they began to grow, and from the moment their little chins rested on the mahogany, Richardson and Fielding began to go under it." James's point is clear enough, though his judgment is questionable. Richardson and Fielding reflected the moral and social infirmities of their age. When society improved itself, so did its novelists or at least those who were more concerned with the "universals" of existence than its messy and sometimes rather exciting particulars. The more respectable and better known individuals who kept alive the latter during the nineteenth century were Sensationalists such as Mary Elizabeth Braddon and Mrs Henry Wood. Their just tolerable counterparts in the crime novel were its pioneers, Poe, and of course Conan Doyle, but each was trailed by a mass of less mannered practitioners whose "penny dreadful" tales of misdeeds and punishment provided recreation for people obliged to spend much of their time in the culturally arid hinterland of the railway station.

James's position is intriguing not least because he appears to treat popular fiction as *too* realistic, unwilling to improve upon the often grotesque raw material of the world in which we live. (He praises Dickens and Scott for abstaining from vividly presented "lovemaking.") Much later Anthony Burgess explains in *The Novel Now* (1968) why he will not soil his hands by reading a certain kind of fiction: "books that make the most money are those which lack both style and subtlety and present a grossly oversimplified picture of life. Such books are poor art, and life is too short to bother with any art that it's not the best of its kind" (Burgess, 1968, p. 20). James and Burgess seem to hold contrary opinions on why popular fiction appeals to the masses but beneath the surface there are parallels. James detected in the bestseller something that ensured the popularity of William Harrison Ainsworth's *Jack Sheppard: A Romance* (1839), an appetite for the vivid, the prurient, even the grotesque that in the early nineteenth century drew massive crowds to public executions, including that of the real Jack Sheppard. Burgess discovered something similar, which might best be described as escapism, a substitute for the world in which readers were obliged to spend most of their time, the former possibly involving the gross fulfilment of their sexual or material fantasies, or something not unlike the story of Jack Sheppard in which complex issues of morality or accountability are sidelined by the question of what happens next. In this respect popular fiction could be classified as a close, if somewhat tainted, relative of the conventional "literary novel." Few if any fans of Dickens or George Eliot would deny that when they first encountered their work they were gripped by what would happen to particular individuals during the course of the narrative and that this experience of captivation involves being able to imagine oneself as part of the created world of the book. However, it is generally accepted by the literary and academic establishment that popular fiction distinguishes itself from its serious counterpart by giving predominant emphasis to the plot at the expense of the style or manner in which the story is told. Here Shklovsky's model of *syuzhet* and *fabula* is instructive. His point is that in the most challenging "literary" novels the former will predominate, drawing our attention primarily to the devices of fiction writing and away from the consecutive events of the story. We might, just, be able to identify a *fabula* in a conventional novel that, in summary, indicates parallels with Joyce's *Ulysses*. It would not be impossible to conceive of a late nineteenth century work called *A Day in the Life of Leopold Bloom* in which, over a 24-hour period, a traditional first person narrator reflects upon his past life, the nature and history of the city in which he lives, his relationship with his wife, and speculates on what goes on in her mind. In synoptic form the two novels might seem closely comparable but we know that *Ulysses* was unprecedented, not because it related a previously untold story but because its true subject is the nature of storytelling. As Shklovsky makes clear we might be able to extrapolate a plot summary from our experience of the novel but without taking into account the ways in which the *syuzhet* informs and interferes with the story we are left with an utterly erroneous perception of what the experience of reading it involves.

Suman Gupta offers some contentious comments on the average reader's experience of one of the most popular series of novels of the last few decades, J.K. Rowling's Harry Potter books. They are, in Gupta's opinion, "unthinkingly real" to the extent that millions of their fans do not discriminate between the original printed versions and their derivative "film versions"; even nonverbal derivatives that are not strictly speaking adaptations of the fictional narrative ("advertisement images and computer and video games and other consumer products") form parts of the virtual world enjoyed by the reader, or in Gupta's terms the consumer (Gupta, 2009, p. 164). Gupta emphasizes the erosion of boundaries between the printed text and various forms of electronic media, yet he implies that his observations on the Potter novels are equally relevant to popular fiction that remains unadapted or predates film, television or video games: they are not "*read*, that is, as being thinkingly understood." In short, we absorb their *fabula* by something close to osmosis, giving little if any attention to the capacities of the *syuzhet* to interfere with this process. The term "page turner" is used routinely by reviewers of bestsellers and repeated as frequently in promotional material. Gupta gives substance to it, arguing that those addicted to certain types of popular fiction are sufficiently obsessed with what happens next and convinced that the people to whom it happens are real that they are no longer distracted by the basics of literacy that connect signs with ideas and things: in bestsellers the words on the page are disposable.

Gupta's thesis gives shape to James's and Burgess's more elastic expressions of distaste, but equally it is difficult to take it seriously. At the other end of the spectrum from the Harry Potter novels we find ourselves, once more, with James Joyce's *Finnegans Wake*. Only professional academic critics who have become so absorbed by the superabundant mythologies and textual densities of the novel will persuade themselves that it possesses anything resembling a *fabula*. The average reader – that is, someone reasonably intelligent and demonstrably sane – will when asked to summarize its plot declare that no such feature exists. *Finnegans Wake* comes as close to any published work to being made up purely and exclusively of *syuzhet*. Such a reader might be able to discern traces of what seem the openings of narratives but each of these becomes so entangled with a profusion of others as to be indistinguishable or extinguishable. What, one wonders, would this hypothetical middlebrow reader make of their first encounter with a Harry Potter novel? Rowling's fan-base is made up predominantly of teenagers but over the span of the series a considerable number of adults have professed to be seriously entertained by the novels. Do these individuals, as Gupta contends, slip effortlessly into the fantastic parallel universe of Potter, Voldemort, and so on, without noticing how they arrived there? Nothing can be proved of course, but it seems unlikely. Consider the opening passage of the concluding novel of the series, *Harry Potter and the Deathly Hallows* (2009).

> The two men appeared out of nowhere, a few yards apart in the narrow, moonlit lane. For a second they stood quite still, wands directed at each other's chests; then, recognising each other, they stowed their wands beneath their cloaks and started walking briskly in the same direction.
> "News?" asked the taller of the two.
> "The best," replied Severus Snape.

Rowling does a reasonable job with one of the mainstay techniques of third person narration. She causes the scene to unfold gradually, creating an effect comparable to the placing of one semi-transparent negative photograph upon another, each incorporating the previous scene while adding something new and as a consequence transfiguring our earlier impression. For the reader unfamiliar with the foregoing works the opening of this one promises more than just fantasy and escapism. We are not gripped simply by what happens next. The manner in which these two figures mutate from indistinct vagueness through familiarity to, eventually, a still compelling yet unspecified sense of conspiracy is in itself something that demands our admiration. Snape and "the taller of the two," Yaxley, are familiar to the dedicated fan who knows the seven other volumes, but Rowling reintroduces them in a neatly choreographed way, adding a nuance of surprise to recognition. Gradually, for the fan, strangers return as intimates and as the passage continues, as they approach a manor house of gloomy yet captivating aspect, the sense of tension increases. Eventually, via noisy gravel paths, alluring, silent, gardens, and the forbidding interior of the manor we encounter Voldemort.

It is possible that the unacademic reader might not be inclined to describe how exactly Rowling operates as a literary technician, but this does not mean that they would be completely oblivious to her strategies and accomplishments. One can surrender oneself to the tensions and thrills of the narrative without becoming inattentive to the methods that empower these effects. The following is from J. Hillis Miller's *On Literature*:

> Good reading ... also demands slow reading ... A good reader is someone on whom nothing in a text is lost ... Such a reader pauses over every key word or phrase, looking circumspectly before and after, walking rather than dancing ... Slow reading, critical reading, means being suspicious at every turn, interrogating every detail of the work, trying to figure out by just what means the magic is wrought. (Hillis Miller, 2002, p. 122)

Hillis Miller does not refer to the kind of literature that demands "good reading" but the concluding phrase – "figure out by just what means the magic is wrought" – is revealing, and rather troubling. He takes it for granted that the good reader (erudite, alert to stylistic intricacies, well practised in the mannerisms of interpretation) will only devote the time and scrutiny of slow reading to books that already qualify for such attention: in short, high cultural, canonized works are the exclusive preserve of the good reader. But what happens when this person turns their attention to novels that are routinely ranked as low cultural products? Barbara Cartland is an extraordinary author at least in the sense that she put words on the page at a rate that almost overtook the seemingly insatiable demand for her work. Her novels, including those in translation, fall short only of the Bible and the Koran as enduring bestsellers. The following is from her *The Naked Battle* (1978) and in scrutinizing it I will try to take on the mantle of Hillis Miller's good reader.

> And as he kissed her, as his lips pressed themselves against her mouth, her eyes, her cheeks and the softness of her neck, Lucilla felt a fire rise within her ignited, she knew, by the fire in him.
>
> "I love ... you ..." she tried to say but her voice was deep and passionate and seemed almost to be strangled in her throat.
>
> "You are mine!" Don Carlos cried. "Mine completely and absolutely."
>
> He kissed her again until she felt the world disappear and once again they were on a secret island of their own surrounded by a boundless sea.
>
> It was what she had felt when she was with him in the little Pavilion; but now it was more real, more wonderful, more intense.
>
> Ever since she has known him she has changed and become alive to new possibilities within herself.
>
> Now she knew she could never go back to what she was before, because she had been reborn! Reborn to a new life and above all to love.

It was a love that was perfect, and Divine, a love that was not only of the body but of the soul and the spirit.

"I love you!! Oh, Carlos ... I love you with ... all of me!" she whispered.

He took the last words from her lips saying fiercely:

"You are mine, my beautiful, adorable wife, now and for all eternity!"

Cartland's passage has two foci: references to bodily contact and its immediate effect ("his lips pressed," "Lucille felt a fire," "He kissed her again"); and shifts of perspective beyond the immediate events to some other part of the story ("It was what she had felt when she was with him in the little Pavilion") or to a less specific condition or state of mind ("Reborn to a new life," and "now and for all eternity!" "Mine completely and absolutely"). As the passage proceeds the second set of foci gradually displace the first. The details of lips, mouth, eyes, cheek, and neck and the hesitant responses of the woman ("I love ... you") in the opening two paragraphs are emphatic enough, but as we read on physicality is at first supplemented by figurative language ("seemed almost to be strangled," "until she felt the world disappear") and eventually replaced entirely by sublime notions of possession, spiritual unity, and submission to an overarching but unspecified condition of "love." The center of gravity of the passage shifts implacably towards a goal of expectations that is, depending on one's point of view, utopian, self-deluding, or pitiable. The paragraphs typify the manner of the rest of the novel and in purely technical terms one must grant some credit to Cartland as a skilled fiction writer. She knows how to use the double pattern, employing the devices of third person narrative very effectively as a means of creating vivid portraits and emotional effects in the mind of the reader. A problem arises, however, when we consider the kind of reader who is a fan of Cartland. Do they care about her skills and accomplishments? The question is, I concede, rhetorical. One might as well ask if a cocaine addict is given to reflect upon the chemical constituents of the powder and means by which it is produced.

Cartland's narrator is particularly good at balancing the immediate aspects of the events described (which in real time occupy probably no more than 2 minutes) against a more universalized fabric of ideals, fantasies, norms, and ambitions. But her proxy employs these skills only as a means of satisfying the fantasies of a certain kind of reader. The mechanisms of fiction are used in a way that is comparable to the techniques of advertising; organizing the imagination of the reader according to a predictable notion of their ongoing fantasy world irrespective of their particular concerns with the true nature of reality. If we are interested in the media it is possible that in watching an advertisement on television we will be engrossed by its style and methodology while remaining largely indifferent to the attractions, or otherwise, of the product. We might even conduct exercises in comparison, evaluating the skills of various advertising agencies in terms of their techniques, particularly their ability to draw the viewers into a narrative and manage their responses to its personnel. But the principal criterion for their success will, inevitably, be how effectively they publicize the product, for someone else. The design of the advertisement might seem accomplished, amusing, even erudite, but if it fails to realize this objective such considerations are immediately despatched to the realm of commendable insignificance. And so it is with Cartland. She does her job as a novelist effectively enough but we know that when we make such judgments we are no more her "reader" than we are the specialist in advertising techniques who both admires the advertisement and then, against their rational instincts, goes out and buys something in which they previously had no interest. In Hillis Miller's terms, it is difficult to conceive of a "good reader" who could reconcile their scrupulous assessment of Cartland's technical accomplishments with an unbiased delight in her product. The appeal of Austen's and Dickens's novels does merit some comparison with the attractions of Cartland. All three cause the reader to return energetically to their books wondering what happens next and whether the character they met at the opening turns out to be quite the person they expect. But with Austen and Dickens we care about other things too. As we wait to see what occurs on the subsequent page we also savor the spectacle of the narrator at work, offering us insights into what really motivates the characters, allowing them to show their true nature – and then shadowing such portraits and withdrawing invitations to indiscretion. We follow the story – suspend disbelief – yet simultaneously we contemplate the manner of the writing as something worthy of admiration in its own right. This is the double pattern at work. If a writer causes us to see through the novel to an imagined world while asking us to appreciate the means by which this process is executed, and as a consequence think again about our perceptions of the characters, their circumstances, their ideas and motivations, then we have encountered quality. Cartland does not qualify for this attribute. Austen and Dickens do.

Before allowing the good reader some sweet repose and rest it seems unfair not to turn his attention to a figure whose popularity rivals that of Cartland and who is still producing fiction at a phenomenal rate, Jeffrey Archer. His recent novel, *Best Kept Secret* (2013) could, charitably, be classed as a piece of historical fiction, set as it is in mid twentieth century England. The plot, roughly summarized, involves two families, the Barringtons (landed aristocracy) and the Cliftons (working class). It begins with Harry Clifton and Emma Barrington's first attempt to get married, a ceremony interrupted and apparently cancelled by the disclosure that he might be her illegitimate half-brother. As we see from the following extract my synopsis must be treated as speculative, given that quite often the *syuzhet* and the *fabula* seem weirdly unsynchronized. The opening chapter is preceded with an extract from the traditional High Church marriage vows; we are, it seems, present at the betrothal of Harry and Emma. Soon, however, the focus of the passage shifts to their lineage.

> At the time of her dalliance with Hugo Barrington, Harry's mother had been walking out with Arthur Clifton, a stevedore who worked at Barringtons' Shipyard. Despite the fact that Maisie had married Arthur soon afterwards, the priest refused to proceed with Harry and Emma's wedding while there was a possibility it might contravene the church's ancient laws on consanguinity.
>
> Moments later, Emma's father Hugo had slipped out of the back of the church, like a coward leaving the battlefield. Emma and her mother had travelled up to Scotland, while Harry, a desolate soul, remained at his college in Oxford, not knowing what to do next. Adolf Hitler made that decision for him.
>
> Harry left the university a few days later and exchanged his academic gown for an ordinary seaman's uniform. But he had been serving on the high seas for less than a fortnight when a German torpedo had scuppered his vessel and the name of Harry Clifton appeared on the list of those reported lost at sea.
>
> *Wilt thou take this woman ...* [the marriage rite is inserted contrapuntally after every 300 word section of the passage]
>
> It was not until the end of hostilities, when Harry had returned from the battlefield scarred in glory, that he discovered that Emma had given birth to their son Sebastian Arthur Clifton. But Harry didn't find out until he had fully recovered that Hugo Barrington had been killed in the most dreadful circumstances and bequeathed the Barrington family another problem.

Slow reading is not so much an option as a necessity here – because Archer reverses the standard polarity between difficult, impenetrable fiction and its accessible user-friendly counterpart: this is a rare instance of unambitious, unpretentious storytelling that is almost impossible to understand. Often we simply lose a clear sense of where we are and what is happening. Certainly, the sentence in the first paragraph informing us that "the priest refused to proceed" with the ceremony is not particularly opaque. It relates a sequence of facts. But we find it difficult to read on because of a nagging residue of questions. Principally, why did it occur to the cleric (who never appears again in the book) only in the midst of the service that the happy couple might be about to commit incest? Did someone pass him a note? Did he recall some faintly sinister piece of gossip and suddenly link it to a more convincing thread of evidence? Each might be possible, or, we should say, plausible as a feature of the plot but Archer's decision to overlook anything resembling an explanation for the priest's decision interrupts our sense of continuity just as abruptly as, say, B.S. Johnson's refusal to complete a chapter. Indeed, on a scale of peculiarity Archer outranks Johnson because we are aware that his omission is not a postmodern gesture: he just cannot be bothered.

The two subsequent paragraphs are equally bizarre. Emma's father leaves the church "Moments later," presumably moments after the priest draws proceedings to a premature conclusion. Next we learn that Emma and her mother "had travelled up to Scotland" and that Harry, after returning to Oxford, volunteers for naval service and is lost at sea. The varying speeds and trajectories of activities undertaken by the figures almost defy known laws of physics. Next, the questions left unanswered by the intervention of the priest pale into insignificance when we are informed that, despite being reported lost at sea, Harry returns from the "battlefield scarred in glory." He could have been rescued, but where was he when Emma carried and gave birth to their child and Hugo was murdered (a period of at least a year, as the slow reader who tracks through the rest of the narrative will calculate)? He might have been a POW but if so the description of him as returning "from the battlefield" is rather baffling. The slow reader, "suspicious at every turn, interrogating every detail of the work," will be further bemused when the war at sea is refashioned as a "battlefield." There were several famous sea battles in World War II, notably the Battle of the Atlantic and the Battle of the River Plate, but none were ever referred to as "battlefields." Did Harry switch services, presumably to the army? Perhaps, but no one else appears to have any knowledge of this.

At last we have found the true heir to McGonagall's legacy in fiction. Archer's disastrous prose might be explained, if not excused, if we assume that he has preplanned the work according to what he assumes his regular audience will expect; specifically, a thrilling tale involving incest, ambition, internecine class conflict plus the always reliable – at least in Britain – voyeuristic contemplation of what remains of the aristocracy at work and play, in sex and death. Creditably, he makes some attempt to anchor these lurid features of the plot to moments in recent history that most readers will find vaguely familiar; mainly World War II and Britain transformed by the post-war Labour government. The problem is that these concessions to historical verisimilitude and the fast-moving plot are horribly, lazily, unco-ordinated. It is as though Archer has a list of preplanned obligations which must be ticked off the column once they are executed. Something like: mention the marriage ceremony as the moment when the possibility of incest and inbreeding can be raised (this will remain in the reader's mind and return as the subtext for Arthur's uneasy friendship with Giles Barrington, Emma's brother); enhance Harry's potential as a bold, courageous figure in preparation for more considered attention to his post-war persona and father of Sebastian.

At each point, however, he appears to be wearily impatient with these duties, so much so that he presses each piece of information into service without giving any thought to its incongruous relationship with the rest of the narrative. It is rather like encountering a third person narrator who is too tired or distracted to orchestrate the various strands of the story.

Here we should drop the pretense that the slow reader of Archer is a literary academic. He is more likely to be the ordinary reader utterly con-founded by the narrator's heedless incompetence, for whom "slow" reading will soon be replaced by infuriation followed by a decision to close the book and return it to the shelf. Yet *Best Kept Secret* has by recent calculations (it was published 3 months before I opened it) sold more than a quarter of a million copies. We face a paradox. For the astute but unpretentious reader the book is virtually unreadable, which is something of an achievement in itself since few other works, apart from *Finnegans Wake*, can make such a claim. But it sells and, we must assume, is consumed in its entirety by its satisfied purchasers. Perhaps there is some truth in Gupta's notion of the attractions of the bestseller. Perhaps, for many, the appeal of the rolling nar-rative, the addictive propulsive energy of the "what happens next" principle, is sufficiently powerful to deaden the effects of its prose vehicle.

As I shall show, the generic notion of "popular fiction" – and for that matter the "bestseller" – is both elastic and terribly misleading. As Archer shows, it generously accommodates works that are, according to the most liberal and indulgent conceptions of quality, intrinsically substandard. Yet there are some authors, particularly crime and thriller writers, placed in the same genre as Archer, who match and often eclipse the achievements of "literary" novelists. The popular, involving the nonelitist combination of quality and entertainment, will always be seen as an aesthetically inferior realm. This prejudice blinds us to the differences within popular fiction, particularly between works that are so outstandingly bad as to rank as monuments to underachievement, and others that show how pure skill and intelligence can be employed as much to demand admiration as to procure excitement. But before we turn our attention to such works let us consider a novel that caused a sensation by becoming almost a sub-genre in its own right, spawning desperate imitations virtually by the month from ambitious ghostwriters and hacks: the *Fifty Shades* trilogy by E.L. James. The third volume, *Fifty Shades Freed* (2011), is concerned with episodes in the compulsive and slightly perverted relationship between the "damaged entrepreneur" Christian Grey and Anastasia Steele, an independent and forbidding woman. They appear to be married but for much of the book their liaisons carry an air of duplicity and subterfuge. This incongruity of mood and apparent context might seem promising, at least for those with an interest in the psychosexual complexities of relationships conducted by their rich, successful, and rather stupid contemporaries. But its potential remains just that, unrealized and never properly explained. The following passage from the book is intriguing and revealing.

> "Turn over. I want to do your back."
>
> Smiling, I roll over, and he undoes a back strap of my hideously expensive bikini.
>
> "I don't think we need this," he says.
>
> My pulse quickens and my breathing shallows. I can't believe it – he's hardly touched me and I feel like this – hot, bothered … ready.
>
> "Please." I lift up the blankets.
>
> "Fuck it." He slips off his shoes and socks, and gingerly climbs in beside me.
>
> He gazes down at me, eyes shining with love, wonder, and wicked thoughts.
>
> Jeez … life is never going to be boring with Christian, and I'm in this for the long haul.
>
> "Kiss me again."
>
> Christian stalls, one hand on my back, the other on my behind.
>
> "Kiss me," I breathe, and I watch his lips part as he inhales sharply. … Then his mouth is on me as he moves his right hand into my hair, holding me in place, and lifts his left to cradle my face. His tongue invades my mouth, and I welcome it. Adrenaline turns to lust and streaks through my body. I clasp his face, running my fingers over his sideburns, relishing the taste of him. He groans at my fevered response, low and deep in his throat, and my belly tightens swift and hard with carnal desire. His hand moves down my body, brushing my breast, my waist, and down to my backside. I shift fractionally.

This is standard mildly erotic fiction, the sort of prose that cultivates images fantasized about or vaguely recollected, but there is something odd about it, something that places it in a slightly different category from, say, the work of Jackie Collins. I have not appended a page reference to the passage because it is assembled from extracts, drawn more or less at random, from different parts of the novel (principally but not exclusively pp. 33, 175, 465, 431, and 103). Archer, frantically driven to get to the next point and open another door on family secrets and the hidden motives of characters, falls over himself to sate what he assumes is his reader's corresponding hunger for sensation. James, conversely, abandons anything resembling a story in favor of a glut of erotic episodes. The narrative is non-existent. Instead, we accompany the mind-sets of Ana and Christian through more than 500 pages of sex, variously anticipated, rehearsed, and fondly recalled. The locations vary, though the implicit convention seems to be that only glamorous, luxurious, and ostentatiously expensive sites are suitable, and we sometimes learn that their lives involve noncarnal activities – employment is sometimes indicated – but information on their more mundane routines is disclosed in a heedless, extemporaneous manner, ensuring that the parade of pornography continues largely without interruption. Despite it being the complete antithesis of Archer's episodic impatience, James's work proved even more popular. It could, in her defense, be argued that she has discovered a version of Beckettian modernism that appeals to the reader with little or no interest in high culture. Beckett's most notable fiction (particularly *Watt*, 1953; *Molloy*, 1955; *Malone Dies*, 1951; and *The Unnameable*, 1953) involves nothing resembling a story or even a recognizable context beyond the imprisoned, self-referring mind-set of the speaking presence. If it can be said to have a subject it is language, particularly its power as a medium of introverted self-possession. Substitute sex for language and the parallels with James become evident. In Malcolm Lowry's *Under the* Volcano (1947) Geoffrey Firmin, alcoholic depressive British Consul to Somewhere, is less a character than a witness to the novel's unbounded concern with the cyclic and unfathomable nature of truth and its quixotic confederate, writing. Ana is similarly fixated with the sensuous, magnetic presence of Christian, so much so that her story, indeed her life, becomes a static, obsessive exchange of continuity for an endlessly repeated sex act.

I am, of course, allowing serious literary criticism to slide into facetiousness. For one thing, James's prose is relentlessly clichéd and unambitious; a transparent vehicle for lurid sex but in its own right extraordinarily tedious.

Nonetheless one has to wonder if there are parallels between a novel that dispenses with characters and narrative energy in favor of an intellectual fancy and one that does the same to flatter a similarly solipsistic instinct, in James's case unaccountable gratification.

Without doubt the sub-genre that raises the most challenging questions about the status, indeed the nature, of popular fiction is crime writing, and its close relatives the thriller and espionage fiction.

From Conan-Doyle's Holmes to Susan Hill's Inspector Serailler, British crime writing has been ranked as a sub-species of fiction per se mainly because of its adherence to and maintenance of a predictable formula. This allows of variations – sometimes despite the best efforts of the detective the suspect might remain at large or the identity of the true perpetrator uncertain – but some elements are inflexible. The detectives – and even their entrepreneurial cousins the private investigators – are always pre-sented as morally superior to the lawbreakers. Certainly, the former will be well laden with character defects largely as a salve to authenticity, but a clear line of demarcation always exists between what they are inclined to do, even in the most arduous circumstances, and the actual offenses committed by the people they investigate.

This is understandable given that the attractions of crime writing are underpinned by a fabric of hypocrisies and self-contradictions. Fiction, along with theater, TV drama, and film, frequently gratifies an enduring but rarely admitted taste among a large number of its readers: the pru-rient thrill that comes from witnessing something terrible or macabre while remaining immune from it or its consequences. For many readers this will be accompanied by commensurate feelings of guilt fueled partly by a personal sense of unease at taking pleasure from the distress of others, albeit fictional, and also by a sense of social responsibility, a sus-picion that an attraction to depictions of criminal misbehavior might carry a trace of condoning or complicity. Hence, most crime writers and their readers appear to have entered into a tacit consensus on how the guilty attraction of reading about crime should be ameliorated by a counterbalance of dependable honesty and attendance to the absolutes of right and wrong.

The genre has by its nature condemned itself to a ranking in the aesthetic second division. In part the lineage of crime fiction includes the hybrid forms of writing that in the eighteenth and nineteenth centuries fed upon the enormous popular taste for capital trials and public executions. The quintessential example of this ghoulish tradition was the 1724 execution of the highwayman Jack Sheppard. Sheppard, sentenced to hang, had escaped from prison on three previous occasions and acquired the reputation of a popular anti-hero mostly through the publication of hack pamphlets documenting his criminal achievements in verse and prose. On the day of his hanging more than 200,000 people packed the streets of London, roughly a third of the population of the metropolis, and at Tyburn more than one thousand copies of his recently printed "autobiography" – allegedly authored by Daniel Defoe – were sold from stalls prior to his arrival. Sheppard's legendary ability to escape the noose almost at the last minute – along with his continued acts of reckless criminality when at large – held the attention of most of the nation and his life, and death, became the subject of prose works, poems, and plays for the subsequent century. People were gripped both by the fantasy of a life conducted with scandalous vigor outside the conformist world of laws and morality and by the grisly fate eventually visited by that society upon the perpetrator of these acts of rebellion and audacity. Sheppard and other figures similarly memorialized by hack writers embodied what would become the two contradictory features of the nineteenth century crime novel and successors: the delight in witnessing the unpredictable consequences of breaking the rules – which incorporates shades of sadomasochism – and the entirely predictable knowledge that the forces of order and righteousness will eventually triumph.

As a consequence of this, mainstream crime fiction is tied to self-limited conventions similar to those that inform the medieval morality play or the kind of Victorian novel that promulgated the ethical norms of the period. Characters and circumstances can be made believable only to the extent that they do not fail in their predetermined functions as indices to abstract codes of behavior. Realism – in its broadest definition as the ability to explore and represent without comment any form of human circumstance, inclination, or activity – is therefore severely constrained.

US crime fiction has shown itself more inclined to transgress this formula, often by shifting the narrative focus away from the mind-set of the investigator and toward that of the perpetrator, a procedure that carries an attendant question: might you, reader, be capable of this? Mid twentieth century classics include James M. Cain's *The Postman Always Rings Twice* (1934) and *Double Indemnity* (1936), and Patricia Highsmith's *Strangers on a Train* (1950) and *The Talented Mr. Ripley* (1955). Soon afterwards US writers began to pose questions regarding the sacrosanct state of the police themselves. In John Ball's *In the Heat of the Night* (1965) endemic racism within Southern policing is exposed, and in virtually all of Elmore Leonard's novels from the 1970s onwards the criminal and the detective are equally dismissive of ethical codes of behavior; the narrative is driven simply by whether the latter or the former will in the end triumph and neither is presented as by their nature the more admirable or amiable. In the same vein Joseph Wambaugh's ground-breaking *The New Centurions* (1971) and *The Choirboys* (1975) offer us California-based police departments made up of alcoholics, racists, drug addicts, perverts, even murderers, albeit via a filter of very dark comedy. Walter Mosley's black private investigator Easy Rawlings acts as a lens for the strata of exploitative violence, corruption, and racism in US society from the 1940s to the 1960s. He is a decent man but no better than he has to be, distrusting the police and the legal system as a whole and often surviving via his ability to incite fear in others. Mosley's exercises in dispassionate naturalism find a more disturbing echo in Lawrence Block's Keller (*Hit List*, 2000). Keller occupies the center of the narrative as a compelling, beguiling presence, a man of dry wit and integrity. His profession? Self-employed hit man. James Ellroy in *American Tabloid* (1995), *White Jazz* (1992), and *The Cold Six Thousand* (2001) intercuts invention with meticulously researched scenarios from US politics and social history of the 1950s and 1960s. J.F. and Edward Kennedy appear alongside, sometimes meet, figures from the Mafia and characters – some fictional, some actual – who frequently cross the line between CIA-sponsored terrorism and pure criminality.

The British writer best known to have made rather modest claims upon the US form of unbridled crime fiction is Ian Rankin, whose series involving the Edinburgh-based Inspector John Rebus began with *Knots and Crosses* (1987). Rebus is prone to depressive bouts and seems by temperament and background to fit in with the rough, urban, working classes who are responsible for much of Edinburgh's day-to-day fabric of criminality. At the same time, however, he never quite dishonors his profession. His litany of failed relationships is presented as a tragic consequence of his commitment to the job and he views, and has the reader view, with circumspect disdain, the pomposities of the Edinburgh middle classes and nouveau riche. Some have treated Rebus's fictional environment as comparable with that created by Irvine Welsh but this is part of the false mythology of the Scottish literary renaissance. In truth, Rebus is only a little more unorthodox than the likes of Reginald Hill's Dalziel and R. D. Wingfield's Frost. He makes something of his existential crises and coat-trails his working-class Scottishness, with its collision of roughness and vulnerability, but beyond that the formulae that inhibit the mainstream of British crime fiction remain undisturbed.

By far the most impressive British crime writer of recent years is Bill James. His novels, involving principally but not exclusively Detective Chief Superintendent Colin Harpur and Assistant Chief Constable Desmond Iles ran from the mid 1980s to the late 2000s. The moral and ethical truancies of his policemen bring to mind Wambaugh and Ellroy. Harpur is a serial adulterer who is particularly besotted with Denise, a local undergraduate student almost half his age. His wife, Megan, begins an affair with his ex-colleague, recently promoted to the Metropolitan Police and in *Roses, Roses* (1993) is stabbed to death – probably by the henchman of a villain Harpur has had sent down, we never know – during her return from London. Iles, a man of lupine sophistication and dry wit, spends some of his time berating the liberal imbecilities of his senior, Lane, while occasionally exploding into almost murderous spasms of rage against both colleagues and villains, particularly those among the former, Harpur included, who have slept with his wife.

Iles attempts, habitually, to seduce one of Harpur's teenage daughters and for downmarket lechery trawls the docks for as yet unfallen virgins who he can rescue from local pimps, but always ensuring that he has sex with them first. Also he murders a local gangster, who seems immune from prosecution, in a particularly sadistic, ritualistic manner. Add to this cast Jack Lamb, a wealthy dealer in stolen art protected by Harpur as his best informer plus "Panicking" Ralph Ember, sex addict, killer, and keeper of the bar where most of the local criminal desolates gather and you have a menu that is the most bizarre and refreshing alternative to conventional British crime writing since Ainsworth's *Jack Sheppard*.

Alongside his fascinatingly grotesque cast James is a consummate stylist, bringing to the rather staid mechanisms of the crime novel a learned, darkly comic bitterness redolent of Waugh or the Amises father and son. In *The Detective is Dead* (1995), Iles, Harpur, and DCI Garland are discussing a recent post office armed robbery allegedly involving a villain called Vine in which a bystander was killed, when Iles allows himself to slip into his erudite psychopathic mode.

Garland, who was standing alongside Harpur's desk, also sat down now, as if aware he'd need all his strength to deal with Iles. Garland was a whizz-kid Chief Inspector, astonishingly brassy and clever, even clever enough to realize Iles was cleverer, when unfeverish.

"You have this wonderful, head-on approach to things, Francis. The way, say, Churchill could chop through the bullshit and get at the essence".

Garland had begun to frown with concentration.

"It's an aristocratic flair and true gift, Francis, often crucial in our work and, of course, most attractive to women."

Harpur stood at once and went to close the door properly. He was just in time.

Iles began to shout, pointing an elegant finger at Garland. "It would be this kind of foul, assertive single-mindedness, this taste for the straight up and down and no thought for others, that led you to screw my wife for as long as it suited you, wouldn't it, Garland?"

Harpur said: "And you will have seen the Traffic account of Vine on the motorway link yesterday, sir."

"Exactly," Iles replied at normal voice. "Clearly, this is the point."

Garland said: "My reading of their meeting is –"

"I know as a certainty my wife now regrets that episode, those episodes with you, Garland, and indeed finds them incomprehensible," Iles yelled. "And the same as regards Harpur. More so. This was a woman looking for something mentally undemanding and merely fleshly, absolutely and totally merely. You're both tailor-made."

"Francis thought they possibly rendezvoused there and ultimately left together, sir," Harpur replied.

"Don't be hard on him, Col," Iles said conversationally. "It's not a totally inane view of the matter. If your brain is in your balls, like Garland, thought processes have a debilitating, uphill trek." (p. 148)

In part, Bill James's fiction undoes the constraints of the British crime novel by caricaturing them, but he goes further than that. Certainly his plots are framed by particular criminal acts but these fall into the background compared with the extraordinary blend of verisimilitude and sublime peculiarity that absorb his characters and their world. To this extent he could be treated as belonging as much to the strain of eccentric realism exemplified by Muriel Spark and Iris Murdoch as he does to standard crime writing. His achievement is considerable but not just because of his ingenious refusal to conform. His work shows how the genre has committed a form of collective suicide, imposing upon itself rules and conventions that are entirely arbitrary and which reinforce the generally accepted distinction between the "literary novel" and it supposedly downmarket relative.

The only other British author who can rival James for unorthodoxy is Jake Arnott. *The Long Firm* (1999) was celebrated as the most original crime novel in living memory but in truth it is an adaptation of the techniques of James Ellroy to a British setting, specifically London in the mid 1960s. The narrative is shared by a young rent boy, a hardened villain called Jack the Hat, a dissolute Tory peer, a fading starlet called Ruby Ryder, and a young sociology teacher, all of whom are drawn into the orbit of the mobster Harry Starks. The technique is impressive because although we never have transparent access to the mind-set of Harry, the five narrators disclose a presence at once charismatic, pitiable, and frighteningly ruthless. Like Ellroy, Arnott furnishes the text with enough period detail to secure authenticity without clogging the narrative, and more significantly he interweaves invented characters and events with some very real ones. The Krays, Tom Driberg, Peter Rachman, Evelyn Waugh, Liza Minnelli, and Johnnie Ray all have cameo roles which both correspond with biographical fact and often cross the line into the realm of the possible and credible. Ruby, Rachman's sometime lover, informs us that he prefers sex on top and facing away from her and Lord "Teddy" Thursby notes in his diary that at the previous night's party he "Nearly tripped over Tom Driberg, Honourable Member for Barking, on his knees, energetically sucking away" (*The Long Firm*, 2003, p. 59).

Arnott's overall objective, one suspects, is to impart to crime fiction a degree of purpose and gravitas, to shift it beyond its popular status as an easy recreational mode to that which engages the reader at a deeper intellectual and temperamental level. His choice of the 1960s testifies to this purpose in that it is routinely regarded as the decade in which Britain finally unshackled itself from the codes of morality and behavior and the class-based social structure that had been its formative elements for the previous century. Arnott addresses many of these issues, most specifically sexuality: he presents Harry Starks as open, energetically homosexual while in all other respects the complete antithesis of the stereotypical figures associated with gayness. Significant political events such as the abolition of the death penalty and the legalization of homosexual acts are strewn into the chronology and it is evident that Arnott is, in part, offering an alternative account of the recent history of British society, obliging us to see behind official mythology to a world in which policemen and politicians are habitually corrupt and certainly not morally superior to professional criminals. It was clearly influenced by Ellroy's *American Tabloid* (1995) in which Peter

Bondurant, Howard Hughes's confidant and fixer, Jimmy Hoffa's hit man and occasional CIA operative, and Kemper Boyd, favorite of FBI boss Hoover, offer us a tour through the hidden, violent, often deranged world of American politics and law enforcement. Ellroy extended his state-of-the-deplorable-nation exercise into *The Cold Six Thousand* (2001), involving new characters and mature versions of the originals, as does Arnott in *He Kills Coppers* (2001). In this Arnott introduces the adhesive tabloid journalist Tony Meehan who witnesses the abundant foulness beneath the tacky spectacle of England from the 1966 World Cup victory to the Thatcher years, and in *Truecrime* (2003) we reach the 1990s accompanied by some of the phlegmatic aging figures from *The Long Firm*, Harry and Ruby included.

Few would deny that crime writing is different from other forms of fiction but does its distinctness automatically qualify it as culturally and aesthetically inferior?

The first attempt to classify crime fiction as a significant intellectual undertaking was Marjorie Nicolson's "The Professor and the Detective" (1929). Nicolson, an academic, bases her argument on the observation, which we must accept on trust, that a considerable number of her peers in the academy, the arts and sciences, are avid fans of detective novels. She asks why this should be, much in the manner of someone who wonders why priests visit brothels, and concludes that this form of writing provides refuge from the ongoing modernist fashion for instability and anarchy. Crime fiction focuses upon the use of reason, by the detective and the reader, and as such "it is an escape not from life but from literature," or at least the kind of literature that employs devices such as "'stream of consciousness' ... to engulf us in its Lethean monotony." Nicolson's piece, while poised and high minded in its manner, is extraordinarily patronizing. It grants crime writing a kind of status by association – comparing it with works by Joyce, for example – while at the same time treating it as a source of effortless relaxation. Despite their apparent differences Nicolson has much in common with Edmund Wilson who, in his famous 1945 article, "Who Cares Who Killed Roger Ackroyd?" stated that "with so many fine books to read ... there is no need to bore ourselves with this rubbish." Wilson treats crime fiction as low cultural idleness and Nicolson regards it as a kind of reassuring crossword puzzle for those unsettled by intellectual radicalism. She indulges it and he does not, but their perception of it as a subsidiary to serious writing is shared.

A far more engaging account of his feelings about crime fiction came from an indisputably high cultural writer. In "The Guilty Vicarage" (1948),

W.H. Auden seems to be following a line similar to that taken by Nicolson but rather than adopt a clinical academic mode he is frank regarding his addiction to the genre and troubled by the different ways in which he responds to it, ranging from guilt to aesthetic appreciation. He feels that detective stories are the least worthy of praise because in most cases the reader identifies with the investigator and joins him or her in an attempt to restore order to society. This, in Auden's view, is not only a misuse of literary writing but a means of denying the genuine attractions of crime writing. In truth, we enjoy the ghoulish thrill of witnessing the apprehension, even the punishment, of the perpetrator but the structure of the detective narrative enables us to pretend that our interest is more virtuous. Auden contends that we should not conceal the unwholesome element of our taste, but rather give greater recognition to the kind of crime fiction that does not easily enable us to do so. He has in mind the kind of novel in which we are invited, sometimes obliged, to share the outlook and emotional preoccupations of killers. He refers to Dostoevsky's *Crime and Punishment* but concedes that Chandler and Hammett could be included in the same category.

In *Bloody Murder* (1972; last revised 1992) Julian Symons came up with a formula for evaluating crime writing as literature that is superior to anything offered in academic studies. Symons concedes that Auden is shrewd and honest but finds fault with his division of the genre into two sub-categories, detective fiction and the crime novel, not because they are different – he accepts that they are – but because Auden and others automatically allocate a potential for artistic quality to the latter while denying it to the former. He compares them with Restoration comedy and Jacobean drama: "nobody condemns Restoration comedy outright because it lacks the profundity of Jacobean drama." There are, he avers, "gradations" within each: some Restoration dramatists outrank a considerable number of their Jacobean counterparts in terms of stylistic acuity, and similarly there are writers of detective novels that transcend the escapist "puzzle" classification of their mode by attaining levels of excellence in dialogue and characterization that match anything in mainstream fiction.

He welcomes what he calls the "double standard": "so that one can say first of all that the characteristic detective story has almost no literary merit, and second that it may still be an ingenious, cunningly deceptive and finely constructed piece of work." Equally, we should not automatically assume that a novel that follows *Crime and Punishment* in its avoidance of the formulaic structure of a puzzle will match the masterful style of Dostoevsky in its execution.

Symons points out the boundaries between crime writing and serious literature can often be blurred but in doing so he reinforces the case that such boundaries endure.

Crime fiction is a genre trapped and limited by its own defining features. It is just possible to imagine a novel that treats the act of murder or the activities of the police in a solidly realist manner, one that does not give undue attention to the interwoven private world of the detectives and the horrid nature of their work nor to the extrapolated crossword puzzle of the reader's own desire to work out who did it and why. But this is all that it will remain – a hypothesis. Deglamorize the criminal act, eliminate the persistent thrill of solving the mystery or catching the perpetrator and then it is no longer crime fiction; it is denuded of those elements that both popularize it and separate from the mainstream of "literary" fiction writing. This aspect of popularity as a rejection of high culture reaches beyond crime.

During its first 2 years in print Helen Fielding's *Bridget Jones's Diary* (1996) sold almost a million copies in the UK alone. The entries of this anxious, hopelessly ambitious, and involuntarily amusing heroine touched a chord of empathy and recognition in women and when the book was published in the USA in 1998 the *New York Times* offered a blunt explanation for its success: "It captures neatly the way modern women teeter between 'I am a woman' independence and a pathetic girlie desire to be all things to all men" (*New York Times*, 31 May 1998). Another reason for the novel's popularity was its form. We learn of Bridget's thoughts and activities predominantly via her diary entries but Fielding sets up a subtle tension in each of these between her public and private personae. The former involves what the *New York Times* refers to as her "'I am a woman' independence," beneficiary as she is of the achievements of the previous generation of feminists and honorable torchbearer for the same. The latter, however, shows us the real Bridget: continually nervous about her weight and appearance, convinced that her "career" in the media will lead nowhere, and concerned ultimately with finding a reliable, handsome, and comfortably off man with whom she will have exuberant sex and play the part of dutiful housewife.

The novel has frequently been cited as initiator of a somewhat amorphous sub-genre known as "chick lit," a term that carries a subtext of tolerant reproval: entertaining, clever, but not on a par with "serious" writing. However, there is cause to treat Fielding's invention as a significant comment upon feminism and women's issues.

The man with whom she finds contentment is Mark Darcy, whose name of course invokes the presence of Jane Austen and her similar account of wish fulfillment, *Pride and Prejudice*. Fielding, who had worked in the media and publishing, would have been fully aware of Emma Tennant's two sequels to this novel. *Pemberley* (1993) and *An Unequal Marriage* (1994) both disclose traits within Elizabeth Bennet and the original Mr Darcy that Austen would have been obliged by the conventions of the period to conceal, or so Tennant indicates. Fielding, contra Tennant, contends that some characteristics are in innate function of gender and immune from the vicissitudes of historical change. Books, she implies, can be rewritten in accordance with a new enlightened perspective, but for women like Bridget – and indeed Elizabeth – a relationship with the likes of Darcy is more important than aspirations to selfhood and independence. Perhaps to dispel any doubts that she is weaving into her entertainment an underhand, sceptical commentary upon literary feminism, in the sequel *Bridge Jones: The Edge of Reason* (1999) Fielding has Bridget interview the actor Colin Firth. Firth famously played Darcy in the BBC version of Austen's *Pride and Prejudice* (1995) and for this reason was later cast as Darcy in the film version of the first *Bridget Jones*. A more peculiar case of intergeneric intertextuality could hardly be envisaged and Fielding makes clever use of it. In Andrew Davies's screenplay Darcy is presented as an arrogantly sexy figure and Bridget asks Firth if he thinks Austen would have approved of this. Their discussion of historical revisionism rapidly spirals into a one-sided sexual fantasy with Bridget struggling to remain coherent as Firth recalls how Davies had insisted that Darcy should have "an enormous sex drive." "At one point" he informs Bridget "Andrew even wrote as a stage direction 'Imagine that Darcy has an erection.'" Bridget appears thereafter to forget the ostensible topic of their exchange and noises replace words (*Bridget Jones: The Edge of Reason*, 2004).

Even in its most recent manifestation, *Mad About The Boy* (2013), Bridget Jones's diary is undiscriminating and ingenuous in its manner; honest yet clearly not intended for the scrutiny of anyone but its author. Look closely, however, and we can discern another figure in the background, orchestrating and, to a degree, caricaturing Jones's exercise in hopeless candor. Like many of her counterparts in crime fiction Fielding writes down to a certain kind of reader, sparing them the unnecessary effort of stylistic decoding and intellectual involvement, while allowing the more discriminating to see the method of representation behind the story; it is an example of the double pattern at its most spare and unaffected.

It would be inappropriate to take leave of the bestseller without giving attention to what some might regard as a sub-species of lyric poetry; popular music. Academia treats rock and pop music with a mixture of condescension and inverse snobbery. On the one hand rock music is dealt with as part of a broader discourse, one that also includes such allegedly high cultural forms as lyric poetry. At the same time, however, few if any are prepared to ask questions about why a song by The Smiths is as good as a lyric by Wordsworth, or vice versa: this would open a door on the forbidden territory of evaluation and aesthetic judgment. Monographs such as *Rimbaud and Jim Morrison, The Rebel as Poet* (W. Fowlie, 1994) and such volumes as *The Cambridge Companion to Bob Dylan* (ed. K.J.H. Dettmar, 2009) bespeak a hierarchy of renown and esteem without actually addressing the implied question of why Morrison and Dylan deserve special treatment. Predominantly, we encounter books and articles where Cultural Theory is let loose upon popular music in much the same way that it has overwhelmed academic literary criticism over the last four decades. The titles of J. Shepherd's *Music as Social Text* (1991) and Paul Friedlander's *Rock and Roll: A Social History* (1997) are self-explanatory: the aesthetic qualities of individual songs are subservient to their status as sociopolitical artefacts. Similarly, *Popular Music, Gender and Postmodernism* (N. Nehring, 1997) and *The Beatles with Lacan* (H.W. Sullivan, 1995) give no consideration to the qualities, or otherwise, of the music; Theory has no time for distinctions between high art, low art, or for the nature of art per se.

I offer this as a preamble to one of the most extraordinary works of literary evaluation of the past few decades, Christopher Ricks's *Dylan's Visions of Sin* (2003). Throughout his career Ricks has avoided the habits that commonly impoverish the work of university-based critics. He has no time for Theory, and relies instead on a blend of discernment and a playful elegance of his own. He does not attempt to outclass his subjects; rather he implies that literary greatness demands a collateral degree of refinement on the part of the commentator. His best known works are on Milton, Keats, T.S. Eliot, Tennyson, and Beckett so when his book on Bob Dylan was published reviewers were dumbfounded. How did this literary meritocrat intend to deal, in excruciating detail, with a man whose verse is comprised entirely of folk-rock songs?

As a student at Cambridge long ago (1928?), the young William Empson impressed his teacher, the not much older I.A. Richards, by his spirited dealings with a Shakespeare sonnet. "Taking the sonnet as a conjurer takes his hat, he produced an endless swarm of rabbits from it and ended by 'You could do that with any poetry, couldn't you?'" But only if the poetry truly teems, and only if the critic only *seems* to be a conjurer. What, then, is the Critic's enterprise? To give grounds for the faith that is in him, in us, in those of us who are grateful. It is a privilege. (Ricks, 2003, p. 1)

Though it postdates Stanley Fish by almost half a century this is the counter-argument against his reader-based thesis. Critical discernment, Ricks contends, alerts us to the inherent qualities of a poem, features created by a talented poet. Bob Dylan is just such an artist, a man who has been waiting for a critic who will treat it as a "privilege" to introduce the reader to his triumphs and profundities.

His case is at once rhapsodic and farcical. In the end Ricks simply asks us to trust him as an honest, reliable guide rather than someone who will prove that a middle-ranking songwriter is a great poet: no convincing evidence to support this case is provided.

The book itself is an embarrassing example of critical coat-trailing. During every encounter with a Dylan lyric he drags in passages from the accepted greats, everyone from Shakespeare to Philip Larkin, as a means of performing exactly the kind of trick that Empson played on Richards; picking out quotations from the canon that in some way echo those from Dylan but which at the same time obscure our sense of the latter's groaning inferiority. His selections and his orchestration of our attention to detail are meticulously calculated. He finds and discloses echoes as adroitly as he disguises and deflects the sheer ordinariness of Dylan as poet. His method is intriguing enough but less interesting than the question of why he employs it.

Rock music has, like football, always exercised an uncomfortable fascination for the intelligentsia. It is quite likely that a number of intellectual high flyers derive a genuine pleasure from both, but two issues arise from this. The first is unproblematic: politicians, top order journalists, and writers of various sorts continue to believe that their well-publicized cultivation of a taste for activities enjoyed by the masses will improve their image. The second is far more troubling. Apart from stating that they have always supported, say, Arsenal, or that they have favored a particular band since their undergraduate years, how do they explain why, in their opinion, this team or that group are superior to others? Most avoid such questions, for obvious reasons. The Monty Python comedy team once ran a sketch in which a plumber with a Cockney accent switched seamlessly from his account of why the boiler had broken down to reflections on Kierkegaard. Imagine this in reverse – shifting from high culture to the mundane – and one has a clear enough idea of what happens when an intellectual moves downmarket; the manner of address is absurdly ill matched with the subject.

At one point Ricks gives attention to Dylan's "Day of Locusts," a lyric on the singer's experience of receiving an honorary doctorate in music from Princeton.

> Oh, the benches were stained with tears and perspiration
> The birdies were flying from tree to tree
> There was little to say, there was no conversation
> As I stepped to the stage to pick up my degree.

As verse, the four lines are engaging in a disposable simplistic way but Ricks is determined to haul them into the higher canon and begins with a quotation from Matthew Arnold, on Wordsworth.

> One can hear them being quoted at a Social Science Congress; one can call up the whole scene. A great room in one of our dismal provincial towns; dusty air and jaded afternoon daylight; benches full of men with bald heads and women in spectacles; an orator lifting up his face from a manuscript written within and without to declaim these lines of Wordsworth; and in the soul of any poor child of nature who may have wandered in thither, an unutterable sense of lamentation, and mourning, and woe! (Ricks, after Arnold, p. 194)

This, in Arnold's view, is the destiny of great literary art once the middle-classes begin to "analyze" it. It is robbed of its life and inspiration. Just as Arnold wished to preserve the likes of Wordsworth from this, so Ricks takes it upon himself to rescue the brilliance of Bob Dylan from the suffocating maul of academe.

This is followed by references to, amongst things, the rhetorical flourishes of Winston Churchill's speeches, and after a page and a half we are still not finished:

> Oh, the benches were stained with tears and perspiration
> The birdies were flying from tree to tree

Why is "birdies" so endearing there? I feel about it as a Kingsley Amis hero did about sex, that he knew why he liked it but why did he like it so much? Partly, the open poeticality of it, its calling up the songs of Robert Burns: "Ye birdies dumb, in with'ring bowers." Yes, the birdies are dumb in this song, they are not singing but flying, and they leave it to the locusts to be the songsters. And those "with'ring bowers"? "Benches stained with tears and Perspiration"?

Or, watching the birdie, the songs of Tennyson: "She sang this baby song. / What does little birdie say / In her nest at peep of Day?" Nothing about a doctorate of music, you may be sure of that – and yet the world of primary education is there, on its way to the tertiary. (Ricks, 2003, p. 195)

Persistently, grievously, Ricks take us on a tour of the top echelons of literary culture, whispering at every point: Bob Dylan belongs here too.

While *Dylan's Visions of Sin* is a colossally embarrassing attempt to salvage popular writing as art it is not an isolated case. Even worse is James Wood's *The Fun Stuff and Other Essays* (2002), and in particular Wood's chapter on The Who drummer, Keith Moon.

The drumming is staggeringly vital, with Moon at once rhythmically tight and massively spontaneous. On both that song ["Won't Get Fooled Again"] and "Behind Blue Eyes" you can hear him do something that was instinctive, probably, but which is hardly ever attempted in ordinary rock drumming: breaking for a fill, Moon fails to stop at the obvious end of the musical phrase and continues with his rolling break, over the line and into the start of the next phrase. In poetry, this failure to stop at the end of the line, this challenge to metrical closure, this desire to *get more in*, is called enjambment. Moon is the drummer of enjambment.

With all due respect to fans of The Who, particularly those drawn to them in their anarchic early years prior to Moon's death in 1978, one has to wonder if any ever thought to themselves: yes indeed, Keith is "the drummer of enjambment," worthy of comparison with Milton and Wordsworth at their best. Throughout the passage Wood appears to be gradually releasing clues towards what will become, for his reader, an epiphany. The two closing sentences are his moments of revelation. Rejoice, he seems to say: Moon is a poet, "the drummer of enjambment." He is trying desperately to reconcile his high cultural state of mind with something else, something that most other people – particularly those who did not attend Eton or gain a First in English from Cambridge – treat simply as entertainment. If he is attempting to enlighten such persons it is an exercise in condescension but I suspect that his intended audience is actually himself. For all I know Wood does indeed enjoy listening to Keith Moon's drumming, just as Ricks takes a good deal of pleasure from the lyrics of Bob Dylan, but for both there is a mismatch between something simple, even visceral, and their scrupulous evaluative mentalities. Perhaps they feel guilty about liking something that is certainly not part of high culture and as a compensation feel they should dress it in the kind of critical language that is the currency of aesthetic superiority. The problem is that the clothes do not fit.

Wood continues:

> For me this playing is like an ideal sentence of prose, a sentence I have always wanted to write and never quite had the confidence to: a long passionate onrush, formally controlled and joyously messy, propulsive but digressively self-interrupted, attired but dishevelled, careful and lawless, right and wrong. (You can encounter such sentences in Lawrence's prose, in Bellow's, some-times in David Foster Wallace's.) Such a sentence would be a breaking out, an escape. And drumming has always represented for me that dream of escape, when the body forgets itself, surrenders its awful self-consciousness.

The last phrase is painfully, inadvertently apt, given that only an onrush of very "awful self-consciousness" would rescue this passage from itself. The thesaurus of descriptive excess leads us into a hushed, bracketed, sequence of grand introductions: "Keith Moon, please meet D.H. Lawrence, Saul Bellow, David Foster Wallace. You too are now one of the Greats"; the subtext being that I, James Wood, gatekeeper to this grand collective, can admit you as a member.

Late 2013 saw the publication of a misery memoir of the kind pioneered by Martin Amis in *Experience* (2000): the artist, now in middle age, revisits his past. This one, *Autobiography*, was by the rock singer and composer, Morrissey. The book invites comparison with Ricks's but not because of what it actually contains. His publisher, at the behest of Morrissey and his agent, chose to bring it out as part of their series, Penguin Modern Classics, alongside, among other greats, the plays of Beckett, the fiction of Saul Bellow, and A.J. Ayer's *Language, Truth and Logic*. Such an attempt at prestige-by-association might attain a special degree of absurdity were it not for the fact that no one found it ridiculous. Many reviewers – generally those habitually concerned with evaluating literature – treated it like the Second Coming. According to Terry Eagleton, Morrissey is "devastatingly articulate", a writer who "could walk off with the Booker Prize" (*Guardian*, 13 November 2013). Neil McCormick in the *Daily Telegraph* complimented him for "a beautifully measured prose style that combines a lilting poetic turn of phrase and acute quality of observation" while Alex Niven of the *Independent* finds it "A brilliant and timely book … reads like a work of genuine literary class." The following is his recollection of how the television set became the altar stone for family rituals.

> Breathing lulls throughout Miss World transmissions as British families ram into chocolate-strewn settees for a genuine glimmer of glamour, where cabaret battles the convent as finalists huddle together backstage awaiting the announcement of the juicy winner in a severe condition of meaningless tragedy.

Is this "devastatingly articulate," "beautifully measured prose," incorporating a "lilting poetic turn of phrase"? I think it could more accurately be described as immature, lazy hyperbole and one wonders why so many of his reviewers present him as a hybrid of Wilde, Waugh, and Julian Barnes. His songs, his history as principal figure in The Smiths and his self-cultivated image as working class prophet of gloom and grievance confer upon him form of sanctity. His prose might involve little more than droning narcissism but the arbiters of high culture rank it in inverse proportion to its worth. I am reasonably certain that few if any of those who celebrate his talents as a prose writer and a lyricist genuinely feel that in the real world he would merit more than the kind of indulgent encouragement offered to a first year on a creative writing course. But they have suspended the real world's guarantees of common sense and elected to perform a curious re-enactment of Hans Christian Anderson's *The Emperor's New Clothes*. Unfortunately, no one seems willing to point out that just as the king is naked, so the notion of Morrissey as a literary genius is a pretense.

8

Is Literature Any Good For Us?

How does the quality of a literary work relate to its impact on our beliefs, our feelings about morality, justice, freedom, even politics? The question fizzes with complications. First of all it rests on the presumption that literature per se has any effect at all beyond the realms of diversion, amusement, escapism, or aesthetic appreciation. Just as significantly it implies that the criteria for literary quality should involve the capacity of a work to make us think differently about the world. Consequently, we find ourselves wondering if literature is not merely an adjunct to the religious tract, the political pamphlet, the essay on humanitarian idealism, or even the newspaper article; its only notable difference being its ability to distract and enchant while it undertakes its primary role of instruction.

F.R. Leavis might have been expected to feature in the chapter on modern criticism but as we will see he deserves special scrutiny here, as the most outspoken twentieth century advocate for literature as a source of improvement, even redemption. Leavis had by the 1950s attained legendary status as a figure who promoted his ideals with a passion which many thought ill-suited to the quiet sensitivities of academia. It was not until 1962, however, that his acerbic temperament featured in a more public controversy when he published in *The Spectator* a lecture he had delivered in Cambridge 2 years earlier in response to C.P. Snow's Rede Lecture of 1959, "The Two Cultures and the Scientific

Is Shakespeare Any Good?: And Other Questions on How to Evaluate Literature, First Edition. Richard Bradford.
© 2015 John Wiley & Sons, Ltd. Published 2015 by John Wiley & Sons, Ltd.

Revolution," also given in Cambridge. Snow was an eminent scientist who had trained under Ernest Rutherford, been elected to a Fellowship at Christ's College, Cambridge, aged 25, served as adviser to the wartime coalition government and later as the Labour Minister of Science. He was also a novelist, whose *Strangers and Brothers* series charted British social, political, and academic life from the 1940s to 1970. Snow was unique in that no one else could make a comparable claim to prominence in both the arts and sciences. His dual perspective was the subject of his lecture – specifically, he called for literary writers and scientists to recognize a shared agenda – and was the prompt for an attack by Leavis that seethed with contempt and sometimes veered towards the foul-mouthed. To Snow's claim that he is able, as a novelist, to speak across the cultural divide between the arts and sciences Leavis responds, "Snow is, of course, a – no, I can't say that; he isn't … as a novelist he doesn't exist. He can't be said to know what a novel is." His novels are "composed for him by an electronic brain called Charlie" (Snow's forenames were Charles Percy). Leavis does not go on to document Snow's failures as a novelist; rather he presumes that the reader will already be aware of the standards set for greatness by one F.R. Leavis and therefore able to judge for themselves that Snow does indeed fall well below them.

Snow angered Leavis for two reasons. First of all he was, at least in Leavis's view, an overreacher. His novels, at their best, invite comparison with those of Anthony Trollope. They are not ostentatiously stylized – indeed his manner sometimes reflects a scientist's cautious attention to detail; he seemed reluctant to leave anything out – yet in terms of basic notions of dialogue and third person characterization they are intelligently informative and thought provoking. Documentary realism might be the best way to classify them. As we will see, this kind of novel was anathema to Leavis's notion of literature's purpose. Second, Snow had in his lecture dared to suggest that literary writers could work alongside scientists as empiricists, discoverers of the real and the actual with a supplementary duty to advertise such disclosures to the reading public in an engaging manner. Leavis was brought close to apoplexy by Snow's casual ascertain that while "Have you read a work of Shakespeare?" is the standard means test for a general attainment of cultural acumen a similar enquiry regarding our knowledge of Rutherford on physics would be thought parochial. Snow's point was that twentieth century intellectuals should attempt to be polymaths, like their Renaissance predecessors, and Leavis replied that "to call the master scientific mind (say Rutherford) a Shakespeare is nothing but cheap journalistic infelicity … There is no scientific equivalent to the question [of have you read Shakespeare]." Leavis became enraged because Snow, a man who was seen as one of the guiding intellects of his generation, seemed to be undermining the basic principle of his, Leavis's, life's work. By comparing a familiarity with Shakespeare to a knowledge of Rutherford's methods and findings Snow was classifying literature as a repository of ideas and while Leavis's writings often appear to suggest something congruous to this – for example he praised *Little Dorrit* for offering "something like a report on Victorian England" – the latter's working principle and credo were resolutely antithetical to Snow's.

Leavis opens *The Great Tradition* with an arresting declaration: "The great English novelists are Jane Austen, George Eliot, Henry James and Joseph Conrad." In later writings he would promote Dickens and D.H. Lawrence to the list but in *The Great Tradition* he goes on to lay out his criteria for selection. First of all they "change the possibilities of the art for practitioners and readers" (Leavis, 1948, p. 2). By this he means that each has in some way invoked and improved upon precedents set by their predecessors. Austen, in Leavis's view, owed much to Fielding and Fanny Burney but surpassed both by bringing to the endeavor of representation an "intense moral preoccupation" (p. 7) which leads him to the second criterion. Great novelists "are significant in terms of the human awareness they promote" (p. 2). Austen, in *Emma*, is judged to have brought to her writing and made available for the reader "a vital capacity for experience, a kind of reverent openness before life, and a marked moral intensity" (p. 9).

Lest we mistakenly assume that he regards literature as a secular annex to Biblical studies Leavis goes on to elide self-improvement with aesthetics, contending that there is a symbiotic relationship between a writer's "reverent openness to life – [and] marked moral intensity" and their "perfection of form." This mantra informs all of Leavis's work and while it is rarely referred to by others as a principle they share – academics tend to be too hubristic to admit to intellectual indebtedness – it underpins the customs and routines of much traditional (i.e. non-Theorized) teaching and critical writing. Even those with only a cursory knowledge of Leavis treat it as received wisdom; that to qualify for greatness literature must be both well-crafted and in some way inculcate wisdom or enlightenment. Routinely, when debates take place on the role of English literature in the national curriculum the same tiresome formula that an intimacy with the works of Shakespeare or Dickens makes us more civilized unites advocates of otherwise contrary policies. Irrespective of differences on other aspects of education there is a naïve and shared belief that good literature is good for us and this originated in the work of Matthew Arnold who can claim to be the founder of English as a scholarly and academic subject. Arnold foresaw the decline of Christian faith as a unifying code of ethics that transcended class. He was also aware of the lower bourgeoisie as potentially the most powerful stratum in the second stage of the industrial revolution, a mass of individuals who were literate, and potentially outspoken, but who were unversed in the Classics, the educational ranking that secured for the upper classes an intellectual superiority over the plebeians, irrespective of their equality before God. The English Canon would, Arnold contended, offer the middle classes a vulgarized substitute for the civilizing agencies of ancient Greek and Roman texts. It would, moreover, encourage patriotism: to appreciate the literature and aesthetic produce of your nation involves a collateral feeling of allegiance. Leavis rarely gave emphatic endorsement to political or ideological ideals, but sometimes the imprint of Arnold's legacy is conspicuous.

> This strength of English belongs to the very spirit of the language – the spirit that was formed when the English people who formed it were predominantly rural ... And how much richer the *life* was in the old, predominantly rural order than in the modern suburban world ... When one adds that speech in the old order was a popularly cultivated art, that people talked (so making Shakespeare possible) instead of reading or listening to the wireless, it becomes plain that the promise of regeneration by American slang, popular city idiom, or invention of *transition* cosmopolitans is a flimsy consolation for our loss. (*Scrutiny*, March 1933)

According to Leavis, Shakespeare made the regenerative properties of high art available to common man and Leavis believes that the degrading influences of urban life and popular culture can only be offset by Shakespeare's modern counterparts, so while he gave considerable attention to poetry his notion of a canonical "tradition" of great works was based mainly on post eighteenth century fiction.

Yet the questions raised by Leavis's observations are numerous. By what means do we discern literary quality? If we require a special level of expertise and erudition (like Leavis himself, for example) the claim that literature can instill both aesthetic and moral enlightenment is undermined because only a tiny minority will have access to this remedy. Moreover, does the relationship between "perfection of form" and a "marked moral intensity" always obtain? Can there be books and poems that are superbly crafted and magnetically engaging but which display an indifference to morality or ideals or perhaps even implicitly endorse such notions as misanthropy or irresponsibility?

René Wellek, a critic steeped in the discipline of European Formalism, wrote to the magazine *Scrutiny* to praise Leavis's *Revaluation* (1936), but he also observed that Leavis had failed to provide a rationale for his assumptions regarding the nature and value of literature. Wellek asked Leavis to become "conscious that large ethical, philosophical and … ultimately aesthetic *choices* are involved" both in the writing and interpretation of literature. The "choices" referred to by Wellek involve all manner of decisions and actions undertaken by writers and readers, including the former's ability to construct a commendable "aesthetic" design while dealing with, or even choosing to avoid, "ethical" and "philosophical" issues and the latter's ability to pick out and appreciate, or find fault with, key elements of what the writer has chosen to do. What Wellek was seeking was an abstract theoretical model which would first enable us to distinguish literature from other discourses (his subtext being that if we don't know what literature is we can't make decisions on its qualities; see Chapters 4–6 above) and also allow us to differentiate between the "ethical and philosophical" choices addressed by, say, religious tracts and political doctrines and those transformed by the "aesthetic" of literature.

Leavis replied in a piece that was later expanded and published in *The Common Pursuit* (1952), and begins by stating that the "complete critic" and the "complete reader" are "concerned with evaluation" but "to figure him as measuring with a norm which he brings up to the object and applies from the outside is to misrepresent the process." In rejecting Wellek's postulate of a general principle of evaluation Leavis also distorts it. Wellek had not appealed for an arbitrary scale of judgment that exists "outside" literature; rather he wondered if there were endemic features through which great literature identified itself. Having sidestepped this issue Leavis goes on to give an account of what evaluation and, crucially, the correlative benefits involve.

> The critic's aim is, first, to realize as sensitively and completely as possible this or that which claims his attention, and a certain valuing is implicit in the realizing. As he matures in experience of the new thing he asks, explicitly and implicitly: Where does this come? How does it stand in relation to …? How relatively important does it seem? And the organization into which it settles as a constituent on becoming "placed" is an organization of similarly "placed" things, things that have found their bearings with regard to one another, and not a theoretical system or a system determined by abstract considerations. No doubt (as I have admitted) a philosophic training might possibly – ideally would – make a critic surer and more penetrating in the perception of significance and relation and in judgement of value. But it is to be noted that the improvement we ask for is of the critic, as critic, and to count on it would be to count on the attainment of an arduous ideal. It would be reasonable to fear – to fear blunting of edge, blurring of focus and muddled misdirection of attention: consequences of queering one discipline with the habits of another. The business of the literary critic is to attain a peculiar completeness of response and to observe a peculiarly strict relevance in developing

his response into commentary; he must be on his guard against abstracting improperly from what is in front of him and against any premature or irrelevant generalizing – of it or from it … My whole effort was to work in terms of concrete judgements and particular analyses: "This – doesn't it? – bears such a relation to that; this kind of thing – don't you find it so? – wears better than that," etc.

The description is ingenuous, sometimes almost impassioned, but it also systematically avoids a proper answer to the questions raised by Wellek, and implicitly by Leavis's own work.

He hints at coherence and harmony as indications of quality ("Where does this come? How does it stand in relation to …?") and goes on to suggest that with literature such matters are governed by different principles from those that obtain in nonliterary writing ("things that have found their bearings with regard to one another, and not a theoretical system or a system determined by abstract considerations"). He appears to be treating literature not only as a singular mode of writing, in terms of its manner and style, but as the source of impressions that are in some way exempt from the real world procedures of "abstracting" and "generalizing." Instead, literature invites "concrete judgements," "particular analyses," opportunes questions that cannot allow for logical or ideological analysis: "This – doesn't it? – bears such a relation to that; this kind of thing – don't you find it so? – wears better than that." This passage is well known and consistent with Leavis's immensely influential critical practice but it is problematic, not in what it states but because it persistently evades a clear statement.

A sceptic might observe, with some justification, that Leavis's notion of "concrete judgements" and "particular analyses," backed up by his implication that all of these are made as part of a companionable, erudite dialogue ("doesn't it," "don't you find"), is vague and conveniently evanescent. All of this can mean whatever he wants it to mean.

Often Leavis describes his encounters with literature in the manner of a quasi-religious epiphany; the boundary between the communication of an idea and a sense of numinous enlightenment is continuously eroded. This is not, I think, due to heedlessness or self-indulgence, rather it stems from single-minded calculation. He is protecting himself against an anomaly that informs his entire rationale for the study and appreciation of literature. As he makes clear, especially in *The Great Tradition*, novelists attain greatness through the inculcation in their work of intellectual challenges, concepts, and cruxes that in some way capture the moral dilemmas of their era. The problem with this model of what the novel does is that it offers to the sceptic, the person who doubts the value of literary studies, indeed literature, an opportunity to question its elevated status.

Why, such a person might ask, read novels when a proper encounter with matters ethical, philosophical, and political is offered by nonliterary thinkers? Do you, they might add, require the assistance of fantasy and entertainment to make such ideas palatable or accessible? Leavis attempts to bypass such enquiries by presenting the novel not as a medium for the communication of ideas but, by its nature, one that reformulates them in a uniquely profound way.

Leavis, despite his influential magnetism, was fettered by his dedication to the concept of literature as a force for transformation and betterment. For each of us, our temperament and expectations will provide a second filter for evaluative open-mindedness but Leavis prejudged fiction according to his particular model of the inspirational purpose of the genre.

For example, he treats Fielding, Richardson, Austen, and George Eliot as embodying a lineage of incremental improvement. Austen takes her cue from Richardson and enhances what she finds in the work of the eighteenth century moralist. "The principle of organization, and the principle of development, in her work is an intense moral interest of her own in life that is in the first place a preoccupation with certain problems that life compels on her as personal ones" (*The Great Tradition*, p. 7). In Leavis's view, the best novelists learn from their predecessors and develop a deeper sense of responsibility to their subject matter – the people and the society that are remodeled for their work – and their technique is enhanced as a consequence. The problem with this model is that it contains an inherent bias against writers who do not subscribe to certain preconditions. Leavis certainly does not hold that novelists should indoctrinate their readers while appearing to entertain them; he endorses a far more sly and pernicious form of instruction. Richardson was a gifted storyteller but he produced novels in an era when the status of fiction was elastic to say the least. Many were reluctant even to treat it as literature and *Pamela*, fine work that it is, comes much closer to a parable than a novel, at least as the genre would later be perceived. Leavis praises Austen not because she bears the imprint of Richardson but for her skill in disguising it. He organized his narratives according to a labored Christian conception of fate and justice; she wrapped a comparable gallery of principles in a distracting fabric of irony and social nuance.

It is interesting that Leavis dismisses in a single paragraph the man who was Richardson's closest rival during the formative decades of the English novel, Henry Fielding. As we have seen in Chapter 1, the reviews, letters to magazines, and private correspondence of the period testify to Fielding's consummate skill as a realist, by which I mean a writer who could cause the distinction between the world he created and the one he shared with his readers to become almost imperceptible. Readers such as Catherine Talbot exemplify a general feeling of being caught between what ethical principle tells her she ought to feel and something far more subjective and less manageable. She feels she should "detest him [Tom Jones] and admire Clarissa" yet she *feels* "things" in the former's story "that must touch and please every good heart, and probe to the quick many a bad one." Similarly, Elizabeth Carter confesses that while "nobody can admire Clarissa more than I do" she finds that "Fielding's book is the most natural representation for what passes in the world, and of the bizarreries which arise from the mixture of good and bad." Both of them might too easily be dismissed as impressionistic unsophisticated readers, dealing as they were with a form that was in its infancy and themselves lacking reliable benchmarks by which it might be judged. I would contend that their comments are, for exactly this reason, instructive and illuminating. At its most primitive the double pattern shifts our awareness between what is profoundly artificial or literary and aspects of the novel that might, without alteration, be found in a nonliterary text, either as recorded speech or writing. As we have seen in Chapter 6, the dynamic between these two elements enables us to evaluate the novelist as a literary craftsman. Talbot, Carter, and most other eighteenth century readers were, albeit involuntarily, provided with a less restricted perspective on the novel than their successors. They benefitted from its uncertain status because they were constantly discovering the boundaries between its literary and nonliterary features rather than coming to it with fixed expectations of what ought to happen. For the eighteenth century reader the uncertainties regarding the generic status of the novel segued into the equally troubling question of what it was supposed to do. Was it merely popular entertainment which, like the theatre, made no great claims to improve its audience's state of mind? Or did it marshal literary devices in the service of some moral or social mission? With this in mind let us consider in more detail the work of Samuel Richardson, and compare it with that of his closest rival, Henry Fielding.

Samuel Richardson's *Pamela* is a cross-breed, part didactic morality tale and part fictitious representation of contemporary England. As a result it achieved immense popularity and cult-like status while attracting scorn, mostly from those also struggling to impose some shape upon the incipient notion of the novel. Like many books of the period, it was published anonymously but as sales increased and its fame spread Richardson's closest friend Aaron Hill wrote to ask him, as its publisher, to disclose the author of this extraordinary work. Hill's praise for it is ecstatic, and he is pleased most by its protean nature: "Who could have dreamt, he should find, under the modest Disguise of a *Novel*, all the *Soul* of Religion, Good-breeding, Discretion, Good-nature, Wit, Fancy, Fine Thought and Morality?" (23 January 1741). Once Richardson's authorship became known among the reading public he was deluged with letters, nearly all unreservedly admiring and each fascinated by his achievement of causing a moral tale to seem so real. His friend George Cheyne reported to him a conversation with Alexander Pope, who would "not bear any faults to be mentioned in the story" and who judged "that it will do more good than a great many of the new Sermons" (12 February 1741). The question of whether Cheyne was deaf to Pope's perpetual taste for irony must remain unanswered, but the poet was most certainly attuned to the popular mood. Typically, an anonymous correspondent to the *Weekly Miscelleny* proclaimed that *Pamela* will "reclaim the Vicious and mend the Age in general" and Ralph Courtville, a publishing associate of Richardson, wrote to him saying that "if all the Books in England were to be burnt, this Book, next to the Bible, ought to be preserved" (27 January 1741).

The book attained a folklorish status with a legend repeated in many magazines throughout the eighteenth century that before the close of 1741 it had become routine in small villages for a literate person to read it aloud to an enthusiastic and presumably illiterate audience, granting it the same rank, as Pope indicated, as the sermon. In one famous recital, allegedly by the blacksmith of a Bedfordshire hamlet, the entire audience burst into applause when Pamela was married and demanded that the church bells be rung in celebration (McKillop, 1949, pp. 325–326). Within a year of its publication *Pamela* had become a multi-media phenomenon, comparable in today's terms with the Harry Potter novels. As well as prints and paintings depicting key scenes, miniature waxworks and statuettes of the main characters sold in abundance along with jars and sets of playing cards carrying quotations from the heroine's letters.

During the early months of his fame the only letters of criticism received by Richardson were constructive – Mary Barber, poet, felt that the scene in which Mr B attempts, and fails, to rape Pamela was "A little too strongly painted." The periodical, *The History of the Works of the Learned*, suggested in an otherwise favorable article, that as an example of virtue and morality Pamela's language sometimes "sinks below the Idea we are constrained to form of the Heroine who is supposed to write it" (December 1740), and one anonymous correspondent wrote to the bookseller Charles Rivington, before Richardson was disclosed as author, suggesting that as Pamela's social elevation progressed so her style of writing should be improved, that when she attained full membership of the gentry she would present herself appropriately (15 November 1740). The common feature of much of this correspondence is an apparent inability to distinguish between Pamela as a moral exemplar, a real person, or a literary character, which reinforces Richardson's achievement – if such it be – in blurring the distinction between different types of writing. Others, far less sympathetic to Richardson's enterprise, were biding their time and the first assailant was already at work on his counterblast before the second volume of *Pamela* was dispatched to the bookseller.

Pamela became an overnight bestseller, a cult, because it side-lined an issue that caused readers to question the attractions of fiction. Sales alone showed that the novel could compete with drama and poetry in terms of popularity but unlike these ancient genres it did not have a prescribed cultural role, let alone a conscience. Each new novelist could alter established precedent as he or she saw fit and some perceived an incipient danger in this. Self-evidently, fiction held up a mirror to contemporary life and it might prove capable of sanctioning, by implication, its foulness and perversity. Suddenly, *Pamela* made readers feel better about an enjoyment previously touched by guilt. They could savor the story of the servant girl relentlessly pursued by the lascivious, though not quite malevolent, Mr B, revel in the episodes that edged towards genteel pornography – mainly attempted ravishment, bordering on rape – but gradually they could ameliorate their prurient pleasures through a knowledge that despite her travails Pamela, as the embodiment of virtue and decency, would triumph.

Some have argued that Fielding wrote *Shamela* as an attempt to cash in on Richardson's profits but we should question this as a motive for the simple reason that it was published barely 6 months after the second part of *Pamela* appeared. When he began his albeit much shorter book Fielding would not have been aware of the impact that Richardson's work would have. I would contend that something more elemental than financial gain prompted Fielding to begin his response to what was still an anonymous work of fiction. He had not yet tried his hand at novel writing but he found something potentially insidious in this most recent contribution to the genre. He saw it as a morality tale, a course of instruction for principle and behavior masquerading as a literary work.

This is Fielding's / Shamela's account of her wedding night.

> Well, at last I went to Bed, and my Husband soon leapt in after me; where I shall only assure you, I acted my Part in such a manner that no Bridegroom was ever better satisfied with Bride's Virginity. And to confess the Truth, I might have been well enough satisfied too, if I had never been acquainted with Parson *Williams*.

Pamela tells a similar story but never allows her correspondent to suspect that the loss of her "Virginity" is an "act," let alone that she is inclined to compare her new husband's performance with Parson Williams's. Routinely, commentators treat Fielding's version of the story as the exposure of what many of us, especially those who cling to Richardson's ideal, would deny, but his purpose is more complex. He knew that *Pamela* would forever be shadowed by his novel and that *Shamela* would never have any autonomy; it depended on the work that prompted it. Pamela and Shamela were in his view components of the same person; without either the other would remain insufficient, like Hamlet without the Prince.

Pamela versus *Shamela* was the opening of an exchange that would continue through the 1740s involving primarily Richardson's *Clarissa* (1747–8) and *Sir Charles Grandison* (1753–4) and Fielding's *Joseph Andrews* (1742), and *Tom Jones* (1749).

Taking the postscripts to *Clarissa* and *Tom Jones* as a guide, Richardson's objective is the more straightforward. He feels himself "well justified by the *Christian system*, in deferring to extricate suffering virtue to the time when it will meet with the *completion* of its reward." In short, Clarissa's contrite admission that it is all her fault, that she is full deserving of her dishonor is an example of "suffering virtue" en route to "the completion of its reward," the afterlife.

Fielding too is honest about his methods and objectives but unlike Richardson he does not include his maxims in a postscript. He allows in practice for a fluid, unpredictable relationship between the narrator, the characters, and the reader. The latter might believe Fielding's inventions to be authentic, or not, and treat his characters as real, and therefore admirable or reprehensible, or unconvincing. Consider the way in which Fielding, or rather his fictional stand-in, describes the exchange between Sophie Western and Blifil.

> Mr Blifil soon arrived; and Mr Western soon after withdrawing left the young couple together.
>
> Here a long silence of near a quarter of an hour ensued; for the gentleman, who was to begin the conversation, had all that unbecoming modesty which consists in bashfulness. He often attempted to speak, and as often suppressed his words just at the very point of utterance. At last, out they broke in a torrent of far-fetched and high-strained compliments, which were answered on her side by downcast looks, half bows, and civil monosyllables. – Blifil, from his inexperience in the ways of women, and from his conceit of himself, took this behaviour for a modest assent to his longer support, Sophia rose up and left the room, he imputed that, too, merely to bashfulness and comforted himself that he should soon have enough of her company.

Most readers, on completing the novel, would be left with an impression of Blifil as faintly repulsive while Sophia comes through as an affable if not faultless presence. The book allows us to form such opinions gradually, much as we judge real people, their motives and actions. The above passage makes subtle implications about Blifil and Sophia but it is only when we encounter the interplay between the narrator's suggestions and what the characters say and do that we begin to ask questions about Fielding's creations and very frequently find ourselves all the more intrigued when we fail to reach a conclusion.

Opinions on which of them had evolved the most satisfactory prototype for the novel differed considerably. Boswell reported in his *Life of Johnson* a conversation between himself, Dr Johnson, and Erskine in which Johnson refers to Fielding as a "blockhead." Boswell asks, "Will you not allow, Sir, that he draws very natural pictures of human life?" Erskine interjects, "Surely, Sir, Richardson is very tedious," and Johnson reframes the principles of Richardson's postscript to *Clarissa* "Why, Sir, if you were to read Richardson for the story, your impatience would be so much fretted that you would hang yourself. But you must read him for the sentiment, and consider the story as only giving occasion to the sentiment." Boswell, though respectful of Johnson's eminence, takes issue with his judgment here. "I cannot refrain from reflecting here my wonder at Johnson's excessive and unaccountable depreciation of one of the best writers England has produced … Fielding's characters, though they do not expand themselves so widely in dissertation, are as just pictures of human nature, and I will venture to say, have more striking features, and nicer touches of the pencil [than Richardson's]." Johnson and Boswell concur on the nature of Fielding's and Richardson's achievements. Their discord arises from their conflicting perceptions of what fiction should be and do. Johnson believes that the novel should improve upon the real world, teach us how we ought to be – a maxim that corresponds with predominant contemporary opinions on the role of poetry – while Boswell contends that it should hold up a mirror to life outside the book, and reflect its flaws and paradoxes.

Their difference encapsulates a much broader series of exchanges that continued unabated through the eighteenth century. As the century wore on opinions remained entrenched but one detects a broad consensus forming in favor of Fielding. Those who continued to defend Richardson tended to be individuals who had known him or often members of the clergy and devout, inflexible nonconformists who regarded all fiction as a potentially dangerous threat to public morality.

Typical of late eighteenth century opinion is Dr John Ogilvie's remarks in his *Philosophical and Critical Observations on the Nature, Characters and Various Species of Composition* (1774).

> [*Clarissa*] is in no respect original. She appears adorned with an assemblage of virtues, and of intellectual endowments ... in order to have the force of an *example*, these are raised considerably beyond the common level ... The *Adams* of Fielding on the contrary, strikes us wholly in the light of an original ... [H]is character is marked with *little strokes* which render it truly comic and there is scarce a single instance in the whole work, in which the originality either ceaseth to appear when it ought to be conspicuous, or is carried beyond nature.

Even the more sanctimonious commentators found themselves praising Fielding's immense craftsmanship while damning his creations as examples to the young and innocent. George Canning cannot quite make up his mind on whether he is addressing a brilliantly fashioned portrait or witnessing the kind of misbehavior from which some should be protected.

> That it [Tom Jones] is a character drawn faithfully from nature, by the hand of a master, most accurately delineated, and most exquisitely finished, is indeed indisputable. But is it not also a character, in whose shades the lines of right and wrong, of propriety and misconduct, are so intimately blended, and softened into each other, as to render it too difficult for the indiscriminating eye of childhood to distinguish between rectitude and error? ("On Novel Writing," *The Microcosm*, Vol. 26, 14 May 1787)

He comes close, albeit involuntarily, to agreeing with those who feted Fielding as the first genuine realist, his representation of indelicate women coming allegedly from his being "accustomed to such company."

Leavis, without referring to a particular eighteenth century reader of Fielding or Richardson, generalizes on why the former novelist found a considerable degree of favor among his contemporaries. "That the eighteenth century, which hadn't much lively reading to choose from, but had much leisure, should have found *Tom Jones* exhilarating is not surprising ... Standards are formed in comparison, and what opportunities had they for that?" (Leavis, 1948, p. 3). Well, Mr Leavis, it could be argued that "standards formed" when under an obligation to compare two diametrically opposed modes of fiction writing, especially in a period when fiction itself was a disputable entity, would cause a sharpening of the evaluative faculties. According to Leavis, "we haven't to read a very large proportion of *Tom Jones* in order to discover the limits of the essential interests it has to offer us. Fielding's attitudes and his concern with human nature, are simple" (p. 4). But because of "Richardson's strength in the analysis of emotional and moral states ... *Clarissa* is a really impressive work" (p. 4). He concedes that Richardson's novel is somewhat primitive compared with its nineteenth century successors but calls for the recognition of its "relevant historical importance ... [as] a major fact in the background of Jane Austen" (p. 4). Whatever status Leavis still retains as a serious literary critic should be thrown into question by these statements. On the one hand his dismissal of Fielding is brusque and unapologetically ground-less – he is a man of "simple interests" apparently – and despite the fact that Leavis seems by implication to align himself alongside Richardson's rather sanctimonious eighteenth century advocates his real strategy is far more opportunistic. He is creating a lineage for the novel which suits his particular model of how its ideal form can be seen to have evolved, and Fielding raises questions about this that it is more convenient to dismiss than to address.

For an alternative view of the respective legacies of Fielding and Richardson a comment by another of Leavis's heroes, D.H. Lawrence, is revealing. In *Phoenix* he accuses Richardson of the prurience that too often accompanies sanctimo-niousness and speaks of his "calico purity and his underclothing excitement." Here the words "pot," "kettle," and "black" come suddenly to mind. True, Lawrence recommended the intellectual and spiritual benefits of energetic sex, but in other more important respects he belonged very much within the tradi-tion founded by Richardson. He used literature to promote a credo, a doctrine for the improvement of the human condition, and we can line up alongside him in this same category Evelyn Waugh, George Eliot, Aldous Huxley, and Fay Weldon, amongst others. Their differences abound but they share with Richardson the handicap of allowing a private agenda to shape their art.

The corollaries of Fielding's model are more commendable because they are also more diffuse and less determinate. His self-conscious fascination with the peculiarities of writing fiction, evident in his habit of suspending the nar-rative to digress on his role as storyteller, anticipated the metafictional habits of dozens of modernist and postmodern writers, though it must be said that, unlike most of his successors, Fielding did not completely abandon a good story for the sake of high-minded self-indulgence. He pioneered a brand of realism that both respects and challenges the reader's own convictions and personal dispositions. They might revel in his unforgiving portraits of their world or be morally repulsed by the spectacle, but that was his intention. He drew them in and obliged then to become part of the experience. In this respect his closest modern counterpart is Kingsley Amis, a writer who revived

Fielding's brand of comedy as a lens for superbly accurate representations of the world. For both writers comedy is generated by the friction between reality and the delusions or ideals that we impose upon it.

The contrasts between Fielding and Richardson are important, not least because the two of them are routinely treated as the initiators of the novel in English and this in turn raises the question of which left the more permeable imprint on what followed. Leavis's version of literary history is partial to say the least, given that he marks out a lineage of writers who maintain a principle of ethical accountability that in his view constitutes the novelist's duty to his calling. He takes it for granted that his notion of fiction as an instrument for intellectual and ethical improvement is unchallengeable and ignores completely the influence of other writers who do not correspond to this ideal.

With this in mind consider a rivalry for which the Fielding and Richardson contest might seem a rehearsal. In a letter to his friend, John Forster, Charles Dickens comments on a man who in terms of popularity and public acclaim he vastly outranked but who was nonetheless being spoken of among the cultural establishment as his literary antithesis: "as far as Thackeray was concerned … I should tell him if he were there, that I thought these things arouse in his jesting much too lightly between what was true and what was false and what he owed to both, and not being sufficiently steady to the former" (9 June 1847). This is generally taken to refer to a private argument involving the three of them but one suspects that Dickens was equally vexed by Thackeray's dealings with the relationship between matters "true" – that is, immutable and just – and "false" – notably our more indulgent, fickle characteristics – in his novels.

Some reviewers hated Thackeray's *Vanity Fair* but their antagonism can be explained by examining the assessments of those who admitted to a blend of puzzlement and fascination. It was a novel that threw readers' sympathies and judgments into a state of confusion. Its two principal characters, Becky and Amelia, are designed to frustrate any straightforward sense of empathy or antipathy, praise or condemnation. They blur the boundaries that novels, in the opinion of many, ought to respect and reinforce, an ideal, again for many, exemplified in the fiction of Dickens.

Many others were struck by the novel's ability to cause uneasiness in the reader, to require him to think again of what he first expected, and then move on. Typically: "his people; they are all individuals … having unmistakable characteristics of men, and not being abstract ideas nor traditional conceptions of character. While reading Thackeray you feel that he is painting 'after nature' …" (George Henry Lewes in *The Morning Chronicle*, 6 March 1848). Most saw Thackeray as having restored to literature the flame lit by Fielding a century earlier and even Forster, a year after the squabble, reviewed *Vanity Fair* with some favor in the *Examiner* (22 July 1848). He too compares Thackeray with Fielding, with telling reservations. "If Mr Thackeray falls short of Fielding … it is because an equal amount of large cordiality had not raised him … into … simple uncontaminated human affection … His is a less comfortable, and on the whole therefore, let us add, a less true view of society than Fielding's." The specific comparison is with his eighteenth century fore-bear but implicitly Forster is invoking the presence of a writer much closer to hand, who deals with his characters in a thoughtful, often benevolent manner. Dickens never allowed wickedness to escape his attention and nor did he ever blur the distinction between good and bad, avarice and kindness, depravity and virtue. But the nuances and ambiguities that cause us to question such easy polarities are foregrounded by Thackeray and banished from Dickens's fiction. The question of which provided the reader with a more or "less true view of society" underpinned comparisons between them thereafter.

An essay written in 1852 made it clear that, irrespective of sales, the two men were sole competitors for the title of foremost novelist of the era. David Masson does not refer to any rumors of private rivalry but he makes it clear that the primary debate among the literary intelligentsia concerned which of them best reflected, in fiction, the mood of their generation.

> THACKERAY and DICKENS, Dickens and Thackeray – the two names now almost necessarily go together … From the printing-house of the same publishers they have simultaneously, during the last few years, sent forth their monthly instalments of amusing fiction. Hence the public had learned to think of them in indissoluble connexion as friendly competitors for the prize of light literature … As the popular novelist of the day Dickens and Thackeray, and again, Thackeray and Dickens divide the public attention … "*Pendennis* and *Copperfield*: Thackeray and Dickens"; *North British Review,* May 1851)

Masson's classification of their fiction as "amusing," "light literature" was not quite as dismissive as it seems today. In the middle of the nineteenth century all fiction was treated as a recreational adjunct to the high art of poetry, and Masson was one of the first literary critics who was also an academic – professor of English first at London and then Edinburgh. English literature as a university discipline was still in its infancy and Masson's weighty article (at 33 pages almost a short monograph) was an attempt to stamp the authority of his profession upon the often ungrounded partialities of freelance reviewers and hack journalists. He conducts an extraordinarily detailed survey of their qualities as stylists, of the "intellectual caliber" of their work and their tendency to allow polemic and opinion to intrude upon representation. Throughout most of Masson's scrupulous evaluation the two writers seem to emerge as equals, at least until we come to the third category where there is a detectable note of dissatisfaction at Dickens's alleged tendency to turn his characters into indices for moral and temperamental abstractions. For Dickens, polarities such as good and bad, endeavor and sloth, greed and benevolence are absolutes and he will not countenance ambiguities in his fiction any more than allow for such in his perception of society. As a consequence, according to Masson, his characters resemble those of Shakespeare who "are not, in any common sense life-like. They are not portraits of existing men and women ... they are grand hyperbolic beings created by the breath of the poet himself out of hints taken from all that is sublime in nature." The comparison is a compliment but an ambiguous one, implying as he does that while Shakespeare is attuned to the "sublime" the novel demands something closer to verisimilitude. Thackeray, meanwhile, "seems to ... give the good and the bad together, in very nearly the same proportions that the cunning apothecary, Nature herself, uses." While Dickens exaggerates our qualities and imperfections by never allowing one to blur the other Thackeray allows their murky interrelationships to inform the texture of his novels.

Masson's assessment endured as the subject of debate throughout the 1850s when there was still no general consensus on what fiction as a genre was supposed to be and achieve. Masson had commended Thackeray as the archetypal realist but, as the latter was aware, those who actually purchased novels continued to offer Dickens their resounding support. The press remained sceptical about the compatibility between mass popularity and aesthetic value. When *David Copperfield* first began to appear, the *Puppet-Show* magazine fabricated a letter from a cockney admirer, whose style resembles that of Dickens's many lower class creations, praising him for extending his appeal from low-brow reader to the intellectual elite, the long-term admirers of Thackeray. The "joke" was that such praise had come from a man barely able to write a sentence which in turn implied that Dickens used his considerable talents to preach simple morality to the simple-minded.

Leavis, who venerated Dickens, has this to say on Thackeray in general and *Vanity Fair* in particular.

> He has (apart from some social history) nothing to offer the reader whose demand goes beyond the "creation of characters" and so on. His attitudes, and the essential substance of interest, are so limited that (though, of course, he provides incident and plot) for the reader it is merely a matter of going on and on; nothing has been done by the close to justify the space taken – except,

of course, that time has been killed (which seems to be all that even some academic critics demand of a novel). (Leavis, 1948, p. 21)

This is not so much the expression of his opinion on the novel as it stands as a gross misrepresentation of what it is in order to serve Leavis's dogmatic agenda.

I dwell upon Leavis because he exemplifies a dilemma faced by all who attempt to reconcile literature with such abstract principles as justice, morality, equity, even truth. His thesis is certainly not simplistic. He does not hold that the novel should serve as an instrument for brainwashing or indoctrinating morally recalcitrant readers; rather his working maxim is that "great" fiction should in some way animate and magnify the ethical choices, decisions, and avoidances that other representations and perceptions of society often elide. Nonetheless, he causes us to wonder whether we should expect the novel to serve any given purpose.

Even if we take seriously Leavis's nuanced concept of the novel-of-ideas we must also accept that novelists, and novels, impose upon their raw material, the world, some shape or form that for the passive observer it might otherwise lack. He is asking us to accept that the novel does more than inculcate principles and ideas – if it served only that purpose literary art would be reduced to the status of one among many communicative discourses. He contends that because of its uniqueness as literature it changes the way that we think about ethical concepts.

It is both instructive to compare Leavis's theory with the work of philosophers of aesthetics. Richard Beardsmore (1971) argues that *what* art teaches us is related affectively to the manner in which it does so. His most notable example is Donne's evocation of love and despair in his extended metaphor involving a pair of compasses in "A Valediction: Forbidding Mourning." He argues that the emotional effects conveyed by the image cause it to become distinct from, say, a psychology treatise on affection and loss. Beardsmore holds that literature is capable of unique cognitive transactions, that the formal and aesthetic features of the text have a transformative effect on the message. In this he seems to be in agreement with Leavis, especially regarding the latter's notion of a symbiotic relationship between the moral tenor of the novel and its literary qualities.

David Novitz expands on Beardsmore's general thesis and examines in detail our encounter with fictional narrative. He presents the reader not as a passive agent but rather as a figure possessed of what he calls a "fanciful imagination," which involves "the ability ... to fabricate or invent by combining ideas, images, beliefs, words or physical objects, however they choose" (Novitz,

1987, p. 27), with limitations. His model is, by implication, based on our encounters with the kind of novel where the motives of characters, their likely response to unforeseen acts and circumstances and the broader progress of the narrative, are anything but predictable. Clues and nuances are sewn into the texture of the work but there are sufficient gaps to encourage us to speculate and draw conclusions. In short, he is dealing with the "literary novel" rather than the standard bestseller.

Martha Nussbaum takes a similar line, arguing that when reading Henry James's *The Golden Bowl* we "work through these sentences and these chapters [and] become involved in an activity of exploration and unravelling that uses abilities, especially abilities of emotion and imagination, rarely tapped by philosophical texts" (Nussbaum, 1990, p. 143). While Nussbaum does not mention Leavis she could easily be describing his ideal reader negotiating the sentences and paragraphs of one of his most valued works and reaping appropriate spiritual reward from the experience. Novitz again, on how literature draws us into a state of "empathetic beliefs": "our imaginative involvement in fiction allows us to respond emotionally or feelingly to the tribulations and triumphs of creatures of fiction. It is as a result of these experiences ... that we often come to hold certain beliefs about what it must feel like to occupy situations akin to those of our favourite heroes and heroines" (Novitz, 1987, p. 120). Sceptics such as Jacobson (1996) and Kieran (1996) have pointed out that while this model is valid it is not necessarily universally beneficial, that fiction might mislead us by sentimentalizing such issues as love or justice – respectively through the popular romantic novel and unadventurous examples of crime fiction. But they add that quality finds its own level, that the more sophisticated reader will be undeceived by popular fiction and drawn naturally to the intellectual challenge and collateral benefits of high quality novels.

Leavis and this cadre of aestheticians appear to agree on two things: that the novel is capable of inculcating various moral principles or philosophical maxims rather than serving merely as verbal entertainment and that it can do so in a manner that taxes the intellect and distinguishes fiction from other communicative discourses, from the sermon through the philosophical treatise to the newspaper article.

Yet there is something deeply problematic and self-contradictory about this postulate. What if a novel fails to allow even the most discerning reader to locate a consistent strand of ideas or conclusions regarding the society or people that are its subjects. Should it be judged inferior to those that achieve this and if so by what criterion; because it is poor literature or because it does not discharge certain duties with regard to the public good? It is all very well to claim that literature is possessed of certain intrinsic characteristics that divorces it from other discourses but to also insist that this is conditional on its capacity to communicate significant ideas surely undermines the foregoing pretext. If literature is fundamentally different, how can it remain so if it serves precisely the same purpose as all other nonliterary discourses?

Judged according to this conjecture Richardson's *Pamela* belongs in the same exalted category as Joyce's *Ulysses*. True, their formal discordances abound but it could be pointed out that both are instructive texts. Richardson shows us how moral certainties are challenged by the vicissitudes of society and the baseness of human nature while Joyce offers us a practical guide to how language both builds and fragments our perceptions of ourselves and others: they are lectures, respectively, in Christian sociology and cultural linguistics disguised as fiction. But if this is how we conceive of fiction in general it follows that it is also the presiding factor in how we evaluate it. Novels such as *Pamela* and *Ulysses* might seem to belong almost in different generic categories but because they serve to improve our sense of worth and our understanding of the world outside the novel they must, by this criterion alone, be great works. Through a bizarre, circuitous formula we have at once defined literature and refused to allow it any independent role beyond the principle that governs all other forms of communication, that is, to expedite a message effectively. Even worse, we have appropriated the essentially literary elements of the double pattern – the features that at once divide *Pamela* and *Ulysses* from each other and unite them against nonliterary works – and allocated to them the role of instruments of instruction.

A single question perplexes the philosophers of fiction and is studiously avoided by literary critics, Leavis included. If we accept that the novel is a meticulously assembled gallery of untruths, a pack of lies, how can we explain, indeed, justify, its existence? If we alter or in some way blur or misrepresent verifiable truth in any other statement – from answering the person who asks us the time of day, through filling our tax returns to preparing a lengthy thesis on our social and political beliefs – we are, everyone would agree, involved in an act of mischief, potentially criminal mischief, or arbitrary deception. This, however, is precisely what the undertaking of fiction writing involves, often accompanied by elaborate and ingenious attempts to cause patent fabrications to seem credible. The novel exists. It is by far the most popular of the three principal literary genres but it leaves those who write about it with an enduring problem. If it is simply the peddling of untruths as a form of recreation, a delusional relief from the verities of the world we know, then it is of minimal value as an art form. If, however, it can be seen to serve some public good, then it is art with a purpose and inevitably virtually every commentator will, with variations, lend their support to this view of it. It is, ultimately, the only reliable failsafe device against the accusation that fiction is merely a form of vulgar entertainment. Yet the more we reformulate novels as educative instruments the more we erode the uniqueness of fiction. Is it possible to enjoy and appreciate the qualities of a novel without feeling, or feeling the need to ascribe to it, a sense of edification or improvement?

In Candia McWilliam's 1988 short story "The Only Only" (in *Wait Till I Tell You*, Bloomsbury, 1997) we are offered an apparently affectionate documentary account of a scene on a Scottish island; groups of locals stand around conversing about their generally agreeable lives, children play, and the ferry prepares to set off for the mainland. McWilliam weaves into the passage an accumulation of information that at first seems gratuitous, appearing to inhibit any sense of a narrative purpose or theme, but gradually it becomes evident that in their abundance these particulars provide for us a special level of omniscience; every aspect of the scene is made known to the reader while its participants give attention only to what immediately concerns them. When the ferry arrives it is tied up with a steel rope, an act so routine as to raise no interest among those not specifically involved with it. It is only the reader who sees that as the ferry steams off the rope remains tied and we watch also, in our minds eye, as it stretches, snaps, and decapitates a group of children. Suddenly their parents share the same level of awareness as the reader and the resonance is disturbing. The standard effect procured by good fiction of causing us to participate is now supplemented by a sense of powerless distress; we watch as fate gradually unleashes a terrible moment, almost wishing that we could warn the victims of what is to occur. McWilliam makes it evident, albeit implicitly, that these impressions, both cognitive and affective, become available by means that are unique to fiction. She orchestrates the perspective so that the relationship between those who are inside the narrative and those who see it from the outside would seem perverse, even grotesque, in a nonliterary account of comparable events. We should, of course, carry from a reading of it a variety of conflicting impressions, some rather unsettling. McWilliam's skill as a storyteller ensures that we allow ourselves to suspend, at least in part, our knowledge that these events are not real. In doing so we also have to deal with the sensation of panic and horror eventually to be visited on the parents, but what happens when common sense returns and reminds us that the decapitated children and their grief-stricken parents are merely verbal constructions, albeit sufficiently well-crafted to create vivid mental images? To feel a sense of relief means that we are still, in part, imagining the story as an actual event: our sense of consolation in their being spared this horrible fate involves a continuation of the illusion that they might have existed. Perhaps, as connoisseurs of literary art, we should suppress emotional registers and simply admire McWilliam's use of technical devices and psychological second-guessing. But in doing so, are we not turning ourselves into cold desensitized observers, immune from a sense of common sympathy with other humans, real or fictional?

It would be wrong to treat the story as a curiosity. On the contrary, it points up a troubling element in all our encounters with fiction. This dates back to Aristotle and Plato's notion that *catharsis,* normally prompted by tragedy, will encourage us to both confront and properly understand the emotions released during the cathartic experience. Catharsis is one of the most widely debated and divisive issues in the history of aesthetics and McWilliam's story illustrates the abundance of problems that attend it. Knowing that characters on the stage or in novels are inventions does not prevent us from responding to them as though they were real. The extent to which we surrender the former to the illusion of the latter depends on a number of factors, but our temperament and our opinions on the world we live in and the skill and intention of the novelist will predominate as the competing elements. Radford (1975), Lamarque (1981), and Walton (1990) are philosophers of aesthetics who have toiled over the vast number of affective and epistemological issues at large in this debate and have come up with three interrelated propositions:

1. We fear for characters in fictions who are in danger.
2. To fear for someone we must believe they are in danger.
3. We do not believe in the dangers described in fictions.

We could substitute "ill" for "in danger," "sympathize with" for "fear for" or redraft the three propositions according to numerous other designations of affect, or, conversely, embitterment or repulsion, but in every instance we are left with what seems an irresolvable paradox. In any reading, each point is dependent on the other two yet each must also undermine the others. I should qualify this by stating that the paradox is irresolvable only if you are a philosopher, or, to broaden the perspective, a person who at least shares the philosopher's belief that fiction should be subjected to the same postulates of logic and reason as everything else. The paradox only persists as a paradox if we are troubled by accepting point three – that is, knowing that fiction is pure illusion – at the same time we experience the effects of points one and two.

The best known example of what appeared to be collective lunacy induced by fiction occurred during the period prior to the final instalment of

Dickens's serialized novel, *The Old Curiosity Shop*. Dickens was bombarded by letters from his British readers begging him to spare the life of "Little Nell" and Dickens himself, when writing to his illustrator George Cattermole, confessed to "breaking my heart over the story [I] cannot bear to finish it." Even for her creator Nell had become more than an invention and when the ship bearing copies of the magazine carrying the final instalment was due to dock in New York the pier head was besieged by crowds of distraught readers screaming, "Save Little Nell." Similarly, we have already noted that many of Richardson's fans celebrated the moral triumphs of Pamela, despite her death, by the ringing of bells in village churches.

To digress, constructively; it would seem that philosophers of aesthetics are hidebound by the compartmentalizations that inform their discipline. I have acknowledged that there are parallels between my own formula of the double pattern and Richard Wollheim's notion of the "twofold" thesis. The principal differences is that Wollheim deals exclusively with the visual arts, and it is striking that none of his fellow philosophers have noted that the twofold thesis is capable of unlocking several questions regarding the novel which continue to trouble them. Just as it is possible to "*see in*" a picture the object it represents while simultaneously remaining aware of, and appreciating, the manner and technique of the artist, so we are able to reconcile in our experience of a novel the three paradoxical propositions. Numbers one and two involve the literary counterpart to "seeing in" the picture the thing that it depicts, while number three is a variation upon our acknowledgment that the skill of the artist is exclusively responsible for this. In the novel our sense of "disbelief" correlates with our awareness of the structure of fiction as the cause of its illusionary effects.

I dwell upon these issues because they provide an illuminating framework for the consideration of the overarching subject of this chapter. If we can in some way be improved by reading novels, does this come from our response to what they contain, from our appreciation of them as literary artefacts, or from some combination of the two?

The best means of addressing this issue is to locate a theme or event in the real world that magnetizes a variety of different, conflicting opinions and consider how fiction deals with it. Key questions are realized: can the novel tell us more than we learn from nonfictional media?; will the novel, by its nature, reinforce or alter our opinions on these matters? In the United Kingdom the most significant transformational decade since World War II was the 1980s, the period when Margaret Thatcher's Conservative governments altered significantly the balance between the state and the private sector and as a consequence challenged our perception of society and its implicit moral and ethical principles. Can novels that address themselves to this decade tell us anything new about it? Can they encourage us to change our preconceived ideas of it? If the answer to either is "yes" do they achieve these effects by means that are exclusive to literary writing? And finally, if the answer to the last question is also the affirmative, are we being deceived and brainwashed, or enlightened?

Justin Cartwright's *Look at it This Way* (1990) was written at the end of the 1980s at a time when media of all types had become conscious of British society as having been transformed, though precisely how and to what long-term effect were matters for conjecture. With commendable subtlety Cartwright manages to recreate in the very texture of his novel a combination of acceptance and perplexity. The characters inhabit a world in which capital has overruled what had once been a balance between fate and choice. Their moods, foreseeable prospects, relationships with lovers, friends, and family all appear to have become conditional, subject to the rarely acknowledged all-powerful presence of money. The only figure who is given to reflect upon all of this is an outsider, Tim Curtiz, a US journalist who reports on the state of Thatcher's Britain to his American readers. About half of the book is narrated in the third person, with Curtiz coming in, first person, for alternate chapters to offer a more incisive account, at once detached and informed. For example:

> Sometimes in London you get great glimpses of enormous wealth, great piles of money [...] money which has grown by leaps and bounds in the last ten years as everything, the very fabric of the country, has reached the point of critical mass. This wealth appears to have no physical limits. Low temperature nuclear fission of wealth has taken place, on a scale which is a surprise even to the beneficiaries [...] How has it happened? Nobody really knows. It is necromancy, it is alchemy. The philosopher's stone has been found. (*Look at it This Way*, Picador, 1991, p. 59)

It is also, as the novel makes evident, a contagion that affects even those who are most certainly not its beneficiaries. Money, its lack or abundance, has taken charge of those shades and dimensions of the human condition once animated by compassion, amiability, aesthetic gratification, even lust. Curtiz is fascinated by what he witnesses, but in a distracted. dispassionate way, much in the manner of an anthropologist. This is appropriate given that his other concern is a lion which eventually escapes from London Zoo and eats one of the main protagonists, Will, an avaricious share dealer. This mildly bizarre subplot might have become a modern morality tale – with the real carnivore exacting revenge upon his human usurper – except that Cartwright does not quite allow the pieces to fit into such convenient slots. He has Curtiz choreograph the killing, which he does with indifference to the consequences; he seems instead to have become part of the dehumanized web of events and causes on which he has reported. What seemed to be impartiality was a kind of crazed connivance and the book's message, if so straightforward a term can be applied to it, is that the society that informs it is too unprecedented, too peculiar, for analysis.

A novel written 5 years earlier in the midst of the Thatcher era does attempt to make sense of contemporary Britain. Julian Rathbone's *Nasty, Very* (1984) is the story of Charlie Bosham, scion of middle-class middle England. It begins on Coronation Day 1953 with Charlie aged 14, and charts his progress up to the second consecutive victory of the Tory government following the Falklands War, in which he becomes a Conservative MP. Charlie is a thoroughly unpleasant individual, a ruthless businessman but without even a veneer of charm to compensate for his feral selfishness. For much of the novel, at least until the late 1970s, Charlie seems to be a grotesque, a curiosity. The people with whom he mixes and frequently exploits and the society in which this occurs are certainly imperfect but he is self-evidently very much worse. With the arrival of Thatcherism, however, Charlie finds himself within a more welcoming, indulgent context. There is a passage towards the end in which Charlie is invited by a senior party grandee to his London club for a final interview to see if he is the sort of person who will sustain a Conservative majority. Charlie has rehearsed his part well. He refers to the working class as "the elves":

> They as always are the key factor in the equation. So long as the top ones are happy, the skilled, the technicians, and those with bottle like the miners, though nukes will see them off in the end, what it comes down to is we're laughing [...] It's a matter of pride. Top eight grand a year in your pay packet and it's buy your council house, face it with reconstituted Portland-type stone, change the front door to one of those with a fanlight and a brass knocker. Catch a bloke who's done that much for himself by voting Labour, and I'll kiss his arse ... (Rathbone, *Nasty, Very*, 1986)

Charlie's, and indeed Rathbone's, analysis of how and why Thatcherism could permanently seize the mandate from Labour is shrewd and, as most subsequent commentators would agree, accurate. Soon after this, when in the toilet, Charlie overhears a conversation between two Old-Party Tories in which one asks "Who was that oick?" that Giles, Charlie's host, was entertaining. An "aspirant from the sticks" answers his friend. Charlie, Rathbone informs us, "is overcome by anger, frustration and humiliation," and the reason is self-evident. The upper-class Conservatives regard the likes of Charlie Bosham as a slightly improved version of the new council-house-owning swathe of the proletariat who have exchanged class solidarity for greed. While Cartwright created an atmosphere of almost horrified incomprehension Rathbone exposes and dissects, but both, however, share an inclination to place at the heart of their picture of contemporaneity something, and in Rathbone's case someone, of unflagging repugnance.

George Crawley, the first person narrator of Tim Parks' *Goodness* (1991), is a rare type of fictional presence: someone who can sustain a tragic story while being pitiably unaware of the part he has played in his own and everyone else's dreadful experience. His manner of discourse reminds one of Mr Pooter, a combination of idiocy and self-importance. The account of his relationship with his wife, Shirley, involves a catalog of events that ought to provoke in the reader a degree of horrified compassion – Shirley's departure and their tearful reunion, the birth of their handicapped child and their decision, ultimately, to kill the infant – but it does not because Crawley seems incapable of disentangling emotions from a perception of the world as composed primarily of material possessions; only the latter seem capable of conferring significance upon life in general.

Bosham and Crawley bear a close resemblance to Michael Parsons of David Caute's *Veronica, Or the Two Nations* (1989), the anonymous narrator of Michael Dibdin's *Dirty Tricks* (1991), and the central character of Terence Blacker's *Fixx* (1989). All are presented as innately unpleasant types for whom the political and social environment has finally provided an arena in which their nastiness accords perfectly with the prevailing ideology.

Never before in the history of English fiction had a group of writers – who might otherwise have differed in temperament and outlook – been so assiduously fascinated by the prevailing political regime and united in their unreserved contempt for it.

Apart from novels written under instruction from a totalitarian regime, which includes most produced in the Soviet bloc until the end of the 1980s, fiction writers who idealize the social and political status quo are rare. Even those who are by temperament and outlook conservative and reactionary will find fault with the mores of the world they depict. Contentment is anathema to the very process of fictional representation, but a feeling of unusual repugnance appears to have gripped a considerable number of writers who engaged with the 1980s. Does the consensual force of their work testify to its value as social history?

Let us return to the "paradox" of the three propositions. It could be argued that those novelists who present the 1980s as a corrosive moral and political nadir do so by manipulating points one and two. We are encouraged to sympathize with some characters and abhor others. This is a standard feature of conventional fiction writing and one which replicates, or at least subordinates, our feelings about figures in the real world. At the same time these writers play a far more unsettling game of assigning affective responses to moral and political states of mind, creating a quiet teleology of nuanced responses and predictable ideological causes.

Jonathan Coe's *What a Carve Up!* (1994) focuses upon the period between August 1990 and January 1991, during which Mrs Thatcher was replaced by John Major and Britain prepared itself for the first Gulf War. Its actual frame of reference reaches beyond this through the preceding decade which, specifically and implicitly, is treated as the cause of the ghastly state of Britain. Its chief characters are composed largely of members of the Winshaw family, minor gentry who gained their wealth in the nineteenth century and despite subsequent misfortunes are revelling in the new economic climate. They are, needless to say, vile individuals and as such the book appears to be an elaborate rerun of Rathbone's *Nasty, Very*. However, there is a significant difference in that the only major non-Winshaw character is Michael Owen, a novelist who has been commissioned to write a history of the family. Owen bears a deliberately contrived resemblance to Coe, at least in the sense that his two published novels carry titles that are virtually paraphrases of Coe's first two novels. More subtly Coe shows us that he and his surrogate also face similar, perhaps intractable problems. Although we are not vouchsafed a glance at how Owen's history of the family is progressing as a text its nature is enacted in the novel. Chapters alternate between first person accounts by Owen of aspects of his ongoing and recent life and chapters that concentrate upon particular members of the Winshaw family. The latter comprise a variety of discourses, including extracts from journals, newspaper articles, transcripts of radio and TV interviews, letters, all threaded along a rather dry third person narrative. This is a patchwork of the basic material that Owen would draw upon in his account of the living Winshaws. Coe creates a beguiling riddle in that throughout the book – both in the parts exclusively involving Owen and those given to the Winshaws – he allows us glimpses into a society entrapped by Thatcherism and, it is implied, its evil consequences: the encroachment of privatization and free enterprise into the National Health Service, the virtual paralysis of an independent media by private sector influences, the stock market as a licensed forum for fraud, the exchange of manufacturing industry for a more controllable service sector, the poisoning of the food chain in pursuit of profit. The novel is self-evidently a state-of-the-nation piece, yet within it we have the spectacle of a writer, not unlike Coe, who when he completes his account of the Winshaws will, we assume, have combined his novelistic skills with a merciless scrutiny of their activities and produced something not unlike the book he is in. How would it have turned out? Coe, cunningly, poses the same question. At one point Owen has an exchange with a character called Graham who contends that novels "today" are "an irrelevance":

> the problem with the English novel is that there's no tradition of political engagement. I mean it's all just a lot of pissing about within the limits set down by bourgeois morality, as far as I can see. There's no radicalism. (*What a Carve Up!*, Penguin, 1995, p. 276)

Graham goes on to mention one notable exception to this alleged state of torpor and Owen is pleased because he has recently produced a hostile review on this same novelist, a figure in his view

> ludicrously over-praised in the national press. Because he made his characters talk in crudely notated dialects and live in conditions of unconvincing squalor, he was hailed as a social realist; because he sometimes played elementary tricks with narrative, in feeble imitation of Sterne and Diderot, he was hailed as an experimental pioneer [...] More annoying than any of this, however, was his reputation for humour. He had been repeatedly credited with a playful irony, a satiric lightness of touch, which seemed to me to be entirely lacking from his work, characterized as it was by lumbering sarcasm and the occasional abject attempt to jog the reader's elbow with well-signposted jokes. (p. 276)

What is needed, according to Owen, are novels "which show an understanding of the ideological hijack which has taken place so recently in this country," novels that would by necessity evolve unprecedented techniques to deal with unprecedented circumstances. Tantalizingly and irritatingly Owen does not provide clues to the nature of such novels, and nor does Coe.

The device of placing an author, within a novel, with ambitions which correspond in some way with the realized text that enables him or her to exist, is as old as Sterne but in the 1980s and 1990s the agenda for its use became a little more predictable. We have already seen how in *Look at it This Way* Cartwright uses the narrative equivalent of a split-screen effect with one half given over to

Curtiz, a writer somewhat perplexed by a society in a state of transition. In Maggie Gee's *Grace* (1988) we encounter Paula who is attempting to write a novel about actual events, actual in hers and Gee's novels and outside of both. Hilda Murrell, an anti-nuclear campaigner, had been preparing a paper for a parliamentary committee on the siting of a nuclear reactor on the Suffolk coast when, in 1984, she was found dead in mysterious circumstances. Articles were written and a question raised in the House of Commons alleging that she had been killed by the intelligence services who by implication were following orders from what was perceived by many as an authoritarian administration. Paula believes that fiction should address directly the most immediate, controversial issues of its age – an opinion she shares with her author – and sets about writing a novel which will, she hopes, reinvigorate interest in what really happened to Murrell and encourage debate on the government's alleged inclination to stifle opposition by force. The Grace of the title is Paula's aunt, who becomes the subject of subtle and intrusive monitoring by a private investigator in the pay of government officials, a rather heavy-handed allusion to Toryism as obsessed with private enterprise. In short, events within the novel about the writer researching the novel about real life take on a very sinister aspect, not unlike those of the Murrell case. Quite how even the more politically motivated reader is supposed to respond to or take inspiration from this clumsy blend of artifice and polemic remains unclear.

The Thatcher decade told us much about the nature of fiction. All of those who wrote of it seemed caught in a creative straightjacket. Their ambition, or perhaps their sense of duty to their vocation, impelled them to engage with it. It was, for more than two decades, the centerpiece of virtually all nonliterary exchanges on the nature of politics, collective morality, and social equity, and novelists of every aesthetic and ideological affiliation felt it necessary to join in. Cartwright, Rathbone, Coe, and others allowed themselves variations upon the standard formulae of classic realism but with each there is a tangible sense of wanting to remould the genre to say something insightful and original about that has happened to Britain tempered with an equally detectable note of self-restraint and caution, as if they knew that too much experiment and formal filtering would obstruct their pursuit of a particular objective, a story that captures the particulars of a milieu. Thatcher is credited with and blamed for many things but we generally overlook that fact that she inspired a contest between the legacy of modernism and the conventions of traditional fiction. In the end the latter were triumphant.

The issue raised here is important because it involves the fundamental question of whether novelists feel an instinctive, innate duty to tailor their work to the gravity of its subject, particularly if the latter is based on actual events. The classic case is Thomas Keneally's Booker Prize winning *Schindler's Ark* (1982). No one disputes that Keneally was meticulous in his research for the book (an endeavor he later wrote of in *Searching For Schindler: A Memoir*, 2007) to the extent that he made certain that unless a "fictional" character had a fully authenticated history as a real person he would not include them, and nor would he speculate on what actually occurred without documentary evidence of the facts. At the same time, however, he makes use of elementary devices – notably the use of a third person narrator to orchestrate perspective, sequence, and dialogue – that are the defining elements of realist fiction. It was agreed by all that the book was exceptionally well-crafted, particularly in terms of the way in which it throws into relief the improbable acts of an otherwise weak and disreputable man. Schindler was a morally dissolute opportunist, a womanizer and a corrupt businessman who made use of his Nazi Party position to rescue 1200 Jews from almost certain death in the concentration camps. This is also what divided readers who otherwise admired Keneally's achievement. Why dress this extraordinary story as a piece of fiction? Certainly the ratcheting up of emotional trauma and narrative tension seizes the attention of readers who might otherwise know little of Oskar Schindler or perhaps even of the nature of the Holocaust. But is this what a novel should do? Does it not reduce an artistic medium to a condescending, didactic mode? Even worse, it might be seen as cheapening unconscionable states of suffering and evil as a form of entertainment, albeit of high-cultural ranking. There is no way in which these questions can be reduced to generalizations. Our judgments depend upon whether an author succeeds, or fails, in striking a balance between what we find in the artefact and what we feel about comparable acts and their emotional and moral registers in the real world. While they do not, like Keneally, deal with undisputed facts, novelists such as Amos Oz and J.M. Coetzee tackle the often horrific dilemmas of existence in, respectively, Israel and South Africa. They are lauded as writers not because they tell us more than historians, political activists, or the news media. Rather they draw us into versions of their worlds without instructing us; while at the same time we do not leave it without having first re-examined our political views and our opinions on literary art. *Looking on Darkness* (1974) by another South African novelist, André Brink, exemplifies this twin compulsion. We are offered the first person reflections of Joseph Malan, a black man, from the condemned cell. He is awaiting execution for the murder of his white lover and throughout we are caught between Malan's significance as allegory personified – irrespective of his immediate plight his account provides a vivid portrait of what apartheid does to individuals – and the voice of a human being who transcends politics.

Brink and others cause us to ask: what is literature for? The novel in particular is immensely significant here because, far more than poetry and drama, it is a medium that absorbs us, draws us into its maze of narrative routes and encounters with people we gradually get to know, an experience that might occupy our attention for days, even weeks. It comes close to being a parallel universe, and it makes us wonder what the novelist is trying to achieve by taking us there. In the case of Richardson we are obviously expected to return to the real world suitably instructed and enlightened; Orwell showed his readers visions of the world they might otherwise have chosen to ignore, without proferring easy solutions; Jeffrey Archer and dozens of other popular writers sell us escapism and fantasy. But the novels that test our assumptions on the purpose of the form most of all are those that close the gap between the actual, recorded horrors of human experience and the process of literary representation. Keneally, Brink, Oz, and Coetzee all blur the boundary between fiction as art or recreation and its potential as a medium for painful truths but others have disregarded it completely, most recently Martin Amis in his *The Zone of Interest* (2014). The novel is about Auschwitz and is divided between three narrative perspectives, dominated by Doll, the camp commandant (a thinly disguised version of Rudolf Hoss the real-life commandant), Thomsen, a bureaucrat responsible for devising the most efficient methods of extermination, and Szmul, a prisoner charged with despatching his fellow Jews to the gas chambers and the disposal of their bodies. Some reviewers praised it for its subdued manner: Amis minimizes his customary linguistic exuberance and postmodern *jeux* – though he retains filaments of perverse humor. Such compliments seem a little backhanded since any other approach would be self-evidently uncouth. Amis appears to acknowledge the difficulties of fictionalizing such matters first by adding a uplifting coda to the narrative followed by an essay on why he wrote the novel and how he felt when conducting the research. In my view it is one of the most unsettling novels ever produced, and not because it is poorly written. What, it prompts us to ask, is it for? Factually it tells us no more about the Holocaust than Martin Gilbert's eponymous history of that foul sequence of events and in this respect it cannot, like Keneally's work, claim to be a faithful dramatization of a single authentic act of humanity; Amis has supplemented historical fact with an arbitrary layer of the grotesque. Are we expected to gain some kind of insight into the motives and states of mind of those involved via Amis's dramatization of them? Doll in particular comes across as a Nazi version of Amis's low-life, fumbling antiheroes, notably John Self, Keith Talent, and Lionel Asbo. Perhaps we are supposed to regard a mass-murderer of unimaginable ruthlessness as in some way the distant relative of an East End buffoon. In the end we have to turn our enquiries inward. Am I enjoying this novel? Amis is an accomplished stylist, even when he tries to subdue his talents, so if the answer to that question is "yes," do you not feel repulsed by yourself, the book, and its author? If you are not enjoying it then the likely reason is that you feel unsettled by Amis's ability to bring the likes of Doll and Thomsen to life. They are not authentic representations of the real perpetrators of the Holocaust and because of their improbable grotesqueness we become far more intrigued by what Amis has created than what actually happened. Literature, the novel in particular, energizes and distorts fact but should it be employed to do so with facts like these? Gilbert's *The Holocaust* (1989) is scrupulously attentive to detail; random shootings of small numbers of Jews, pre-Final Solution, do not escape his attention but the most memorable feature of the book is its resolutely impersonal nonliterary style. Its subtext appears to be: literature is fraudulent and engrossing and has no place in accounts of these events. To compare Gilbert's endeavor with Amis's might seem erroneous – they are after all writing, respectively, a history book and a novel, aren't they? Not quite. Amis, in his essay on the novel, makes it clear that he relied little on imagination. His narrative is built on recorded facts, despite his splicings and refractions. So we return to the issue of the suitability of fiction to such matters. Even if we perceive Doll as by parts bizarre, farcical, and repulsive – Amis is, as he puts it himself, "dramatizing the mind of the babbler, the monologuist, the man on the milk crate with the flickering eyes" – we find ourselves checking our response with a troubled uncertainty as to what exactly we are responding *to*. Are we reading through the text an image of what Rudolf Hoss, Auschwitz's commandant, was really like, or do we accept that Doll is a commendable contrivance, mercurial evil assembled from words, and as a consequence a testament to Amis's skill as a literary artist? The former brings some discredit on both the reader and the author: there are far more suitable ways to learn of perpetrators of the Holocaust than via fictional "dramatizations." Many reviewers saw it as one of Amis's best executed novels since the 1980s but then found themselves facing a dilemma, which they could not explain, but which prevented them from offering unreserved praise. Their problem was that it is improper to write well – to put it crudely, splendidly or entertainingly – about matters such as this. It might be possible of course to reduce the literary elements of a novel about actual horrific events, its *syuzhet*, to a bare minimum, which returns us to the original question; why choose fiction as the means of engaging with the Holocaust? Is this, we have to ask ourselves, the use of literature as a uniquely revealing mirror for the human condition, or is it the exploitation of both as a means to boost the writer's egotistical self-image?

Shortly after the publication of Amis's book, *The Guardian* (20 September 2014) offered its readers a short story by Hilary Mantel which begs comparison with it. "The Assassination of Margaret Thatcher" is set in 1983. It ends with a sniper, an IRA terrorist, taking aim and we are left in little doubt that he will kill the then Prime Minister. Certainly the event itself is pure fiction but it is assembled from a very authentic fabric of truths and impressions. In 1984 the IRA came close to killing Mrs Thatcher with the Brighton bomb. The flat occupied by the fictional marksman is identical to the one where Mantel lived in 1983; it overlooked the back door that Mrs Thatcher used, along with her security staff, when visiting her private optician. Mantel, thinly disguised, is the narrator and observer, talking with the assassin as he explains his background and intention. Most significantly, Mantel, like Amis, permits herself a reflective appendix on her feelings about the story, or in her case an interview with a *Guardian* journalist, Damian Barr, who states that "Mantel succeeds where terrorists failed. It's an unexpectedly funny exploration of the Maggie mythos, delivered with sniper-like skill. It's a horror story for Thatcher's fans, a wish-fulfillment fantasy for her detractors." And Mantel concedes that she is writing mainly for the latter: "When I think of her, I can still feel that boiling detestation." The right to voice our utter contempt for others, politicians in particular, is a mainstay of free speech; but what of murderous contempt? It would seem that this is permissible, at least as "wish-fulfillment fantasy" disguised as literary fiction. Mantel: "She did longstanding damage in many areas of national life ... She imitated masculine qualities to the extent that she had to get herself a good war [the Falklands] ... She was not of woman born. She was a psychological transvestite." One has to ask. Has Mantel exchanged invention for, as Barr puts it, "wish-fulfillment"? More significantly, does she feel that there is an implicit alliance between the educated reading public and a political consensus on Thatcherism sufficient to ensure a predictable affective and ethical reaction similar to that which Amis can expect in his representation of the Holocaust? Both make use of the devices of fiction to compel and energize our opinions about actual people and events in the real world, but in different ways make us wonder about the exploitation of fiction for purposes that have more to do with ideological prejudice and egotism than art.

Nussbaum (1990) argued that knowledge or even a collective ideological consensus can be better conveyed in imaginative writing than in, say, philosophical or historical discourses. The former has the advantage of being an affective medium; the expression or dramatization of emotion is more effective than its description. But we should remember that Amis can take it for granted that his reader will begin the novel with reasonably secure, and predictable, knowledge of and opinions on the Holocaust. Even if some Holocaust-denier were to voice their opinion that the novel involves too great an imaginative leap, they would be treated as a deranged curiosity. But with Mantel we find ourselves in more difficult territory. Certainly neither the author nor her fictional proxy goes quite so far as to fully endorse the assassin's objective but it is clear enough that their dialogue is comprised of various aspects of today's leftish historical consensus, with Mantel as its inquisitive uncertain conscience and the gunman as (admit it quietly) the embodiment of its backdated desires.

One of Leavis's closest allies, especially during his altercation with Snow, was Lionel Trilling. Trilling, however, is a far more brutal apologist for the novel as a dramatized political pamphlet.

> Not, it may be granted, by reason of the essence of literature but certainly by reason of prevailing accident, the judgement of literature is overtly and explicitly a moral and intellectual judgment ... Literature doesn't easily submit to the category of aesthetic contemplative disinterestedness – so much of it insists "*De TE fabula* – this means *you*" and often goes on to say, "And you'd better *do* something about it quick." Time and tradition diminish our awareness of literature's nasty unaesthetic tendency to insist upon some degree of immediate practicality, and the aestheticians take all possible advantage of this effect of time and tradition. But if human experience – human danger and pain – is made the material of an artistic creation, the judgment that is directed upon that creation will involve important considerations of practicality and thus of cogency, relevance, appositeness, logicality, and truth. Unless we get the clear signal from the literary work itself that we are not to ask the question, we inevitably do ask, "Is this true, is this to be believed, is this to shape our future judgments of experience?" And even when the literary work does give us the clear signal that we are not to apply this standard, we are sure to ask some such question as, "What is being implied about logic and truth by this wilful departure from logic and truth?" (Trilling, 1955, pp. 135–136)

The most disturbing phrase here is the condemnatory "when the literary work does not give us the clear signal." In Trilling's view we should have opinions served to us disguised as literature, and even when the author fails to deliver a clear message we should go looking for it, for in a worthy piece of writing it will be present somewhere – a procedure also known as brainwashing. He would probably have admired Mantel greatly.

According to Trilling, the person who demands that the novel challenges, or at least engages with, their political or moral preconceptions (and such were his ideal readers) will be severely disappointed by the likes of Kingsley Amis, Anthony Powell, Fielding, and Thackeray who forestall such questions as "Is this true, is this to be believed, is this to shape our future judgments of experience?" Trilling and Leavis were fans of D.H. Lawrence because his fiction never allows us to leave it without having made demands on what we think about life in general. The following can be taken as Lawrence's creative manifesto.

> And of all the art forms, the novel most of all demands the trembling and oscillating of the balance. The "sweet" novel is more falsified, and therefore more immoral, than the blood-and-thunder novel.
>
> The same with the smart and smudgily cynical novel, which says it doesn't matter what you do, because one thing is as good as another, anyhow, and prostitution is just as much "life" as anything else.
>
> This misses the point entirely. A thing isn't life just because somebody does it. This the artist ought to know perfectly well. The ordinary bank clerk buying himself a new straw hat isn't "life" at all: it is just existence, quite all right, like everyday dinners: but not "life."
>
> By life, we mean something that gleams, that has the fourth-dimensional quality. If the bank clerk feels really piquant about his hat, if he establishes a lively relation with it, and goes out the shop with the new straw on his head, a changed man, be-aureoled, then that is life.
>
> The same with the prostitute. If a man establishes a living relation to her, if only for one moment, then it is life. But if it *doesn't*: if it is just money and function, then it is not life, but sordidness, and a betrayal of living. (Lawrence, 1925, pp. 270–272)

In Shklovskian terms, Lawrence has not so much discarded as grossly insulted the *syuzhet*. He gives no attention whatsoever to the notion of good, or bad, writing. Instead, the novel should be a vehicle for the extraordinary, an obligation that we look again at a world we might otherwise treat with complacent familiarity. Neither the "sweet" novel nor its "smudgily cynical" counterpart can achieve this because, apparently, each refuses to force shocking impressions upon us. It sounds exhilarating and such pronouncements buttressed Lawrence's reputation and popularity as something more than a literary radical; he was celebrated as a figure who advocated revolutionary ideas, particularly regarding sex. But how did he put this into practice in his fiction? Open one of his best known works at random and quite soon one will begin to detect that the narrator is not really interested in the characters and what they do. He – it is Lawrence speaking – certainly exploits them very effectively and this amounts to his principal failing as a literary writer.

Consider the famous passage in *Women in Love* when Brangwen and Anna visit Lincoln Cathedral.

> Then he pushed open the door, and the great, pillared gloom was before him, in which his soul shuddered and rose from her nest. His soul leapt, soared up into the great church. His body stood still, absorbed by the height. His soul leapt up into the gloom, into possession, it reeled, it swooned with a great escape, it quivered in the womb, in the hush and the gloom of fecundity, like seed of procreation in ecstasy.
>
> Here, the very first dawn was breaking, the very last sunset sinking, and the immemorial darkness, whereof life's day would blossom and fall away again, re-echoed peace and profound immemorial silence.
>
> Away from the time, always outside of time! Between east and west, between dawn and sunset, the church lay like a seed in silence, dark before germination, silenced after death. Containing birth and death, potential with all the noise and transition of life, the cathedral remained hushed, a great involved seed ... whereof the flower would be radiant life inconceivable, but whose beginning and whose end were the circle of silence. (p. 201)

Lawrence continues in this manner for another three pages, informing us of how "the stone leapt up from the plain of earth, leapt up in a manifold, clustered desire each time, up, away from the horizontal earth ..." (p. 202). Eventually it – the stone, that is – reaches a "timeless ecstasy," consumated, twice: "the climax of eternity, the apex of the arch" (p. 202). By this point we might begin to wonder what has happened to the man and the woman whose visit to the cathedral enables Lawrence to distill from its quasi-sexual symbolism such of moment of transcendence. It is some time since we – the reader and the narrator – left them standing in the transept. One might imagine them glancing at each other, puzzled, perhaps slightly disappointed, and wondering: "Where has he [our narrator] gone now?" One might because the passage exemplifies Lawrence's tendency to turn events and people into vehicles for what really interests him (his own conception of life, individuality, the self, and so on) and return to them only because he has to: someone, he knows, has to carry this irksome story forward and bring it to a close. The novel, for him, is more a means to an end than a literary artefact. Leavis's failure to notice this, or his decision to blind himself to it, tells us a great deal about conceptions of literature in which the communication of ideas is promoted above craftsmanship.

In the light of these arguments on relevance let us return to the 1980s, to a novel that caused a controversy far more visceral than any raised by Thatcher or the elevated symposia joined by the likes of Leavis, Snow, Trilling, and Lawrence.

The first review in Iran of Salman Rushdie's *The Satanic Verses* (1988) appeared in December 1988 in *Kayhan Farangi*, one of the leading literary magazines of the Islamic Republic and, like all publications, subject to monitoring by the agencies of the largely fundamentalist government. It was not a particularly sympathetic piece, but no more vitriolic than one would expect from, say, a *Church Times* review of a novel about Christ's baser inclinations and unrecorded activities. It "contains a number of false interpretations about Islam and gives wrong portrayals of the Koran and the Prophet Mohammed. It also draws a caricature-like and distorted image of Islamic principles which lacks even the slightest artistic credentials." This seems even-handed, one might say tolerant, given that 2 months earlier the Ministry of Finance in India had put the book on its list of proscribed texts, an unusual gesture by a nation whose constitution committed it to secularism.

It is probable that the ban in India provided the initial momentum for what would very soon become an avalanche of protests, government rulings, and violence. On 11 October, 6 days after the banning was announced UK-based Muslims and Muslim groups founded the UK Action Committee on Islamic Affairs whose sole purpose was to mobilize opinion against the book and campaign for a ban in the United Kingdom. On 28 October the *Gazette*, the official mouthpiece for the government of South Africa, announced that under the section of the Publications Act dealing with blasphemy, *The Satanic Verses* would be banned. The Congress of South African Writers, under pressure from Muslim organizations and following threats of bombings, withdrew its invitation to Rushdie who was due to speak in the country in November, and the South African *Weekly Mail*, facing similar threats, refused to withdraw its invitation but on the advice of security forces interviewed Rushdie from London via a telephone link. The novel was awarded the Whitbread Best Novel prize in London on 8 November but during the following week the governments of Bangladesh and Sudan banned it. In December the Islamic Defense Council organized a protest rally in London which was followed a few days later by large marches in northern cities with sizeable Muslim populations, notably Bradford and Bolton. In the latter the turnout was estimated at more than 7000, but a good deal more press attention would be drawn to the march in Bradford on 14 January 1989 where copies of the book were publically burned and shortly afterwards the British Muslim Action Front sent a petition to Penguin to withdraw the book and a demand that the government ban it. On 31 January the Home Secretary, Douglas Hurd, announced that there would be no ban and that blasphemy laws would not be changed to accommodate the protesters' demands. In the interim the book was banned in Sri Lanka (14 December 1988) and Pakistan (8 February 1989). Following the decree by Pakistan's National Assembly public protests in the subcontinent became more frequent and violent, beginning in Bombay and Dhaka, Bangladesh, and culminating in riots in Islamabad on 12 February at which six people were killed and more than 100 injured, and in Kashmir the following day leaving one person dead. The day after that Ayatollah Ruhollah Khomeini of Iran pronounced a fatwa (religious edict) which was broadcast on Tehran radio. "I inform the proud Muslim people of the world that the author of *The Satanic Verses* book which is against Islam, the Prophet and the Koran, and all involved in its publications who were aware of its content, are sentenced to death." Rushdie would remain in hiding and under constant protection by the police and the security forces until March 2002. His marriage did not survive the experience. On 15 January, Rushdie and Marianne Wiggins left their home for the last time and Hojatoleslam Hassani Sanei, a senior Iranian cleric and associate of Khomeini, offered a bounty of $3 million to any Iranian who killed Rushdie.

Throughout the next 12 months more countries with sizable Muslim populations banned the book. In contrast, petitions were signed and meetings held by human rights and writers groups, principally the International Rushdie Defence Committee, to protest against the fatwa. Several bookshops in the United States, Britain, and Australia which sold the book were bombed. On 7 March 1989 Iran broke off diplomatic relations with the United Kingdom and on 27 May the British Muslim Action organized the largest demonstration so far in the United Kingdom involving more than 30,000 protesters in Hyde Park.

William Nygaard, Rushdie's publisher in Norway, was shot twice in the back outside his home on 11 October 1993 and closely escaped death. Shortly after the fatwa was issued many of the colleagues and neighbors of Peter Mayer, chief executive of Viking/Penguin, petitioned him, for their own safety, to suspend publication. Letters written in blood were pushed under the front door of his house promising to kill him and he received phone calls in the middle of the night which described in lurid detail how his wife and children would be tortured and murdered before he was executed. A year later, on 11 July 1991, Hitoshi Igarashi was stabbed to death on the campus of Tsukuba University. He had translated *The Satanic Verses* into Japanese. Later that day a spokesman for the Pakistan Association in Japan commented for the press: "Today we have been congratulating each other. Everyone was really happy." Ettore Capriolo of Milan had translated the novel into Italian in 1989. Exactly a week before the murder of Igarishi he was stabbed repeatedly and beaten by a man, claiming to be an Iranian, who demanded Rushdie's address. He refused to reply and somehow managed to survive after his assailant fled. I have provided only a brief account of the horrible events that followed the fatwa. There were many others, not least the murder by car bomb of the Turkish journalist and advocate of Rushdie, Ugur Mumcu, and the attempt on the life of his fellow Turk, Aziz Nesin, who had written articles condemning the fatwa.

A question that has not been properly addressed by those who have documented and commented on these events is why a book initially judged in Iran merely as a falsification of Islamic history with only slight "artistic credentials" could then move millions of seemingly sane individuals worldwide to campaign for the execution of its author, as well as causing the numerous deaths and serious injuries that surrounded the dispute. It is an important question and not simply because it obliges us to examine the meaning of "free speech," the campaigning principle of most of Rushdie's supporters. It also involves a more nuanced but equally significant issue, involving the difference, if any, between literature and other forms of writing and expression.

The sense of incomprehension experienced by most Western writers during the first few years of the fatwa, Rushdie included, is exemplified by John Walsh in an article for *The Sunday Times* (19 February 1989):

> At no point in these imaginings does Rushdie refer to the prophet Muhammad by name, nor to the city Mecca, nor to the Sheria law, nor anything directly concerned with Islamic faith.
>
> All the fundamentalists' objections concern the *symbolic* representation of religious figures and events – as one might condemn George Orwell's fictional Ministry of Love for satirising the Ministry of Defence.
>
> What is altogether more odd is that the book's status as a novel cuts no ice with its Muslim critics. The grand sheikh of Cairo's Al-Azhar, the 1,000-year-old seat of Islamic theology, said when calling on all the nations in the Islamic Conference Organization to suppress the book that it contained "lies and figments of the imagination" about Islam, which were "passed off as facts," and that the Jahilia sequences were insulting distortions of Islamic history.
>
> That Rushdie has always presented his material as fictional "figments of the imagination" is not considered an excuse.

Walsh's difficulty in making sense of a culture seemingly mired in what Christianity began to shrug off around the time of the Reformation is made more starkly evident when we compare his piece with a lecture delivered at Cornell University by Ali Muzrui 2 weeks later on 1 March 1989.

> When I was in Pakistan, in November 1988, this book was already being discussed. I was very intrigued by the analogy, which was being made by Pakistanis in the circles in which I moved. They said: "It's as if Rushdie had composed a brilliant poem about the private parts of his parents, and then gone to the market place to recite that poem to the applause of strangers, who invariable laughed at the jokes he cracks about his parents' genitalia, and he's taking money for doing it."
>
> At the time, I hadn't really gone into the book, and I wondered whether it was fair or not. Now, at least I understand where the Pakistanis were coming from – that this is an invasion of one's ancestry – almost as basic as the private parts of one's parents: and that, to go around making fun of it to the cheer of the enemies of the faith, and be paid $850,000 before publication is like composing that poem from the market place. Hence, they are wondering what is his motive, what could make anybody like that.

The analogy chorused by the Pakistanis depends upon an assumed perception of literature as a record of the world in which we live. Since the Renaissance, Western cultures have routinely classified literary writing as exempt from the responsibilities of truth-telling, a basic precondition for all other discourses. Rushdie and his peers took the deregulation of literature even further, causing it continually to question the distinction between reality and representation in language. It should be noted the Muzrui was not co-opted by Cornell to demonstrate its openmindedness to patent Fundamentalists. He might sound like a fanatic brought in by academia to advertise its indulgent liberalism but in truth he was playing on home territory, being Professor of Political Science and Afro-American and African Studies at the University of Michigan, an equally prestigious institution. One would assume that as a senior academic in the field of Humanities he was not entirely ignorant of developments that had occurred in the arts, literature, and language over the previous half century in the United Staes and Europe yet he overlooks completely the glaringly obvious reason for the reaction of the Pakistanis, and by implication all other Muslims, to the book: that is, with regard to their perception of "literature" and "fiction" they exist in a different universe from that of literate Westerners.

Had he pointed this out he would have undermined his plea for an understanding of Islamic rage, given that Rushdie would be seen to be not guilty by virtue of the fact that his postmodern technique exempted him from the potential effects of his writings upon those whose legacy was his subject. It was not quite that Rushdie was naïve enough to assume that the rest of the Muslim world partook of his inclination towards creative speculation, but he did think that those more resolute in their beliefs had by 1988 reached a stage where his liberal vacillation would be tolerated. As Professor Muzrui shows, even Western-assimilated Muslims were not willing to allow him the freedom to write about their shared legacy in the way he wished. Muzrui goes on to compare *The Satanic Verses* with *Mein Kamf*, the only difference, as far as he is concerned, being that the former is anti-Muslim while Hitler's work is "anti Jewish." The fact that one is a deranged pseudo-autobiographical political manifesto and the other a self-proclaimed fantasy is not mentioned.

These events prompt comparison with what happened in England during the mid eighteenth century. Certainly supporters and opponents of Fielding, Richardson, and others did not accompany their observations with threats of violence or death yet there was a similar sense of unreconciled perceptions: some treated fiction as a replica, perhaps an improvement, of the world, while others accepted that the novel created its own world and was unaccountable to what went on in real life.

If we can learn anything from this it is that the arrival of fiction, at least in the West, signaled an important moment of maturity in the relationship between literature and society. The latter began to release its claims on literary art. Writers started to make their own rules, devised conventions that broke the chain between the predominant religious, ethical, or social dimensions of citizenship and what writers allowed for in their novels, poems, or plays. It is impossible to ignore the parallels between Rushdie and the fatwa and the argument between Leavis and C.P. Snow; indeed, if it were not for the fact that the former wrecked and ended many lives it might seem like a darkly comic satire on the state of fiction and criticism. The two esteemed dons differed on virtually every aspect of what literature, particularly the novel, was supposed to be and do. Leavis regarded literature as limitless in range and significance; something that outranks empiricism, the discourses of science, as a means of addressing the essential questions of human existence. Conversely, supporters of the fatwa refused to draw a line between the world portrayed by fiction and such ultimate truths as those recorded in the Koran.

Despite their apparent differences they had one thing in common. Both refused to treat literature as, by its nature, perversely dysfunctional, an activity that causes us to think as much about the way it operates as what it says, and one that is therefore exempt from the rules and expectations that obtain for everything else written or spoken.

This chapter has, so far, concentrated on fiction; justifiably because the novel constantly provokes the question of whether the suspension of disbelief involves a collateral alteration of perception or trust. I finish this book with a short piece on poetry which according to Auden "makes nothing happen"; unlike Rushdie's novel.

There have been numerous attempts to provide a raison d'être for the existence and attractions of poetry and these have been remarkable in their lack of conviction and their inconsistencies. As we have seen, Plato was ambivalent to say the least on the value of poetry as a means of representation or persuasion. Horace's much quoted formula that the end of poetry is "*aut prodesses aut delectare,*" to instruct or to delight, is finely ambiguous: entertainment and didacticism are generally speaking not compatible activities. The first recorded case of scholarly engagement with poetry involved teams of scrutineers in the Great Library in Alexandria poring over the, dated, third century BC version of Homer and attempting to intuit the "real" text beneath what they believed to be the untidy work of previous scribes. Homer's work, indeed poetry per se, was accorded an almost sacred ranking but no one ventured that it might have an obvious purpose. The grounds on which Renaissance critics and poets defended the newly revived classical models of poetry, particularly the epic, were ethical: poetry promoted virtue by representing noble actions in an ostensibly edifying manner. Virgil, Spenser, Rapin, and Le Bossu all held that the various sub-genres of verse made their own contribution to the inculcation of key ideas about human conduct. But by the time that the Renaissance began to inspire poetic writing in England in the early sixteenth century these didactic formulae were becoming self-evidently obsolete. The period was awash with competing and contradictory models of belief and behavior typified by the tension between humanism and religious orthodoxy and the often incompatible versions of Christian doctrine thrown up by the Reformation. One might assume therefore that poetry had an ample amount of material upon which to practice its cautiously rehearsed role as moral arbiter. In fact, the birth of modern methods for the distribution of ideas and dogma, predominantly the printing press, ensured that verse would thereafter have no more than a secondary role in public debate.

Within just over two centuries, from the early 1500s to the mid eighteenth century, England had exchanged its condition as a feudal, largely agrarian state governed by an autocratic monarch and humbly attendant upon a single monotheistic doctrine for an assembly of competing factions, an extended debating chamber in which matters such as governance and religious conviction were open for disputation. Trade, colonial settlement, and the incipient growth of urban centers were preparing the ground for the Industrial Revolution. As a consequence the printed text became the forum for this new multiplicity of issues, causes, and perspectives and each of the growing panoply of sub-genres had a self-evident purpose and objective. A pamphlet on architecture or animal husbandry was simply what it claimed to be. Poetry, unlimited in its range of subjects, was now beginning to find itself in the invidious position as a redundant supplement to other genres, mostly nonliterary, whose existence was guaranteed by their subject and function. Indeed, Milton's Christian epic, *Paradise Lost,* is a quintessential example of the Renaissance poem at the tipping point between relevance and obsolescence. It adapted the grand expectation of its Classical predecessors to the post-Classical topic of a Christian perception of the Creation and the Fall and much of the debate which it fueled during the eighteenth and nineteenth centuries involved the issue of appropriateness. In short, were such fundamental theological and existential topics suitable for poetry? Few disputed the magnificence of Milton's achievement but equally there was the implicit question of what he was attempting to achieve. If his objective was to re-ignite theological disputes regarding key Biblical issues then surely a more apposite vehicle would be the prose pamphlet – of which he was an adept practitioner – rather than an elaborate blank verse narrative strewn with grand conceits and monologues reminiscent of Shakespeare.

Consider also the shift in the mood and sense of purpose in poetry after the Restoration of the monarchy at the end of the seventeenth century. For much of the subsequent hundred years poets endeavored to compete with prose hacks and pamphleteers as commentators on topical contemporary subjects, with a correlative paring down of the intrinsic, some would say definitive, stylistic extravagances of verse. Poetry, briefly, was attempting to imitate the function and status of prose discourse. To varying degrees it was successful but it could not by its nature achieve anything resembling full equality. Despite their puritanical stylistic restraint Augustan poems were still indisputably poems. They belonged to a generic family with recognizable characteristics but with no clear purpose or role. Poems could indeed address any idea or theme but they could do so only as ostentatious subsidiaries to the work undertaken by prose.

The reaction against Augustanism by the Romantics and the maintenance of various forms of the Romantic ideal during the nineteenth century further testify to the collective feelings of unease among poets – a fear that their vocation might be seen as dysfunctional and purposeless. The Augustans had attempted to adapt poetry to the conventions of prose, promoting such notions as order, clarity, and logic above imagination or inspiration while the Romantics, driven by a similar dread of redundancy, took their verse in the opposite direction, attempting to establish for it a special ranking as an autonomous vehicle for existential contemplation, even enlightenment, outside the routines of conventional religion or philosophy. It can be no accident that the emergence of Romanticism brought with it a collateral program of writings that sought to justify the independence of poetry according to purely aesthetic principles. The genesis of this can be traced to writers and philosophers of the German Romantic movement. Kant stressed the purity and disinterestedness of the poem as a work of art, Goethe and Schiller emphasized the poem's status as an independent organism, and Schelling averred that poetry involved the unique revelation of the universal. All of these beliefs resurfaced in the ex-cathedra writings of the English Romantic poets, particularly in the prose of Coleridge, and later in the work of Carlyle and Arnold.

The French Symbolist movement, pioneered by Mallarmé and Verlaine, carries the influence of these Romantic manifestoes and although their verse differs stylistically from that of their German and English predecessors the notion of the poem as capable of operating independently of all other discourses and creating a unique revelatory fabric of meaning is a key enduring feature of their beliefs. Eliot and Pound, the originators of modernism in English, drew inspiration in their early work from Arthur Symons's *The Symbolist Movement in Literature* (1899) and what fascinated them most was Symons's concept of the impersonal and objective existence of the poem, a maxim that would in due course be disseminated through many of the sub-categories of the modernist aesthetic. A version of this same principle is a key element of New Criticism and Formalism, with critics such as Wimsatt and Beardsley insisting that the poem itself should be the exclusive subject of the reader's scrutiny, and that circumstantial, biographical material should not be allowed to contaminate our awareness of its unique operations.

At the other end of the Theoretical spectrum the Frankfurt School Marxist critics – precursors of the New Historicists and Cultural Materialists – saw poetry as standing at the apex of what they called the "culture industry," which also incorporated other traditional high arts along with radio, television, and film. Poetry, according to the Frankfurt thinkers, feeds a self-perpetuating milieu of docility. It has, they aver, fulfilled the Arnoldian prophecy and become a substitute for religion, or rather a means of avoiding confrontation with the world beyond bourgeois culture. Irrespective of one's opinion on the ideology of this approach it bears a remarkable resemblance to the consensus that has accompanied poetry on its uneasy journey from classical civilization to the present; it is an activity with no purpose.

It would of course be absurd to claim that since the eighteenth century the idea of the poem as a structure immune from the logic and vagaries of the real world has obtained without challenge. Nonetheless, there persists an enduring, powerful perception of a poem as a cryptogram, a palimpsest, a special form of writing capable of encoding or revealing messages not obtainable elsewhere or by other means. However, there is a problem with this model. Even if we accept that poems are, by their nature, capable of sustaining within themselves a fugitive, anomalous thread of meaning, how can we describe what this is? As we have seen in our considerations of naturalization we face, in all of our engagements with poetry, a dilemma. The only means by which we can discuss, write about, or even privately reflect upon the special characteristics of a poem is by effectively translating it into nonpoetic discourse; we can only articulate the operations of the double pattern by entering an alliance with one dimension of it, the referential function. Once we begin to talk or write about poetry the sense of beguilement that draws us to it, its self-evident aversion to logic or reason, is extinguished.

This dilemma is at once irresolvable and a clue to the enduring, addictive power of poetry. We read poems in different ways. Sometimes we clumsily appropriate some element of their fabric as an essential theme and telescope this into an overarching "interpretation." On other occasions – and as I have indicated above, more wisely – we accept their skewed logic and devise a response that is respectfully indeterminate. In all respects, however, we are aware that something unusual, indeed unique, is occurring.

We are drawn, simultaneously, in two directions. On the one hand we attempt to form a paraphrase of the poem, yet the poem by its nature resists us. It is the dynamic between these two trajectories that holds the key to our attraction to poetry. A single sequence of words catches us between opposing states of response, and by this I do not refer to a version of Empson's concept of ambiguity or Brooks's paradox. Rather, poetry involves us in an experience far more fundamental, a dizzying combination of visceral and intellectual questions. Our desire, our elemental need to understand the poem is instinctive, but so is our guilty fascination with a piece of writing that refuses to submit to the standard ordinances of logic, transparency, even intention. We want to tease out its essential meaning while at the same time we are aware that our desire to do so is fed by its enigmatic character, that the latter propitiates the former and thus should remain immune from our interpretive impulse. As Mallarmé put it, "the power of a line of poetry comes from an indefinable harmony between what it *says*, and what it is." This is the double pattern. The poem, being made of language, deceives us into the same state of expectations provoked by all of our other encounters with words, yet once this offer is made all further arrangements are forsworn.

When a stranger asks us the time or the way to the nearest Tube station the process of decoding the message, establishing its intention is reflexive and unproblematic. We become part of a dialogue or a shared discourse. At a more elevated level, when we listen to a lecture on biochemistry or tackle a work by Wittgenstein we become similarly attuned to what we perceive as the demands of the message, its context and apparent purpose. In all instances the participants – writer, speaker, listener, reader – become subject to the conventions and operations of the discourse, accept these as serving a practical purpose. The role of language in all of this is comparable to that of doorkeeper, the functionary who enables one to pass through the process of interpretation and advance toward what is always the objective, the substantiation of unambiguous truth. This is why we cannot prevent ourselves from operating against the texture of the poem when we attempt to make sense of it. Poetry, however, catches us in a double bind. It plays the doorkeeper and draws us in yet as it does so it refuses to stand aside and allow us to continue our search for a determinate meaning. Instead it takes control of our cognitive registers, lays out perverse spirals of meaning and deploys linguistic devices that have no purposive logic. The language of poetry – the double pattern – draws upon the language of human beings but it is not the language we use. At the same time poetry, far more effectively than any poststructuralist, exposes, indeed celebrates, the arbitrary nature of our sign system, exploits the fugitive capabilities of language as material (meter, rhyme, enjambment, shaped poetry, and so on) to generate disparate channels of meaning, and demonstrates that language is unfettered by the commands of some prelinguistic substratum of truths and can indeed rewrite the rules of perception and rationalization.

This might seem to give credence to the Frankfurt School model of poetry as a form of erudite escapism, but the opposite is the case. The most controversial statement by a Frankfurt Theorist on poetry came from Theodor Adorno in *Prisms* (1955); that "to write poetry after Auschwitz is barbaric." What he means is that since the range of subjects that can be covered by poetry is limitless this must now include the Holocaust. Therefore, in his opinion, poets face two incontestable prohibitions. They cannot pretend to be ignorant of the Holocaust as an index to the horrible potentialities of humankind. At the same time there is a ghastly incompatibility between something so transparently horrific and a genre that by its nature, abjures transparency. Adorno was wrong. Poets have written about the Holocaust and their work is by no means "barbaric" (and one can assume here that Adorno means that poetry must by its nature trivialize its subject). At one extreme we come upon the work of the Polish poet, Tadeusz Różewicz, who in his first two volumes (1947 and 1948) prefigured Adorno by virtually reinventing the modes and idioms of Polish verse as a suitable medium for writing about the war. His pieces are stripped bare of rhetorical posturing; there is no meter, rhyme, or metaphor. Others attempted to reconcile the humane elegance of verse with inhumane subjects. Consider the following extracts from Dannie Abse's "White Balloon":

> Dear love, Auschwitz made me
> more of a Jew than Moses did.
> But the world's not always with us.
> Happiness enters here again tonight
> like an unexpected guest
>
> …
>
> into our night living room
> where, under the lampshade's ciliate,
> an armchair's occupied by a white balloon.
>
> …
>
> But what does it matter now
> as the white balloon is thrown up high?
> Quiet, so quiet, the moon above Masada
> and closed, abandoned for the night,
> the icecream van at Auschwitz.

There is an unsettling disjunction between the statement that opens the poem and the fissiparous, unfixed images of the balloon, the embodied state of "happiness" ("with no memory of the future") and the intimate domestic setting shared, we assume, by Abse and his wife. These closing lines return us to Auschwitz, surreally attended at night by an ice-cream van. This is not, in my opinion, "barbaric." Abse assumes that, once invoked, the Holocaust requires no elucidation – and in this respect he is in accord with Adorno. It is something that immunizes itself from speculative discourse; it simply exists as a record of gargantuan suffering and systematic inhumanity. For Abse, however, it carries a special resonance. It has "made me / more of a Jew than Moses did." He did not, he implies, witness it but at the same time the entire spectrum of his consciousness carries a trace of it. We are tempted by this contextual placement to comb for resonances the curious dreamlike sequence sandwiched between the two specific references to Auschwitz. Is the ghostly embodiment of happiness symbolic of a sense of resignation and despair? It leads them up the "lit staircase / towards the landing's darkness." Does the whiteness of the balloon indicate unaffiliation, innocence, naivety, or any other of the various states of hope that are now foreshadowed by dread: it sits on an armchair "as if there'd been a party." Virtually every phrase in the poem is puzzling, pointing to no clear extrinsic fabric of meanings. But having been introduced to the poem's one unambiguous theme we cannot help but use this as an interpretive key to what would otherwise be a tantalizingly incoherent sequence. This, as I have stated, is the effect that attracts us most to poetry: being caught between our desire to interpret and make sense and our equally powerful impulse to submit to illogic and leave the text to its own devices. In this instance, however, the experience goes far beyond an intellectual or aesthetic exercise. We recoil from interpreting the images as symbols of the Holocaust because to do so we would be interfering with a very personal, very tragic example of mimesis. Abse is using the unique capacities of verse to simulate a state of mind that is too conflicted and shifting for prose. He is fully, brutally aware of what happened at Auschwitz; it has become part of his life, yet he implicitly raises the question of how he can describe this condition. His answer is "The White Balloon," a poem that invites us into its web of interpretive possibilities and allows us to go no further. We have a picture of an unsettled consciousness, restlessly, painfully connecting the minutiae of his everyday world – ice-cream vans, armchairs, balloons, and so on – with something that is both ever present and inexplicable. The poem begs comparison with Martin Amis's novel on the same subject. The feelings of disquiet prompted by the latter do not attend readings of Abse's piece and numerous explanations could be offered for this. We can rule out the notion of Abse's background earning him a special dispensation. Certainly, the fact that he is Jewish is self-evidently relevant to the poem but it would not cause us to ignore aspects of his work that we might otherwise find distasteful or unsuitable; what is also evident is his ability to combine something almost unutterable with a demonstration of exquisite literary skill. Poetry, at least in the hands of an artist as sensitive and accomplished as Abse, allows for vacillation without evasion, enables the writer to confront such horrors as Auschwitz while freeing them from the belligerent preconditions of prose fiction.

Abse's lyric tells us much about the seemingly irreconcilable views on the purpose of poetry that have attended its history. Some treat verse as pure performance, a demonstration of language at its most brittle, magical, untrustworthy, and arbitrary while others see it as a special vehicle for various forms of exaltation, insight, and revelation. "The White Balloon" shows how both can inform the same piece of writing. Its subject is treated with respectful circumvention but is at the same time made abundantly present. We watch with admiration as Abse performs a linguistic confidence trick and continually find ourselves reminded that this is something more than an artist's demonstration of his skills, that these skills are employed to refine a brief monument in words to something terrible and profound. Abse does with language what others less accomplished would recoil from attempting, and he shows that poetry is a unique and uniquely demanding medium. Poems that prevent us completely from encountering a prevailing theme, even a story, and instead swallow us in incessant linguistic perversity are of negligible value, as are verses in which the poet is unable or unwilling to counterpoint self-evident skill and stylistic exuberance against some discernible notion of presence. This is not an arbitrary evaluative criterion. To at once have a sense of what a poem means alongside an awareness of its purely literary peculiarities is to understand why poetry is unique. If one of these dimensions is squandered or allowed to suffocate the other the text will relinquish its special generic qualities and as a consequence be aesthetically diminished.

References

Acheson, J. and Huk, R. (eds) (1996) *Contemporary British Poetry: Essays in Theory and Criticism*, State University of New York Press, New York, NY.

Ackroyd, P. (1976) *Notes for a New Culture*, Vision Press, London.

Adorno, T. (1997) *Aesthetic Theory*, trans. R. Hullot-Kentor, vol. 8, *Theory and History of Literature* (eds G. Adorno and R. Tiedmann), University of Minnesota, Minneapolis, MN.

Andrews, B. and Bernstein, C. (eds) (1984) *The Language Book*, Southern Illinois University Press, IL.

Bagehot, W. (1853[1965–86]) Shakespeare the individual, in *The Collected Works*, vol. 1 (ed. N. St John Stevas), The Economist, London.

Barthes, R. (1967) The death of the author, in *The Norton Anthology of Theory and Criticism*, (ed. V. Leitch), Norton, New York, NY.

Barthes, R. (1970) *S/Z: An Essay*, Cape, London.

Bate, J. (1997a) *The Genius of Shakespeare*, Picador, London.

Bate, J. (ed.) (1997b) *The Romantics on Shakespeare*, Penguin, London.

Beardsmore, R.W. (1971) *Art and Morality*, Macmillan, London.

Bennett, A. and Royle, N. (eds) (1995) *An Introduction to Literature, Criticism and Theory*, Pearson, Edinburgh.

Bersani, L. (1978) *A Future for Astyanax: Character and Desire in Literature*, Marion Boyars, London.

Bloom, H. (1998) *Shakespeare: The Invention of the Human*, Fourth Estate, New York, NY.

Is Shakespeare Any Good?: And Other Questions on How to Evaluate Literature,
First Edition. Richard Bradford.
© 2015 John Wiley & Sons, Ltd. Published 2015 by John Wiley & Sons, Ltd.

Bradbury, M. and McFarlane, J. (eds) (1970) *Modernism: A Guide to European Literature*, Penguin, London.

Brooks, C. (1939) *Modern Poetry and the Tradition*, University of North Carolina Press, Chapel Hill, NC.

Brooks, C. ([1947]1968) *The Well Wrought Urn: Studies in the Structure of Poetry*, Methuen, London.

Burgess, A. (1968) *The Novel Now*, Faber, London.

Cartwright, J. (1990) *Look at it This Way*, Picador.

Coleridge, S.T. (1957–1990) *The Notebooks of Samuel Taylor Coleridge* (eds K. Coburn and M. Christensen), Princeton University Press, Princeton and Routledge, London.

Culler, J. (1975) *Structuralist Poetics: Structuralism*, Routledge and Kegan Paul, London.

Daiches, D. (1940) *Poetry and the Modern World: A Study of Poetry in England Between 1900 and 1939*, University of Chicago Press, Chicago, IL.

de Man, P. (1979) *Allegories of Reading*, Yale University Press, New Haven, CT.

de Saussure, F. ([1919]1959) *Course in General Linguistics*, trans. W. Baskin, McGraw Hill, New York, NY.

Drabble, M (ed.) (2000) *Oxford Companion to English Literature*, 6th edn, Oxford University Press, Oxford.

Drakakis, J. (ed.) (1985) *Alternative Shakespeares*, Methuen, London.

Drew, E. (1933) *Discovering Poetry*, Norton, New York, NY.

Eagleton, T. (1983) *Literary Theory: An Introduction*, Blackwell, Oxford.

Eagleton T. (2006) *How To Read a Poem*, Blackwell, Oxford.

Easthope, A. and Thompson, J.O. (eds) (1991) *Contemporary Poetry Meets Modern Theory*, University of Toronto Press, Buffalo and London.

Eliot, T.S. ([1919](1975) Tradition and the individual talent, in *Twentieth Century Poetry* (eds G. Martin and P.N. Firbank), Open University Press, Milton Keynes.

Eliot, T.S. ([1921]1973) The metaphysical poets, in *Oxford Anthology of English Literature*, vol. 3 (eds F. Kermode and J. Hollander), Oxford University Press, London.

Empson, W. ([1930]1961) *Seven Types of Ambiguity*, Chatto & Windus, London,

Esslin, M. (1969) *The Theatre of the Absurd*, Doubleday, London.

Evans, M (1989) *Signifying Nothing: Truth's True Contends in Shakespeare's Text*, Harvester, London.

Fish, S. (1980) How to recognise a poem when you see one, in *Is There a Text in this Class? The Authority of Interpretive Communities* (ed. S. Fish), Harvard University Press, Cambridge, MA.

Forrest-Thomson, V. (1978) *Poetic Artifice: A Theory of Twentieth Century Poetry*, Manchester University Press, Manchester.

Genette, G. (1980) *Narrative Discourse*, Cornell University Press, Ithaca, NY.

Greenblatt, S. (1998) *Shakespearean Negotiations: The Circulation of Social Energy in Renaissance England*, Clarendon Press, Oxford.

Grierson, H. (ed.) (1921) *Metaphysical Lyrics and Poems of the Seventeenth Century*, Oxford University Press, Oxford.

Grigson, G. (1972) The Methodism of Ezra Pound, in *Ezra Pound: The Critical Heritage*, Routledge and Kegan Paul, London.

Gupta, S. (2009) *Re-Reading Harry Potter*, Palgrave, Basingstoke.

Hartman, G. (1980) *Criticism in the Wilderness: The Study of Literature Today*, Yale University Press, Newhaven, CT.

Hawkes, T. (1977) *Structuralism and Semiotics*, Methuen, London.

Hawkes, T. (ed.) (1996) *Alternative Shakespeares 2*, Routledge, London.

Henderson, D.E. (ed.) (2008) *Alternative Shakespeares 3*, Routledge, Abingdon.

Hillis Miller, J. (1982) *Fiction and Repetition: Seven English Novels*, Blackwell, Oxford.

Hillis Miller, J. (1995) The critic as host, in *Deconstruction and Criticism* (eds H. Bloom, P. de Man, J. Derrida, G. Hartman and J. Hillis Miller), Continuum, London.

Hillis Miller, J. (2002) *On Literature*, Routledge, London.

Jacobson, D. (1996) Sir Philip Sidney's dilemma: on the ethical function of narrative art. *Journal of Aesthetics and Art Criticism*, 54, 327–336.

Jakobson, R. (1960) Closing statement: linguistics and poetics, in *Style in Language* (ed. T. Sebeok), MIT Press, Cambridge, MA. [Reprinted in D. Lodge (1988) *Modern Criticism and Theory: A Reader*, Longman, London.]

James, H. ([1899]1962) The future of the novel, in *The House of Fiction* (ed. L. Edel), Mercury, London.

Johnson, S. ([1779–1781]1973) The lives of the poets, in *Oxford Anthology of English Literature* (general eds F. Kermode and J. Hollander), Oxford University Press, London.

Kieran, M. (1996) Art, imagination, and the cultivation of morals. *Journal of Aesthetics and Art Criticism*, 54, 337–351.

Lamarque, P. (1981) How can we fear and pity fictions? *British Journal of Aesthetics*, 21, 291–305.

Leavis, F.R. (1948) *The Great Tradition*, Chatto & Windus, London.

Leavis, F.R. (1952) *The Common Pursuit*, Chatto & Windus, London.

Leavis, F.R. (1972) Two cultures? The significance of Lord Snow, in *Nor Shall My Sword: Discourse on Pluralism, Compassion and Social Hope*, Chatto & Windus, London.

Leavis, Q.D. ([1932]1965) *Fiction and the Reading Public*, Chatto & Windus, London.

Lawrence, D.H. (1925) Morality and the novel, in *The Calendar of Modern Letters*, vol. 2, no. 10.

Lodge, D. (ed.) (1972) *Twentieth Century Literary Criticism: A Reader*, Longman, London.

Lodge, D. (ed.) (1988) *Modern Criticism and Theory: A Reader*, Longman, London.

Lodge, D. and Wood, N. (eds) (2008) *Modern Criticism and Theory*, Longman, Harlow.

Masson, D. (1851) Pendennis and Copperfield: Thackeray and Dickens. *North British Review,* May 1851.

McKillop, A.D. (1949) Wedding bells for Pamela. *Philological Quarterly*, 28, 325–326.

Moore, M. (1986) Feeling and precision, in *The Complete Prose of Marianne Moore*, Viking, New York, NY, pp. 396–402. [First published in *Sewanee Review*, 1944, 52, 449–507.]

Murray, D (ed.) (1989) *Literary Theory and Poetry: Extending the Canon*, Batsford, London.

Murphy, G. (1938) Introduction, in *The Modern Poet* (ed. G. Murphy), Sidgwick and Jackson, London.

Nicholls, P. (1991) Difference spreading: From Gertrude Stein to L-A-N-G-U-A-G-E poetry, in *Contemporary Poetry Meets Modern Theory* (eds A. Easthope and J.O. Thompson), University of Toronto Press, Toronto.

Novitz, D. (1987) *Knowledge, Fiction and Imagination*, Temple University Press, Philadelphia, PA.

Nussbaum, M. (1990) *Love's Knowledge*, Oxford University Press, Oxford.

Plato (1888) *The Republic*, trans. B. Jowett, Clarendon Press, Oxford.

Pound, E. (1914) The audience. *Poetry* 5, 29–30.

Puttenham, G. (1589) *The Arte of English Poesie*, R. Field, London.

Radford, C. (1975) How can we be moved by the fate of Anna Karenina? *Aristotelian Society Supplementary Volume*, 49, 67–80.

Ransom, J.C. (1937) Criticism Inc. in *Twentieth Century Literary Criticism: A Reader* (ed. D. Lodge), Longman, London.

Richards, I.A. ([1924]1966) *Principles of Literary Criticism*, Kegan Paul, London.

Ricks, C. (2003) *Dylan's Visions of Sin*, HarperCollins, London.

Riffaterre, M. (1966) Describing poetic structures: two approaches to Baudelaire's "Les Chats." *Yale French Studies*, 367, 200–242.

Shklovsky, V. ([1917]1965) Art as technique, in *Russian Formalist Criticism: Four Essays* (eds L. Lemon and M. Reis), University of Nebraska Press, Lincoln, NE.

Sinfield, A. and Dollimore, J. (1985) *Political Shakespeare*, Cornell University Press, New York, NY.

Sitwell, E. (1926) *Poetry and Criticism*, Henry Hold and Company, New York, NY.

Smith, B.H. (1978) *On the Margins of Discourse*, Chicago University Press, Chicago, IL.

Snow, C.P. ([1959] Canto edition, 1993) *The Two Cultures* (ed. S. Collini), Cambridge University Press, Cambridge.

Sockal, A. and Bricmont, J. (2003) *Intellectual Impostures*, Profile, London.

Sprat, T. ([1667]1908) The history of the Royal Society, in *Critical Essays of the 17th Century* (ed. J.E. Springarm), Clarendon Press, Oxford.

Squire, J.C. (1924) The man who wrote free verse. *London Mercury*, June, 121–137.

Symons, J. (1996) *A Sort of Virtue*, Macmillan, London.

Taylor, G. (1990) *Reinventing Shakespeare: A Cultural History from the Restoration to the Present*, Oxford University Press, Oxford.

Trilling, L. (1955) *A Gathering of Fugitives*, Secker & Warburg, London.

Van Doran, M. (1930) Introduction, in *Prize Poems -1929* (ed. C.A. Wagner) Charles Boni, New York, NY, pp. 5- 20.

Vickers, B. (1993) *Appropriating Shakespeare: Contemporary Critical Quarrels*, Yale University Press, London.

Walton, K. (1990) *Mimesis as Make-Believe*, Harvard University Press, Cambridge, MA.

Wellek, R. (1937) Correspondence: literary criticism and philosophy. *Scrutiny*, 6(2), 195–196.

Werth, P. (1976) Roman Jakobson's verbal analysis of poetry. *Journal of Linguistics*, 12, 21–73.

Wimsatt, W.K. Jr and Beardsley, M.C. ([1946]1954) The intentional fallacy, in *The Verbal Icon: Studies in the Meaning of Poetry* (ed. W.K. Wimsatt Jr), University of Kentucky Press, Lexington, KY.

Wimsatt, W.K. Jr and Beardsley, M.C. ([1949]1954) The affective fallacy, in *The Verbal Icon: Studies in the Meaning of Poetry* (ed. W.K. Wimsatt Jr), University of Kentucky Press, Lexington, KY.

Wimsatt, W.K. and Brooks, C. (1957) *Romantic Criticism*, Routledge, London.

Wolfe, T. (1970) Letter to Maxwell E. Perkins (15 December 1936), in *James Joyce: The Critical Heritage*, vol. 2, Routledge and Kegan Paul, London, p. 642.

Wollheim, R. (1980) *Art and Its Objects*, Faber, London.

Index

Is Shakespeare Any Good?: And Other Questions on How to Evaluate Literature,
First Edition. Richard Bradford.
© 2015 John Wiley & Sons, Ltd. Published 2015 by John Wiley & Sons, Ltd.